Ultimate Bootstrap for Responsive Web Design

Master the Art of Building Mobile-First, Responsive Websites with Bootstrap for Effortless Cross-Device Compatibility

Amit Diwan

www.orangeava.com

First Published: November 2024

Published By: Orange Education Pvt Ltd, AVA®

Address: 9, Daryaganj, Delhi, 110002, India

275 New North Road Islington Suite 1314 London,
N1 7AA, United Kingdom

ISBN (PBK): 978-93-48107-25-1
ISBN (E-BOOK): 978-93-48107-54-1

Scan the QR code to explore our entire catalogue

www.orangeava.com

Dedicated To

My Parents, Wife, and Sisters,

and

My Love for Teaching and Cricket

About the Author

Amit Diwan is the founder of **Studyopedia.com**. He is also running **Amit Thinks**, a tech YouTube channel with over 215k+ subscribers.

His interest in developing educational projects grew after completing his basic schooling. He subsequently pursued BCA and MCA from GGSIPU. As he approached the final year of MCA and faced career decisions, freelancing appealed to him more than traditional employment. At the age of 22, he embarked on his first freelancing endeavor, working on a Python programming project.

Following the completion of his MCA, Amit was offered a position at Accenture. However, due to a three-month gap before joining, he seized the opportunity to work at IIT, Delhi. This experience proved invaluable, ultimately leading him to decline the Accenture offer.

From the outset, Amit harbored the ambition of establishing his own IT company. Therefore, he dedicated himself to his role at IIT while simultaneously pursuing freelance assignments.

Amit's freelancing clients included prominent E-learning platforms like Tutorialspoint and Sitepoint from India and Australia. He has contributed to over 30 technologies, creating and publishing codes, articles, blogs, and more. Amit has produced an impressive body of work, with over 50,000 codes, articles, posts, and blogs, including video guidance and discussions.

In addition to his freelance work, Amit has developed E-learning courses for students, engineers, and professionals of all levels. His diverse experiences, spanning government, private sectors, and freelancing, have equipped him with valuable insights.

Driven by entrepreneurial aspirations, Amit launched Learnofy, an educational app designed to assist children with learning and writing challenges. Although the app was discontinued after a year, Amit's entrepreneurial journey continued. In August 2024, he launched Studyopedia Certifications, offering QR code verified certificates that are ATS compatible. These certificates can be easily shared on LinkedIn, validating a student's course completion.

Recognizing the value of educational courses and content, Amit is passionate about sharing his knowledge and inspiring others to achieve their Bootstrap development goals through this book.

About the Technical Reviewer

Jeppe Schaumburg Jensen is an experienced front-end developer with a deep interest in teaching Bootstrap and other UI frameworks. He holds a master of science degree in Information Technology with a specialization in interaction design and user experience. Over the last few years, he has been successful in establishing himself as an independent Instructor by creating online courses on different frontend development topics for various online course providers. His courses on Bootstrap have garnered over 35,000 students and consistently receive high ratings, achieving Bestseller and Highest rated badges on Udemy. Besides teaching, Jeppe is a Senior Software Engineer on the Design System Team at Siteimprove, a multinational and industry-leading Software-as-a-Service (SaaS) company.

Acknowledgements

I am deeply grateful to the many individuals who have supported me throughout the writing of this book. First and foremost, I would like to express my sincere thanks to my family for their unwavering encouragement and belief in my abilities. Their support has been invaluable in helping me complete this project.

I am also indebted to the Orange AVA team for their exceptional support and guidance. Their patience and understanding allowed me to dedicate the necessary time to complete this book. Their valuable suggestions and insights were instrumental in ensuring the quality and accuracy of the content.

I am truly grateful for the contributions of everyone who has been involved in this journey. Their support has made this book possible.

Preface

This book serves as a comprehensive resource for mastering Bootstrap, a powerful front-end framework for building responsive and visually appealing websites. From the fundamentals of setting up Bootstrap to advanced techniques like optimizing performance, this book covers all aspects of the framework.

Throughout the chapters, you will explore various Bootstrap components, including forms, navigation menus, layouts, and more. You will learn how to effectively utilize these components to create interactive and engaging web pages. Additionally, the book delves into essential optimization strategies to ensure your Bootstrap websites load quickly and perform efficiently across different devices.

Whether you are a beginner or an experienced web developer, this book will equip you with the knowledge and skills to create stunning websites using Bootstrap. With clear explanations, practical examples, and step-by-step guidance, you will be able to leverage the full potential of Bootstrap to build exceptional web applications.

This book is divided into 10 chapters. It will cover Bootstrap basics, followed by both basic and advanced topics in responsive web design. The book will explain why Bootstrap is a preferred framework for responsive web design while designing a website for all devices with consistency, accessibility, and reliability. The detailed outline is as follows:

Chapter 1. Introduction to Bootstrap and Responsive Web Design: This chapter introduces Bootstrap, a free front-end framework for creating responsive websites. Responsive web design ensures a website looks good on all devices. Bootstrap 5 is the latest version and eliminates the dependency on jQuery. Key features of Bootstrap include responsiveness, ease of use, and accessibility. It comes with pre-defined CSS styles and utility classes for layout and formatting. Setting up Bootstrap involves downloading the framework or using a CDN link. The chapter concludes by creating a simple web page with and without a header using Bootstrap.

Chapter 2. Bootstrap Layout: This chapter explores the layout of web pages using containers and grids. We will delve into the grid system's functionality across various devices, from small to extra-large screens. The chapter will demonstrate how containers, rows, and columns are used to structure content. We will also examine how to implement the grid system at different breakpoints and create unequal columns with ease.

Chapter 3. Set the Content with Bootstrap: This chapter introduces Bootstrap tables, which are used to display data in rows and columns. We will learn how to create basic tables, add styles like borders, stripes, and hover effects, and make tables responsive for different screen sizes. We will also explore features like contextual classes for table cells and dark-colored tables.

Chapter 4. Bootstrap Navs: This chapter introduces Bootstrap navs, which are used to create navigation menus on web pages. We will learn how to create horizontal and vertical navigation menus, use tabs and pills for different styles, and customize the appearance of navigation bars. We will also explore concepts like navbar toggling and Scrollspy for enhanced user interaction.

Chapter 5. Bootstrap Components: This chapter covers Bootstrap components, which are essential building blocks for web pages. We will learn how to create badges, progress bars, cards, list groups, spinners, buttons, button groups, and alerts. These components offer various styles and functionalities to enhance the visual appeal and interactivity of your web pages.

Chapter 6. Bootstrap Popup Components: This chapter introduces Bootstrap pop-up components, which are used to create interactive elements on web pages. We will learn how to create collapsible content, modal dialog boxes, offcanvas sidebars, dropdown menus, tooltips, and toasts. These components enhance the user experience by providing additional information or actions on demand.

Chapter 7. Bootstrap Forms: This chapter introduces Bootstrap forms, which are essential for creating interactive web pages. We will learn how to create stacked and inline forms, and work with various form elements including input fields, labels, buttons, checkboxes, radio buttons, select menus, and range sliders. We will also explore how to style and customize these elements using Bootstrap classes.

Chapter 8. Bootstrap Helpers: This chapter introduces Bootstrap helper classes, which provide convenient tools for web developers. These classes simplify tasks like clearing floats, managing aspect ratios, and controlling element visibility. By using helper classes, you can enhance your web page layout and design without writing complex CSS code.

Chapter 9. Bootstrap Utilities: This chapter introduces Bootstrap utility classes, which provide pre-defined CSS styles for various layout and styling tasks. We will learn how to control content display, alignment, spacing, overflow, and more using these classes. By leveraging utility classes, you can efficiently design and customize web pages without writing extensive custom CSS code.

Chapter 10. Optimization Techniques for Bootstrap Websites: This chapter introduces techniques for optimizing Bootstrap websites, focusing on responsiveness and performance. It covers the use of media queries to create responsive layouts for different screen sizes. Additionally, the chapter explores modifier classes for styling components and z-index scales for controlling element stacking. To optimize performance, the chapter recommends using Sass imports to include only necessary components, minifying code, and leveraging the Bootstrap Icons library. By following these techniques, you can create responsive and efficient Bootstrap websites.

Get a Free eBook

We hope you are enjoying your recently purchased book! Your feedback is incredibly valuable to us, and to all other readers looking for great books.

If you found this book helpful or enjoyable, we would truly appreciate it, if you could take a moment to leave a short review with a 5 star rating on Amazon. It helps us grow, and lets other readers discover our books.

As a thank you, we would love to send you a free digital copy of this book, and a **30%** discount code on your next cart value on our official websites:

www.orangeava.com

www.orangeava.in (For Indian Subcontinent)

☑ **Here's how:**

Leave a review for the book on Amazon.

Take a screenshot of your review, and send an email to **info@orangeava.com** (it can be just the confirmation screen).

Once, we receive your screenshot, we will send you the digital file, within 24 hours.

Thank you so much for your support – it means a lot to us!

Downloading the code bundles and colored images

Please follow the links or scan the QR codes to download the
Code Bundles and Images of the book:

https://github.com/ava-orange-education/Ultimate-Bootstrap-for-Responsive-Web-Design

The code bundles and images of the book are also hosted on
https://rebrand.ly/18ffe4

In case there's an update to the code, it will be updated on the existing GitHub repository.

Errata

We take immense pride in our work at **Orange Education Pvt Ltd,** and follow best practices to ensure the accuracy of our content to provide an indulging reading experience to our subscribers. Our readers are our mirrors, and we use their inputs to reflect and improve upon human errors, if any, that may have occurred during the publishing processes involved. To let us maintain the quality and help us reach out to any readers who might be having difficulties due to any unforeseen errors, please write to us at :

errata@orangeava.com

Your support, suggestions, and feedback are highly appreciated.

DID YOU KNOW

Did you know that Orange Education Pvt Ltd offers eBook versions of every book published, with PDF and ePub files available? You can upgrade to the eBook version at **www.orangeava.com** and as a print book customer, you are entitled to a discount on the eBook copy. Get in touch with us at: **info@orangeava.com** for more details.

At **www.orangeava.com**, you can also read a collection of free technical articles, sign up for a range of free newsletters, and receive exclusive discounts and offers on AVA® Books and eBooks.

PIRACY

If you come across any illegal copies of our works in any form on the internet, we would be grateful if you would provide us with the location address or website name. Please contact us at **info@orangeava.com** with a link to the material.

ARE YOU INTERESTED IN AUTHORING WITH US?

If there is a topic that you have expertise in, and you are interested in either writing or contributing to a book, please write to us at **business@orangeava.com**. We are on a journey to help developers and tech professionals to gain insights on the present technological advancements and innovations happening across the globe and build a community that believes Knowledge is best acquired by sharing and learning with others. Please reach out to us to learn what our audience demands and how you can be part of this educational reform. We also welcome ideas from tech experts and help them build learning and development content for their domains.

REVIEWS

Please leave a review. Once you have read and used this book, why not leave a review on the site that you purchased it from? Potential readers can then see and use your unbiased opinion to make purchase decisions. We at Orange Education would love to know what you think about our products, and our authors can learn from your feedback. Thank you!

For more information about Orange Education, please visit **www.orangeava.com**.

Table of Contents

CHAPTER 1
Introduction to Bootstrap and Responsive Web Design

Introduction

This chapter will cover the basics of responsive web design and the role of Bootstrap in it. We will introduce the concept of the current version of Bootstrap, that is, Bootstrap 5, and how to set it up.

The enhancements of Bootstrap 5 over Bootstrap 4 are also discussed. Some coding examples to create our first web page with Bootstrap. This will be a benchmark for us in the upcoming chapters.

Structure

In this chapter, we will discuss the following topics:

- Introduction to Responsive Web Design
- Overview of Bootstrap
- Features of Bootstrap
- Bootstrap 5 Enhancements
- Setting Up a Bootstrap Environment
  - Download on the local system
  - Use CDN
- Creating your first Bootstrap web page
- Create a Bootstrap web page with a header

Introduction to Responsive Web Design

The first website ever came online in 1991. The era of website development and design boomed and never stopped. In the 2000s, the wave of mobile phones came, and the first iPhone was also launched in 2007. The same desktop website accessible on mobile was leading to a poor user experience and needed to be tackled. A desktop website accessed on a mobile device brought an experience that fell short of expectations.

Mobile Version of Websites

This brought a need for mobile-specific websites, that is, a separate mobile version of a website. A new version of a website for mobile started developing. In the late 2000s, mobile web browsers were also introduced, leading to the need for mobile-specific website versions. Around this time, you must have seen different websites for desktop and mobile. Some developers added sub-domains or even different directories to host these websites.

A website, let us say example.com, was developing a different mobile version of the website. This was hosted either in a sub-domain, **`m.example.com`**, or a different directory, **`/mobile`**, as follows:

```
m.example.com
example.com/mobile
```

Even Facebook followed this with the following desktop version:

```
www.facebook.com
```

The mobile version is on a sub-domain, like:

```
m.facebook.com
```

The mobile version was optimized to work on mobile web browsers. However, this worked for some years but had the hassle of being too cumbersome and costly. The reason was self-explanatory, that is, the need to maintain two websites, one for desktop and another for mobile.

Such issues brought the need for a platform to create a single website for all the devices and let it work according to the screen size. This was needed to enhance the user experience, performance, and accessibility.

Understanding Frameworks

A framework is a set of pre-defined styles that can be easily worked on to create a platform. A CSS framework is a set of ready-to-use and prepared CSS styles and stylesheets to implement consistent websites.

The CSS frameworks came to the rescue for responsive website design, since CSS was also booming. The CSS frameworks allowed the developers to work on pre-defined and standardized CSS styles and components. This led to the development of a CSS framework, Bootstrap.

Now, many frameworks are available to achieve responsive web design, but Bootstrap still leads the race because of its ease of creating responsive and mobile-friendly websites.

Benefits of Responsive Web Design

Responsive web design means designing a website for all these devices with consistency, accessibility, and reliability. These days, a user can access a website from any device of different sizes, like a mobile, tablet, or laptop.

Responsiveness means, let us say, a user is using a tablet. The sections on that website should stack to make them visible to the user. Likewise, on a mobile device, the sections should stack completely to make it easier for the user to understand the layout and navigate the content accordingly. This means automatically resizing, shrinking, and enlarging a website's layout and adapting to different screen sizes, that is, desktops, tablets, and mobile devices.

The following is how a website looks on different screen sizes:

Figure 1.1: *A website on different devices*

Overview of Bootstrap

Bootstrap is a free and open-source front-end framework developed by Mark Otto and Jacob Thornton in 2011. They both worked for Twitter. First, it was released on

GitHub in the same year. The current version is Bootstrap v5.3.3. It is currently one of the most popular frameworks for building responsive and mobile-first websites.

Bootstrap 5 is a front-end framework and has an enhanced grid system with additional support for large screens, that is, xxl screens above 1400px. The Bootstrap 5 switch from jQuery to Vanilla JavaScript has led to no dependency on jQuery. This also made the framework faster.

Features of Bootstrap

Bootstrap has a lot of features to create responsive websites, including:

- **Responsive:** Bootstrap is a CSS framework to build responsive websites that work for different devices, including mobile, tablet, and desktop.
- **Open-Source:** It is a free and open-source framework.
- **Modern Websites**: Bootstrap supports building modern responsive websites, that is, a single website that works for all devices.
- **Compatible with modern browsers:** Bootstrap is compatible with all modern web browsers, such as Google Chrome, Mozilla Firefox, Safari, Opera, and so on.
- **Accessibility:** Bootstrap cares about accessibility as well and came up with a class to let the content be visually hidden but remain accessible to screen readers.

Bootstrap 5 Enhancements

Bootstrap 5 is the current version of Bootstrap. It came up with the following enhancements on Bootstrap 4:

- **Utility Classes:** Bootstrap 5 added some utilities to set the position, spacing, alignment, visibility, and more.
- **Helper Classes**: Some helper classes were also added in Bootstrap to truncate the text, clear floated content, maintain the aspect ratio, and so on.
- **Focus on Accessibility:** Bootstrap 5 focused more on accessibility and came up with the visually-hidden class to let the content be visually hidden but remain accessible to screen readers.
- **More lightweight:** Bootstrap 5 removed the mandatory inclusion of jQuery.
- **XXLarge Devices:** The XXL breakpoint introduced in Bootstrap 5, that is, a new class, `col-xxl-` came for the xxlarge devices. These are the devices with a screen width equal to or greater than 1400 pixels.
- **Floating labels:** The floating labels are now supported for forms in Bootstrap.

Setting Up a Bootstrap Environment

There are various ways to set up the Bootstrap environment on the Windows, Mac, and Linux operating systems. We can either download it on the local system or directly use the CDN link.

Download on the Local System

To download Bootstrap on the local system, go to the official website and download Bootstrap. This will host Bootstrap on your system. Let us see the steps:

Step 1: Go to the web browser and open the official website (https://getbootstrap.com/docs/5.3/getting-started/download/). Download ready-to-use compiled CSS and JavaScript:

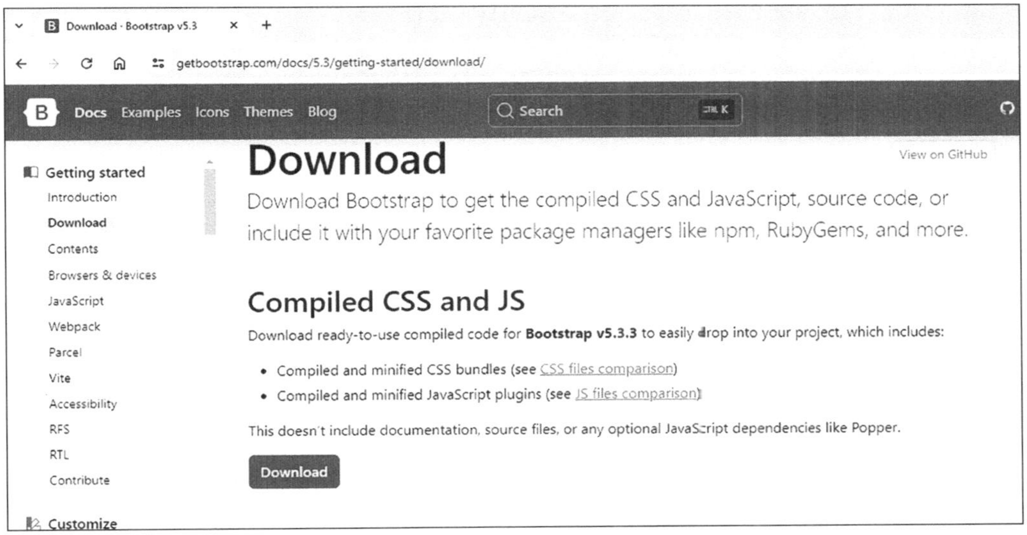

***Figure 1.2**: Download Bootstrap from the official website*

The downloaded files would be in zip format, that is, for this version:

```
bootstrap-5.3.3-dist.zip
```

Step 2: Extract the downloaded files and save the downloaded files in a folder on your local system. Let us say we saved it in a new folder, **`AmitProject`,** in the **`D: Drive`**. This will be our project folder:

```
D:\AmitProject\
```

To ease your work, rename the extracted file to **`bootstrap`**. After adding the compressed folder to the project folder, the path will be the following:

```
D:\AmitProject\bootstrap\
```

Step 3: Open the folder and reach the individual **CSS** and **JS** folders.

Now, get the compiled CSS and JavaScript paths:

Compiled CSS path:

```
D:\AmitProject\bootstrap\css\bootstrap.min.css
```

Compiled JavaScript path:

```
D:\AmitProject\bootstrap\css\bootstrap.bundle.min.js
```

Step 4: Create a new HTML file, **`index.html`** in the project folder. This is our first web page:

```
<!DOCTYPE html>
<html lang="en">
<head>
  <title>Bootstrap First Example</title>
  <meta charset="utf-8">
  <meta name="viewport" content="width=device-width,
initial-scale=1">
</head>
<body>

</body>
</html>
```

Now, our project folder looks like the following screenshot with the **`index.html`** file and the **`bootstrap`** folder:

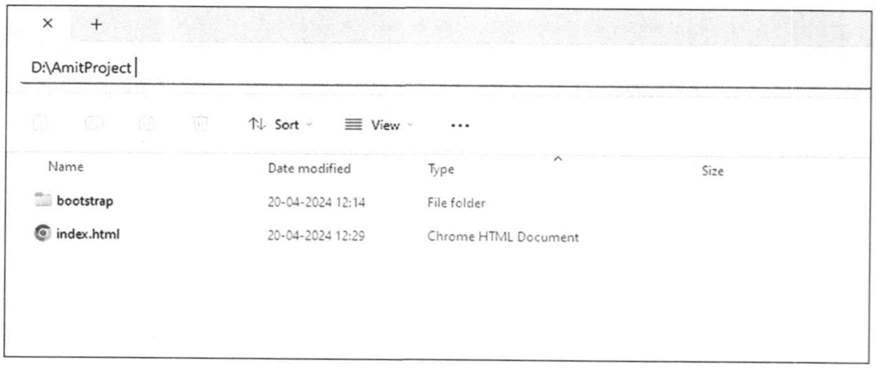

***Figure 1.3**: Our project folder*

Step 4: Set the path of the downloaded files in it. Finally, the HTML file, that is, our first web page, should look like this:

```
<!DOCTYPE html>
<html lang="en">
<head>
```

```
  <title>Bootstrap First Example</title>
  <meta charset="utf-8">
  <meta name="viewport" content="width=device-width,
  initial-scale=1">
  <!-- Our Bootstrap CSS -->
  <link rel="stylesheet"
href="/bootstrap/css/bootstrap.min.css/bootstrap.min.css">
</head>
<body>

    <!-- Content -->

    <!-- Our Bootstrap JS -->
    <script src="/bootstrap/js/bootstrap.bundle.min.js"></script>

</body>
</html>
```

Use CDN

To avoid the hassles of downloading Bootstrap, use CDN. CDN is a content delivery network that provides access to the cached version. CDN is very useful for speeding up the execution and loading of images and videos. We can use it for Bootstrap without deploying it on our local system.

To use CDN, add the compiled JavaScript and CSS using the **jsDelivr CDN**. Here, **jsDelivr** is the CDN to deliver the cached version of Bootstrap's compiled CSS and JS. This speeds up your project execution.

The compiled CSS would be added using the **<link>** element. This is like adding an external stylesheet to a web page. It provides the cached version of Bootstrap's compiled CSS.

Copy and directly add the following to your web page:

```
<link href="https://cdn.jsdelivr.net/npm/bootstrap@5.3.3/dist/
css/bootstrap.min.css" rel="stylesheet">
```

The compiled JavaScript would get added using the **<script>** element with the **jsDelivr** CDN:

```
<script src="https://cdn.jsdelivr.net/npm/bootstrap@5.3.3/dist/
js/bootstrap.bundle.min.js"></script>
```

Creating your first Bootstrap Web Page

Let us create and run our web page using the Bootstrap framework. In the example, we would create a **`div`** container using the **`.container`** class. This is a responsive container:

```
<!DOCTYPE html>
<html lang="en">
<head>
  <title>Bootstrap First Example</title>
  <meta charset="utf-8">
  <meta name="viewport" content="width=device-width, initial-scale=1">
  <link
href="https://cdn.jsdelivr.net/npm/bootstrap@5.3.3/dist/css/bootstrap.
min.css" rel="stylesheet">
  <script
src="https://cdn.jsdelivr.net/npm/bootstrap@5.3.3/dist/js/bootstrap.
bundle.min.js"></script>
</head>
<body>

<div class="container">
  <h1>Demo Heading1</h1>
  <h2>Demo Heading2</h2>
  <p>This is a demo text.</p>
  <h2>Demo Heading2</h2>
  <p>This is another demo text.</p>
  <p>We have used the container class.</p>
  <p>To see the difference, try to resize the web browser window</p>
</div>

</body>
</html>
```

After running the code, the web page will look as follows:

Screen Size: 1366 x 633

Note: We have mentioned the screen size for every output screenshot as shown above.

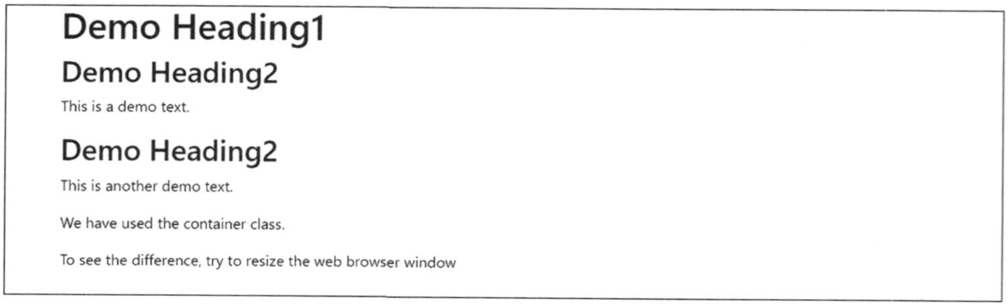

***Figure 1.4**: First Bootstrap web page*

In the preceding example, we have used the **<meta>** in the **<head>** element. This is done to set the initial zoom level of the web page when it is loaded:

```
initial-scale=1
```

Also, the following sets the page's width and follows the device's screen width:

```
width=device-width
```

Create a Bootstrap Web Page with a Header

Let us create and run our web page using the Bootstrap framework. In the example, we would create a full-width container for the header using the **.container-fluid** class in Bootstrap. The header spans the entire width of the viewport, except for some padding in the sides and this is what we will achieve. We will discuss more about this in the next chapter.

For the responsive container, a fixed-width div container is set using the **.container** class. A container has a different fixed width for each breakpoint.

Let us see an example. We have set four columns in the following example:

```
<!DOCTYPE html>
<html lang="en">
<head>
  <title>Bootstrap Example with a header</title>
  <meta charset="utf-8">
  <meta name="viewport" content="width=device-width, initial-scale=1">
  <link
href="https://cdn.jsdelivr.net/npm/bootstrap@5.3.3/dist/css/bootstrap.
min.css" rel="stylesheet">
  <script
src="https://cdn.jsdelivr.net/npm/bootstrap@5.3.3/dist/js/bootstrap.
bundle.min.js"></script>
</head>
<body>

<div class="container-fluid bg-info text-center">
  <h1>Header</h1>
</div>

<div class="container">
  <div class="row">
    <div class="col-sm-3">
      <h3>Column 1</h3>
      <p>This is a demo text. This is Column 1.</p>
```

```
      <p>This is another demo text. This is Column 1.</p>
    </div>
    <div class="col-sm-3">
      <h3>Column 2</h3>
     <p>This is a demo text. This is Column 2.</p>
      <p>This is another demo text. This is Column 2.</p>
    </div>
    <div class="col-sm-3">
      <h3>Column 3</h3>
     <p>This is a demo text. This is Column 3.</p>
      <p>This is another demo text. This is Column 3.</p>
    </div>
     <div class="col-sm-3">
      <h3>Column 4</h3>
     <p>This is a demo text. This is Column 4.</p>
      <p>This is another demo text. This is Column 4.</p>
    </div>
  </div>
</div>

</body>
</html>
```

After running the code, the web page will look as follows:

Screen Size: 1366 x 633

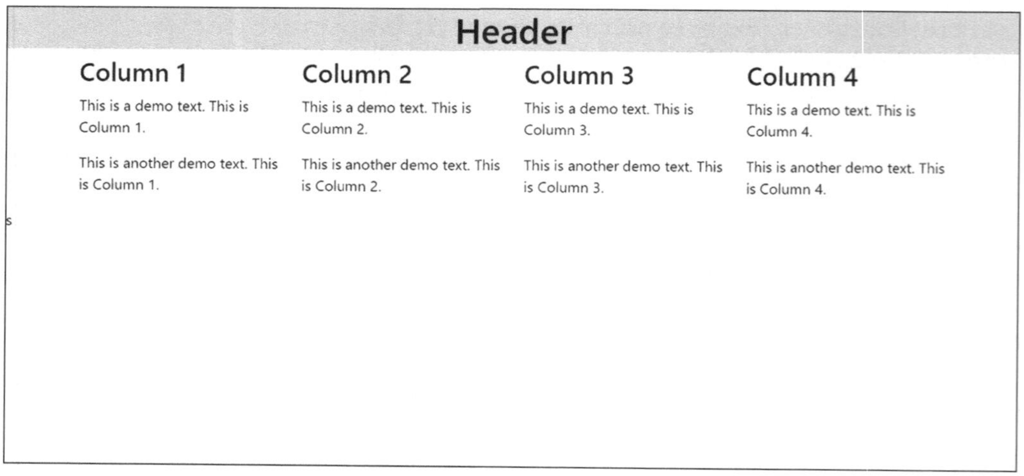

***Figure 1.5**: A web page with a header and columns*

Explanation

The preceding class **`col-sm-*`** is for small devices. On a web page, we have 12 columns according to Bootstrap's Grid System. We will discuss it in the next chapter.

The `col-sm-3` is used four times, that is, a total of 12 columns. As shown in the preceding figure, the web page is divided into 12 columns. The columns would get placed next to each other if the screen size is small, that is, >=576px and <768px. The small screen devices have a screen width of 576px to 767px.

The above example would have a 25% split for each column on every device except the extra small devices. On those devices, it would stack 100%. That means for screen size <576px, it would stack completely, that is, 100%.

Note: *The* ***`bg-info`*** *is a contextual class to set the background color.*

All these grid system concepts are discussed in the next chapter with examples.

Conclusion

Bootstrap is a free front-end framework that is easy to install. To avoid the hassles of deployment, use the CDN and add the compiled CSS and JS directly to the web page. We created our first web page using Bootstrap with and without a header.

In the next lesson, we will discuss the grid system of a web page layout. A web page layout can be managed based on the device sizes, such as small, medium, large, extra-large, and so on.

Points to Remember

- Bootstrap is a free and open-source framework.
- Bootstrap 5 is an enhancement of Bootstrap 4.
- Bootstrap 5 focuses more on accessibility.
- The XXL breakpoint introduced in Bootstrap 5 is for devices with a screen width equal to or greater than 1400 pixels.

Multiple Choice Questions

1. Does Bootstrap support modern web browsers?
   a. True
   b. False
2. A web page is divided into __ columns.
   a. 10
   b. 12
   c. 15
   d. 20

3. What is CDN?
    a. Container Delivery Network
    b. Content Delivery Network

Answers

1. a
2. b
3. b

Questions

- What is a responsive web design?
- What is the need for Bootstrap?
- How is Bootstrap 5 different from Bootstrap 4?
- Can we run Bootstrap without installing it?

Key Terms

- **Framework**: A set of pre-defined styles and stylesheets to assist in implementing consistent websites.
- **Utility Classes:** Classes to set the position, spacing, alignment, visibility, and more.
- **Helper Classes:** Classes to truncate the text, clear floated content, maintain the aspect ratio, and so on.
- **CDN**: CDN is a content delivery network that speeds up web page loading.
- **`jsDelivr`**: The **`jsDelivr`** is a CDN to deliver the cached version of Bootstrap's compiled CSS and JS. This speeds up your project execution.

CHAPTER 2
Bootstrap Layout

Introduction

This chapter covers the layout of a web page with containers and grids. The grid system is also covered on different devices, such as small, medium, large, extra-large, and so on, with examples. The grid system uses the container, rows, and columns to set the content.

We will see the implementation of the grid system on different breakpoints. Unequal columns can also be created on a web page and the extra space can be easily removed.

Structure

In this chapter, we will discuss the following topics:

- Bootstrap Container
- Bootstrap Grids
- Grid XSmall
- Grid Small
- Grid Medium
- Grid Large
- Grid XLarge
- Grid XXLarge
- Unequal columns
- Row Cols
- Gutters

Bootstrap Container

To add content to a web page, we need to wrap it inside a container. Consider a container as a box within which all the elements are placed. The following are the two types of containers:

- **Fixed Width Container**
  The **.container** class is used to create a fixed-width container. It is a responsive, fixed-width container.
- **Full-Width Container**
  The **.container-fluid** class is used to create a full-width container.

Let us see some examples:

The following is an example of a fixed-width container:

```
<!DOCTYPE html>
<html lang="en">
<head>
  <title>Bootstrap Fixed Width Container</title>
  <meta charset="utf-8">
  <meta name="viewport" content="width=device-width, initial-scale=1">
  <link
href="https://cdn.jsdelivr.net/npm/bootstrap@5.3.3/dist/css/bootstrap.
min.css" rel="stylesheet">
  <script
src="https://cdn.jsdelivr.net/npm/bootstrap@5.3.3/dist/js/bootstrap.
bundle.min.js"></script>
</head>
<body>

<div class="container">
  <h1>Sports</h1>
  <p>The following are some popular sports played widely:</p>
  <p>Note: Resize the browser window to see the changes.</p>
  <ul>
     <li>Football</li>
     <li>Golf</li>
     <li>Cricket</li>
     <li>Tennis</li>
     <li>Badminton</li>
  </ul>
</div>

</body>
</html>
```

After running the code, the web page will look as follows: :

Screen Size: 1366 x 633

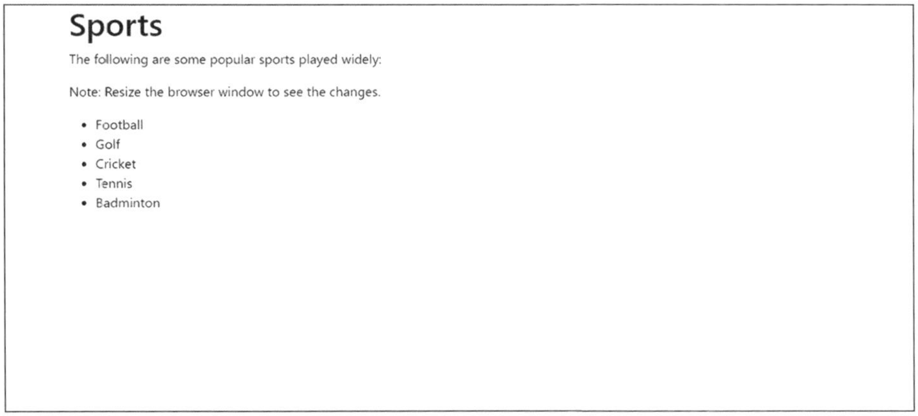

***Figure 2.1**: Display a Bootstrap container*

The following is an example of a full-width container:

```
<!DOCTYPE html>
<html lang="en">
<head>
  <title>Bootstrap Full-Width Container</title>
  <meta charset="utf-8">
  <meta name="viewport" content="width=device-width, initial-scale=1">
  <link
href="https://cdn.jsdelivr.net/npm/bootstrap@5.3.3/dist/css/bootstrap.
min.css" rel="stylesheet">
  <script
src="https://cdn.jsdelivr.net/npm/bootstrap@5.3.3/dist/js/bootstrap.
bundle.min.js"></script>
</head>
<body>

<div class="container-fluid">
  <h1>Sports</h1>
  <p>The following are some popular sports played widely:</p>
  <p>Note: Resize the browser window to see the changes.</p>
  <ul>
     <li>Football</li>
     <li>Golf</li>
     <li>Cricket</li>
     <li>Tennis</li>
     <li>Badminton</li>
  </ul>
</div>

</body>
</html>
```

After running the code, the web page will look as follows:

Screen Size: 1366 x 633

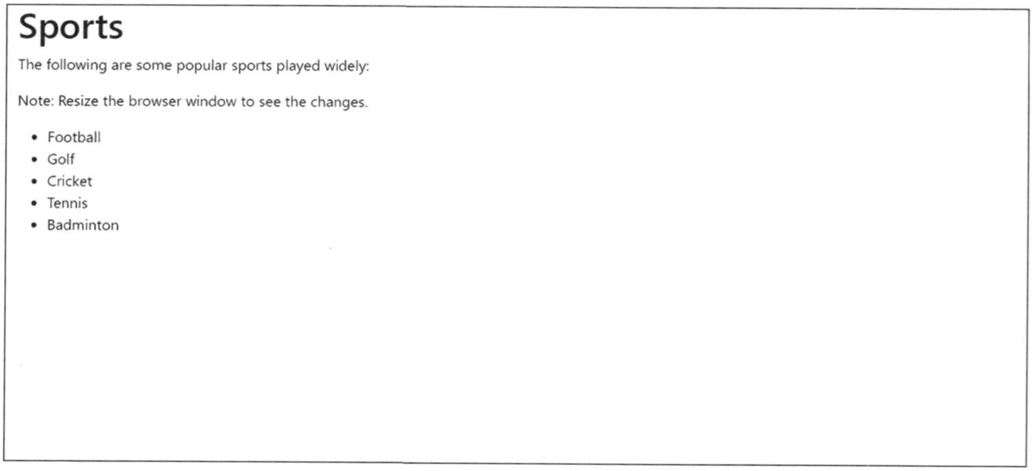

Figure 2.2: *A full-width container*

We saw two examples above covering both the fixed-width as well as the full-width container using the .container and .container-fluid classes, respectively. Before moving to the Bootstrap Grids topic, let us see the differences:

In Bootstrap 5, .container and .container-fluid are two classes used for layout and responsive design.

.container

1. Centers content horizontally.
2. Sets a fixed max-width based on screen size (responsive).
3. Adds horizontal padding (15px by default).
4. Used for most layout scenarios.

.container-fluid

1. Takes full width of parent element (100% width).
2. No max-width, spans entire container.
3. No horizontal padding.
4. Ideal for:
    - Full-width backgrounds or images.

- Full-screen layouts.
- Edge-to-edge content.

Differences

Here are the differences:

- **Width**: .container has fixed max-width, while .container-fluid has 100% width.
- **Padding**: .container has horizontal padding, whereas .container-fluid does not.

Bootstrap Grids

For the web page layout and to align the content within it, we have Bootstrap Grid. The Grid system uses the container, rows, and columns to set the content. Bootstrap works on a grid system to arrange rows and columns on a web page. As per the standards, 12 columns per row are allowed.

Here are some examples that form 12 columns on a web page for small devices and up:

```
For six equal columns, use six .col-sm-2
For four equal columns, use four .col-sm-3

For six equal columns, use two .col-sm-2
For four equal columns, use four .col-sm-3

For three equal columns, use three .col-sm-4

For two equal columns, use two .col-sm-6
```

If you want to create a group of columns, then use the `.row` class.

Note: *In the examples, we have set the div background color using the contextual classes in Bootstrap. The contextual classes are covered in detail in the section Background Color of Chapter 9, Bootstrap Utilities.*

Grid XSmall

In Bootstrap, we use the following classes to implement the grid system on extra-small devices. This grid is always horizontal:

```
.col-
```

The **xsmall** devices have a screen width of:

```
<576px
```

Until now, you must have understood the class prefix we use in Bootstrap for extra small devices, that is,

```
.col-
```

Three Equal Columns

Let us create three equal columns on a web page using the Bootstrap Grid System. In the following example, the 33% wide is on all devices:

```
<div class="container-fluid">
  <div class="row">
    <div class="col-4 bg-primary text-white">Column A</div>
    <div class="col-4 bg-dark text-white">Column B</div>
    <div class="col-4 bg-primary text-white">Column C</div>
  </div>
</div>
```

Here, the total is 12, that is, three equal columns.

The following is the complete example:

```
<!DOCTYPE html>
<html lang="en">
<head>
  <title>Bootstrap Grids on Extra Small Devices</title>
  <meta charset="utf-8">
  <meta name="viewport" content="width=device-width, initial-scale=1">
  <link
href="https://cdn.jsdelivr.net/npm/bootstrap@5.3.3/dist/css/bootstrap.
min.css" rel="stylesheet">
  <script
src="https://cdn.jsdelivr.net/npm/bootstrap@5.3.3/dist/js/bootstrap.
bundle.min.js"></script>
</head>
<body>

<div class="container-fluid">
  <h1>Bootstrap Grids on Extra Small Devices</h1>
  <p>Resize the browser window.</p>
  <p>The 33.3%/33.3%/ 33.3% split is set on all devices</p>
  <div class="row">
    <div class="col-4 bg-primary text-white">Column A</div>
    <div class="col-4 bg-info text-white">Column B</div>
    <div class="col-4 bg-success text-white">Column C</div>
  </div>
</div>

</body>
</html>
```

After running the code, the web page will look as follows:

Screen Size: 1366 x 633

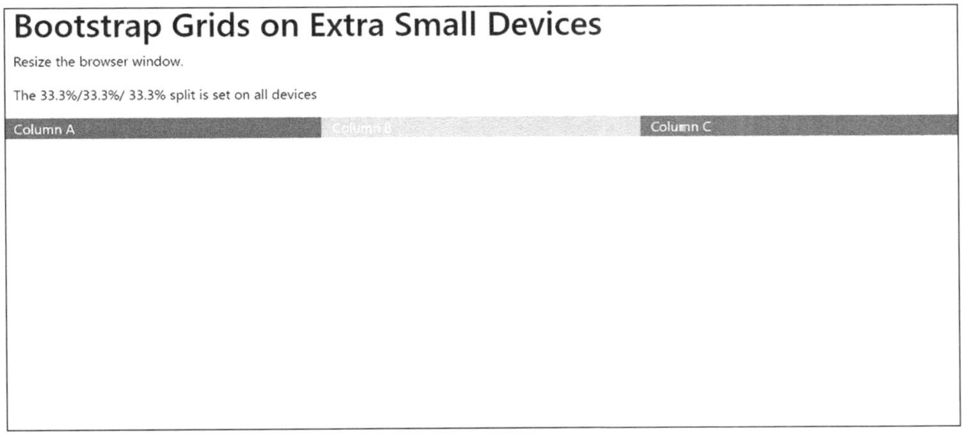

***Figure 2.3**: Grids on extra small devices*

The output remains the same even when the screen size is less than 576px.

Creating Five Equal-Width Columns

To set the equal width of columns, directly use the **`.col`** class. For our example, we will set the **`.col`** class five times to give equal width to each column. The Bootstrap would recognize and provide a layout with each column 20%, that is, the same width:

```
<!DOCTYPE html>
<html lang="en">
<head>
  <title>Bootstrap Grids with equal columns</title>
  <meta charset="utf-8">
  <meta name="viewport" content="width=device-width, initial-scale=1">
  <link
href="https://cdn.jsdelivr.net/npm/bootstrap@5.3.3/dist/css/bootstrap.
min.css" rel="stylesheet">
  <script
src="https://cdn.jsdelivr.net/npm/bootstrap@5.3.3/dist/js/bootstrap.
bundle.min.js"></script>
</head>
<body>

<div class="container-fluid">
  <h1>Bootstrap Grids with equal columns</h1>
  <p>Resize the browser window.</p>
  <p>The 20% each split is set on all devices</p>
  <div class="row">
    <div class="col bg-primary text-white">Column A</div>
    <div class="col bg-info text-white">Column B</div>
    <div class="col bg-success text-white">Column C</div>
```

```
    <div class="col bg-secondary text-white">Column D</div>
    <div class="col bg-warning text-white">Column E</div>
  </div>
</div>

</body>
</html>
```

After running the code, the web page will look as follows:

Screen Size: 1366 x 633

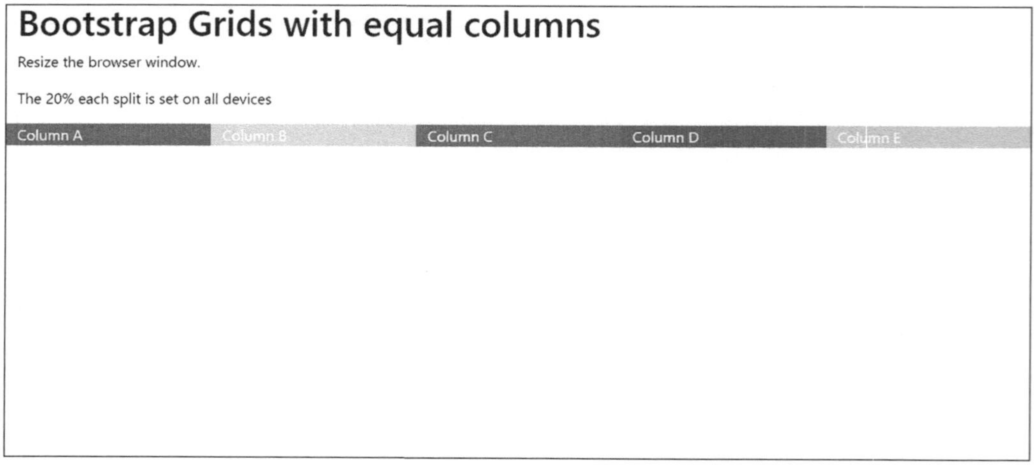

***Figure 2.4**: Grids on equal columns*

The output remains the same even when the screen size is less than 576px.

Grid Small

In Bootstrap, we use the following classes to implement the grid system on small devices:

```
.col-sm-*
```

The **small** devices have a screen width of:

```
576px to 767px
```

Until now, you must have understood the class prefix we use in Bootstrap for small devices, that is,

```
.col-sm-
```

Three Equal Columns

Let us create three equal columns on a web page using the Bootstrap Grid System. In the following example, the 33.3% wide is on small, medium, large, and xlarge devices, that is, 576px and above.

The columns will stack on top of each other when the screen width is less than 576px. On extra small devices, it will stack, that is, 100% width:

```
<div class="container-fluid">
  <div class="row">
    <div class="col-sm-4 bg-primary text-white">Column A</div>
    <div class="col-sm-4 bg-dark text-white">Column B</div>
    <div class="col-sm-4 bg-primary text-white">Column C</div>
  </div>
</div>
```

Here, the total is 12, that is, three equal columns.

The following is the complete example:

```
<!DOCTYPE html>
<html lang="en">
<head>
  <title>Bootstrap Grids on small devices</title>
  <meta charset="utf-8">
  <meta name="viewport" content="width=device-width, initial-scale=1">
  <link
href="https://cdn.jsdelivr.net/npm/bootstrap@5.3.3/dist/css/bootstrap.
min.css" rel="stylesheet">
  <script
src="https://cdn.jsdelivr.net/npm/bootstrap@5.3.3/dist/js/bootstrap.
bundle.min.js"></script>
</head>
<body>

<div class="container-fluid">
  <h1>Bootstrap Grids on Small Devices</h1>
  <p>Resize the browser window.</p>
  <p>The 33.3%/33.3%/ 33.3% split is set on small, medium, large and
xlarge devices i.e. 576px and above.</p>
<p>The columns will stack on top of each other, when the screen width
is less than 576px i.e. on extra small devices, it will stack (100%
width).</p>
  <div class="row">
    <div class="col-sm-4 bg-primary text-white">Column A</div>
    <div class="col-sm-4 bg-info text-white">Column B</div>
    <div class="col-sm-4 bg-success text-white">Column C</div>
  </div>
</div>
```

```
</body>
</html>
```

After running the code, the web page will look as follows:

Screen Size: 1366 x 633

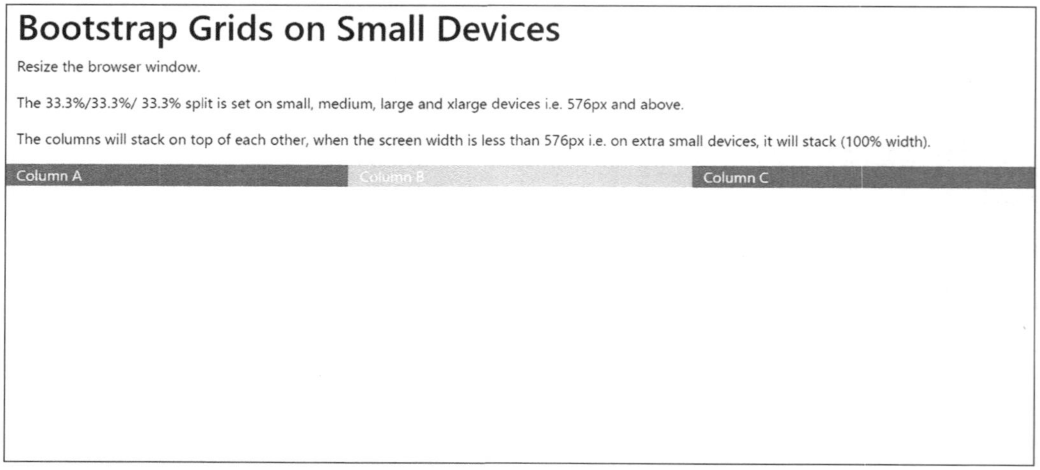

Figure 2.5: *The Three Columns won't stack when the device size is more than 576px*

Let us now resize the screen size. The columns will stack on top of each other when the screen width is less than 576px:

Screen Size: 570 x 633

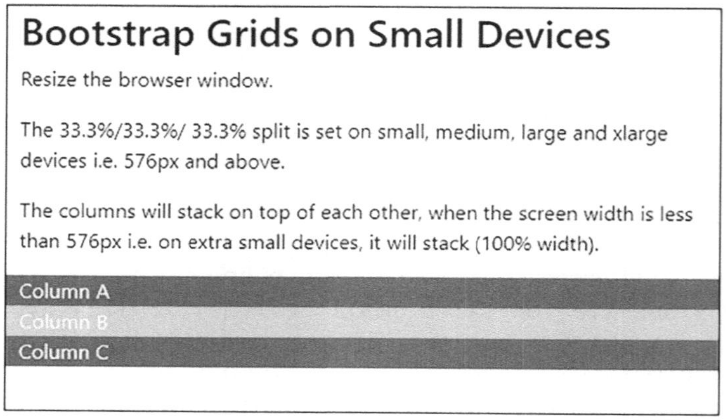

Figure 2.6: *The Three Columns will stack when the device size is less than 576px*

Creating Five Equal-Width Columns to Stack

To set the equal width of columns, directly use the **`.col-sm`** class. For our example, we will set the **`.col-sm`** class five times to give equal width to each column. The Bootstrap would recognize and provide a layout with each column as 20%, that is, the same width:

```
<!DOCTYPE html>
<!DOCTYPE html>
<html lang="en">
<head>
  <title>Bootstrap Grids with equal columns</title>
  <meta charset="utf-8">
  <meta name="viewport" content="width=device-width, initial-scale=1">
  <link
href="https://cdn.jsdelivr.net/npm/bootstrap@5.3.3/dist/css/bootstrap.
min.css" rel="stylesheet">
  <script s
rc="https://cdn.jsdelivr.net/npm/bootstrap@5.3.3/dist/js/bootstrap.bun-
dle.min.js"></script>
</head>
<body>

<div class="container-fluid">
  <h1>Bootstrap Grids with equal columns</h1>
  <p>Resize the browser window.</p>
  <p>The 20% each split is set on small, medium, large and xlarge
devices i.e. 576px and above.</p>
<p>The columns will stack on top of each other, when the screen width
is less than 576px i.e. on extra small devices, it will stack (100%
width).</p>
  <div class="row">
    <div class="col-sm bg-primary text-white">Column A</div>
    <div class="col-sm bg-info text-white">Column B</div>
    <div class="col-sm bg-success text-white">Column C</div>
    <div class="col-sm bg-secondary text-white">Column D</div>
    <div class="col-sm bg-warning text-white">Column E</div>
  </div>
</div>

</body>
</html>
```

After running the code, the web page will look as follows:

Screen Size: 1366 x 633

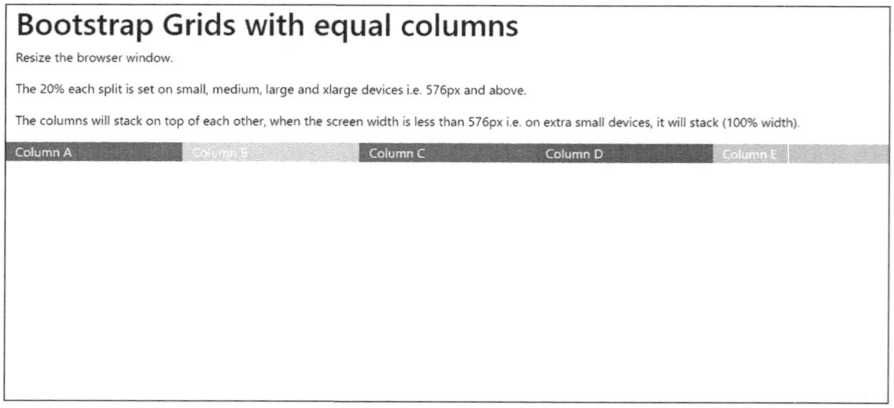

Figure 2.7*: The Five Columns won't stack when the device size is more than 576px*

Let us now resize the screen size. All five columns will stack on top of each other when the screen width is less than 576px:

Screen Size: 570 x 633

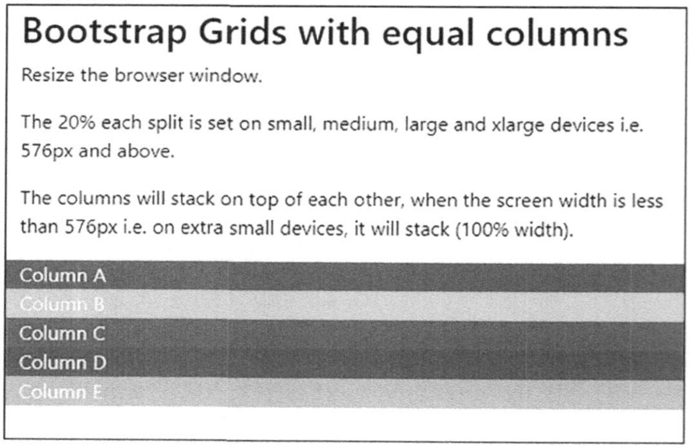

Figure 2.8*: The Five Columns will stack when the device size is less than 576px*

Grid Medium

In Bootstrap, we use the following classes to implement the grid system on **medium** devices:

```
.col-md-*
```

The **medium** devices have a screen width of:

```
768px to 991px
```

Until now, you must have understood the class prefix we use in Bootstrap for medium devices, that is,

```
.col-md-
```

Three Equal Columns

Let us create three equal columns on a web page using the Bootstrap Grid System. In the following example, the 33.3% wide is on medium, large, and xlarge devices, that is, 768px and above.

The columns will stack on top of each other when the screen width is less than 768px. On small and extra small devices, it will stack, that is, 100% width.

```
<div class="container-fluid">
  <div class="row">
    <div class="col-md-4 bg-primary text-white">Column A</div>
    <div class="col-md-4 bg-dark text-white">Column B</div>
    <div class="col-md-4 bg-primary text-white">Column C</div>
  </div>
</div>
```

Here, the total is 12, that is, three equal columns.

The following is the complete example:

```
<!DOCTYPE html>
<!DOCTYPE html>
<html lang="en">
<head>
  <title>Bootstrap Grids on Medium Devices</title>
  <meta charset="utf-8">
  <meta name="viewport" content="width=device-width, initial-scale=1">
  <link
href="https://cdn.jsdelivr.net/npm/bootstrap@5.3.3/dist/css/bootstrap.
min.css" rel="stylesheet">
  <script
src="https://cdn.jsdelivr.net/npm/bootstrap@5.3.3/dist/js/bootstrap.
bundle.min.js"></script>
</head>
<body>

<div class="container-fluid">
  <h1>Bootstrap Grids on Medium Devices</h1>
  <p>Resize the browser window.</p>
  <p>The 33.3%/33.3%/ 33.3% split is set on medium, large and xlarge
devices i.e. 768px and above.</p>
  <p>The columns will stack on top of each other, when the screen width
is less than 768px. On small and extra small devices, it will stack
```

```
(100% width).</p>
  <div class="row">
    <div class="col-md-4 bg-primary text-white">Column A</div>
    <div class="col-md-4 bg-info text-white">Column B</div>
    <div class="col-md-4 bg-success text-white">Column C</div>
  </div>
</div>

</body>
</html>
```

After running the code, the web page will look as follows:

Screen Size: 1366 x 633

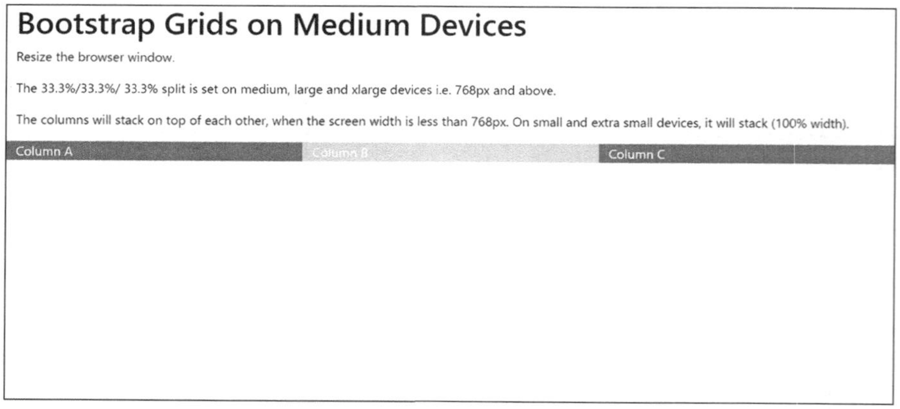

***Figure 2.9**: The Three Columns won't stack when the device size is more than 768px*

Let us now resize the screen size. The columns will stack on top of each other when the screen width is less than 768 pixels:

Screen Size: 760x 633

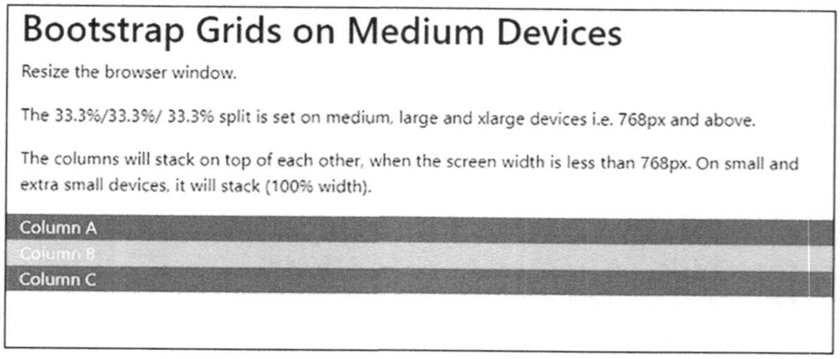

***Figure 2.10**: The Five Columns will stack when the device size is less than 768px*

Creating Five Equal-Width Columns to Stack

To set the equal width of columns, directly use the **.col-md** class. For our example, we will set the **.col-md** class five times to give equal width to each column. The Bootstrap would recognize and provide a layout with each column 20%, that is, the same width:

```
<!DOCTYPE html>
<html lang="en">
<head>
  <title>Bootstrap Grids with equal columns</title>
  <meta charset="utf-8">
  <meta name="viewport" content="width=device-width, initial-scale=1">
  <link
href="https://cdn.jsdelivr.net/npm/bootstrap@5.3.3/dist/css/bootstrap.
min.css" rel="stylesheet">
  <script
src="https://cdn.jsdelivr.net/npm/bootstrap@5.3.3/dist/js/bootstrap.
bundle.min.js"></script>
</head>
<body>

<div class="container-fluid">
  <h1>Bootstrap Grids with equal columns</h1>
  <p>Resize the browser window.</p>
  <p>The 20% each split is set on medium, large and xlarge devices i.e.
768px and above.</p>
  <p>The columns will stack on top of each other, when the screen width
is less than 768px. On small and extra small devices, it will stack
(100% width).</p>
  <div class="row">
    <div class="col-md bg-primary text-white">Column A</div>
    <div class="col-md bg-info text-white">Column B</div>
    <div class="col-md bg-success text-white">Column C</div>
    <div class="col-md bg-secondary text-white">Column D</div>
    <div class="col-md bg-warning text-white">Column E</div>
  </div>
</div>

</body>
</html>
```

After running the code, the web page will look as follows:

Screen Size: 1366 x 633

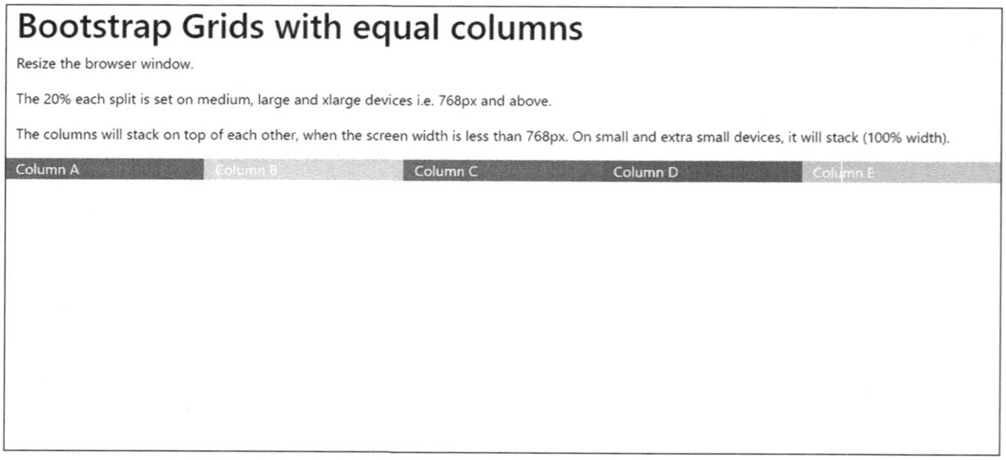

Figure 2.11: *The Five Columns won't stack when the device size is more than 768px*

Let us now resize the screen size. All five columns will stack on top of each other when the screen width is less than 768px:

Screen Size: 760 x 633

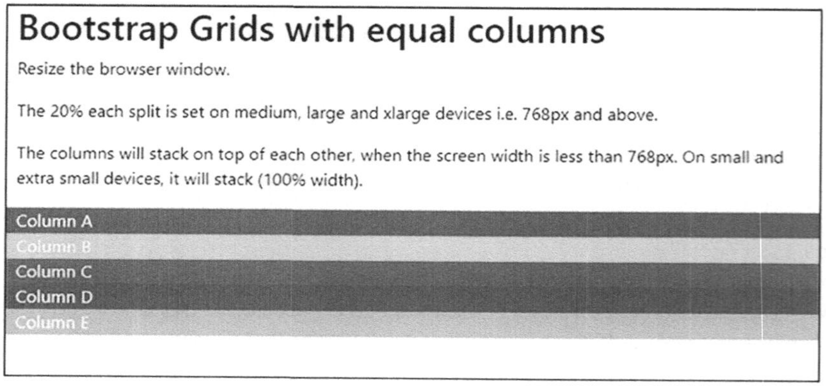

Figure 2.12: *The Five Columns will stack when the device size is less than 768px*

Grid Large

In Bootstrap, we use the following classes to implement the grid system on large devices:

```
.col-lg-*
```

The **large** devices have a screen width of:

```
992px to 1200px
```

Until now, you must have understood the class prefix we use in Bootstrap for large devices, that is,

```
.col-lg-
```

Three Equal Columns

Let us create three equal columns on a web page using the Bootstrap Grid System. In the following example, the 33% wide is on large and xlarge devices, that is, 992px and above.

The columns will stack on top of each other when the screen width is less than 992px. On medium, small, and extra small devices, it will stack, that is, 100% width.

```
<div class="container-fluid">
  <div class="row">
    <div class="col-lg-4 bg-primary text-white">Column A</div>
    <div class="col-lg-4 bg-dark text-white">Column B</div>
    <div class="col-lg-4 bg-primary text-white">Column C</div>
  </div>
</div>
```

Here, the total is 12, that is, three equal columns.

The following is the complete example:

```
<!DOCTYPE html>
<html lang="en">
<head>
  <title>Bootstrap Grids on Large Devices</title>
  <meta charset="utf-8">
  <meta name="viewport" content="width=device-width, initial-scale=1">
  <link
href="https://cdn.jsdelivr.net/npm/bootstrap@5.3.3/dist/css/bootstrap.
min.css" rel="stylesheet">
  <script
src="https://cdn.jsdelivr.net/npm/bootstrap@5.3.3/dist/js/bootstrap.
bundle.min.js"></script>
</head>
<body>

<div class="container-fluid">
  <h1>Bootstrap Grids on Large Devices</h1>
  <p>Resize the browser window.</p>
  <p>The 33.3%/33.3%/ 33.3% split is set on large and xlarge devices
i.e. 992px and above.</p>
  <p>The columns will stack on top of each other, when the screen width
is less than 992px i.e. on medium, small, and extra small devices, it
will stack (100% width).</p>
```

```
  <div class="row">
    <div class="col-lg-4 bg-primary text-white">Column A</div>
    <div class="col-lg-4 bg-info text-white">Column B</div>
    <div class="col-lg-4 bg-success text-white">Column C</div>
  </div>
</div>

</body>
</html>
```

After running the code, the web page will look as follows:

Screen Size: 1366 x 633

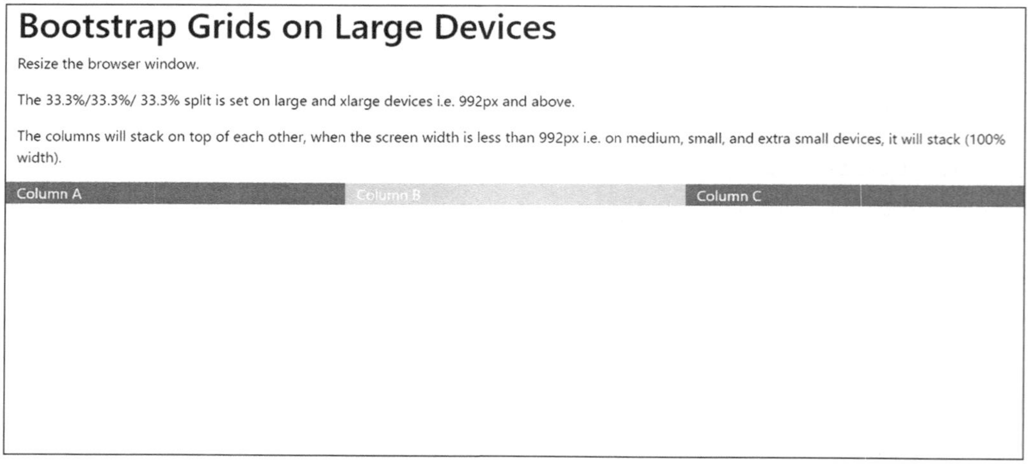

***Figure 2.13**: The Three Columns won't stack when the device size is more than 992px*

Let us now resize the screen size. All three columns will stack on top of each other when the screen width is less than 992px:

Screen Size: 980 x 633

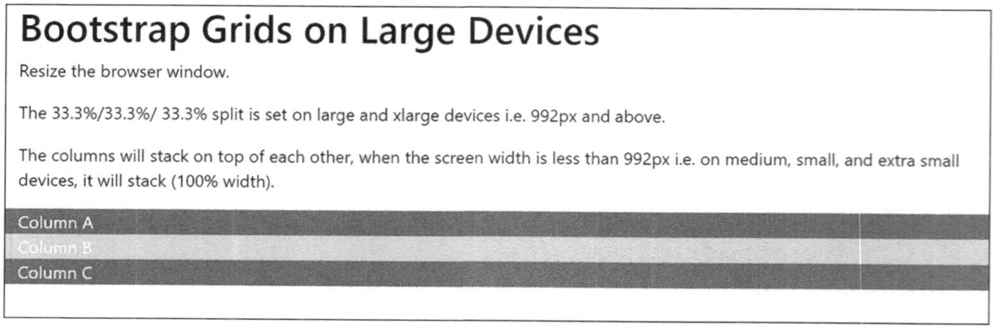

***Figure 2.14**: The Three Columns will stack when the device size is less than 992px*

Creating Equal-Width Columns

To set the equal width of columns, directly use the **.col-lg** class. For our example, we will set the **.col-lg** class five times to give equal width to each column. The Bootstrap would recognize and provide a layout with each column 20%, that is, the same width.

```
<!DOCTYPE html>
<html lang="en">
<head>
  <title>Bootstrap Grids with equal columns</title>
  <meta charset="utf-8">
  <meta name="viewport" content="width=device-width, initial-scale=1">
  <link
href="https://cdn.jsdelivr.net/npm/bootstrap@5.3.3/dist/css/bootstrap.
min.css" rel="stylesheet">
  <script
src="https://cdn.jsdelivr.net/npm/bootstrap@5.3.3/dist/js/bootstrap.
bundle.min.js"></script>
</head>
<body>

<div class="container-fluid">
  <h1>Bootstrap Grids with equal columns</h1>
  <p>Resize the browser window.</p>
  <p>The 20% each split is set on large and xlarge devices i.e. 992px
and above.</p>
  <p>The columns will stack on top of each other, when the screen width
is less than 992px i.e. on medium, small, and extra small devices, it
will stack (100% width).</p>
  <div class="row">
    <div class="col-lg bg-primary text-white">Column A</div>
    <div class="col-lg bg-info text-white">Column B</div>
    <div class="col-lg bg-success text-white">Column C</div>
    <div class="col-lg bg-secondary text-white">Column D</div>
    <div class="col-lg bg-warning text-white">Column E</div>
  </div>
</div>


</body>
</html>
```

After running the code, the web page will look as follows:

Screen Size: 1366 x 633

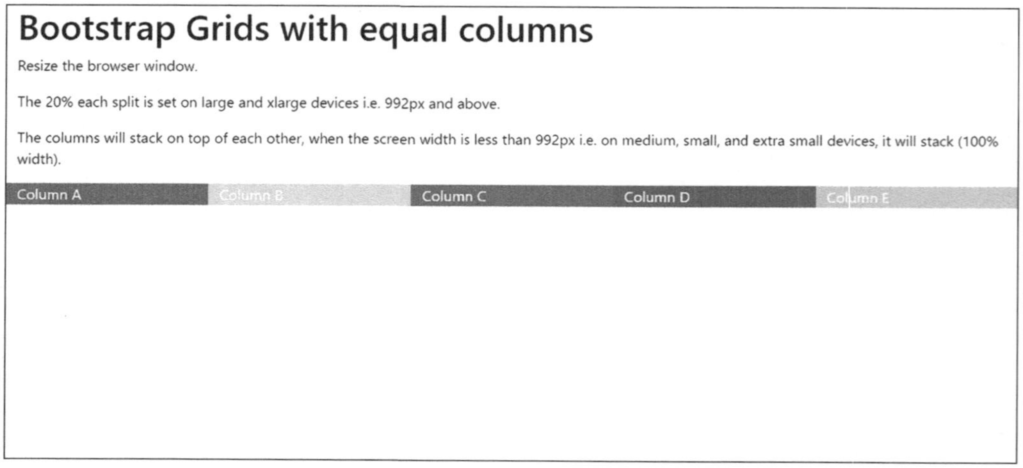

***Figure 2.15**: The Five Columns won't stack when the device size is more than 992px*

Let us now resize the screen size. All five columns will stack on top of each other when the screen width is less than 992px:

Screen Size: 980 x 633

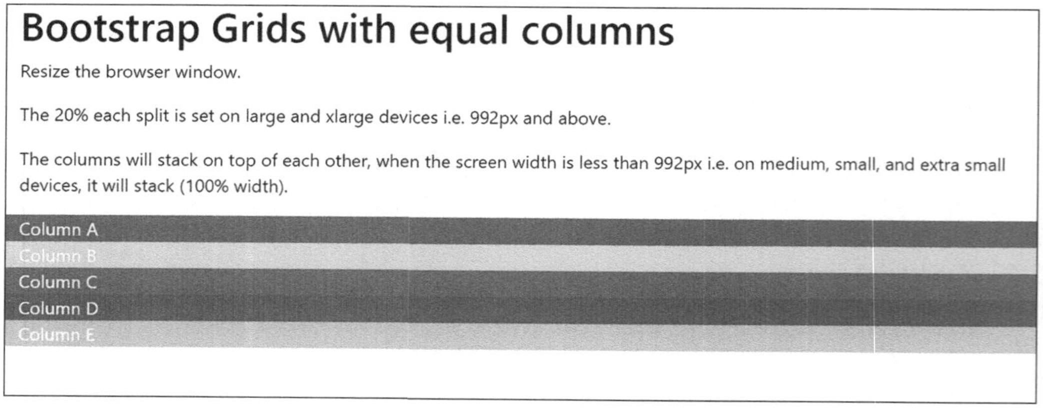

***Figure 2.16**: The Five Columns will stack when the device size is less than 992px*

Grid XLarge

In Bootstrap, we use the following classes to implement the grid system on extra-large devices, that is, **XLarge**:

```
.col-xl-*
```

The **XLarge** devices have a screen width of:

```
1200px to 1400px
```

Until now, you must have understood the class prefix we use in Bootstrap for extra-large devices, that is,

```
.col-xl-
```

Three Equal Columns

Let us create three equal columns on a web page using the Bootstrap Grid System. In the following example, the 33.3% wide is on xlarge devices, that is, 1200px and above.

The columns will stack on top of each other when the screen width is less than 1200px.

On large, medium, small, and extra small devices, it will stack, that is, 100% width:

```
<div class="container-fluid">
  <div class="row">
    <div class="col-xl-4 bg-primary text-white">Column A</div>
    <div class="col-xl-4 bg-dark text-white">Column B</div>
    <div class="col-xl-4 bg-primary text-white">Column C</div>
  </div>
</div>
```

Here, the total is 12, that is, three equal columns.

The following is the complete example:

```
<!DOCTYPE html>
<html lang="en">
<head>
  <title>Bootstrap Grids on Extra Large Devices</title>
  <meta charset="utf-8">
  <meta name="viewport" content="width=device-width, initial-scale=1">
  <link
href="https://cdn.jsdelivr.net/npm/bootstrap@5.3.3/dist/css/bootstrap.
min.css" rel="stylesheet">
  <script
src="https://cdn.jsdelivr.net/npm/bootstrap@5.3.3/dist/js/bootstrap.
bundle.min.js"></script>
</head>
<body>

<div class="container-fluid">
  <h1>Bootstrap Grids on Extra Large Devices</h1>
  <p>Resize the browser window.</p>
  <p>The 33.3%/33.3%/ 33.3% split is set on xlarge devices i.e. 1200px
and above.</p>
  <p>The columns will stack on top of each other, when the screen width
is less than 1200px i.e. on large, medium, small, and extra small
devices, it will stack (100% width).</p>
```

```
  <div class="row">
    <div class="col-xl-4 bg-primary text-white">Column A</div>
    <div class="col-xl-4 bg-info text-white">Column B</div>
    <div class="col-xl-4 bg-success text-white">Column C</div>
  </div>
</div>

</body>
</html>
```

After running the code, the web page will look as follows:

All three columns will stack on top of each other when the screen width is less than 1200px.

Screen Size: 1100 x 633

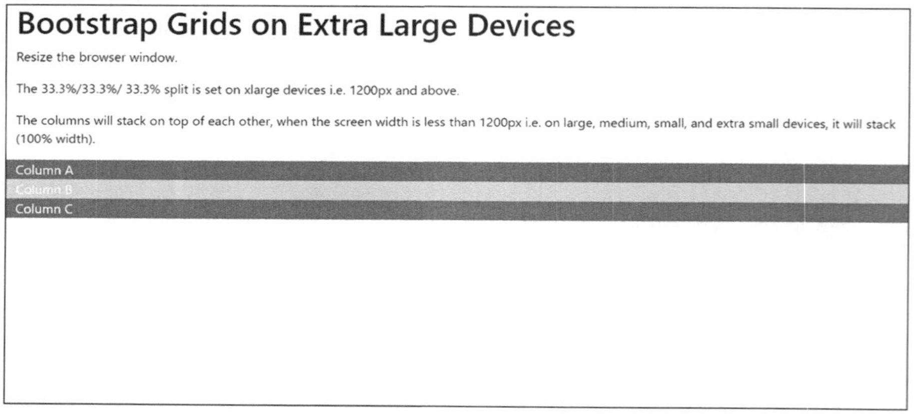

Figure 2.17: *The Three Columns will stack when the device size is less than 1200px*

Let us now resize the screen size.

Screen Size: 1366 x 633

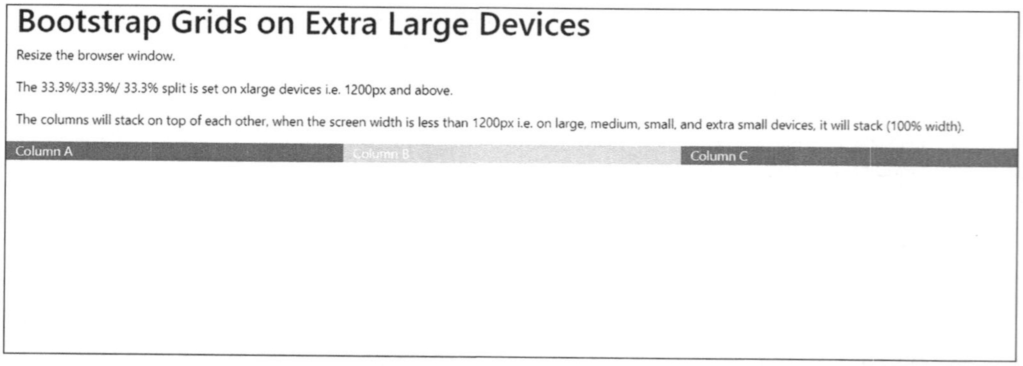

Figure 2.18: *The Three Columns won't stack when the device size is more than 1200px*

Creating Equal-Width Columns

To set the equal width of columns, directly use the **.col-xl** class. For our example, we will set the **.col-xl** class five times to give equal width to each column. The Bootstrap would recognize and provide a layout with each column 20%, that is, the same width:

```
<!DOCTYPE html>
<!DOCTYPE html>
<html lang="en">
<head>
  <title>Bootstrap Grids with equal columns</title>
  <meta charset="utf-8">
  <meta name="viewport" content="width=device-width, initial-scale=1">
  <link
href="https://cdn.jsdelivr.net/npm/bootstrap@5.3.3/dist/css/bootstrap.
min.css" rel="stylesheet">
  <script
src="https://cdn.jsdelivr.net/npm/bootstrap@5.3.3/dist/js/bootstrap.
bundle.min.js"></script>
</head>
<body>

<div class="container-fluid">
  <h1>Bootstrap Grids with equal columns</h1>
  <p>Resize the browser window.</p>
  <p>The 20% each split is set on xlarge devices i.e. 1200px and
above.</p>
  <p>The columns will stack on top of each other, when the screen width
is less than 1200px i.e. on large, medium, small, and extra small
devices, it will stack (100% width).</p>
  <div class="row">
    <div class="col-xl bg-primary text-white">Column A</div>
    <div class="col-xl bg-info text-white">Column B</div>
    <div class="col-xl bg-success text-white">Column C</div>
    <div class="col-xl bg-secondary text-white">Column D</div>
    <div class="col-xl bg-warning text-white">Column E</div>
  </div>
</div>

</body>
</html>
```

After running the code, the web page will look as follows:

All three columns will stack on top of each other when the screen width is less than 1200px:

Screen Size: 1100 x 633

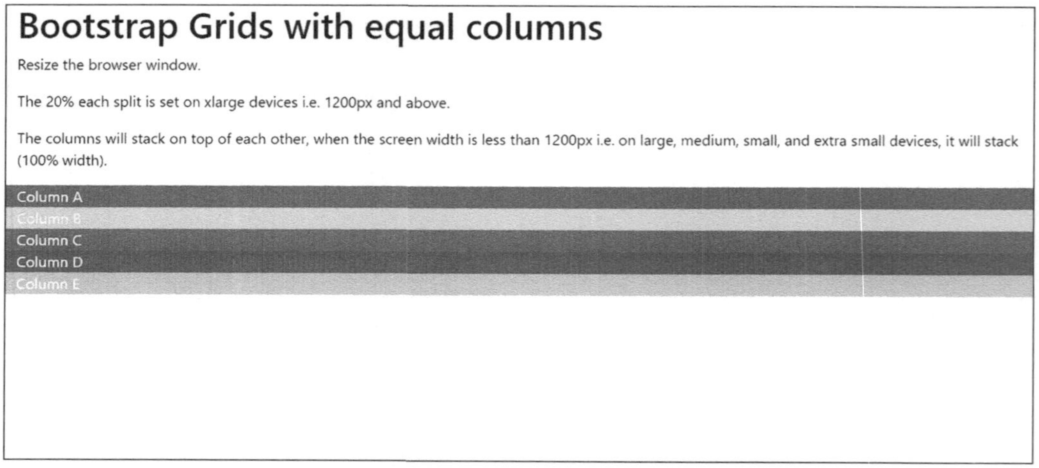

***Figure 2.19**: The Five Columns will stack when the device size is less than 1200px*

Let us now resize the screen size.

Screen Size: 1366 x 633

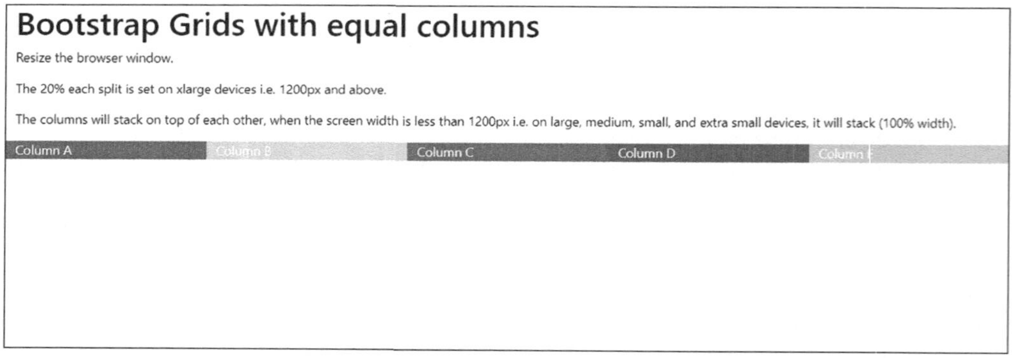

***Figure 2.20**: The Five Columns won't stack when the device size is more than 1200px*

Grid XXLarge

Bootstrap 5 came up with support for the XXL Breakpoint, that is, the extra-large devices.

We use the following classes to implement the grid system on **xxlarge** devices:

```
.col-xxl-*
```

The **xxlarge** devices have a screen width of:

```
>=1400px
```

Until now, you must have understood the class prefix we use in Bootstrap for **xxlarge** devices, that is,

```
.col-xxl-
```

Three Equal Columns

Let us create three equal columns on a web page using the Bootstrap Grid System. In the following example, the 33% split on **xxlarge** devices that is, 1400px and above.

The columns will stack on top of each other when the screen width is less than 1400px.

On extra-large, large, medium, small, and extra small devices, it will stack, that is,, 100% width:

```
<div class="container-fluid">
  <div class="row">
    <div class="col-xxl-4 bg-primary text-white">Column A</div>
    <div class="col-xxl-4 bg-dark text-white">Column B</div>
    <div class="col-xxl-4 bg-primary text-white">Column C</div>
  </div>
</div>
```

Here, the total is 12, that is, three equal columns.

The following is the complete example:

```
<!DOCTYPE html>
<html lang="en">
<head>
  <title>Bootstrap Grids on xx Large Devices</title>
  <meta charset="utf-8">
  <meta name="viewport" content="width=device-width, initial-scale=1">
  <link
href="https://cdn.jsdelivr.net/npm/bootstrap@5.3.3/dist/css/bootstrap.
min.css" rel="stylesheet">
  <script
src="https://cdn.jsdelivr.net/npm/bootstrap@5.3.3/dist/js/bootstrap.
bundle.min.js"></script>
</head>
<body>

<div class="container-fluid">
  <h1>Bootstrap Grids on xx Large Devices</h1>
  <p>Resize the browser window.</p>
  <p>The 33.3%/33.3%/ 33.3% split is set on xxlarge devices i.e. 1400px
and above.</p>
  <p>The columns will stack on top of each other, when the screen width
```

```
is less than 1400px i.e. on extra large, large, medium, small, and extra
small devices, it will stack (100% width).</p>
  <div class="row">
    <div class="col-xxl-4 bg-primary text-white">Column 1</div>
    <div class="col-xxl-4 bg-info text-white">Column 2</div>
    <div class="col-xxl-4 bg-success text-white">Column 3</div>
  </div>
</div>

</body>
</html>
```

After running the code, the web page will look as follows:

Screen Size: 1366 x 633

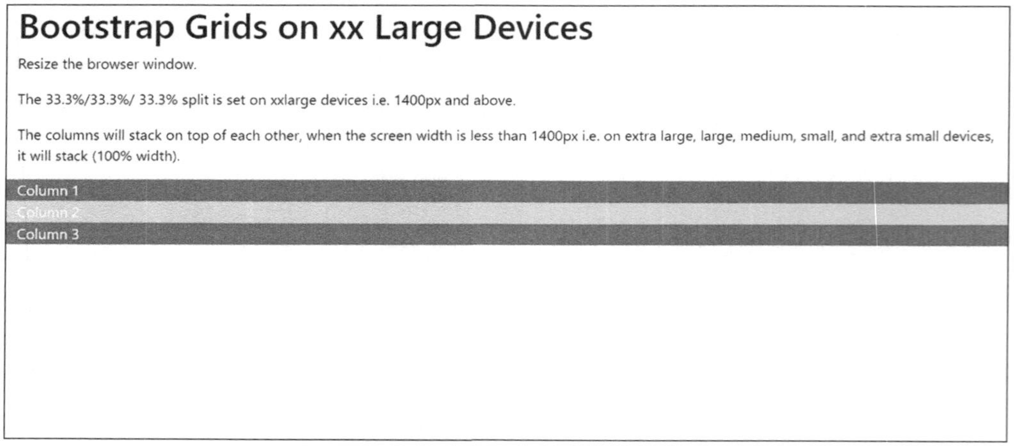

***Figure 2.21**: The Five Columns will stack when the device size is less than 1400px*

Let us now resize the screen size.

Screen Size: 1420 x 633

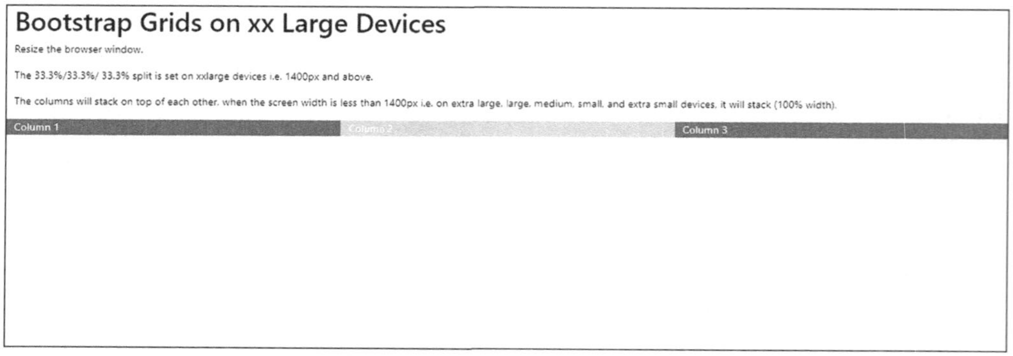

***Figure 2.22**: The Five Columns won't stack when the device size is more than 1400px*

Creating Equal-Width Columns

To set the equal width of columns, directly use the **.col-xxl** class. For our example, we will set the **.col-xxl** class five times to give equal width to each column. The Bootstrap would recognize and provide a layout with each column as 20%, that is, the same width:

```
<!DOCTYPE html>
<html lang="en">
<head>
  <title>Bootstrap Grids with equal columns</title>
  <meta charset="utf-8">
  <meta name="viewport" content="width=device-width, initial-scale=1">
  <link
href="https://cdn.jsdelivr.net/npm/bootstrap@5.3.3/dist/css/bootstrap.
min.css" rel="stylesheet">
  <script
src="https://cdn.jsdelivr.net/npm/bootstrap@5.3.3/dist/js/bootstrap.
bundle.min.js"></script>
</head>
<body>

<div class="container-fluid">
  <h1>Bootstrap Grids with equal columns</h1>
  <p>Resize the browser window.</p>
  <p>The 20% each split is set on xxlarge devices i.e. 1400px and
above.</p>
  <p>The columns will stack on top of each other, when the screen width
is less than 1400px i.e. on extra large, large, medium, small, and extra
small devices, it will stack (100% width).</p>
  <div class="row">
    <div class="col-xxl bg-primary text-white">Column A</div>
    <div class="col-xxl bg-info text-white">Column B</div>
    <div class="col-xxl bg-success text-white">Column C</div>
    <div class="col-xxl bg-secondary text-white">Column D</div>
    <div class="col-xxl bg-warning text-white">Column E</div>
  </div>
</div>

</body>
</html>
```

After running the code, the web page will look as follows:

Screen Size: 1366 x 633

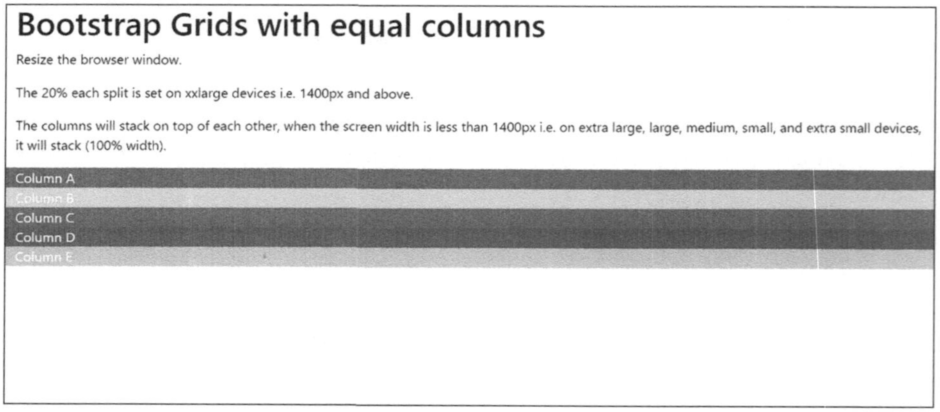

Figure 2.23: *The Five Columns will stack when the device size is less than 1400px*

Let us now resize the screen size.

Screen Size: 1420 x 633

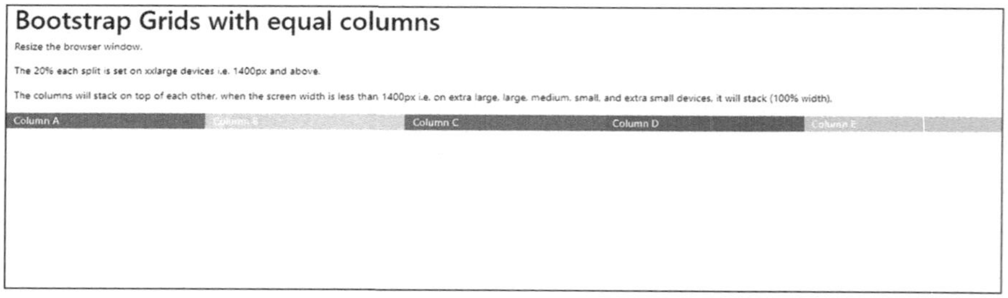

Figure 2.24: *The Five Columns won't stack when the device size is more than 1400px*

Unequal Columns

On a web page, you can easily create unequal columns. Let's say you want four unequal columns:

```
Column 1: 20%
Column 2: 30%
Column 3: 20%
Column 4: 30%
```

We can set a row with unequal columns as follows. We have used numbers:

```
<div class="row">
  <div class="col-2 bg-primary">C#</div>
  <div class="col-5 bg-secondary">Python and Java</div>
  <div class="col-2 bg-warning">C</div>
  <div class="col-3 bg-danger">C++</div>
</div>
```

Let us see an example of creating unequal columns on a web page:

```
<!DOCTYPE html>
<html lang="en">
<head>
  <title>Bootstrap Grids</title>
  <meta charset="utf-8">
  <meta name="viewport" content="width=device-width, initial-scale=1">
  <link
href="https://cdn.jsdelivr.net/npm/bootstrap@5.3.3/dist/css/bootstrap.
min.css" rel="stylesheet">
  <script
src="https://cdn.jsdelivr.net/npm/bootstrap@5.3.3/dist/js/bootstrap.
bundle.min.js"></script>
</head>
<body>

<div class="container-fluid mt-3">
  <h2>Products</h2>
  <p>The following are our products:</p>
  <div class="row">
       <div class="col-2 bg-primary">C#</div>
       <div class="col-5 bg-secondary">Python and Java</div>
       <div class="col-2 bg-warning">C</div>
       <div class="col-3 bg-danger">C++</div>
  </div>
</div>

</body>
</html>
```

The following is how the web page will look after running the code:

Screen Size: 1366 x 633

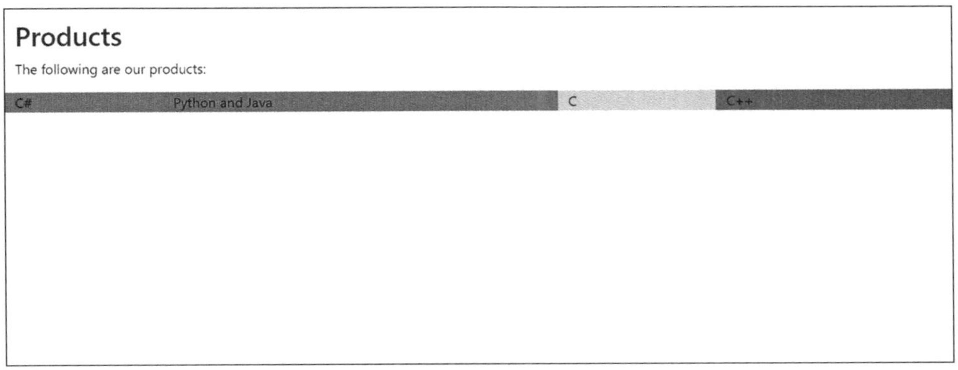

Figure 2.25: *Grid with unequal columns*

Row cols

The **.rows-cols-*** class can be used on a web page to control the number of columns appearing next to each other. Let's say we want to display two columns next to each other. For that, use the **.row-cols-2** as follows to display two columns on each row:

```
<div class="row row-cols-2">
  <div class="col bg-primary">1 of 4</div>
  <div class="col bg-secondary">2 of 4</div>
  <div class="col bg-danger">3 of 4</div>
  <div class="col bg-warning">4 of 4</div>
</div>
```

Let us see an example of displaying multiple rows and columns:

```
<!DOCTYPE html>
<html lang="en">
<head>
  <title>Bootstrap Row Cols</title>
  <meta charset="utf-8">
  <meta name="viewport" content="width=device-width, initial-scale=1">
  <link
href="https://cdn.jsdelivr.net/npm/bootstrap@5.3.3/dist/css/bootstrap.
min.css" rel="stylesheet">
  <script
src="https://cdn.jsdelivr.net/npm/bootstrap@5.3.3/dist/js/bootstrap.
bundle.min.js"></script>
</head>
<body>

<div class="container-fluid mt-2">
  <h2>Row Cols</h2>
  <div class="row row-cols-1">
       <div class="col bg-primary">1 of 2</div>
       <div class="col bg-secondary">2 of 2</div>
  </div>
  <br>
  <div class="row row-cols-1">
       <div class="col bg-primary">1 of 3</div>
       <div class="col bg-secondary">2 of 3</div>
       <div class="col bg-danger">3 of 3</div>
  </div>
  <br>
  <div class="row row-cols-2">
       <div class="col bg-primary">1 of 6</div>
       <div class="col bg-secondary">2 of 6</div>
       <div class="col bg-danger">3 of 6</div>
```

```
        <div class="col bg-warning">4 of 6</div>
        <div class="col bg-success">5 of 6</div>
        <div class="col bg-info">6 of 6</div>
    </div>
    <br>
    <div class="row row-cols-2">
        <div class="col bg-primary">1 of 4</div>
        <div class="col bg-secondary">2 of 4</div>
        <div class="col bg-danger">3 of 4</div>
        <div class="col bg-warning">4 of 4</div>
    </div>
</div>

</body>
</html>
```

After running the code, the web page will look as follows:

Screen Size: 1366 x 633

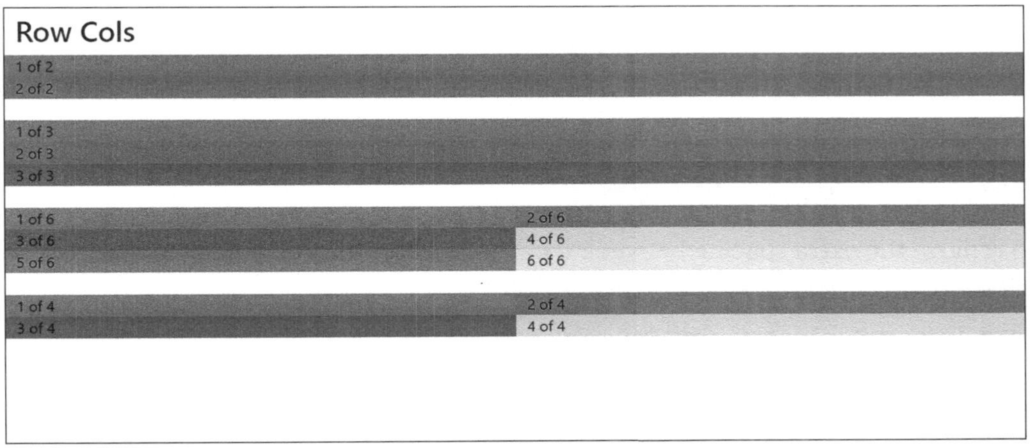

***Figure 2.26**: Columns appearing next to each other*

Gutters in Bootstrap

In Bootstrap, gutters are the gaps between columns in a grid layout. They are used to create spacing between elements to ensure a clean and organized look. Gutters are typically implemented with padding.

The following are the types of gutters:

- **Horizontal Gutters:** These are the spaces between columns across the row.
- **Vertical Gutters:** These are the spaces between rows.

Note: *Bootstrap applies a horizontal gutter of 30px. This is 15px on each side of a column by default.*

Horizontal Gutters

The Bootstrap classes, such as **.gx-1**, **.gx-2**, **.gx-3**, and so on, can be used to set horizontal gutter sizes. For example:

```
<div class="row gx-2">
  <div class="col">...</div>
  <div class="col">...</div>
</div>
```

Vertical Gutters

The Bootstrap classes, such as **.gy-1**, **.gy-2**, **.gy-3**, and so on, can be used to set vertical gutter sizes. For example:

```
<div class="row gy-2">
  <div class="col">...</div>
  <div class="col">...</div>
</div>
```

Remove Gutter Spacing

To remove the extra spacing between columns, that is, the gutters completed, use the **g-0** class. You can also use **.g-1|2|3|4|5** classes.

Note: *The* **.g-4 class** *is default.*

Let us see an example of removing the gutter spacing between columns:

```
<!DOCTYPE html>
<html lang="en">
<head>
  <title>Bootstrap Example</title>
  <meta charset="utf-8">
  <meta name="viewport" content="width=device-width, initial-scale=1">
  <link
href="https://cdn.jsdelivr.net/npm/bootstrap@5.3.3/dist/css/bootstrap.
min.css" rel="stylesheet">
  <script
src="https://cdn.jsdelivr.net/npm/bootstrap@5.3.3/dist/js/bootstrap.
bundle.min.js"></script>
</head>
<body>
```

```
<div class="container-fluid mt-2">
  <h1>Types of Learning</h1>
  <div class="container-fluid">
       <div class="row g-0">
       <div class="col-3 bg-primary">
       Under Inductive learning, the learner observes instances and
discover rules based on defined principles to draw conclusion.
       </div>
       <div class="col-9 bg-danger">
       Under Deductive learning, the conclusion is drawn from experiences.
The deductive approach applies known principles to derive specific out-
comes.
       </div>
       </div>
  </div>
</div>

</body>
</html>
```

The following is how the web page will look after running the code:

Screen Size: 1366 x 633

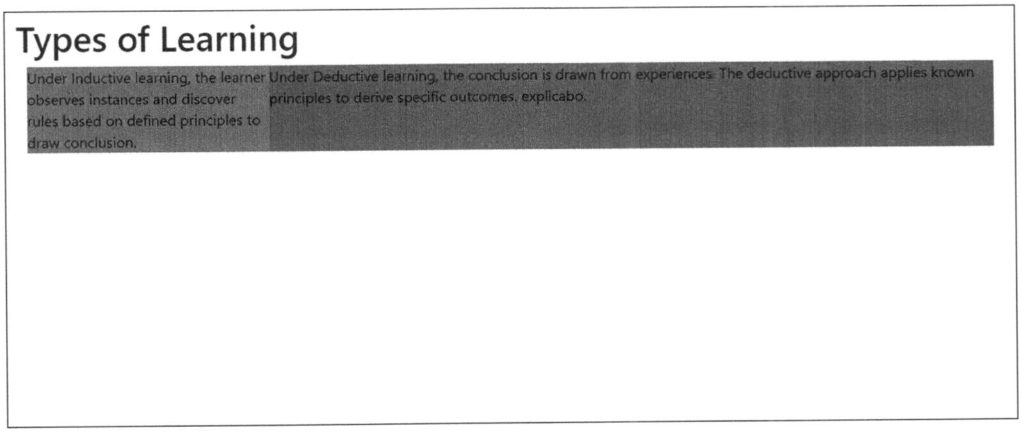

Figure 2.27: *Removing gutter spacing from columns*

Conclusion

We are now familiar with the Bootstrap Grid System. A container and grid are quite vital to understanding the layout of a web page since all the content goes inside them.

In the next chapter, we will see how to set the content on the web page in the form of images, tables, and so on.

Points to Remember

- A container on a web page is either fixed or full-width
- 12 columns on a web page are allowed
- The six classes of the grid system are extra small, small, medium, large, extra-large, and xxlarge devices.
- The `.rows-cols-*` class can be used on a web page to control the number of columns appearing next to each other
- The Bootstrap classes, such as `.gx-1`, `.gx-2`, `.gx-3`, and so on, can be used to set horizontal gutter sizes.
- The Bootstrap classes, such as `.gy-1`, `.gy-2`, `gy-3`, and so on, can be used to set vertical gutter sizes.

Multiple Choice Questions

1. The `.container` class is used to create a _______ container.
   a. fixed-width
   b. full-width
2. How many columns are allowed on a web page?
   a. 3
   b. 6
   c. 9
   d. 12
3. The medium devices have a screen width of:
   a. 768–991 px
   b. 768–992 px
   c. 992–1199 px
   d. 992–1200 px
4. For three equal columns, use _____ `.col-sm-4`
   a. One
   b. Two
   c. Three
   d. Four

5. To remove the extra spacing between columns, that is, the gutters completely, use the ____ class.

    a. `g-1`

    b. `g-0`

    c. `g-2`

    d. `g-3`

Answers

1. a
2. d
3. a
4. c
5. b

Questions

1. What is a container on a web page?
2. What are fixed-width and full-width containers?
3. How many columns are on a web page according to the Grid System?
4. What is the role of the Grid System?
5. What are the classes of the Bootstrap 5 Grid System?
6. Explain the Bootstrap classes for the screen width 992 to 1400px.
7. What is a Gutter in Bootstrap?

Key Terms

- **Container:** Consider, a container as a box on a web page within which all the elements are placed. All the elements are wrapped inside it.
- **Grid:** For the web page layout and to align the content within it, we have Bootstrap Grid. The Grid system uses the container, rows, and columns to set the content.
- **XSmall Grid:** The grid system on extra small devices is called an XSmall Grid.

This grid is always horizontal. The XSmall devices have a screen width of < 576px.

- **XLarge Grid:** The grid system on extra-large devices is called an XLarge Grid. The xlarge devices have a screen width of 1200–1400px
- **XXLarge Grid:** The grid system on extra-large devices is called an XXLarge Grid. The xxlarge devices have a screen width of > 1400px.
- **Gutters:** In Bootstrap, gutters are the gaps between columns in a grid layout. They are used to create spacing between elements to ensure a clean and organized look

CHAPTER 3
Set the Content with Bootstrap

Introduction

This chapter covers how to set the content on a web page with Bootstrap. This includes how to set and style the text, images, tables, and so on on a web page with Bootstrap. The global settings applied to a web page are also discussed.

Structure

In this chapter, we will discuss the following topics:

- Typography
- Images
- Tables
- Responsive Tables

Typography

Bootstrap typography refers to the set of styles and classes provided by the Bootstrap framework to design and format text content. It includes a variety of features to help you create visually appealing and consistent text across your web pages.

The Bootstrap Typography on a web page, includes,

- Global settings
- Bootstrap heading classes
- Creating a paragraph to stand out from the default
- Set a smaller font size for abbreviations
- Make the text look fine print

Global Settings

The following are the global settings provided by Bootstrap on a web page:

- The default font size is **`1rem`**, that is, **`16px`** by default for text.
- The default line height is **`1.5`**.
- The **`<p>`** elements have **`margin-top: 0`** and **`margin-bottom: 1rem`**, that is, **`16px`** by default.
- Use a **native font stack** that selects the best font family for each OS and device.

Headings

To set headings, HTML already provides **`<h1>`** to **`<h6>`**. The same can be used in Bootstrap. However, Bootstrap also provided the following separate classes to do the same work:

- **`.h1`** to **`.h6`**
- Display headings

The `.h1` to `.h6` Bootstrap Headings

The **`<p>`** element can also be used to set the headings using the **`.h1`** to **`.h6`** headings:

```
<p class="h1">h1. Bootstrap heading</p>
<p class="h2">h2. Bootstrap heading</p>
<p class="h3">h3. Bootstrap heading</p>
<p class="h4">h4. Bootstrap heading</p>
<p class="h5">h5. Bootstrap heading</p>
<p class="h6">h6. Bootstrap heading</p>
```

Let us see an example:

```
<!DOCTYPE html>
<html lang="en">
<head>
  <title>Bootstrap Headings</title>
  <meta charset="utf-8">
  <meta name="viewport" content="width=device-width, initial-scale=1">
  <link
href="https://cdn.jsdelivr.net/npm/bootstrap@5.3.3/dist/css/bootstrap.
min.css" rel="stylesheet">
  <script
src="https://cdn.jsdelivr.net/npm/bootstrap@5.3.3/dist/js/bootstrap.
bundle.min.js"></script>
</head>
<body>
<h1>Bootstrap Headings</h1>
```

```
<p class="h1">Bootstrap Heading (Heading1)</p>
<p class="h2">Bootstrap Heading (Heading2)</p>
<p class="h3">Bootstrap Heading (Heading3)</p>
<p class="h4">Bootstrap Heading (Heading4)</p>
<p class="h5">Bootstrap Heading (Heading5)</p>
<p class="h6">Bootstrap Heading (Heading6)</p>
</body>
</html>
```

After running the code, the web page will look as follows:

Screen Size: 1366 x 633

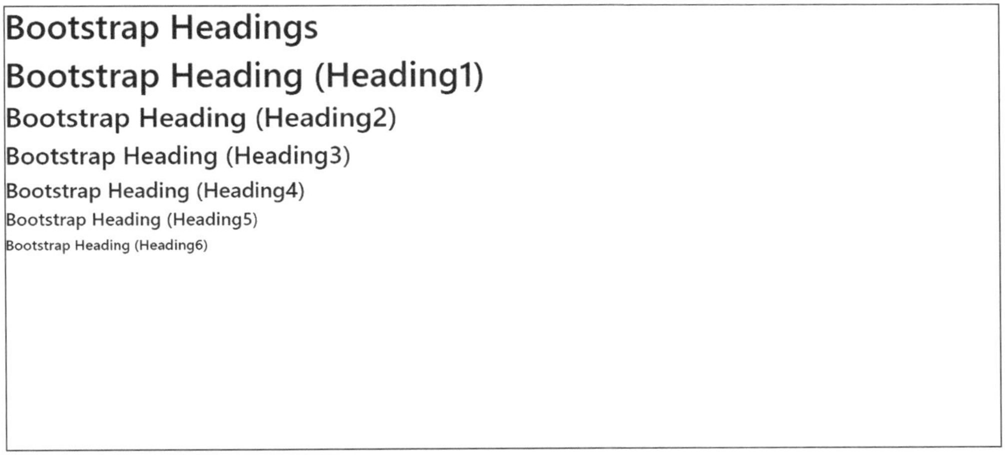

***Figure 3.1**: Bootstrap Headings*

The Bootstrap Display Heading

For larger and differently styled headings on a webpage, use the display headings, that is, the Bootstrap classes **`.display-1`** to **`.display-6`**:

```
<h1 class="display-1">Display Heading 1</h1>
<h1 class="display-2">Display Heading 2</h1>
<h1 class="display-3">Display Heading 3</h1>
<h1 class="display-4">Display Heading 4</h1>
<h1 class="display-5">Display Heading 5</h1>
<h1 class="display-6">Display Heading 6</h1>
```

Let us see an example:

```
<!DOCTYPE html>
<html lang="en">
<head>
  <title>Bootstrap Display Headings</title>
  <meta charset="utf-8">
```

```
  <meta name="viewport" content="width=device-width, initial-scale=1">
  <link
href="https://cdn.jsdelivr.net/npm/bootstrap@5.3.3/dist/css/bootstrap.
min.css" rel="stylesheet">
  <script
src="https://cdn.jsdelivr.net/npm/bootstrap@5.3.3/dist/js/bootstrap.
bundle.min.js"></script>
</head>
<body>
<h1>Bootstrap Display Headings</h1>
<h1 class="display-1">Display Heading 1</h1>
<h1 class="display-2">Display Heading 2</h1>
<h1 class="display-3">Display Heading 3</h1>
<h1 class="display-4">Display Heading 4</h1>
<h1 class="display-5">Display Heading 5</h1>
<h1 class="display-6">Display Heading 6</h1>

</body>
</html>
```

After running the code, the web page will look as follows:

Screen Size: 1366 x 633

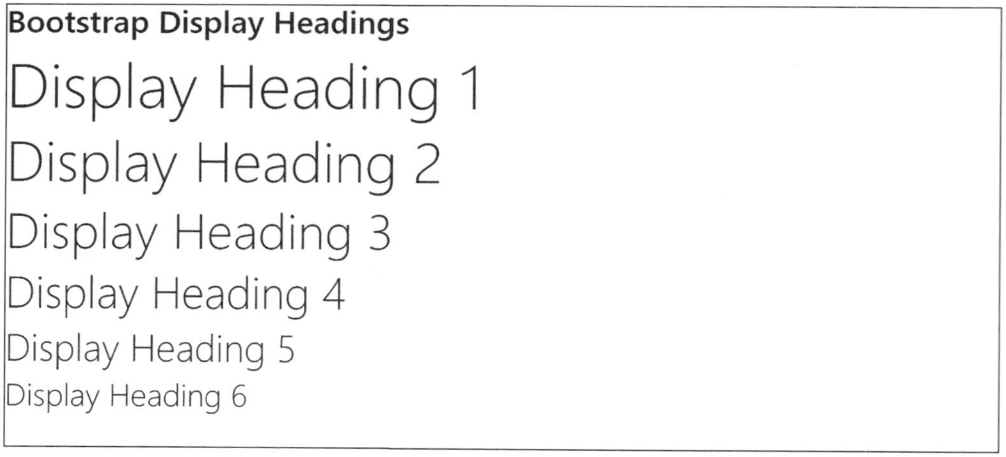

***Figure 3.2**: Bootstrap Display Headings*

A Paragraph to Stand Out from the Default

On a web page, a paragraph is set using the **<p>** element. To make a paragraph stand out from the default size, weight, and line height, use the Bootstrap class **.lead**.

```
<p class="lead">
```

Let us see an example:

```
<!DOCTYPE html>
<html lang="en">
<head>
  <title>Bootstrap Paragraphs</title>
  <meta charset="utf-8">
  <meta name="viewport" content="width=device-width, initial-scale=1">
  <link href="https://cdn.jsdelivr.net/npm/bootstrap@5.3.3/dist/css/
bootstrap.min.css" rel="stylesheet">
  <script src="https://cdn.jsdelivr.net/npm/bootstrap@5.3.3/dist/js/
bootstrap.bundle.min.js"></script>
</head>
<body>
<h1>Bootstrap Paragraphs</h1>
<p>This is a normal default usage of the paragraph tag on a web page.</
p>
<p class ="lead">This paragraph is using the Bootstrap class lead to get
a different look on a web page.</p>
</body>
</html>
```

After running the code, the web page will look as follows: :

Screen Size: 1366 x 633

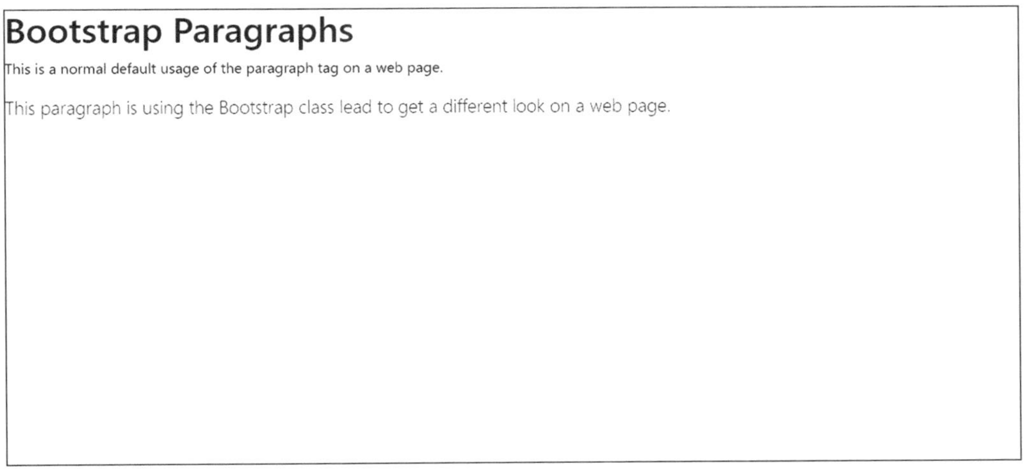

Figure 3.3: *Bootstrap Paragraphs*

Setting a Smaller Font Size for Abbreviations

On a web page, an abbreviation is set using the **`<abbr>`** element. To make the abbreviation look different than the default size, use the Bootstrap class **`.initialism`**.

The class **`.initialism`** also converted the characters to uppercase.

Let us see an example to set a smaller font size for abbreviations. To explain the different uses of initialism, we have the characters to be in lowercase:

```
<!DOCTYPE html>
<html lang="en">
<head>
  <title>Bootstrap Abbreviation</title>
  <meta charset="utf-8">
  <meta name="viewport" content="width=device-width, initial-scale=1">
  <link
href="https://cdn.jsdelivr.net/npm/bootstrap@5.3.3/dist/css/bootstrap.
min.css" rel="stylesheet">
  <script
src="https://cdn.jsdelivr.net/npm/bootstrap@5.3.3/dist/js/bootstrap.
bundle.min.js"></script>
</head>
<body>
<h1>Abbreviations</h1>
<p>Below are two abbreviations. The 2nd one is set using a Bootstrap
class:</p>
<abbr title="Solid State Drive">ssd</abbr><br>
<abbr title="Hard Disk Drive"class ="initialism">hdd</abbr>
</body>
</html>
```

After running the code, the web page will look as follows:

Screen Size: 1366 x 633

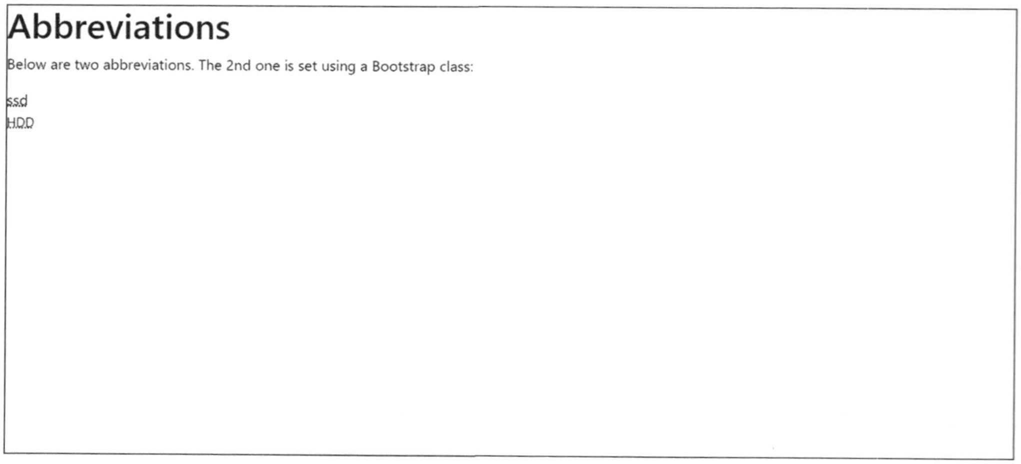

Figure 3.4: *Bootstrap Abbreviations*

Create a Smaller Secondary Heading

The **<small>** element is used in Bootstrap for multiple purposes:

- To create a small secondary heading.
- To make a text look fine print

Let us see an example of creating a small secondary heading using the **<small>** element:

```
<!DOCTYPE html>
<html lang="en">
<head>
  <title>Bootstrap Smaller Headings</title>
  <meta charset="utf-8">
  <meta name="viewport" content="width=device-width, initial-scale=1">
  <link
href="https://cdn.jsdelivr.net/npm/bootstrap@5.3.3/dist/css/bootstrap.
min.css" rel="stylesheet">
  <script
src="https://cdn.jsdelivr.net/npm/bootstrap@5.3.3/dist/js/bootstrap.
bundle.min.js"></script>
</head>
<body>
<h1>The h1 Heading <small>smaller secondary text</small></h1>
<h2>The h2 Heading <small>smaller secondary text</small></h2>
<h3>The h3 Heading <small>smaller secondary text</small></h3>
<h4>The h4 Heading <small>smaller secondary text</small></h4>
<h5>The h5 Heading <small>smaller secondary text</small></h5>
<h6>The h6 Heading <small>smaller secondary text</small></h6>
</body>
</html>
```

After running the code, the web page will look as follows:

Screen Size: 1366 x 633

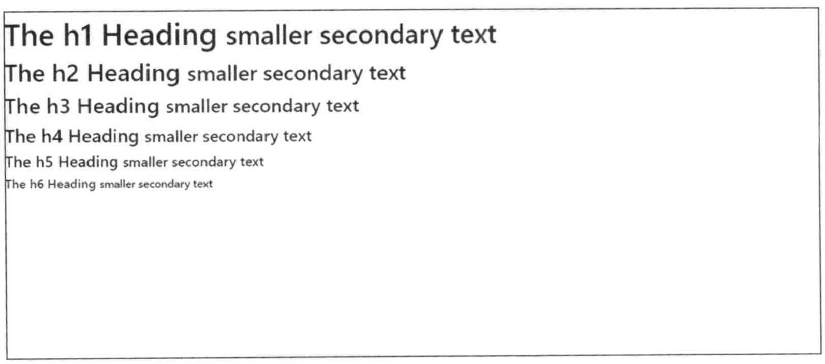

Figure 3.5: *Bootstrap Small Headings*

Let us see an example of creating a text that looks fine print using the Bootstrap **`.small`** class:

```
<!DOCTYPE html>
<html lang="en">
<head>
  <title>Bootstrap Fine Print Paragraphs</title>
  <meta charset="utf-8">
  <meta name="viewport" content="width=device-width, initial-scale=1">
  <link
href="https://cdn.jsdelivr.net/npm/bootstrap@5.3.3/dist/css/bootstrap.
min.css" rel="stylesheet">
  <script
src="https://cdn.jsdelivr.net/npm/bootstrap@5.3.3/dist/js/bootstrap.
bundle.min.js"></script>
</head>
<body>
<h1>Bootstrap Paragraphs</h1>
<p>This is a normal default usage of the paragraph tag on a web page.</
p>
<p class ="small">This paragraph is using the Bootstrap class small to
get a fine print text.</p>
</body>
</html>
```

After running the code, the web page will look as follows:

Screen Size: 1366 x 633

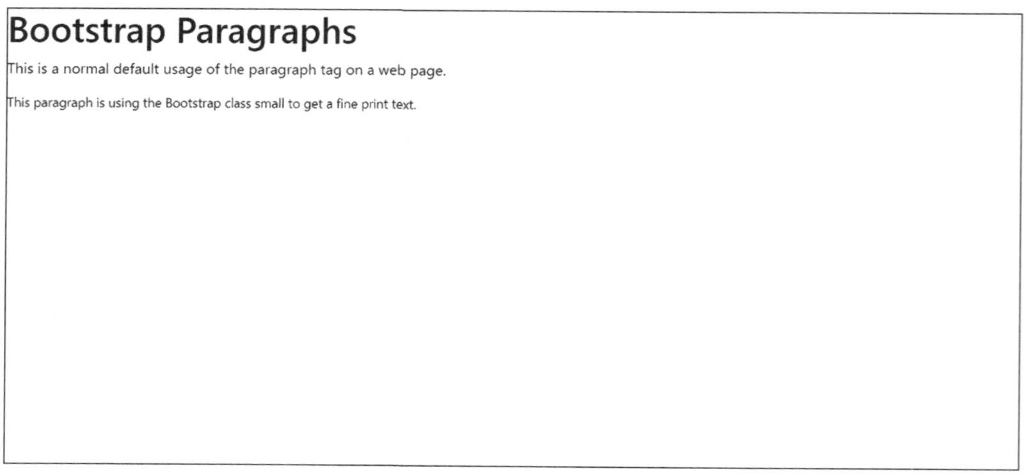

***Figure 3.6**: Bootstrap Small Text*

Images

Learn how to work with Images in Bootstrap, such as:

- How to create responsive images
- How to create a Circular Image
- How to create Rounded Corners of an image
- Create Image Thumbnail
- Align image

Creating a Responsive Image

A responsive image is an image that fits and scales according to the size of the screen or the web browser.

To set an image as responsive, use the **img-fluid** class:

```
<!DOCTYPE html>
<html lang="en">
<head>
  <title>Bootstrap Responsive Image</title>
  <meta charset="utf-8">
  <meta name="viewport" content="width=device-width, initial-scale=1">
  <link
href="https://cdn.jsdelivr.net/npm/bootstrap@5.3.3/dist/css/bootstrap.
min.css" rel="stylesheet">
  <script
src="https://cdn.jsdelivr.net/npm/bootstrap@5.3.3/dist/js/bootstrap.
bundle.min.js"></script>
</head>
<body>
<h2>Quizzes</h2>
<img class="img-fluid" src="https://studyopedia.com/wp-content/up-
loads/2017/02/Studyopedia-Quizzes.png" alt="Attempt Quizzes" width="700"
height="500">
</body>
</html>
```

After running the code, the web page will look as follows:

Screen Size: 1366 x 633

***Figure 3.7**: Create a responsive image*

Creating a Circular Image

The following Bootstrap class is used to create a circular Image:

.rounded-circle

Let us see an example:

```
<!DOCTYPE html>
<html lang="en">
<head>
  <title>Bootstrap Circular Image</title>
  <meta charset="utf-8">
  <meta name="viewport" content="width=device-width, initial-scale=1">
  <link
href="https://cdn.jsdelivr.net/npm/bootstrap@5.3.3/dist/css/bootstrap.
min.css" rel="stylesheet">
  <script
src="https://cdn.jsdelivr.net/npm/bootstrap@5.3.3/dist/js/bootstrap.
bundle.min.js"></script>
</head>
<body>
<h2>Quizzes</h2>
<img class="rounded-circle" src="https://studyopedia.com/wp-content/up-
loads/2017/02/Studyopedia-Quizzes.png" alt="Attempt Quizzes" width="700"
height="500">

</body>
</html>
```

After running the code, the web page will look as follows:

Screen Size: 1366 x 633

Figure 3.8: *Create a circular image*

Creating Rounded Corners of An Image

The following Bootstrap class is used to create rounded corners of an image:

```
.rounded
```

We can also set rounded corners only on certain sides (instead of on all four corners) using Bootstrap classes, such as rounded-top, rounded-bottom, and so on.

Note: *We have discussed rounded borders in the section* **Borders** *of Chapter 9,* **Bootstrap Utilities**.

Let us see an example:

```
<!DOCTYPE html>
<html lang="en">
<head>
  <title>Bootstrap Image with Rounded Corners</title>
  <meta charset="utf-8">
  <meta name="viewport" content="width=device-width, initial-scale=1">
  <link
href="https://cdn.jsdelivr.net/npm/bootstrap@5.3.3/dist/css/bootstrap.
min.css" rel="stylesheet">
  <script
src="https://cdn.jsdelivr.net/npm/bootstrap@5.3.3/dist/js/bootstrap.
bundle.min.js"></script>
</head>
```

```
<body>
<h2>Quizzes</h2>
<img class="rounded" src="https://studyopedia.com/wp-content/uploads/
2017/02/Studyopedia-Quizzes.png" alt="Attempt Quizzes" width="700"
height="500">

</body>
</html>
```

After running the code, the web page will look as follows:

Screen Size: 1366 x 633

***Figure 3.9**: Create rounding corners of an image*

We have set rounded corners of the preceding image. Now let us see how to create an image thumbnail on a web page.

Creating Image Thumbnail

To create an Image Thumbnail, use the following bootstrap class:

`.img-thumbnail`

The thumbnail adds a border and border-radius to the image. The border is white with grey edges. This makes the image look like a thumbnail. Let us see an example:

```
<!DOCTYPE html>
<html lang="en">
<head>
  <title>Bootstrap Image Thumbnail</title>
  <meta charset="utf-8">
  <meta name="viewport" content="width=device-width, initial-scale=1">
  <link
```

```
href="https://cdn.jsdelivr.net/npm/bootstrap@5.3.3/dist/css/bootstrap.
min.css" rel="stylesheet">
  <script
src="https://cdn.jsdelivr.net/npm/bootstrap@5.3.3/dist/js/bootstrap.
bundle.min.js"></script>
</head>
<body>
<h2>Quizzes</h2>
<img class="img-thumbnail" src="https://studyopedia.com/wp-content/up-
loads/2017/02/Studyopedia-Quizzes.png" alt="Attempt Quizzes" width="700"
height="500">

</body>
</html>
```

After running the code, the web page will look as follows:

Screen Size: 1366 x 633

Figure 3.10: *Create image thumbnail*

Aligning an Image to the Left

Images can be easily aligned to the left with Bootstrap float utilities. The float utilities not only align the image but also make the content collapse if not using the **.clearfix** helper class on the parent elements.

To align an image to the left, use the following bootstrap class:

.float-start

Let us see an example to align an image to the left on a web page:

```
<!DOCTYPE html>
<html lang="en">
<head>
  <title>Bootstrap Image Left Alignment</title>
  <meta charset="utf-8">
  <meta name="viewport" content="width=device-width, initial-scale=1">
  <link
href="https://cdn.jsdelivr.net/npm/bootstrap@5.3.3/dist/css/bootstrap.
min.css" rel="stylesheet">
  <script
src="https://cdn.jsdelivr.net/npm/bootstrap@5.3.3/dist/js/bootstrap.
bundle.min.js"></script>
</head>
<body>
<h2>Quizzes</h2>
<img class="float-start" src="https://studyopedia.com/wp-content/up-
loads/2017/02/Studyopedia-Quizzes.png" alt="Attempt Quizzes" width="700"
height="500">

</body>
</html>
```

After running the code, the web page will look as follows:

Screen Size: 1366 x 633

***Figure 3.11**: Align an image to the left*

Aligning an Image to the Right

Images can be easily aligned to the right with Bootstrap float utilities. The float utilities not only align the image but also make the content collapse if the **.clearfix** helper class is not used on the parent elements.

To align an image to the right, use the following bootstrap class:

.float-end

Let us see an example to align an image to the right on a web page:

```
<!DOCTYPE html>
<html lang="en">
<head>
  <title>Bootstrap Image Right Alignment</title>
  <meta charset="utf-8">
  <meta name="viewport" content="width=device-width, initial-scale=1">
  <link
href="https://cdn.jsdelivr.net/npm/bootstrap@5.3.3/dist/css/bootstrap.
min.css" rel="stylesheet">
  <script
src="https://cdn.jsdelivr.net/npm/bootstrap@5.3.3/dist/js/bootstrap.
bundle.min.js"></script>
</head>
<body>
<h2>Quizzes</h2>
<img class="float-end" src="https://studyopedia.com/wp-content/uploads/
2017/02/Studyopedia-Quizzes.png" alt="Attempt Quizzes" width="700"
height="500">

</body>
</html>
```

After running the code, the web page will look as follows:

Screen Size: 1366 x 633

Figure 3.12: *Align an image to the right*

Tables

Tables are still the best way to display the data in the form of rows and columns. On a web page, a table with rows and columns can be easily created with Bootstrap. In this lesson, learn how to create a table from scratch on a web page.

Creating a Table

To create a table on a web page with Bootstrap, use the **`.table`** class. Let us see an example:

```
<!DOCTYPE html>
<html lang="en">
<head>
  <title>Bootstrap Tables</title>
  <meta charset="utf-8">
  <meta name="viewport" content="width=device-width, initial-scale=1">
  <link
href="https://cdn.jsdelivr.net/npm/bootstrap@5.3.3/dist/css/bootstrap.
min.css" rel="stylesheet">
  <script
src="https://cdn.jsdelivr.net/npm/bootstrap@5.3.3/dist/js/bootstrap.
bundle.min.js"></script>
</head>
<body>
<h1>Create a Table</h1>
<table class="table">
    <thead>
      <tr>
        <th>Rank</th>
        <th>Player</th>
        <th>Points</th>
      </tr>
    </thead>
    <tbody>
      <tr>
        <td>1</td>
        <td>Virat</td>
        <td>120</td>
      </tr>
      <tr>
        <td>2</td>
        <td>Steve</td>
        <td>100</td>
      </tr>
      <tr>
```

```
        <td>3</td>
        <td>David</td>
        <td>90</td>
      </tr>
      <tr>
        <td>4</td>
        <td>Ken</td>
        <td>80</td>
      </tr>
    </tbody>
</table>

</body>
</html>
```

After running the code, the web page will look as follows:

Screen Size: 1366 x 633

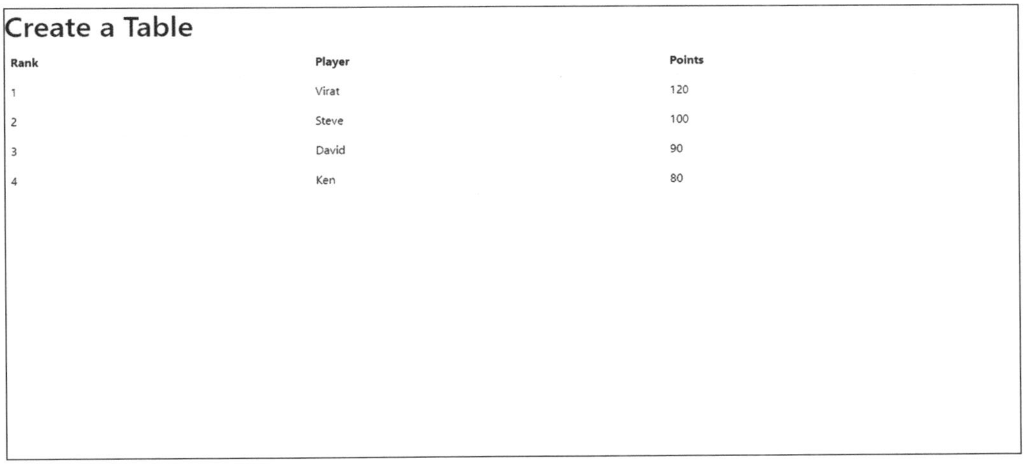

Figure 3.13: *Create a Table*

Creating a Striped Table

Creating a striped table means adding zebra stripes to the rows. For that, Bootstrap has provided the **`.table-striped`** class. Let us see an example:

```
<!DOCTYPE html>
<html lang="en">
<head>
  <title>Bootstrap Striped Table</title>
  <meta charset="utf-8">
  <meta name="viewport" content="width=device-width, initial-scale=1">
```

```
  <link
href="https://cdn.jsdelivr.net/npm/bootstrap@5.3.3/dist/css/bootstrap.
min.css" rel="stylesheet">
  <script
src="https://cdn.jsdelivr.net/npm/bootstrap@5.3.3/dist/js/bootstrap.
bundle.min.js"></script>
</head>
<body>
<h1>Create a Striped Table</h1>
<table class="table table-striped">
    <thead>
      <tr>
        <th>Rank</th>
        <th>Player</th>
        <th>Points</th>
      </tr>
    </thead>
    <tbody>
      <tr>
        <td>1</td>
        <td>Virat</td>
        <td>120</td>
      </tr>
      <tr>
        <td>2</td>
        <td>Steve</td>
        <td>100</td>
      </tr>
      <tr>
        <td>3</td>
        <td>David</td>
        <td>90</td>
      </tr>
      <tr>
        <td>4</td>
        <td>Ken</td>
        <td>80</td>
      </tr>
    </tbody>
</table>

</body>
</html>
```

After running the code, the web page will look as follows:

Screen Size: 1366 x 633

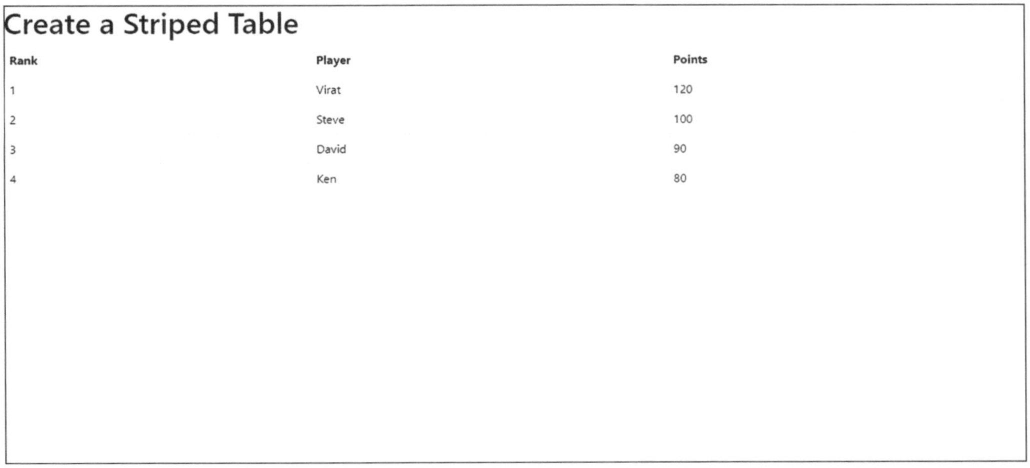

Create a Striped Table

Rank	Player	Points
1	Virat	120
2	Steve	100
3	David	90
4	Ken	80

Figure 3.14: *Create a Striped Table*

Adding a Border to a Table

To add a border to a table on a web page, use the **`.table-bordered`** class. Let us see an example:

```
<!DOCTYPE html>
<html lang="en">
<head>
  <title>Bootstrap Bordered Table</title>
  <meta charset="utf-8">
  <meta name="viewport" content="width=device-wicth, initial-scale=1">
  <link
href="https://cdn.jsdelivr.net/npm/bootstrap@5.3.3/dist/css/bootstrap.
min.css" rel="stylesheet">
  <script
src="https://cdn.jsdelivr.net/npm/bootstrap@5.3.3/dist/js/bootstrap.
bundle.min.js"></script>
</head>
<body>
<h1>Create a Table with borders</h1>
<table class="table table-bordered">
    <thead>
      <tr>
        <th>Rank</th>
        <th>Player</th>
        <th>Points</th>
      </tr>
    </thead>
    <tbody>
```

```
        <tr>
          <td>1</td>
          <td>Virat</td>
          <td>120</td>
        </tr>
        <tr>
          <td>2</td>
          <td>Steve</td>
          <td>100</td>
        </tr>
        <tr>
          <td>3</td>
          <td>David</td>
          <td>90</td>
        </tr>
        <tr>
          <td>4</td>
          <td>Ken</td>
          <td>80</td>
        </tr>
      </tbody>
</table>

</body>
</html>
```

After running the code, the web page will look as follows:

Screen Size: 1366 x 633

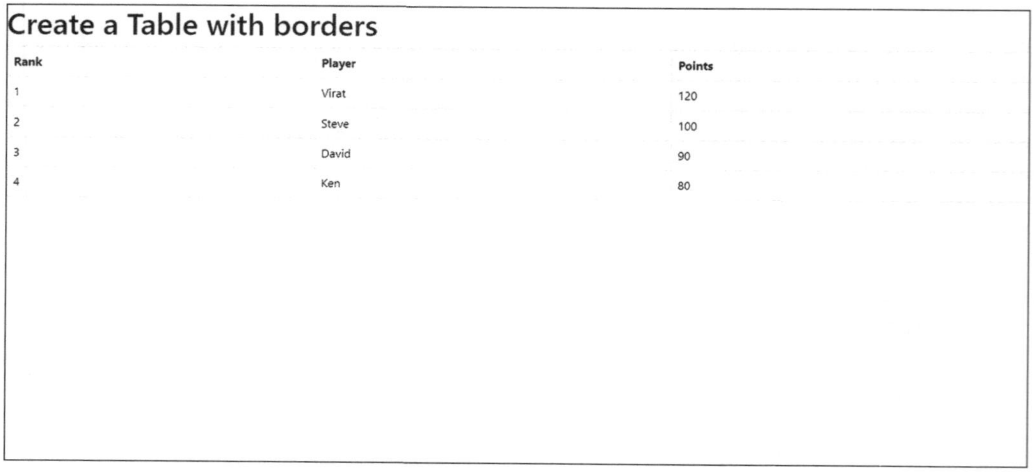

Figure 3.15: *Create a table with borders*

Creating a Borderless Table

The **.table-borderless** Bootstrap class is used to remove borders from the table. Let us see an example:

```
<!DOCTYPE html>
<html lang="en">
<head>
  <title>Bootstrap Borderless Table</title>
  <meta charset="utf-8">
  <meta name="viewport" content="width=device-width, initial-scale=1">
  <link
href="https://cdn.jsdelivr.net/npm/bootstrap@5.3.3/dist/css/bootstrap.
min.css" rel="stylesheet">
  <script
src="https://cdn.jsdelivr.net/npm/bootstrap@5.3.3/dist/js/bootstrap.
bundle.min.js"></script>
</head>
<body>
<h1>Create a Table with no border</h1>
<table class="table table-borderless">
    <thead>
      <tr>
        <th>Rank</th>
        <th>Player</th>
        <th>Points</th>
      </tr>
    </thead>
    <tbody>
      <tr>
        <td>1</td>
        <td>Virat</td>
        <td>120</td>
      </tr>
      <tr>
        <td>2</td>
        <td>Steve</td>
        <td>100</td>
      </tr>
      <tr>
        <td>3</td>
        <td>David</td>
        <td>90</td>
      </tr>
      <tr>
        <td>4</td>
```

```
            <td>Ken</td>
            <td>80</td>
        </tr>
    </tbody>
</table>

</body>
</html>
```

After running the code, the web page will look as follows:

Screen Size: 1366 x 633

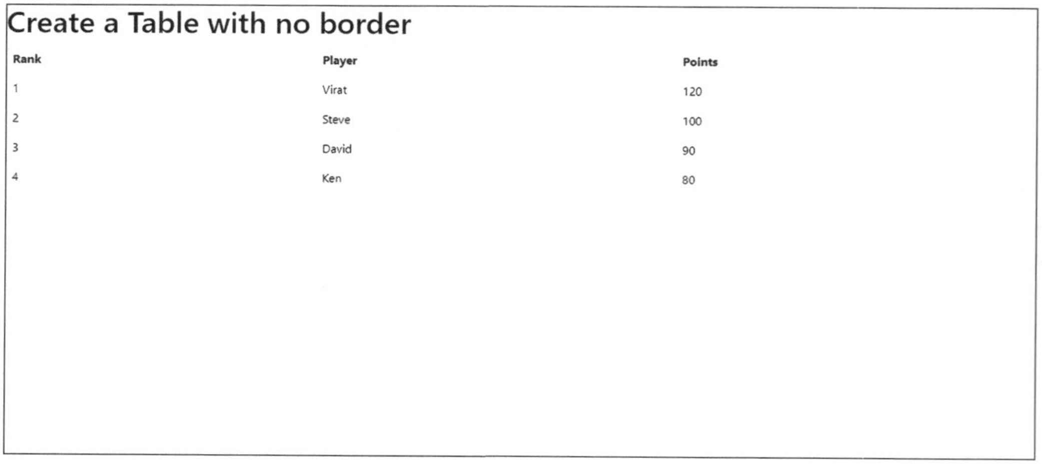

***Figure 3.16**: Create a table with no border*

Adding a Hover Effect to the Table

The hover effect on a table can be set using the **`.table-hover`** Bootstrap class. On keeping the mouse cursor on the table, the hover effect will be visible on that specific row. Let us see an example:

```
<!DOCTYPE html>
<html lang="en">
<head>
  <title>Bootstrap Table with hover effect</title>
  <meta charset="utf-8">
  <meta name="viewport" content="width=device-width, initial-scale=1">
  <link
href="https://cdn.jsdelivr.net/npm/bootstrap@5.3.3/dist/css/bootstrap.
min.css" rel="stylesheet">
  <script
src="https://cdn.jsdelivr.net/npm/bootstrap@5.3.3/dist/js/bootstrap.
bundle.min.js"></script>
```

```
</head>
<body>
<h1>Create a table with a hover effect</h1>
<table class="table table-hover">
    <thead>
      <tr>
        <th>Rank</th>
        <th>Player</th>
        <th>Points</th>
      </tr>
    </thead>
    <tbody>
      <tr>
        <td>1</td>
        <td>Virat</td>
        <td>120</td>
      </tr>
      <tr>
        <td>2</td>
        <td>Steve</td>
        <td>100</td>
      </tr>
      <tr>
        <td>3</td>
        <td>David</td>
        <td>90</td>
      </tr>
      <tr>
        <td>4</td>
        <td>Ken</td>
        <td>80</td>
      </tr>
    </tbody>
</table>

</body>
</html>
```

After running the code, the web page will look as follows:

Screen Size: 1366 x 633

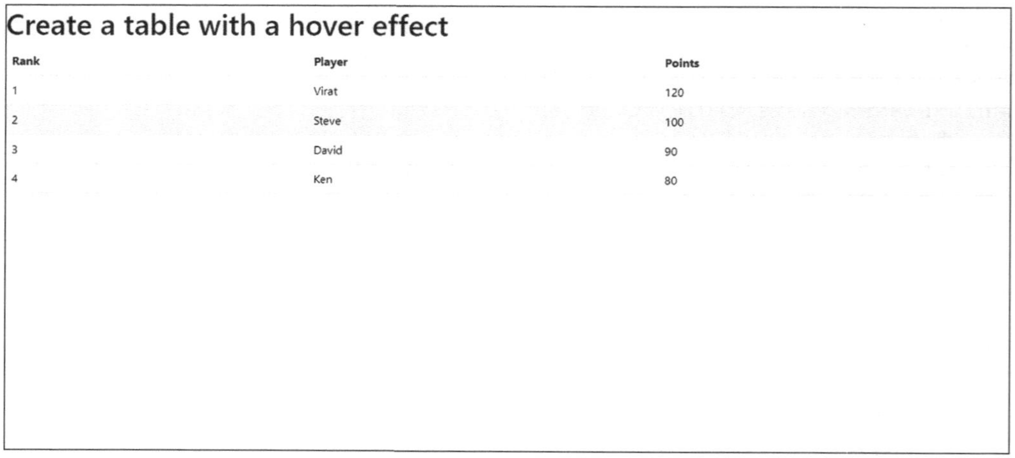

***Figure 3.17**: Create a table with a hover effect*

Contextual Class for Table Cells

The contextual classes allow for adding background color. The following are the contextual classes for table cells:

- **`.table-primary`**: important info
- **`.table-success`**: success action
- **`.table-danger`**: danger action
- **`.table-info`**: add info
- **`.table-warning`**: warning action
- **`.table-active`**: highlighted
- **`.table-secondary`**: less important info
- **`.table-dark`**: dark grey color
- **`.table-light`**: light grey color

Let us see an example. Here, we set different colors to the table body and rows:

```
<!DOCTYPE html>
<html lang="en">
<head>
  <title>Bootstrap Tables</title>
  <meta charset="utf-8">
  <meta name="viewport" content="width=device-width, initial-scale=1">
  <link
href="https://cdn.jsdelivr.net/npm/bootstrap@5.3.3/dist/css/bootstrap.
min.css" rel="stylesheet">
```

```
  <script
src="https://cdn.jsdelivr.net/npm/bootstrap@5.3.3/dist/js/bootstrap.
bundle.min.js"></script>
</head>
<body>
<h1>Create a table and color it</h1>
<table class="table">
    <thead>
      <tr class="table-primary">
        <th>Rank</th>
        <th>Player</th>
        <th>Points</th>
      </tr>
    </thead>
    <tbody>
      <tr class="table-secondary">
        <td>1</td>
        <td>Virat</td>
        <td>120</td>
      </tr>
      <tr class="table-info">
        <td>2</td>
        <td>Steve</td>
        <td>100</td>
      </tr>
      <tr class="table-success">
        <td>3</td>
        <td>David</td>
        <td>90</td>
      </tr>
      <tr class="table-warning">
        <td>4</td>
        <td>Ken</td>
        <td>80</td>
      </tr>
  </tbody>
  </table>

</body>
</html>
```

After running the code, the web page will look as follows:

Screen Size: 1366 x 633

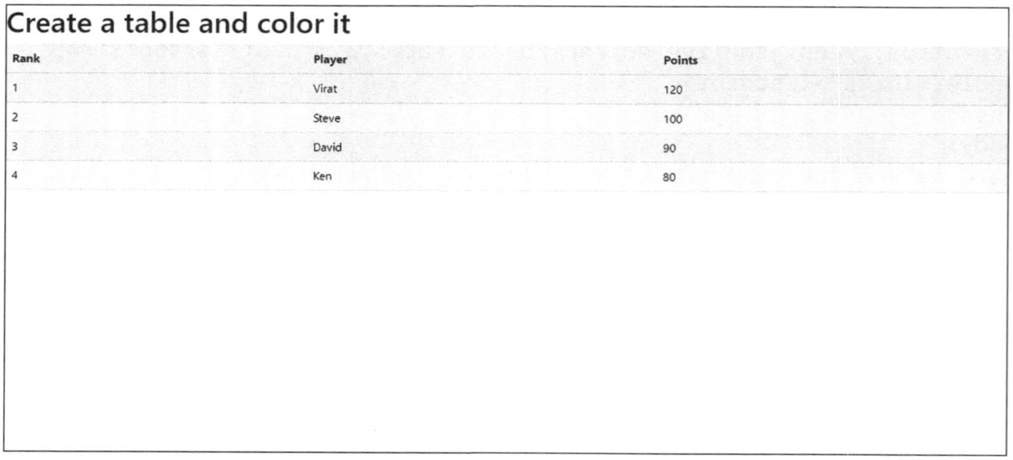

***Figure 3.18**: Add a color to a table*

Here, we have created a table and also added colors to the table cells. Now let us see how to create a dark-colored table.

Creating a Dark Colored Table

The **`.table-dark`** Bootstrap class is used to set a dark color to the table. Let us see an example:

```
<!DOCTYPE html>
<html lang="en">
<head>
  <title>Bootstrap Dark Colored Table</title>
  <meta charset="utf-8">
  <meta name="viewport" content="width=device-width, initial-scale=1">
  <link
href="https://cdn.jsdelivr.net/npm/bootstrap@5.3.3/dist/css/bootstrap.
min.css" rel="stylesheet">
  <script
src="https://cdn.jsdelivr.net/npm/bootstrap@5.3.3/dist/js/bootstrap.
bundle.min.js"></script>
</head>
<body>
<h1>Create a dark table</h1>
<table class="table table-dark">
    <thead>
      <tr>
        <th>Rank</th>
        <th>Player</th>
        <th>Points</th>
      </tr>
```

```
    </thead>
    <tbody>
      <tr>
        <td>1</td>
        <td>Virat</td>
        <td>120</td>
      </tr>
      <tr>
        <td>2</td>
        <td>Steve</td>
        <td>100</td>
      </tr>
      <tr>
        <td>3</td>
        <td>David</td>
        <td>90</td>
      </tr>
      <tr>
        <td>4</td>
        <td>Ken</td>
        <td>80</td>
      </tr>
    </tbody>
</table>

</body>
</html>
```

After running the code, the web page will look as follows:

Screen Size: 1366 x 633

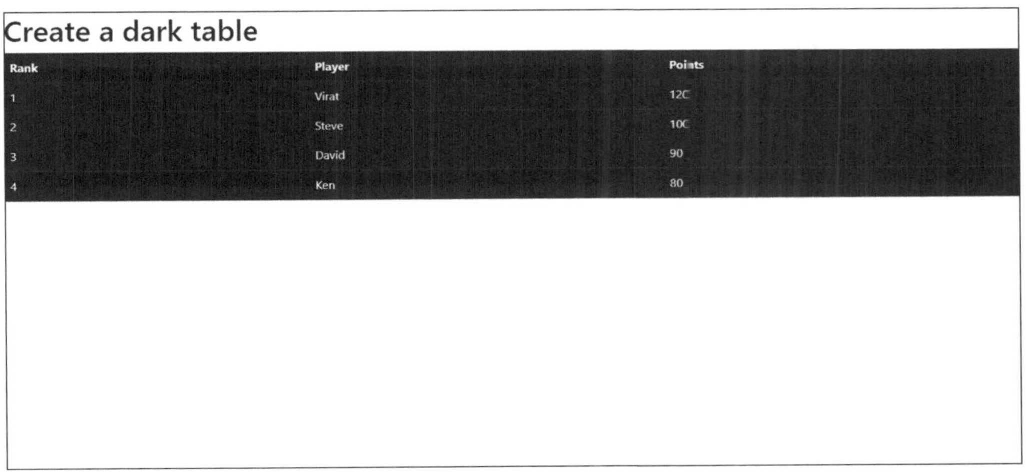

Figure 3.19: *Create a dark-colored table*

Setting the Table Header Color to Dark Color

Set the dark color to the table header using the **`.table-dark`** Bootstrap class. Let us see an example:

```
<!DOCTYPE html>
<html lang="en">
<head>
  <title>Bootstrap Table</title>
  <meta charset="utf-8">
  <meta name="viewport" content="width=device-width, initial-scale=1">
  <link
href="https://cdn.jsdelivr.net/npm/bootstrap@5.3.3/dist/css/bootstrap.
min.css" rel="stylesheet">
  <script
src="https://cdn.jsdelivr.net/npm/bootstrap@5.3.3/dist/js/bootstrap.
bundle.min.js"></script>
</head>
<body>
<h1>Create a table with dark colored table header</h1>
<table class="table">
    <thead class="table-dark">
      <tr>
        <th>Rank</th>
        <th>Player</th>
        <th>Points</th>
      </tr>
    </thead>
    <tbody>
      <tr>
        <td>1</td>
        <td>Virat</td>
        <td>120</td>
      </tr>
      <tr>
        <td>2</td>
        <td>Steve</td>
        <td>100</td>
      </tr>
      <tr>
        <td>3</td>
        <td>David</td>
        <td>90</td>
      </tr>
      <tr>
        <td>4</td>
```

```
        <td>Ken</td>
        <td>80</td>
      </tr>
    </tbody>
</table>

</body>
</html>
```

After running the code, the web page will look as follows:

Screen Size: 1366 x 633

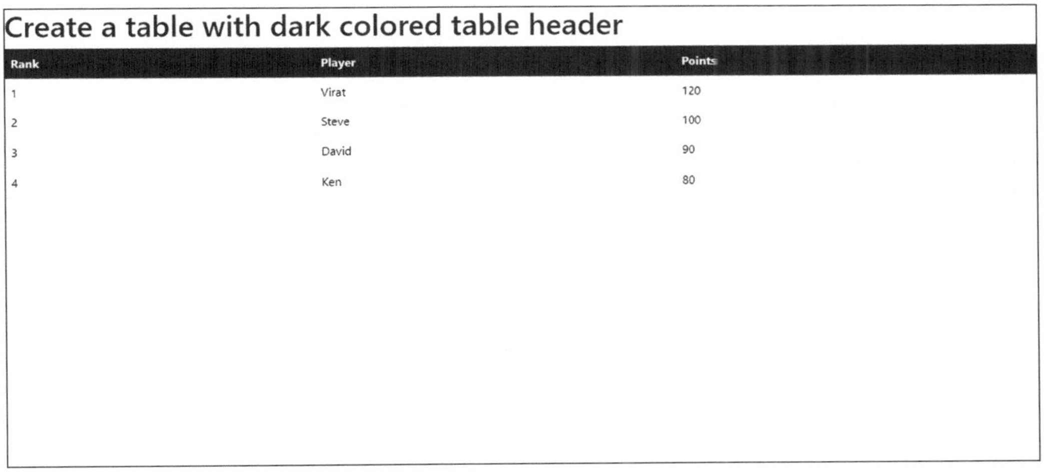

***Figure 3.20**: Create a table with dark-colored header*

Setting the Table Header Color to Light Color

Set the light color to the table header using the **`table-light`** Bootstrap class. Let us see an example:

```
<!DOCTYPE html>
<html lang="en">
<head>
  <title>Bootstrap Table</title>
  <meta charset="utf-8">
  <meta name="viewport" content="width=device-width, initial-scale=1">
  <link
href="https://cdn.jsdelivr.net/npm/bootstrap@5.3.3/dist/css/bootstrap.
min.css" rel="stylesheet">
  <script
src="https://cdn.jsdelivr.net/npm/bootstrap@5.3.3/dist/js/bootstrap.
bundle.min.js"></script>
</head>
```

```
<body>
<h1>Create a table with light colored table header</h1>
<table class="table">
    <thead class="table-light">
      <tr>
        <th>Rank</th>
        <th>Player</th>
        <th>Points</th>
      </tr>
    </thead>
    <tbody>
      <tr>
        <td>1</td>
        <td>Virat</td>
        <td>120</td>
      </tr>
      <tr>
        <td>2</td>
        <td>Steve</td>
        <td>100</td>
      </tr>
      <tr>
        <td>3</td>
        <td>David</td>
        <td>90</td>
      </tr>
      <tr>
        <td>4</td>
        <td>Ken</td>
        <td>80</td>
      </tr>
    </tbody>
</table>

</body>
</html>
```

After running the code, the web page will look as follows:

Screen Size: 1366 x 633

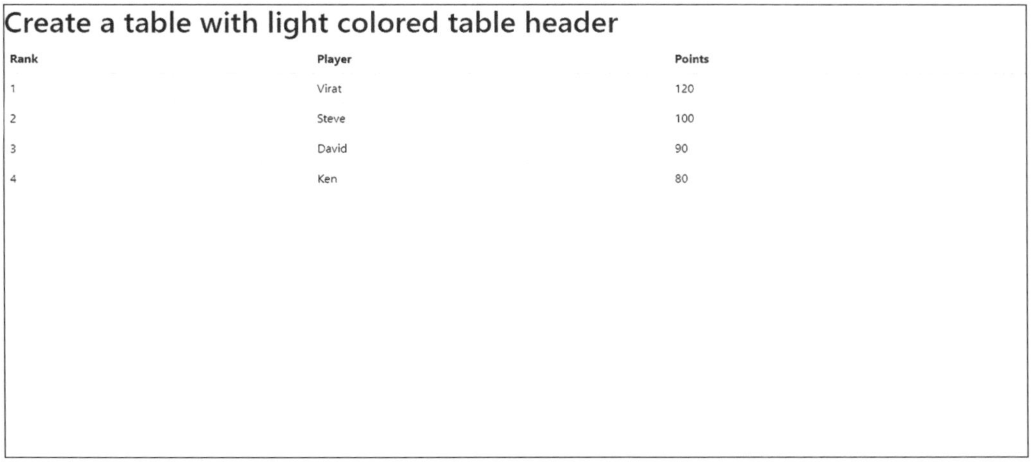

Figure 3.21: *Create a table with light colored header*

Responsive Tables

Learn how to create a responsive table. With live running examples, get thorough knowledge about designing a responsive table on small, medium, large, and extra-large devices. To create a responsive table, use the following Bootstrap class that would add a scrollbar for horizontal scrolling:

`table-responsive`

The following are the Bootstrap classes to create a responsive table based on the device it is being accessed. The screen width for a responsive table:

```
.table-responsive-sm  for < 576px
.table-responsive-md  for < 768px
.table-responsive-lg  for < 992px
.table-responsive-xl  for < 1200px
.table-responsive-xxl  for <1400 px
```

Creating a Responsive Table

The Bootstrap **`.table-responsive`** class is used to create a responsive table on a web page. You need to add this class to a wrapping HTML element, like:

`<div class="table-responsive">`

Let us create a responsive table:

```
<!DOCTYPE html>
<html lang="en">
<head>
  <title>Bootstrap Responsive Table</title>
```

```
  <meta charset="utf-8">
  <meta name="viewport" content="width=device-width, initial-scale=1">
  <link
href="https://cdn.jsdelivr.net/npm/bootstrap@5.3.3/dist/css/bootstrap.
min.css" rel="stylesheet">
  <script
src="https://cdn.jsdelivr.net/npm/bootstrap@5.3.3/dist/js/bootstrap.
bundle.min.js"></script>
</head>
<body>
<h1>Create a responsive table</h1>
<div class="table-responsive">
  <table class="table">
    <thead>
      <tr>
        <th>Player</th>
        <th>Team</th>
        <th>Age</th>
        <th>Batsman</th>
        <th>ODI Debut</th>
        <th>Test Debut</th>
        <th>T20 Debut</th>
        <th>Rank</th>
        <th>Points</th>
        <th>ODI Avg.</th>
        <th>Test Avg.</th>
        <th>T20 Avg.</th>
        <th>RCB</th>
        <th>Delhi Capitals</th>
        <th>Sydney Thunders</th>
        <th>Sydney Sixers</th>
        <th>Dubai Capitals</th>
        <th>Toronto Nations</th>
        <th>Comilla Victorians</th>
      </tr>
    </thead>
    <tbody>
      <tr>
        <td>Virat</td>
        <td>IND</td>
        <td>35</td>
        <td>Right-Handed</td>
        <td>2008</td>
        <td>2011</td>
        <td>2010</td>
        <td>1</td>
        <td>120</td>
```

```
    <td>58</td>
    <td>49</td>
    <td>52</td>
    <td>Yes</td>
    <td>No</td>
    <td>No</td>
    <td>No</td>
    <td>No</td>
    <td>No</td>
    <td>No</td>
  </tr>
  <tr>
    <td>Steve</td>
    <td>AUS</td>
    <td>33</td>
    <td>Right-Handed</td>
    <td>2012</td>
    <td>2013</td>
    <td>2012</td>
    <td>2</td>
    <td>100</td>
    <td>45</td>
    <td>60</td>
    <td>35</td>
    <td>No</td>
    <td>No</td>
    <td>Yes</td>
    <td>Yes</td>
    <td>No</td>
    <td>Yes</td>
    <td>Yes</td>
  </tr>
  <tr>
    <td>David</td>
    <td>AUS</td>
    <td>36</td>
    <td>Left-Handed</td>
    <td>2007</td>
    <td>2008</td>
    <td>2008</td>
    <td>3</td>
    <td>90</td>
    <td>46</td>
    <td>50</td>
    <td>32</td>
    <td>No</td>
    <td>Yes</td>
```

```
        <td>Yes</td>
        <td>Yes</td>
        <td>Yes</td>
        <td>No</td>
        <td>No</td>
      </tr>
    </tbody>
  </table>
</div>
</body>
</html>
```

After running the code, the web page will look as follows:

Screen Size: 1366 x 633

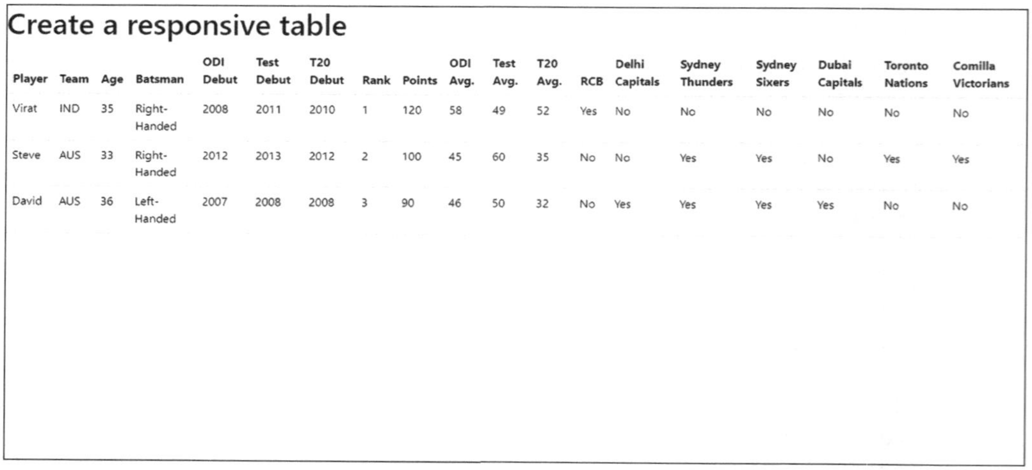

Create a responsive table

Player	Team	Age	Batsman	ODI Debut	Test Debut	T20 Debut	Rank	Points	ODI Avg.	Test Avg.	T20 Avg.	RCB	Delhi Capitals	Sydney Thunders	Sydney Sixers	Dubai Capitals	Toronto Nations	Comilla Victorians
Virat	IND	35	Right-Handed	2008	2011	2010	1	120	58	49	52	Yes	No	No	No	No	No	No
Steve	AUS	33	Right-Handed	2012	2013	2012	2	100	45	60	35	No	No	Yes	Yes	No	Yes	Yes
David	AUS	36	Left-Handed	2007	2008	2008	3	90	46	50	32	No	Yes	Yes	Yes	Yes	No	No

Figure 3.22: *Create a responsive table*

Let us resize the screen to understand how the responsive table works. The scrollbar is now visible:

Screen Size: 900x 633

Create a responsive table

Player	Team	Age	Batsman	ODI Debut	Test Debut	T20 Debut	Rank	Points	ODI Avg.	Test Avg.	T20 Avg.	RCB	Delhi Capitals	Sydney Thunders
Virat	IND	35	Right-Handed	2008	2011	2010	1	120	58	49	52	Yes	No	No
Steve	AUS	33	Right-Handed	2012	2013	2012	2	100	45	60	35	No	No	Yes
David	AUS	36	Left-Handed	2007	2008	2008	3	90	46	50	32	No	Yes	Yes

***Figure 3.23**: The horizontal scrollbar is visible in a responsive table*

Responsive Table for a Small Screen

For a small screen, the screen width is less than 576px. The responsive table will scroll horizontally on screens with a width < 576px. Let us see the example:

```
<!DOCTYPE html>
<html lang="en">
<head>
  <title>Bootstrap Responsive Table</title>
  <meta charset="utf-8">
  <meta name="viewport" content="width=device-width, initial-scale=1">
  <link
href="https://cdn.jsdelivr.net/npm/bootstrap@5.3.3/dist/css/bootstrap.
min.css" rel="stylesheet">
  <script
src="https://cdn.jsdelivr.net/npm/bootstrap@5.3.3/dist/js/bootstrap.
bundle.min.js"></script>
</head>
<body>
<h1>Create a responsive table</h1>
<p>The responsive table will horizontally scroll on screens with a width
of less than 576px because we have used the Bootstrap table-respon-
sive-sm class.</p>
<div class="table-responsive-sm">
  <table class="table">
    <thead>
      <tr>
        <th>Player</th>
```

```
        <th>Team</th>
        <th>Age</th>
        <th>Batsman</th>
        <th>ODI Debut</th>
        <th>Test Debut</th>
        <th>T20 Debut</th>
        <th>Rank</th>
        <th>Points</th>
        <th>ODI Avg.</th>
        <th>Test Avg.</th>
        <th>T20 Avg.</th>
      </tr>
    </thead>
    <tbody>
      <tr>
        <td>Virat</td>
        <td>IND</td>
        <td>35</td>
        <td>Right-Handed</td>
        <td>2008</td>
        <td>2011</td>
        <td>2010</td>
        <td>1</td>
        <td>120</td>
        <td>58</td>
        <td>49</td>
        <td>52</td>
      </tr>
      <tr>
        <td>Steve</td>
        <td>AUS</td>
        <td>33</td>
        <td>Right-Handed</td>
        <td>2012</td>
        <td>2013</td>
        <td>2012</td>
        <td>2</td>
        <td>100</td>
        <td>45</td>
        <td>60</td>
        <td>35</td>
      </tr>
      <tr>
        <td>David</td>
        <td>AUS</td>
        <td>36</td>
        <td>Left-Handed</td>
```

```
        <td>2007</td>
        <td>2008</td>
        <td>2008</td>
        <td>3</td>
        <td>90</td>
        <td>46</td>
        <td>50</td>
        <td>32</td>
      </tr>
    </tbody>
  </table>
</div>
</body>
</html>
```

After running the code, the web page will look as follows:

Screen Size: 1366 x 633

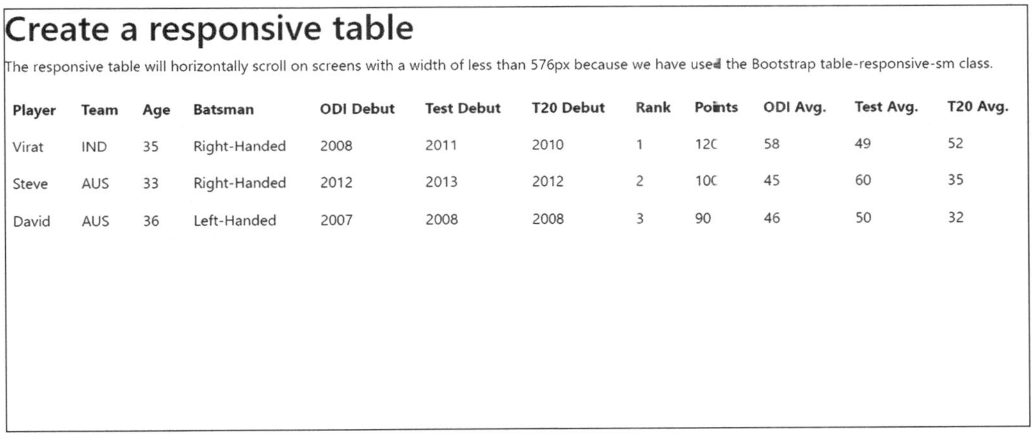

Figure 3.24: *Create a responsive table for a small screen*

Let us resize the screen to understand how the responsive table works for a small screen. The scrollbar will be visible when the screen size is less than 576 px:

Screen Size: 570x633

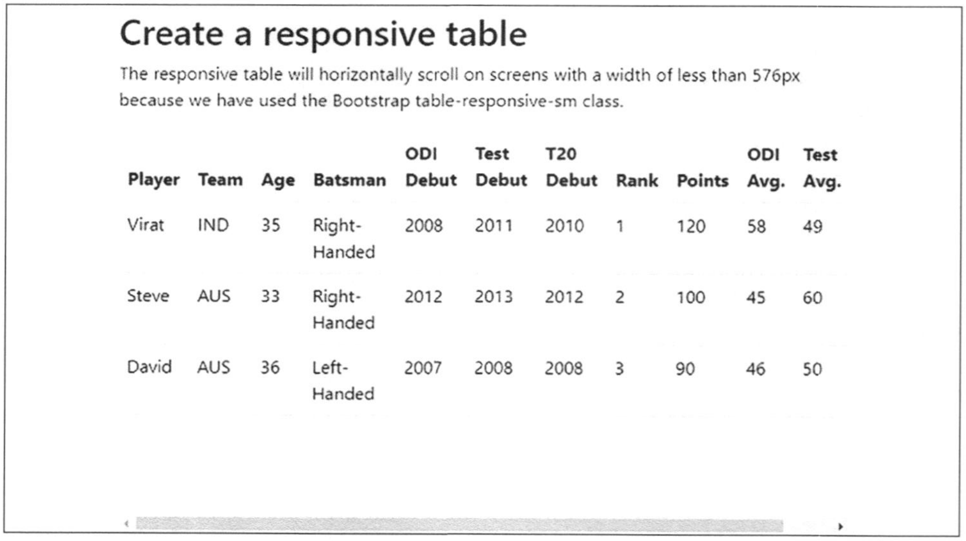

Create a responsive table

The responsive table will horizontally scroll on screens with a width of less than 576px because we have used the Bootstrap table-responsive-sm class.

Player	Team	Age	Batsman	ODI Debut	Test Debut	T20 Debut	Rank	Points	ODI Avg.	Test Avg.
Virat	IND	35	Right-Handed	2008	2011	2010	1	120	58	49
Steve	AUS	33	Right-Handed	2012	2013	2012	2	100	45	60
David	AUS	36	Left-Handed	2007	2008	2008	3	90	46	50

***Figure 3.25**: Horizontal scrollbar is visible in a responsive table when the screen size is less than 576 px*

Responsive Table for a Medium Screen

For a medium screen, the screen width is less than 768px. The responsive table will scroll horizontally on screens with a width of < 768px. Let us see an example:

```
<!DOCTYPE html>
<html lang="en">
<head>
  <title>Bootstrap Responsive Table</title>
  <meta charset="utf-8">
  <meta name="viewport" content="width=device-width, initial-scale=1">
  <link
href="https://cdn.jsdelivr.net/npm/bootstrap@5.3.3/dist/css/bootstrap.
min.css" rel="stylesheet">
  <script
src="https://cdn.jsdelivr.net/npm/bootstrap@5.3.3/dist/js/bootstrap.
bundle.min.js"></script>
</head>
<body>
<h1>Create a responsive table</h1>
<p>For medium screen, the screen width is less than 768px. The respon-
sive table will horizontally scroll on screens with widths less than
768px</p>
<div class="table-responsive-md">
  <table class="table">
    <thead>
```

```
      <tr>
        <th>Player</th>
        <th>Team</th>
        <th>Age</th>
        <th>Batsman</th>
        <th>ODI Debut</th>
        <th>Test Debut</th>
        <th>T20 Debut</th>
        <th>Rank</th>
        <th>Points</th>
        <th>ODI Avg.</th>
        <th>Test Avg.</th>
        <th>T20 Avg.</th>
        <th>RCB</th>
        <th>Delhi Capitals</th>
        <th>Sydney Thunders</th>
        <th>Sydney Sixers</th>
        <th>Dubai Capitals</th>
        <th>Toronto Nations</th>
        <th>Comilla Victorians</th>
      </tr>
    </thead>
    <tbody>
      <tr>
        <td>Virat</td>
        <td>IND</td>
        <td>35</td>
        <td>Right-Handed</td>
        <td>2008</td>
        <td>2011</td>
        <td>2010</td>
        <td>1</td>
        <td>120</td>
        <td>58</td>
        <td>49</td>
        <td>52</td>
        <td>Yes</td>
        <td>No</td>
        <td>No</td>
        <td>No</td>
        <td>No</td>
        <td>No</td>
        <td>No</td>
      </tr>
      <tr>
        <td>Steve</td>
        <td>AUS</td>
```

```
          <td>33</td>
          <td>Right-Handed</td>
          <td>2012</td>
          <td>2013</td>
          <td>2012</td>
          <td>2</td>
          <td>100</td>
          <td>45</td>
          <td>60</td>
          <td>35</td>
          <td>No</td>
          <td>No</td>
          <td>Yes</td>
          <td>Yes</td>
          <td>No</td>
          <td>Yes</td>
          <td>Yes</td>
        </tr>
        <tr>
          <td>David</td>
          <td>AUS</td>
          <td>36</td>
          <td>Left-Handed</td>
          <td>2007</td>
          <td>2008</td>
          <td>2008</td>
          <td>3</td>
          <td>90</td>
          <td>46</td>
          <td>50</td>
          <td>32</td>
          <td>No</td>
          <td>Yes</td>
          <td>Yes</td>
          <td>Yes</td>
          <td>Yes</td>
          <td>No</td>
          <td>No</td>
        </tr>
      </tbody>
    </table>
</div>
</body>
</html>
```

After running the code, the web page will look as follows:

Screen Size: 1366 x 633

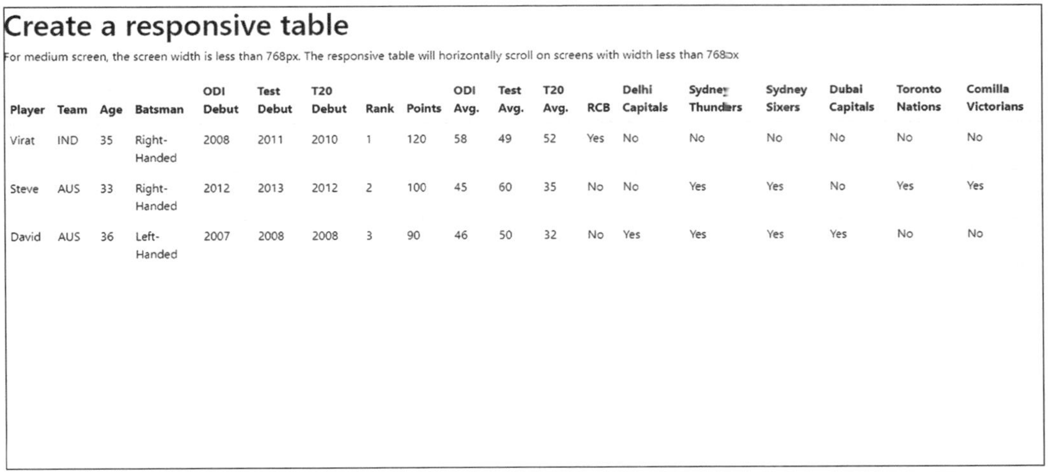

Figure 3.26: *Create a responsive table for a medium screen*

Let us resize the screen to understand how the responsive table works for a medium screen. The scrollbar will be visible when the screen size is less than 768 px:

Screen Size: 760x633

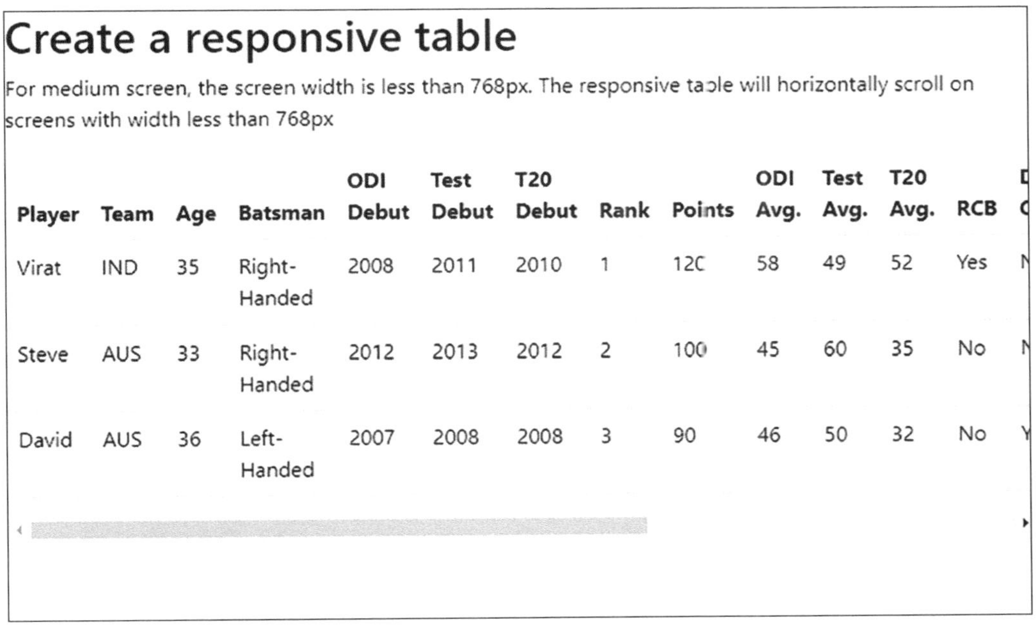

Figure 3.27: *Horizontal scrollbar is visible in a responsive table when the screen size is less than 768 px*

Responsive Table for a Large Screen

For a large screen, the screen width is less than 992px. The responsive table will scroll horizontally on screens with a width less than 992px. Let us see an example:

```
<!DOCTYPE html>
<html lang="en">
<head>
  <title>Bootstrap Responsive Table</title>
  <meta charset="utf-8">
  <meta name="viewport" content="width=device-width, initial-scale=1">
  <link
href="https://cdn.jsdelivr.net/npm/bootstrap@5.3.3/dist/css/bootstrap.
min.css" rel="stylesheet">
  <script
src="https://cdn.jsdelivr.net/npm/bootstrap@5.3.3/dist/js/bootstrap.
bundle.min.js"></script>
</head>
<body>
<h1>Create a responsive table</h1>
<p>For large screen, the screen width is less than 992px. The responsive
table will horizontally scroll on screens with width less than 992px</p>
<div class="table-responsive-lg">
  <table class="table">
    <thead>
      <tr>
        <th>Player</th>
        <th>Team</th>
        <th>Age</th>
        <th>Batsman</th>
        <th>ODI Debut</th>
        <th>Test Debut</th>
        <th>T20 Debut</th>
        <th>Rank</th>
        <th>Points</th>
        <th>ODI Avg.</th>
        <th>Test Avg.</th>
        <th>T20 Avg.</th>
        <th>RCB</th>
        <th>Delhi Capitals</th>
        <th>Sydney Thunders</th>
        <th>Sydney Sixers</th>
        <th>Dubai Capitals</th>
        <th>Toronto Nations</th>
        <th>Comilla Victorians</th>
      </tr>
```

```
    </thead>
    <tbody>
      <tr>
        <td>Virat</td>
        <td>IND</td>
        <td>35</td>
        <td>Right-Handed</td>
        <td>2008</td>
        <td>2011</td>
        <td>2010</td>
        <td>1</td>
        <td>120</td>
        <td>58</td>
        <td>49</td>
        <td>52</td>
        <td>Yes</td>
        <td>No</td>
        <td>No</td>
        <td>No</td>
        <td>No</td>
        <td>No</td>
        <td>No</td>
      </tr>
      <tr>
        <td>Steve</td>
        <td>AUS</td>
        <td>33</td>
        <td>Right-Handed</td>
        <td>2012</td>
        <td>2013</td>
        <td>2012</td>
        <td>2</td>
        <td>100</td>
        <td>45</td>
        <td>60</td>
        <td>35</td>
        <td>No</td>
        <td>No</td>
        <td>Yes</td>
        <td>Yes</td>
        <td>No</td>
        <td>Yes</td>
        <td>Yes</td>
      </tr>
      <tr>
        <td>David</td>
        <td>AUS</td>
```

```
        <td>36</td>
        <td>Left-Handed</td>
        <td>2007</td>
        <td>2008</td>
        <td>2008</td>
        <td>3</td>
        <td>90</td>
        <td>46</td>
        <td>50</td>
        <td>32</td>
        <td>No</td>
        <td>Yes</td>
        <td>Yes</td>
        <td>Yes</td>
        <td>Yes</td>
        <td>No</td>
        <td>No</td>
      </tr>
    </tbody>
  </table>
</div>
</body>
</html>
```

After running the code, the web page will look as follows:

Screen Size: 1366 x 633

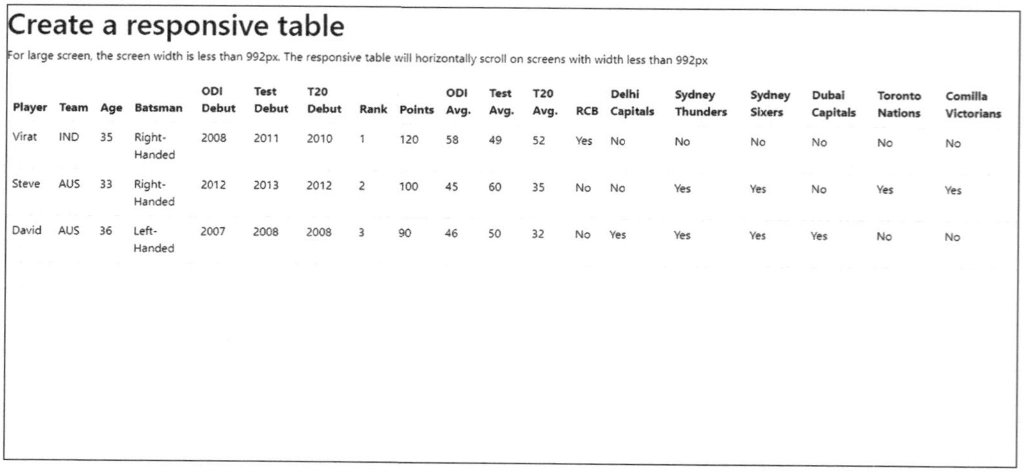

Create a responsive table

For large screen, the screen width is less than 992px. The responsive table will horizontally scroll on screens with width less than 992px

Player	Team	Age	Batsman	ODI Debut	Test Debut	T20 Debut	Rank	Points	ODI Avg.	Test Avg.	T20 Avg.	RCB	Delhi Capitals	Sydney Thunders	Sydney Sixers	Dubai Capitals	Toronto Nations	Comilla Victorians
Virat	IND	35	Right-Handed	2008	2011	2010	1	120	58	49	52	Yes	No	No	No	No	No	No
Steve	AUS	33	Right-Handed	2012	2013	2012	2	100	45	60	35	No	No	Yes	Yes	No	Yes	Yes
David	AUS	36	Left-Handed	2007	2008	2008	3	90	46	50	32	No	Yes	Yes	Yes	Yes	No	No

***Figure 3.28**: Create a responsive table for a large screen*

Let us resize the screen to understand how the responsive table works for a large screen. The scrollbar will be visible when the screen size is less than 992px:

Screen Size: 980x633

Create a responsive table

For large screen, the screen width is less than 992px. The responsive table will horizontally scroll on screens with width less than 992px

Player	Team	Age	Batsman	ODI Debut	Test Debut	T20 Debut	Rank	Points	ODI Avg.	Test Avg.	T20 Avg.	RCB	Delhi Capitals	Sydney Thunders	Sydney Sixers
Virat	IND	35	Right-Handed	2008	2011	2010	1	120	58	49	52	Yes	No	No	No
Steve	AUS	33	Right-Handed	2012	2013	2012	2	100	45	60	35	No	No	Yes	Yes
David	AUS	36	Left-Handed	2007	2008	2008	3	90	46	50	32	No	Yes	Yes	Yes

***Figure 3.29**: Horizontal scrollbar is visible in a responsive table when the screen size is less than 992px*

Conclusion

We are now familiar with how to set the content on a web page. Beginning with the global settings, we saw the standards followed by Bootstrap. The responsive images and tables were also created.

In the next chapter, we will learn how to create a menu on a web page with Bootstrap.

Points to Remember

- The headings on a web page can also be set using the Bootstrap classes **`.h1`** to **`.h6`**
- A different-styled paragraph can be created on a web page using the Bootstrap class **`.lead`**.
- A small secondary heading can be set using the using the **`<small>`** tag.
- A responsive image is an image that fits and scales according to the size of the screen or the web browser. Create it using the **`.img-fluid`** Bootstrap class.
- To create a table on a web page with Bootstrap, use the **`.table`** class.

Multiple Choice Questions

1. What is the default line height on a web page using Bootstrap?
   a. 1
   b. 1.5
   c. 2
   d. 2.5
2. Which class is used in Bootstrap to create responsive images?
   a. `responsive`
   b. `responsive-width`
   c. `img-fluid`
   d. `fluid`
3. Which class is used in Bootstrap to create a responsive table?
   a. `responsive`
   b. `table-responsive`
   c. `responsive-table`
   d. `table`
4. How do you create a borderless table on a web page with Bootstrap?
   a. `<table class="table table-borderless">`
   b. `<table class="table table-noborder">`
   c. `<table class="table table-no-border">`
   d. `<table class="table">`

Answers

1. c
2. c
3. b
4. a

Questions

- What does Typography include?
- What are the different ways to set headings on a web page?
- How is the text made look fine print?
- How is an image responsive set on a web page?
- How is a table on a web page created?
- What is a striped table?
- How is a responsive table on a web page created?
- How are responsive tables for devices of different screen sizes created?

Key Terms

- **Typography**: Typography is how the font and text appear on a web page.
- **Abbreviations**: It allows the writer to avoid repeating long words and phrases.
- **Responsive Image**: A responsive image is an image that fits and scales according to the size of the screen or the web browser.
- **Responsive Table**: A table that adjusts itself on any device, mobile, laptop, desktop, larger screen, and so on.
- **Striped Table:** A table that adds zebra stripes to the table rows.

CHAPTER 4
Bootstrap Navs

Introduction

This chapter covers how to create a navigation menu on a web page. We will create a navigation bar section where a logo can also be placed. The navigation bar can be collapsed and placed on the top or bottom of the web page.

We will also see how to add pagination to a website with a lot of pages and place it on the left, right, or center of the web page. The concept of Scrollspy is also discussed with examples.

Structure

In this chapter, we will discuss the following topics:

- Navs
- Navbar
- Pagination
- Scrollspy

Navs

To set navigation on a web page, use the nav. Learn how to create a menu on a web page, set nav alignment, and so on. With that, learn the following from this section:

- How to create a Horizontal Nav
- Set Nav Alignment
- How to create a Vertical Nav
- How to create navigation tabs
- How to create navigation pills

Creating a Horizontal Menu

To create a horizontal menu on a web page, use the following Bootstrap classes:

- **`.nav`**: Set for the **`<ul>`** element
- **`.nav-item`**: Set for each **`<li>`** of the **`<ul>`** element
- **`.nav-link`**: Set for each **`<a>`** for the links

Let us see an example of creating a horizontal menu:

```
<!DOCTYPE html>
<html lang="en">
<head>
  <title>Bootstrap Navs</title>
  <meta charset="utf-8">
  <meta name="viewport" content="width=device-width, initial-scale=1">
  <link
href="https://cdn.jsdelivr.net/npm/bootstrap@5.3.3/dist/css/bootstrap.
min.css" rel="stylesheet">
  <script
src="https://cdn.jsdelivr.net/npm/bootstrap@5.3.3/dist/js/bootstrap.
bundle.min.js"></script>
</head>
<body>

<div class="container mt-2">
   <ul class="nav">
      <li class="nav-item">
         <a class="nav-link" href="#">Cricket</a>
      </li>
      <li class="nav-item">
         <a class="nav-link" href="#">Football</a>
      </li>
      <li class="nav-item">
         <a class="nav-link" href="#">Rugby</a>
      </li>
      <li class="nav-item">
         <a class="nav-link" href="#">Tennis</a>
      </li>
   </ul>
</div>
</body>
</html>
```

After running the code, the web page will look as follows:

Screen Size: 1366 x 633

***Figure 4.1**: Create a Horizontal Menu*

Setting Nav Alignment

To align the nav, use any of the following cases:

- **`.justify-content-center`:** Center-align a nav
- **`.justify-content-end`:** Right-align a nav

Let us see an example. Here, we have right-aligned the nav:

```
<!DOCTYPE html>
<html lang="en">
<head>
  <title>Bootstrap Navs</title>
  <meta charset="utf-8">
  <meta name="viewport" content="width=device-width, initial-scale=1">
  <link
href="https://cdn.jsdelivr.net/npm/bootstrap@5.3.3/dist/css/bootstrap.
min.css" rel="stylesheet">
  <script
src="https://cdn.jsdelivr.net/npm/bootstrap@5.3.3/dist/js/bootstrap.
bundle.min.js"></script>
</head>
<body>

<div class="container mt-2">
  <ul class="nav justify-content-end">
    <li class="nav-item">
      <a class="nav-link" href="#">Cricket</a>
    </li>
    <li class="nav-item">
```

```
      <a class="nav-link" href="#">Football</a>
    </li>
    <li class="nav-item">
      <a class="nav-link" href="#">Rugby</a>
    </li>
    <li class="nav-item">
      <a class="nav-link" href="#">Tennis</a>
    </li>
  </ul>
</div>
</body>
</html>
```

After running the code, the web page will look as follows:

Screen Size: 1366 x 633

***Figure 4.2**: Set Nav Alignment*

Creating Vertical Nav

The nav is by default horizontal. For vertical navigation, use the **`.flex-column`** Bootstrap class. Let us see an example:

```
<!DOCTYPE html>
<html lang="en">
<head>
  <title>Bootstrap Navs</title>
  <meta charset="utf-8">
  <meta name="viewport" content="width=device-width, initial-scale=1">
  <link
href="https://cdn.jsdelivr.net/npm/bootstrap@5.3.3/dist/css/bootstrap.
min.css" rel="stylesheet">
```

```
  <script
src="https://cdn.jsdelivr.net/npm/bootstrap@5.3.3/dist/js/bootstrap.
bundle.min.js"></script>
</head>
<body>
<div class="container mt-2">
  <ul class="nav flex-column">
    <li class="nav-item">
      <a class="nav-link" href="#">Cricket</a>
    </li>
    <li class="nav-item">
      <a class="nav-link" href="#">Football</a>
    </li>
    <li class="nav-item">
      <a class="nav-link" href="#">Rugby</a>
    </li>
    <li class="nav-item">
      <a class="nav-link" href="#">Tennis</a>
    </li>
  </ul>
</div>
</body>
</html>
```

After running the code, the web page will look as follows:

Screen Size: 1366 x 633

Figure 4.3: *Create Vertical Nav*

Creating Navigation Tabs

With Bootstrap, easily set the nav as navigation tabs using the **.nav-tabs** Bootstrap class:

```
<ul class="nav nav-tabs">
```

The active state of the Nav is set using the **.active** class:

```
<a class="nav-link active" href="#">Cricket</a>
```

Let us see an example to create navigation tabs on a web page:

```
<!DOCTYPE html>
<html lang="en">
<head>
  <title>Bootstrap Navs</title>
  <meta charset="utf-8">
  <meta name="viewport" content="width=device-width, initial-scale=1">
  <link
href="https://cdn.jsdelivr.net/npm/bootstrap@5.3.3/dist/css/bootstrap.
min.css" rel="stylesheet">
  <script
src="https://cdn.jsdelivr.net/npm/bootstrap@5.3.3/dist/js/bootstrap.
bundle.min.js"></script>
</head>
<body>

<div class="container mt-2">
  <ul class="nav nav-tabs">
    <li class="nav-item">
      <a class="nav-link active" href="#">Cricket</a>
    </li>
    <li class="nav-item">
      <a class="nav-link" href="#">Football</a>
    </li>
    <li class="nav-item">
      <a class="nav-link" href="#">Rugby</a>
    </li>
    <li class="nav-item">
      <a class="nav-link" href="#">Tennis</a>
    </li>
  </ul>
</div>
</body>
</html>
```

After running the code, the web page will look as follows:

Screen Size: 1366 x 633

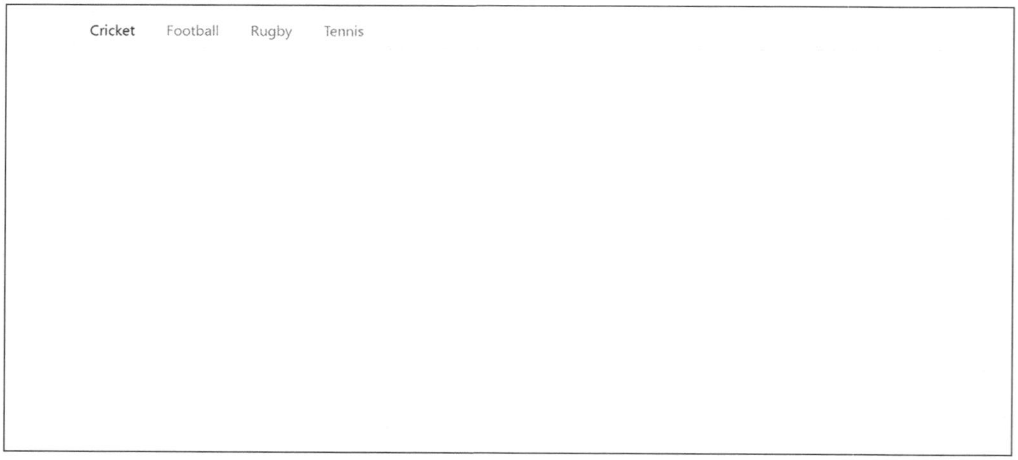

Figure 4.4: *Create Navigation Tabs*

Creating Navigation Pills

With Bootstrap, easily set the nav as navigation pills using the `.nav-pills` Bootstrap class:

```
<ul class="nav nav-pills">
```

The active state of the Nav is set using the `.active` class:

```
<a class="nav-link active" href="#">Cricket</a>
```

Let us see an example to create navigation pills:

```
<!DOCTYPE html>
<html lang="en">
<head>
  <title>Bootstrap Navs</title>
  <meta charset="utf-8">
  <meta name="viewport" content="width=device-width, initial-scale=1">
  <link
href="https://cdn.jsdelivr.net/npm/bootstrap@5.3.3/dist/css/bootstrap.
min.css" rel="stylesheet">
  <script
src="https://cdn.jsdelivr.net/npm/bootstrap@5.3.3/dist/js/bootstrap.
bundle.min.js"></script>
</head>
<body>
```

```
<div class="container mt-2">
  <ul class="nav nav-pills">
    <li class="nav-item">
      <a class="nav-link active" href="#">Cricket</a>
    </li>
    <li class="nav-item">
      <a class="nav-link" href="#">Football</a>
    </li>
    <li class="nav-item">
      <a class="nav-link" href="#">Rugby</a>
    </li>
    <li class="nav-item">
      <a class="nav-link" href="#">Tennis</a>
    </li>
  </ul>
</div>
</body>
</html>
```

After running the code, the web page will look as follows:

Screen Size: 1366 x 633

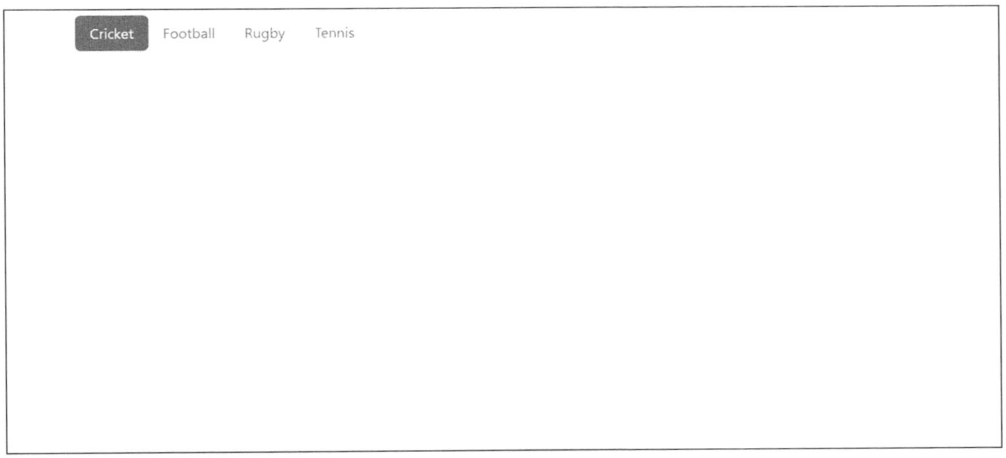

Figure 4.5: *Create Navigation Pills*

Navbar

A navbar is a navigation bar on a web page. Learn how to create a navigation bar in Bootstrap, and with that, get a thorough understanding of the following in this section:

- Create a navigation bar
- Center a navigation bar

- Change the background color of the navigation bar
- Change the text color of the navigation bar items
- Set the logo on the navigation bar
- Fix the navigation bar on the top
- Fix the navigation bar on the bottom
- Navbar Toggle

Creating a Navigation Bar

To create a navigation bar on a web page, use the **`.navbar`** class within the **`<nav>`** element. The **`<nav>`** is used to set the navigation section on a web page:

```
<nav class="navbar">
```

In Bootstrap 5, you also need to set a responsive collapsing class. This would assist the navigation bar to work perfectly on different screen sizes, that is, devices:

The navbar will stack vertically on screens smaller than 576px. The following **`sm`** is for small devices:

```
<nav class="navbar navbar-expand-sm">
```

The navbar will stack vertically on screens smaller than 768px. The following **`md`** is for medium devices:

```
<nav class="navbar navbar-expand-md">
```

The navbar will stack vertically on screens smaller than 992px. The following **`lg`** is for large devices:

```
<nav class="navbar navbar-expand-lg">
```

The navbar will stack vertically on screens smaller than 1200px. The following **`xl`** is for extra-large devices:

```
<nav class="navbar navbar-expand-xl">
```

The navbar will stack vertically on screens smaller than 1400px. The following **`xxl`** is for xx-large devices:

```
<nav class="navbar navbar-expand-xxl">
```

Let us see an example to create a navigation bar. We have used the **`.navbar-nav`** class to set the links with **`<ul>`**. The list items, that is, the menus, are set using the **`.nav-item`** class.

Since the **.navbar-expand-md** class is set, the navbar will stack vertically on a screen size less than 768px.

```
<!DOCTYPE html>
<html lang="en">
<head>
  <title>Bootstrap Navbar</title>
  <meta charset="utf-8">
  <meta name="viewport" content="width=device-width, initial-scale=1">
  <link
href="https://cdn.jsdelivr.net/npm/bootstrap@5.3.3/dist/css/bootstrap.
min.css" rel="stylesheet">
  <script
src="https://cdn.jsdelivr.net/npm/bootstrap@5.3.3/dist/js/bootstrap.
bundle.min.js"></script>
</head>
<body>
  <nav class="navbar navbar-expand-md">
    <ul class="navbar-nav">
      <li class="nav-item">
        <a class="nav-link" href="#">Home</a>
      </li>
      <li class="nav-item">
        <a class="nav-link" href="#">Features</a>
      </li>
      <li class="nav-item">
        <a class="nav-link" href="#">Products</a>
      </li>
      <li class="nav-item">
        <a class="nav-link" href="#">Contact</a>
      </li>
    </ul>
  </nav>
</body>
</html>
```

After running the code, the web page will look as follows:

Screen Size: 1366 x 633

Figure 4.6.1: *Create a Navigation Bar*

Let us resize the screen. The navbar stacks vertically when the screen size is less than 768px:

Screen Size: 760x 633

Figure 4.6.2: *Navigation Bar stacks*

Centering a Navigation Bar

To center a navigation bar, use the **`.justify-content-center`** class. Place it with the **`<nav>`** element:

```
<nav class="navbar navbar-expand-md justify-content-center">
```

Let us see an example of centering a navigation bar:

Screen Size: 1366 x 633

```
<!DOCTYPE html>
<html lang="en">
<head>
  <title>Bootstrap Navbar</title>
  <meta charset="utf-8">
  <meta name="viewport" content="width=device-width, initial-scale=1">
  <link
href="https://cdn.jsdelivr.net/npm/bootstrap@5.3.3/dist/css/bootstrap.
min.css" rel="stylesheet">
  <script
src="https://cdn.jsdelivr.net/npm/bootstrap@5.3.3/dist/js/bootstrap.
bundle.min.js"></script>
</head>
<body>
  <nav class="navbar navbar-expand-md justify-content-center">
    <ul class="navbar-nav">
      <li class="nav-item">
        <a class="nav-link" href="#">Home</a>
      </li>
      <li class="nav-item">
        <a class="nav-link" href="#">Features</a>
      </li>
      <li class="nav-item">
        <a class="nav-link" href="#">Products</a>
      </li>
      <li class="nav-item">
        <a class="nav-link" href="#">Contact</a>
      </li>
    </ul>
  </nav>
</body>
</html>
```

After running the code, the web page will look as follows:

Screen Size: 1366 x 633

***Figure 4.7**: Centering a Navigation Bar*

Changing the Background Color of the Navigation Bar

To change the background color of the navigation bar, use any of the following contextual classes. Each class represents a color to provide a meaning, that is, a representation.

Let us see all the contextual classes:

- **`.bg-primary`:** Represents important text.
- **`.bg-secondary`:** Represents secondary text.
- **`.bg-success`:** Represents a successful action.
- **`.bg-danger`:** Represents danger.
- **`.bg-warning`:** Represents warning.
- **`.bg-info`:** Represents information.
- **`.bg-light`:** Light grey
- **`.bg-dark`:** Dark grey

Let us see an example to change the background color of the navigation bar:

```
<!DOCTYPE html>
<html lang="en">
<head>
  <title>Bootstrap Navbar</title>
  <meta charset="utf-8">
  <meta name="viewport" content="width=device-width, initial-scale=1">
```

```
  <link
href="https://cdn.jsdelivr.net/npm/bootstrap@5.3.3/dist/css/bootstrap.
min.css" rel="stylesheet">
  <script
src="https://cdn.jsdelivr.net/npm/bootstrap@5.3.3/dist/js/bootstrap.
bundle.min.js"></script>
</head>
<body>
<nav class="navbar navbar-expand-md bg-info">
  <ul class="navbar-nav">
    <li class="nav-item">
      <a class="nav-link" href="#">Home</a>
    </li>
    <li class="nav-item">
      <a class="nav-link" href="#">Features</a>
    </li>
    <li class="nav-item">
      <a class="nav-link" href="#">Products</a>
    </li>
    <li class="nav-item">
      <a class="nav-link" href="#">Contact</a>
    </li>
  </ul>
</nav>
</body>
</html>
```

After running the code, the web page will look as follows:

Screen Size: 1366 x 633

***Figure 4.8**: Change the background color of the Navigation Bar*

Changing the Text Color of the Navigation Bar Items

To change the text of the navbar items, use any of the below items:

- **.navbar-light:** Black color
- **.navbar-dark:** White color

Let us see an example to change the text color of the navigation bar items:

```
<!DOCTYPE html>
<html lang="en">
<head>
  <title>Bootstrap Navbar</title>
  <meta charset="utf-8">
  <meta name="viewport" content="width=device-width, initial-scale=1">
  <link
href="https://cdn.jsdelivr.net/npm/bootstrap@5.3.3/dist/css/bootstrap.
min.css" rel="stylesheet">
  <script
src="https://cdn.jsdelivr.net/npm/bootstrap@5.3.3/dist/js/bootstrap.
bundle.min.js"></script>
</head>
<body>
<nav class="navbar navbar-expand-md bg-primary navbar-dark">
  <ul class="navbar-nav">
    <li class="nav-item">
      <a class="nav-link" href="#">Home</a>
    </li>
    <li class="nav-item">
      <a class="nav-link" href="#">Features</a>
    </li>
    <li class="nav-item">
      <a class="nav-link" href="#">Products</a>
    </li>
    <li class="nav-item">
      <a class="nav-link" href="#">Contact</a>
    </li>
  </ul>
</nav>
</body>
</html>
```

After running the code, the web page will look as follows:

Screen Size: 1366 x 633

Figure 4.9: *Change the text color of the Navigation Bar items*

Setting the Brand Logo on the Navigation Bar

To set the brand logo on the navigation bar, use the **`.navbar-brand`** class:

```
<a class="navbar-brand" href="#">Logo</a>
```

Let us see an example to set a brand logo on the navigation bar:

```
<!DOCTYPE html>
<html lang="en">
<head>
  <title>Bootstrap Navbar</title>
  <meta charset="utf-8">
  <meta name="viewport" content="width=device-width, initial-scale=1">
  <link
href="https://cdn.jsdelivr.net/npm/bootstrap@5.3.3/dist/css/bootstrap.
min.css" rel="stylesheet">
  <script
src="https://cdn.jsdelivr.net/npm/bootstrap@5.3.3/dist/js/bootstrap.
bundle.min.js"></script>
</head>
<body>
<nav class="navbar navbar-expand-sm bg-dark navbar-dark">
  <div class="container-fluid">
    <a class="navbar-brand" href="#">Logo</a>
  </div>
</nav>
</body>
</html>
```

After running the code, the web page will look as follows:

Screen Size: 1366 x 633

***Figure 4.10**: Set the brand color on the Navigation Bar*

Fixing the Navigation Bar on the top

Fix the navigation on the top of the web page using the **`.fixed-top`** Bootstrap class:

```
<nav class="navbar navbar-expand-md bg-primary navbar-dark fixed-top">
```

Let us see an example. Try to scroll the web page and notice the fixed navbar at the top:

```
<!DOCTYPE html>
<html lang="en">
<head>
  <title>Bootstrap Navbar</title>
  <meta charset="utf-8">
  <meta name="viewport" content="width=device-width, initial-scale=1">
  <link
href="https://cdn.jsdelivr.net/npm/bootstrap@5.3.3/dist/css/bootstrap.
min.css" rel="stylesheet">
  <script
src="https://cdn.jsdelivr.net/npm/bootstrap@5.3.3/dist/js/bootstrap.
bundle.min.js"></script>
</head>
<body style="height:1500px">
  <nav class="navbar navbar-expand-md bg-primary navbar-dark fixed-top">
    <ul class="navbar-nav">
      <li class="nav-item">
```

```
        <a class="nav-link" href="#">Home</a>
      </li>
      <li class="nav-item">
        <a class="nav-link" href="#">Features</a>
      </li>
      <li class="nav-item">
        <a class="nav-link" href="#">Products</a>
      </li>
      <li class="nav-item">
        <a class="nav-link" href="#">Contact</a>
      </li>
    </ul>
  </nav>
</body>
</html>
```

After running the code, the web page will look as follows:

Screen Size: 1366 x 633

***Figure 4.11**: Fix the Navigation Bar on the top*

Fixing the Navigation Bar on the Bottom

Fix the navigation on the bottom of the web page using the **`.fixed-bottom`** Bootstrap class:

```
<nav class="navbar navbar-expand-md bg-primary navbar-dark fixed-bottom">
```

Let us see an example. Try to scroll the web page and notice the fixed navbar at the bottom:

```
<!DOCTYPE html>
<html lang="en">
<head>
  <title>Bootstrap Navbar</title>
  <meta charset="utf-8">
  <meta name="viewport" content="width=device-width, initial-scale=1">
  <link
href="https://cdn.jsdelivr.net/npm/bootstrap@5.3.3/dist/css/bootstrap.
min.css" rel="stylesheet">
  <script
src="https://cdn.jsdelivr.net/npm/bootstrap@5.3.3/dist/js/bootstrap.
bundle.min.js"></script>
</head>
<body style="height:1300px">
  <nav class="navbar navbar-expand-md bg-primary navbar-dark fixed-bottom">
    <ul class="navbar-nav">
      <li class="nav-item">
        <a class="nav-link" href="#">Home</a>
      </li>
      <li class="nav-item">
        <a class="nav-link" href="#">Features</a>
      </li>
      <li class="nav-item">
        <a class="nav-link" href="#">Products</a>
      </li>
      <li class="nav-item">
        <a class="nav-link" href="#">Contact</a>
      </li>
    </ul>
  </nav>
</body>
</html>
```

After running the code, the web page will look as follows:

Screen Size: 1366 x 633

***Figure 4.12**: Fix the Navigation Bar on the bottom*

Navbar Toggle

The **`.navbar-toggler`** in Bootstrap can be used to hide navbar items inside a menu in small screens which can then be toggled by the click of a menu button. Consider it as a collapsible navbar.

A collapsible navigation bar can be created using the following classes and attributes:

```
class="navbar-toggler"
data-bs-toggle="collapse"
data-bs-target="#mytarget"
```

Wrap the navbar links in a <div> element with the following:

```
class="collapse navbar-collapse"
```

The preceding code should be followed by an id that matches the **`data-bs-target`** of the button: **"`mytarget`"**.

Let us see an example of creating a collapsible navigation bar to toggle the navbar items:

```
<!DOCTYPE html>
<html lang="en">
<head>
  <title>Bootstrap Navbar Toggle</title>
  <meta charset="utf-8">
  <meta name="viewport" content="width=device-width, initial-scale=1">
  <link
href="https://cdn.jsdelivr.net/npm/bootstrap@5.3.3/dist/css/bootstrap.
min.css" rel="stylesheet">
```

```
  <script
src="https://cdn.jsdelivr.net/npm/bootstrap@5.3.3/dist/js/bootstrap.
bundle.min.js"></script>
</head>
<body>

<nav class="navbar navbar-expand-sm bg-primary navbar-dark">
  <div class="container-fluid">
    <a class="navbar-brand" href="#">Website Logo</a>
    <button class="navbar-toggler" type="button" data-bs-toggle="col-
lapse" data-bs-target="#mytarget">
      <span class="navbar-toggler-icon"></span>
    </button>
    <div class="collapse navbar-collapse" id="mytarget">
      <ul class="navbar-nav">
        <li class="nav-item">
          <a class="nav-link" href="#">Tutorials</a>
        </li>
        <li class="nav-item">
          <a class="nav-link" href="#">Study Material</a>
        </li>
        <li class="nav-item">
          <a class="nav-link" href="#">Quizzes</a>
        </li>
        <li class="nav-item">
          <a class="nav-link" href="#">Blog</a>
        </li>
        <li class="nav-item">
          <a class="nav-link" href="#">Contact</a>
        </li>
      </ul>
    </div>
  </div>
</nav>

<div class="container-fluid mt-2">
  <h2>Navbar Toggle</h2>
  <p>Displaying how collapsible navigation works. On smaller devices,
the navbar items will collapse.</p>
</div>

</body>
</html>
```

After running the code, the web page will look as follows:

Screen Size: 1366 x 633

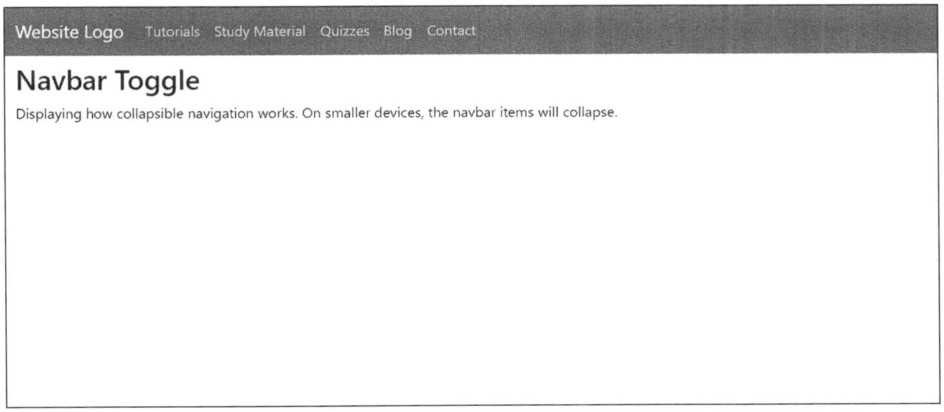

Figure 4.13: *Navigation Bar*

Let us change the screen size. On smaller devices, the navbar items hide:

Screen Size: 570 x 633

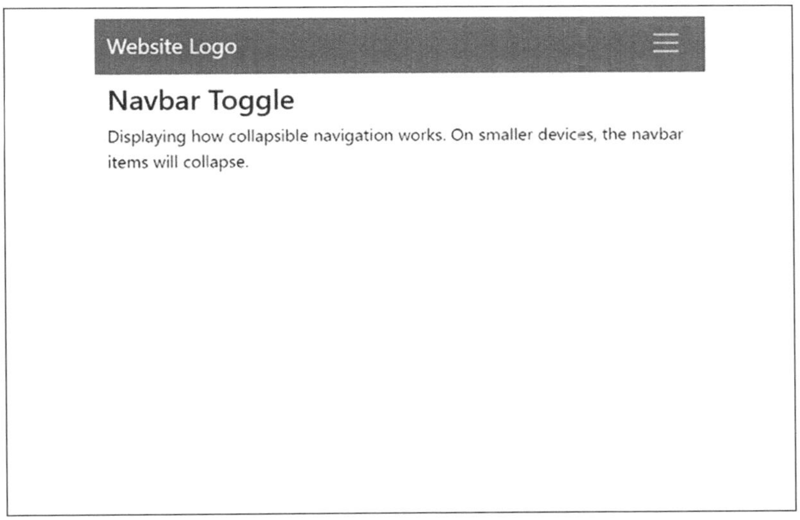

Figure 4.14: *Display Navbar Toggle*

Pagination

To provide navigation to your website with several pages, set pagination for every page. In this section, learn how to create a pagination in Bootstrap. With that, learn:

- How to highlight a link
- How to disable a link
- Resize Pagination

Creating Pagination

To create a pagination on a web page, use the **.pagination** Bootstrap class. This is to be set for the **<ul>** element. With that, we need to use two more Bootstrap classes:

- Add the **.page-item** class to each list item, that is, the **<li>** element
- Add the **.page-link** class to each **<a>** inside **<li>**.

Let us see an example to create a pagination:

```
<!DOCTYPE html>
<html lang="en">
  <head>
    <title>Bootstrap Pagination</title>
    <meta charset="utf-8">
    <meta name="viewport" content="width=device-width, initial-scale=1">
    <link
href="https://cdn.jsdelivr.net/npm/bootstrap@5.3.3/dist/css/bootstrap.
min.css" rel="stylesheet">
    <script
src="https://cdn.jsdelivr.net/npm/bootstrap@5.3.3/dist/js/bootstrap.
bundle.min.js"></script>
</head>
<body>
<div class="container mt-2">
  <h1>Demo Heading</h1>
  <p>Here, we are showing how a pagination looks like. It consists of a
previous and next link also:</p>
  <ul class="pagination">
    <li class="page-item"><a class="page-link" href="#">Previous</a></li>
    <li class="page-item"><a class="page-link" href="#">1</a></li>
    <li class="page-item"><a class="page-link" href="#">2</a></li>
    <li class="page-item"><a class="page-link" href="#">3</a></li>
    <li class="page-item"><a class="page-link" href="#">4</a></li>
    <li class="page-item"><a class="page-link" href="#">5</a></li>
    <li class="page-item"><a class="page-link" href="#">Next</a></li>
  </ul>
</div>
</body>
</html>
```

After running the code, the web page will look as follows:

Screen Size: 1366 x 633

***Figure 4.15**: Create pagination*

Highlighting a Link

A single link is always active and should be highlighted. This active link is the current page visited by a user. To highlight the active link, use the **`.active`** Bootstrap class.

Let us see an example and consider that we are on page 4:

```
<!DOCTYPE html>
<html lang="en">
  <head>
    <title>Bootstrap Pagination</title>
    <meta charset="utf-8">
    <meta name="viewport" content="width=device-width, initial-scale=1">
    <link
href="https://cdn.jsdelivr.net/npm/bootstrap@5.3.3/dist/css/bootstrap.
min.css" rel="stylesheet">
    <script
src="https://cdn.jsdelivr.net/npm/bootstrap@5.3.3/dist/js/bootstrap.
bundle.min.js"></script>
</head>
<body>
<div class="container mt-2">
  <h1>Demo Heading</h1>
  <p>Here, we are showing how a pagination looks like. It consists of a
previous and next link also:</p>
  <ul class="pagination">
    <li class="page-item"><a class="page-link" href="#">Previous</a></li>
    <li class="page-item"><a class="page-link" href="#">1</a></li>
    <li class="page-item"><a class="page-link" href="#">2</a></li>
    <li class="page-item"><a class="page-link" href="#">3</a></li>
```

```
    <li class="page-item active"><a class="page-link" href="#">4</a></li>
    <li class="page-item"><a class="page-link" href="#">5</a></li>
    <li class="page-item"><a class="page-link" href="#">Next</a></li>
  </ul>
</div>
</body>
</html>
```

After running the code, the web page will look as follows:

Screen Size: 1366 x 633

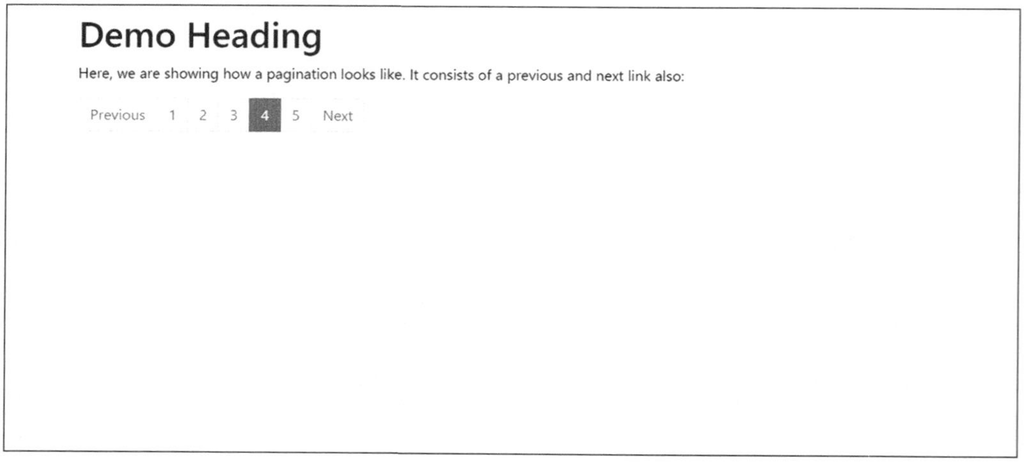

***Figure 4.16**: Highlight a link*

Disabling a Link

To disable a link in a pagination, use the **`.disabled`** class. If you are on page 1, then definitely the previous link will be disabled as there is no previous page. Similarly, when you are on the last page, the **`Next`** link will be disabled as there is no next page.

The active page is the last:

```
<li class="page-item active"><a class="page-link" href="#">5</a></li>
```

Therefore, the **`Next`** pagination will be disabled:

```
<li class="page-item disabled"><a class="page-link" href="#">Next</a></li>
```

Let us see an example to disable a link:

```
<!DOCTYPE html>
<html lang="en">
  <head>
    <title>Bootstrap Pagination</title>
    <meta charset="utf-8">
```

```
    <meta name="viewport" content="width=device-width, initial-scale=1">
    <link
href="https://cdn.jsdelivr.net/npm/bootstrap@5.3.3/dist/css/bootstrap.
min.css" rel="stylesheet">
    <script
src="https://cdn.jsdelivr.net/npm/bootstrap@5.3.3/dist/js/bootstrap.
bundle.min.js"></script>
</head>
<body>
<div class="container mt-2">
  <h1>Demo Heading</h1>
  <p>Here, we are showing how a pagination looks like. It consists of a
previous and next link also:</p>
  <ul class="pagination">
    <li class="page-item"><a class="page-link" href="#">Previous</a></li>
    <li class="page-item"><a class="page-link" href="#">1</a></li>
    <li class="page-item"><a class="page-link" href="#">2</a></li>
    <li class="page-item"><a class="page-link" href="#">3</a></li>
    <li class="page-item"><a class="page-link" href="#">4</a></li>
    <li class="page-item active"><a class="page-link" href="#">5</a></li>
    <li class="page-item disabled"><a class="page-link" href="#">Next</
a></li>
  </ul>
</div>
</body>
</html>
```

After running the code, the web page will look as follows:

Screen Size: 1366 x 633

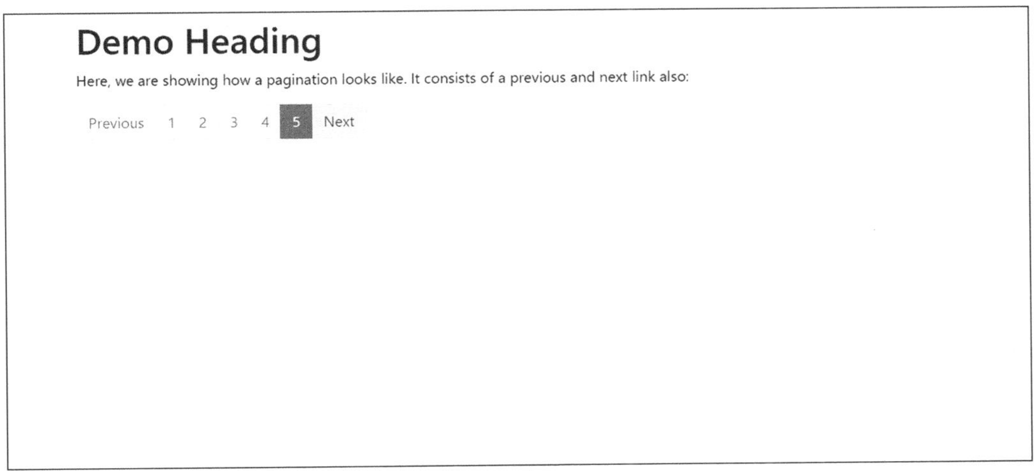

***Figure 4.17**: Disable a link*

Resizing Pagination

With Bootstrap, you can easily create and even resize a pagination on a web page. The following classes are provided:

- **.pagination-lg** for large pagination
- **.pagination-sm** for smaller pagination

Let us see an example. Here, we have created a pagination larger than the default size:

```
<!DOCTYPE html>
<html lang="en">
  <head>
    <title>Bootstrap Pagination</title>
    <meta charset="utf-8">
    <meta name="viewport" content="width=device-width, initial-scale=1">
    <link
href="https://cdn.jsdelivr.net/npm/bootstrap@5.3.3/dist/css/bootstrap.
min.css" rel="stylesheet">
    <script
src="https://cdn.jsdelivr.net/npm/bootstrap@5.3.3/dist/js/bootstrap.
bundle.min.js"></script>
</head>
<body>
<div class="container mt-2">
  <h1>Demo Heading</h1>
  <p>Here, we are showing how a pagination looks like. It consists of a
previous and next link also:</p>
  <ul class="pagination pagination-lg">
    <li class="page-item"><a class="page-link" href="#">Previous</a></li>
    <li class="page-item"><a class="page-link" href="#">1</a></li>
    <li class="page-item"><a class="page-link" href="#">2</a></li>
    <li class="page-item"><a class="page-link" href="#">3</a></li>
    <li class="page-item"><a class="page-link" href="#">4</a></li>
    <li class="page-item active"><a class="page-link" href="#">5</a></li>
    <li class="page-item"><a class="page-link" href="#">Previous</a></li>
  </ul>
</div>
</body>
</html>
```

After running the code, the web page will look as follows:

Screen Size: 1366 x 633

***Figure 4.18**: Resize pagination*

Align Pagination

With Bootstrap, you can easily align the pagination on the left, right, or center. The default is left-aligned. The following classes are provided:

- **`.justify-content-center`** for center-aligned pagination
- **`.justify-content-end`** for right-aligned pagination

Let us see an example. Here, we have aligned the pagination to the center:

```
<!DOCTYPE html>
<html lang="en">
  <head>
    <title>Bootstrap Pagination</title>
    <meta charset="utf-8">
    <meta name="viewport" content="width=device-width, initial-scale=1">
    <link
href="https://cdn.jsdelivr.net/npm/bootstrap@5.3.3/dist/css/bootstrap.
min.css" rel="stylesheet">
    <script
src="https://cdn.jsdelivr.net/npm/bootstrap@5.3.3/dist/js/bootstrap.
bundle.min.js"></script>
</head>
<body>
<div class="container mt-2">
  <h1>Demo Heading</h1>
  <p>Here, we are showing how a pagination looks like. It consists of a
previous and next link also:</p>
  <ul class="pagination justify-content-center">
    <li class="page-item"><a class="page-link" href="#">Previous</a></li>
```

```
    <li class="page-item"><a class="page-link" href="#">1</a></li>
    <li class="page-item"><a class="page-link" href="#">2</a></li>
    <li class="page-item"><a class="page-link" href="#">3</a></li>
    <li class="page-item"><a class="page-link" href="#">4</a></li>
    <li class="page-item active"><a class="page-link" href="#">5</a></li>
    <li class="page-item"><a class="page-link" href="#">Previous</a></li>
  </ul>
</div>
</body>
</html>
```

After running the code, the web page will look as follows:

Screen Size: 1366 x 633

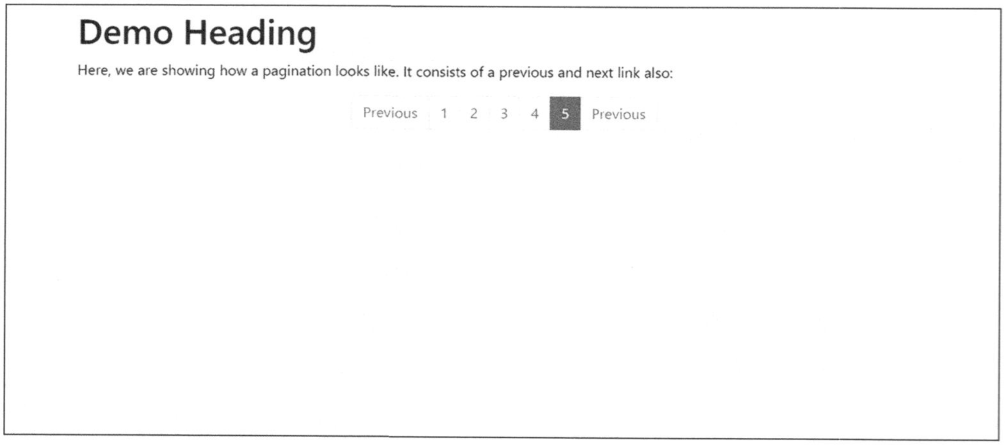

***Figure 4.19**: Align pagination*

Scrollspy

The Bootstrap Nav or List Group can be automatically updated indicating the current active link. The update is based on the scroll position. The scrollspy is mostly used with Bootstrap Nav or List Group. Also, feel free to use it with any anchor elements on the web page.

Let's see how scrollspy works:

- The scrollspy needs a navigation, list group, or a set of links, and a scrollable container. The container can be the **`<body>`** or a custom element with a set height and **`overflow-y: scroll`**.
- On the scrollable container, add **`data-bs-spy="scroll"`** and **`data-bs-target="#navId"`** where navId is the unique id of the associated navigation. If there is no focusable element inside the element, be sure to also include a **`tabindex="0"`** to ensure keyboard access.

- While scrolling, the container, a **.active** class is added and removed from anchor links within the associated navigation.
- The invisible target elements will be ignored.

Scrollspy with List Groups

Let us see an example of using scrollspy with list groups. The active class will update whenever you scroll the page:

```
<!DOCTYPE html>
<html lang="en">
<head>
  <title>Bootstrap Scrollspy</title>
  <meta charset="utf-8">
  <meta name="viewport" content="width=device-width, initial-scale=1">
  <link
href="https://cdn.jsdelivr.net/npm/bootstrap@5.3.3/dist/css/bootstrap.
min.css" rel="stylesheet">
  <script
src="https://cdn.jsdelivr.net/npm/bootstrap@5.3.3/dist/js/bootstrap.
bundle.min.js"></script>
</head>
<body>
<div class="row">
  <div class="col-4">
    <div id="list-example" class="list-group">
      <a class="list-group-item list-group-item-action"
href="#list-item-1">Furniture</a>
      <a class="list-group-item list-group-item-action"
href="#list-item-2">Accessories</a>
      <a class="list-group-item list-group-item-action" href="#
list-item-3">Books</a>
      <a class="list-group-item list-group-item-action" href="#
list-item-4">Equipments</a>
      <a class="list-group-item list-group-item-action" href="#
list-item-5">Toys</a>
    </div>
  </div>
  <div class="col-8">
    <div data-bs-spy="scroll" data-bs-target="#list-example" data-bs-
smooth-scroll="true" class="scrollspy-example" tabindex="0">
      <h4 id="list-item-1">Furniture</h4>
      <p>The product furniture is still available. This is a demo text.
This is a demo text. This is a demo text. This is a demo text. This is a
demo text. This is a demo text. This is a demo text </p>
      <h4 id="list-item-2">Accessories</h4>
```

```
      <p>The product accessories are still available. This is a demo
text. This is a demo text. This is a demo text. This is a demo text.
This is a demo text. This is a demo text. This is a demo text</p>
      <h4 id="list-item-3">Books</h4>
      <p>The product books are still available. This is a demo text.
This is a demo text. This is a demo text. This is a demo text. This is a
demo text. This is a demo text. This is a demo text</p>
      <h4 id="list-item-4">Equipments</h4>
      <p>The product equipment is still available. This is a demo text.
This is a demo text. This is a demo text. This is a demo text. This is a
demo text. This is a demo text. This is a demo text</p>
      <h4 id="list-item-5">Toys</h4>
      <p>The product toy is still available. This is a demo text. This
is a demo text. This is a demo text. This is a demo text. This is a demo
text. This is a demo text. This is a demo text</p>
    </div>
  </div>
</div>
</body>
</html>
```

After running the code, the web page will look as follows:

Screen Size: 1366 x 633

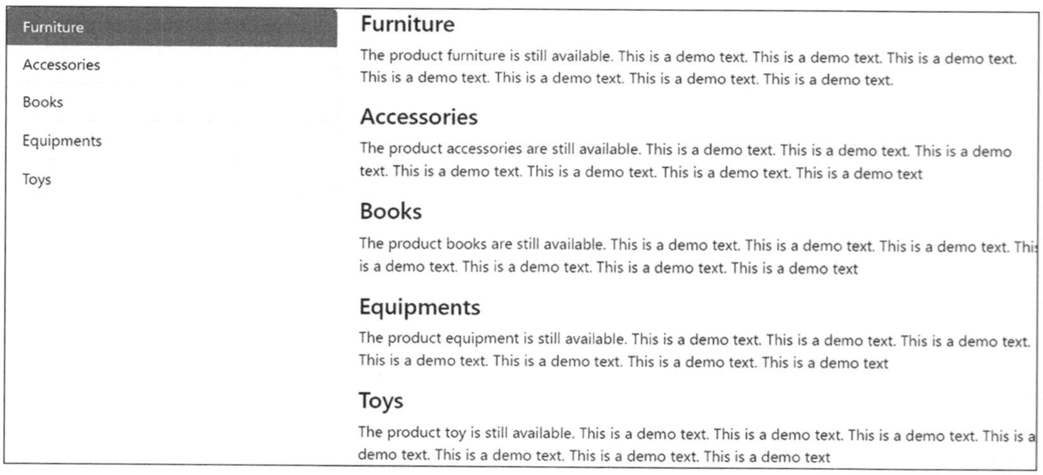

Figure 4.20: *Scrollspy with list groups*

Scrollspy with Navbar

Let us see an example of using scrollspy with **.navbar**. The active class will update whenever you scroll the page:

```
<!DOCTYPE html>
<html lang="en">
<head>
  <title>Bootstrap Scrollspy</title>
  <meta charset="utf-8">
  <meta name="viewport" content="width=device-width, initial-scale=1">
  <link
href="https://cdn.jsdelivr.net/npm/bootstrap@5.3.3/dist/css/bootstrap.
min.css" rel="stylesheet">
  <script
src="https://cdn.jsdelivr.net/npm/bootstrap@5.3.3/dist/js/bootstrap.
bundle.min.js"></script>
</head>
<body>
<nav id="navbar-example2" class="navbar bg-body-tertiary px-3 mb-3">
  <a class="navbar-brand" href="#">Logo</a>
  <ul class="nav nav-pills">
    <li class="nav-item">
      <a class="nav-link" href="#scrollspyHeading1">Furniture</a>
    </li>
    <li class="nav-item">
      <a class="nav-link" href="#scrollspyHeading2">Accessories</a>
    </li>
    <li class="nav-item">
      <a class="nav-link" href="#scrollspyHeading3">Books</a>
    </li>
    <li class="nav-item dropdown">
      <a class="nav-link dropdown-toggle" data-bs-toggle="dropdown"
href="#" role="button" aria-expanded="false">Electronics</a>
      <ul class="dropdown-menu">
        <li><a class="dropdown-item" href="#scrollspyHeading4">Camera</
a></li>
        <li><a class="dropdown-item" href="#scrollspyHeading5">Mobile</
a></li>
        <li><a class="dropdown-item" href="#scrollspyHeading6">Laptop</
a></li>
      </ul>
    </li>
  </ul>
</nav>
```

```
<div data-bs-spy="scroll" data-bs-target="#navbar-example2" data-bs-
root-margin="0px 0px -40%" data-bs-smooth-scroll="true" class="scroll-
spy-example bg-body-tertiary p-3 rounded-2" tabindex="0">
  <h4 id="scrollspyHeading1">Furniture</h4>
  <p>The product furniture is still available. This is a demo text. This
is a demo text. This is a demo text. This is a demo text. This is a demo
text. This is a demo text. This is a demo text</p>
  <h4 id="scrollspyHeading2">Accessories</h4>
  <p>The product accessories is still available. This is a demo text.
This is a demo text. This is a demo text. This is a demo text. This is a
demo text. This is a demo text. This is a demo text</p>
  <h4 id="scrollspyHeading3">Books</h4>
  <p>The product books is still available. This is a demo text. This is
a demo text. This is a demo text. This is a demo text. This is a demo
text. This is a demo text. This is a demo text</p>
  <h4 id="scrollspyHeading4">Camera</h4>
  <p>The product camera is still available. This is a demo text. This is
a demo text. This is a demo text. This is a demo text. This is a demo
text. This is a demo text. This is a demo text</p>
  <h4 id="scrollspyHeading5">Mobile</h4>
  <p>The product mobile is still available. This is a demo text. This is
a demo text. This is a demo text. This is a demo text. This is a demo
text. This is a demo text. This is a demo text</p>
  <h4 id="scrollspyHeading6">Laptop</h4>
  <p>The product laptop is still available. This is a demo text. This is
a demo text. This is a demo text. This is a demo text. This is a demo
text. This is a demo text. This is a demo text</p>
</div>
</body>
</html>
```

After running the code, the web page will look as follows:

Screen Size: 1366 x 633

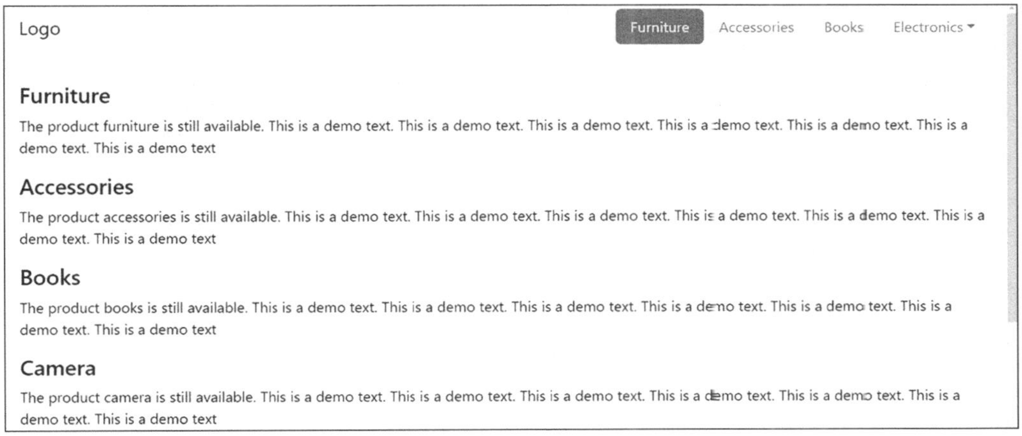

Figure 4.21: *Use scrollspy with Navbar*

Conclusion

We are now familiar with how to set navigation on a web page. Beginning with the navs and navigation bar, we saw how to set the navigation section on a web page. The pagination on every page was set to ease navigation on a website with multiple web pages.

In the next chapter, we will learn how to work with Bootstrap components on a web page, such as badges, cards, list groups, spinners, buttons, and so on.

Points to Remember

- To create a navigation menu on a web page, use the **`.nav`**, **`nav-item`**, and **`nav-link`** Bootstrap classes.
- Set the navs as navigation tabs using the **`.nav-tabs`** class.
- With Bootstrap, easily set the navs as navigation pills using the **`.nav-pills`** class.
- To create a navigation bar on a web page, use the **`.navbar`** class.
- To set the logo on the navigation bar, use the **`.navbar-brand`** class.
- To create a pagination on a web page, use the **`.pagination`**, **`.page-item`**, and **`.page-link`** classes.
- Use the **`.pagination-lg`** to create a larger pagination.
- Use the **`.pagination-sm`** to create a smaller pagination.

Multiple Choice Questions

1. Which class is used in Bootstrap to center align a nav?
    a. `center`
    b. `justify-content-center`
    c. `justify-center`
    d. `justify-center-nav`
2. The nav on a web page is by default ______.
    a. vertical
    b. horizontal
3. Which class is used in Bootstrap to stack the navbar vertically on small screens?
    a. `navbar-md`
    b. `nav-expand-md`
    c. `navbar-expand-md`
    d. `nav-md`
4. Which class is used in Bootstrap to set the brand logo on the navigation bar?
    a. `nav-brand`
    b. `nav-logo`
    c. `navbar-logo`
    d. `navbar-brand`

Answers

1. b
2. a
3. c
4. d

Questions

1. How is navigation set on a web page?
2. How is a nav aligned in the center?
3. How is a navigation bar created on a web page?
4. What is the Bootstrap class to set the logo on the navigation bar?
5. How is the navbar vertically stacked on small screens?
6. What is pagination?
7. What is Scrollspy?

Key Terms

- **Navbar:** A navbar is a navigation bar on a web page.
- **Navs:** To set navigation on a web page, use the navs.
- **Pagination:** To set pagination for every page to provide navigation to your website with several pages.
- **Scrollspy**: It is a Bootstrap feature that automatically updates links in a navigation list based on the user's scroll position.

Chapter 5
Bootstrap Components

Introduction

This chapter covers components for the web page in Bootstrap that allow adding progress bars, cards, list groups, and more, to a web page. We will also learn to create drop-down menus, list groups, and spinners.

Toast messages that mimic push notifications will also be set. Also, buttons would be created on a web page and customized. We will also learn how to add alerts to a web page and customize them.

Structure

In this chapter, we will discuss the following topics:

- Badges
- Progress Bars
- Cards
- List Groups
- Spinners
- Buttons
- Button Groups
- Alerts

Badges

Learn about Badges in Bootstrap and how they are used. Additionally, create a new badge on a web page and style it. With that, get a thorough understanding of the following in this lesson:

- Creating a badge

- Making badges round
- Setting badge inside a button

Creating a Badge

A badge is used to add any extra information to a piece of content. Let's say you launched a new course. Just set the "**New**" badge where the course name is mentioned, that is, inside the element.

Use the **.badge** Bootstrap class to create a badge on a web page. Badges are mainly rectangular and set in a **<span>** element.

In the following example, we have marked one of the courses, that is, Python, with a badge to represent it as a new course. The badge color is set using the contextual class **.bg-primary**:

```
<!DOCTYPE html>
<html lang="en">
<head>
  <title>Bootstrap Badges</title>
  <meta charset="utf-8">
  <meta name="viewport" content="width=device-width, initial-scale=1">
  <link
href="https://cdn.jsdelivr.net/npm/bootstrap@5.3.3/dist/css/bootstrap.
min.css" rel="stylesheet">
  <script
src="https://cdn.jsdelivr.net/npm/bootstrap@5.3.3/dist/js/bootstrap.
bundle.min.js"></script>
</head>
<body>
<div class="container">
  <h1>Our Courses</h1>
  <p>The following are our programming courses:</p>
  <h2>Java</h2>
  <h2>C</h2>
  <h2>C++</h2>
  <h2>Python<span class="badge bg-primary">New</span></h2>
</div>
</body>
</html>
```

After running the code, the web page will look as follows:

Screen Size: 1366 x 633

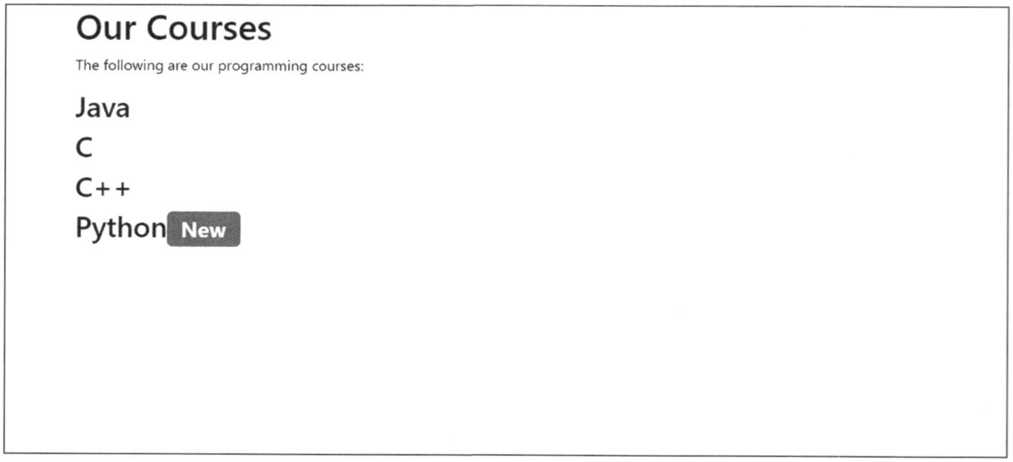

***Figure 5.1**: Create a Badge*

To change the badge color, use any of the following contextual classes. Each class represents a color to provide a meaning, that is, a representation.

In the previous example, we used one of such classes, that is, **`bg-primary`**. Let us see all the contextual classes:

- **`.bg-primary`**: Represents important text
- **`.bg-secondary`**: Represents secondary text
- **`.bg-success`**: Represents a successful action
- **`.bg-danger`**: Represents danger
- **`.bg-warning`**: Represents warning
- **`.bg-info`**: Represents information
- **`.bg-light`**: Light grey
- **`.bg-dark`**: Dark grey

Making Badges Round

The **`.rounded-pill`** class is used in Bootstrap to change the shape of a badge:

```
<span class="badge rounded-pill bg-primary">
```

Let us see an example to make the badges more rounded:

```
<!DOCTYPE html>
<html lang="en">
<head>
  <title>Bootstrap Badges</title>
  <meta charset="utf-8">
```

```
  <meta name="viewport" content="width=device-width, initial-scale=1">
  <link
href="https://cdn.jsdelivr.net/npm/bootstrap@5.3.3/dist/css/bootstrap.
min.css" rel="stylesheet">
  <script
src="https://cdn.jsdelivr.net/npm/bootstrap@5.3.3/dist/js/bootstrap.
bundle.min.js"></script>
</head>
<body>
<div class="container">
  <h1>Our Courses</h1>
  <p>The following are our programming courses:</p>
  <h2>Java</h2>
  <h2>C<span class="badge rounded-pill bg-primary">Updated</span></h2>
  <h2>C++</h2>
  <h2>Python<span class="badge rounded-pill bg-primary">New</span></h2>
</div>
</body>
</html>
```

After running the code, the web page will look as follows:

Screen Size: 1366 x 633

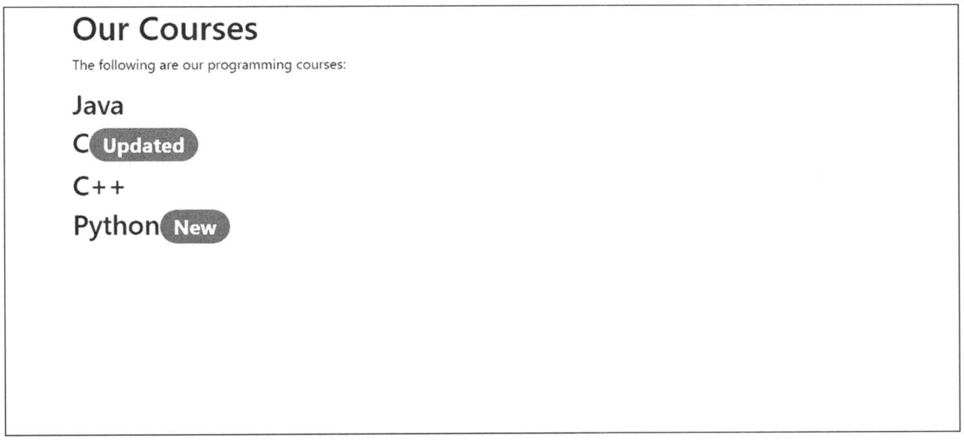

***Figure 5.2**: Make badges round*

Setting Badge Inside a Button

To make the badges look more professional, place them inside a button. Set the **<span>** class inside a button and represent the colors using the contextual classes;

Let us see an example of setting a badge inside a button:

```
<!DOCTYPE html>
<html lang="en">
```

```
<head>
  <title>Bootstrap Badges</title>
  <meta charset="utf-8">
  <meta name="viewport" content="width=device-width, initial-scale=1">
  <link
href="https://cdn.jsdelivr.net/npm/bootstrap@5.3.3/dist/css/bootstrap.
min.css" rel="stylesheet">
  <script
src="https://cdn.jsdelivr.net/npm/bootstrap@5.3.3/dist/js/bootstrap.
bundle.min.js"></script>
</head>
<body>
<div class="container">
  <h1>Interview QA</h1>
  <p>The following Interview QA are provided with each technology cover-
ing over 10 questions and answers:</p>
  <button type="button" class="btn btn-primary">
    Python <span class="badge bg-danger">15</span>
  </button>
  <button type="button" class="btn btn-warning">
    Java <span class="badge bg-secondary">20</span>
  </button>
</div>
</body>
</html>
```

After running the code, the web page will look as follows:

Screen Size: 1366 x 633

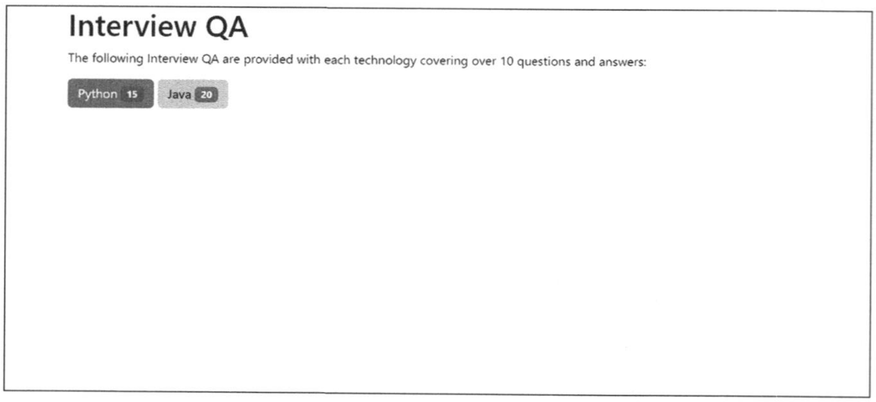

***Figure 5.3**: Set a badge inside a button*

Progress Bars

A progress bar is a visual indicator used to show the progress of a task or process.

Learn how to create a progress bar on a web page with Bootstrap. With that, get a thorough understanding of the following in this lesson:

- Creating a progress bar
- Changing the progress bar color
- Adding stripes to the progress bar
- Setting a label for the progress bar
- Animating progress bar

Let us first see how to create a progress bar:

Creating a Progress Bar

To create a progress bar on a web page, use the following Bootstrap classes:

- **`.progress class`**
- **`.progress-bar class`**

The default color of the progress bar is blue. The width of the progress bar is used to set it; otherwise, the progress will not be visible. Use the width property to achieve this. The width is set for the **`.progress-bar`** class:

```
style="width:85%"
```

The default height of the progress bar is 16px. To change the default height, set the height property of the progress bar with CSS. The height is set for the **`.progress`** class:

```
style="height:25px"
```

Let us see an example to create a progress bar on a web page:

```
<!DOCTYPE html>
<html lang="en">
<head>
  <title>Bootstrap Progress Bar</title>
  <meta charset="utf-8">
  <meta name="viewport" content="width=device-width, initial-scale=1">
  <link
href="https://cdn.jsdelivr.net/npm/bootstrap@5.3.3/dist/css/bootstrap.
min.css" rel="stylesheet">
  <script
src="https://cdn.jsdelivr.net/npm/bootstrap@5.3.3/dist/js/bootstrap.
bundle.min.js"></script>
</head>
<body>
<div class="container">
  <h2>Download Progress</h2>
  <p>Let the download continue:</p>
```

```
  <div class="progress" style="height:25px">
    <div class="progress-bar" style="width:85%;"></div>
  </div>
</div>
</body>
</html>
```

After running the code, the web page will look as follows:

Screen Size: 1366 x 633

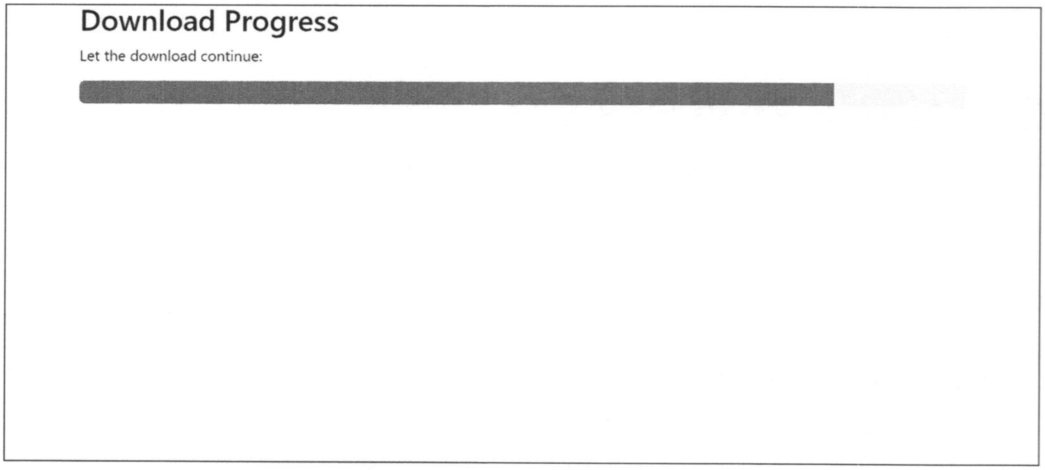

***Figure 5.4**: Create a Progress Bar*

Setting a Label to Progress Bar

A progress bar with a label representation will add more understanding regarding what the Progress Bar wants to convey. To set a label for the progress bar, set the text within the Progress Bar:

```
<div class="progress-bar" style="width:85%;">85%</div>
```

Let us see an example to set a label to the progress bar:

```
<!DOCTYPE html>
<html lang="en">
<head>
  <title>Bootstrap Progress Bar</title>
  <meta charset="utf-8">
  <meta name="viewport" content="width=device-width, initial-scale=1">
  <link
href="https://cdn.jsdelivr.net/npm/bootstrap@5.3.3/dist/css/bootstrap.
min.css" rel="stylesheet">
  <script
```

```
src="https://cdn.jsdelivr.net/npm/bootstrap@5.3.3/dist/js/bootstrap.
bundle.min.js"></script>
</head>
<body>
<div class="container">
  <h2>Download Progress</h2>
  <p>Let the download continue:</p>
  <h3>Java Study Material</h3>
  <div class="progress" style="height:25px">
    <div class="progress-bar" style="width:85%;">85%</div>
  </div>
  <h3>Python Study Material</h3>
  <div class="progress" style="height:25px">
    <div class="progress-bar" style="width:60%;">60%</div>
  </div>
</div>
</body>
</html>
```

After running the code, the web page will look as follows:

Screen Size: 1366 x 633

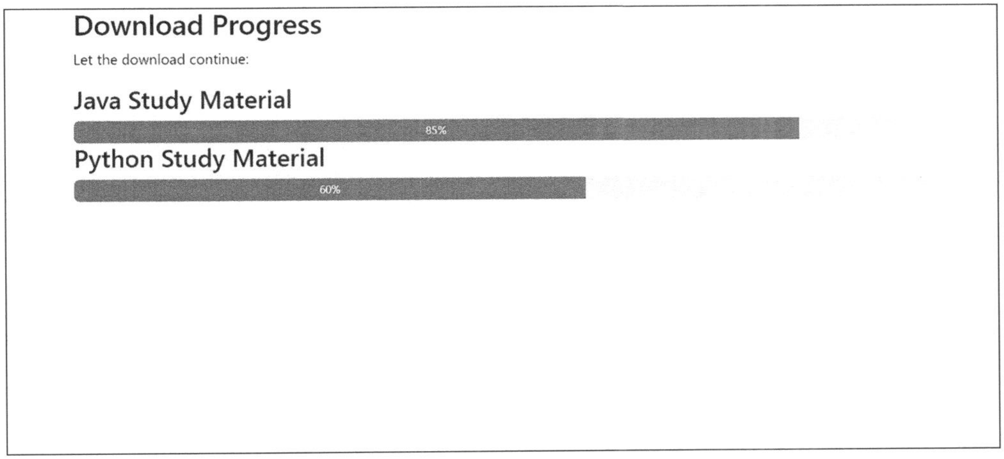

***Figure* 5.5**: *Set a label to Progress Bar*

Changing Progress Bar Color

We created a Progress Bar and added a label to it. The default color of the progress bar can be changed easily. To change the progress bar color, use contextual classes. Each class represents a color to provide a meaning, that is, a representation. In the preceding example, the default color is set, that is, blue.

Let us see an example of how to create progress bars with different colors:

```
<!DOCTYPE html>
<html lang="en">
<head>
  <title>Bootstrap Progress Bar</title>
  <meta charset="utf-8">
  <meta name="viewport" content="width=device-width, initial-scale=1">
  <link
href="https://cdn.jsdelivr.net/npm/bootstrap@5.3.3/dist/css/bootstrap.
min.css" rel="stylesheet">
  <script
src="https://cdn.jsdelivr.net/npm/bootstrap@5.3.3/dist/js/bootstrap.
bundle.min.js"></script>
</head>
<body>
<div class="container">
  <h2>Download Progress</h2>
  <p>Let the download continue:</p>
  <h3>Java Study Material</h3>
  <div class="progress" style="height:25px">
    <div class="progress-bar" style="width:85%;">85%</div>
  </div>
  <h3>Python Study Material</h3>
  <div class="progress" style="height:25px">
    <div class="progress-bar bg-secondary" style="width:50%;">50%</div>
  </div>
    <h3>SQL Study Material</h3>
  <div class="progress" style="height:25px">
  <div class="progress-bar bg-success" style="width:60%;">60%</div>
  </div>
  <h3>CSS Study Material</h3>
  <div class="progress" style="height:25px">
    <div class="progress-bar bg-danger" style="width:30%;">30%</div>
  </div>
  <h3>JavaScript Study Material</h3>
  <div class="progress" style="height:25px">
  <div class="progress-bar bg-warning" style="width:55%;">55%</div>
  </div>
  <h3>jQuery Study Material</h3>
  <div class="progress" style="height:25px">
  <div class="progress-bar bg-info" style="width:90%;">90%</div>
  </div>

  <h3>MongoDB Study Material</h3>
  <div class="progress" style="height:25px">
  <div class="progress-bar bg-dark" style="width:60%;">60%</div>
```

```
  </div>
</div>
</body>
</html>
```

After running the code, the web page will look as follows:

Screen Size: 1366 x 633

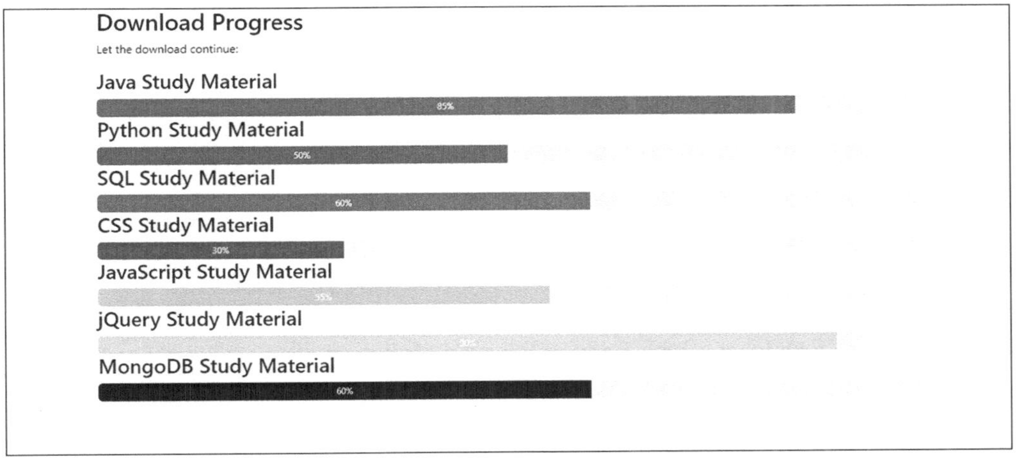

***Figure 5.6**: Change the Progress Bar color*

Adding Stripes to a Progress Bar

We created a progress bar and learned how to change the default color. Besides adding the color, we can also add stripes to it. The **`.progress-bar-striped`** Bootstrap class is used to add stripes to a progress bar:

```
<div class="progress-bar progress-bar-striped" style="width:85%;">85%</
div>
```

Let us see an example of adding stripes to a progress bar on a web page:

```
<!DOCTYPE html>
<html lang="en">
<head>
  <title>Bootstrap Progress Bar</title>
  <meta charset="utf-8">
  <meta name="viewport" content="width=device-width, initial-scale=1">
  <link
href="https://cdn.jsdelivr.net/npm/bootstrap@5.3.3/dist/css/bootstrap.
min.css" rel="stylesheet">
  <script
src="https://cdn.jsdelivr.net/npm/bootstrap@5.3.3/dist/js/bootstrap.
bundle.min.js"></script>
```

```
</head>
<body>
<div class="container">
  <h2>Download Progress</h2>
  <p>Let the download continue:</p>
  <h3>Java Study Material</h3>
  <div class="progress" style="height:25px">
    <div class="progress-bar progress-bar-striped"
style="width:85%;">85%</div>
  </div>
  <h3>Python Study Material</h3>
  <div class="progress" style="height:25px">
    <div class="progress-bar progress-bar-striped"
style="width:60%;">60%</div>
  </div>
</div>
</body>
</html>
```

After running the code, the web page will look as follows:

Screen Size: 1366 x 633

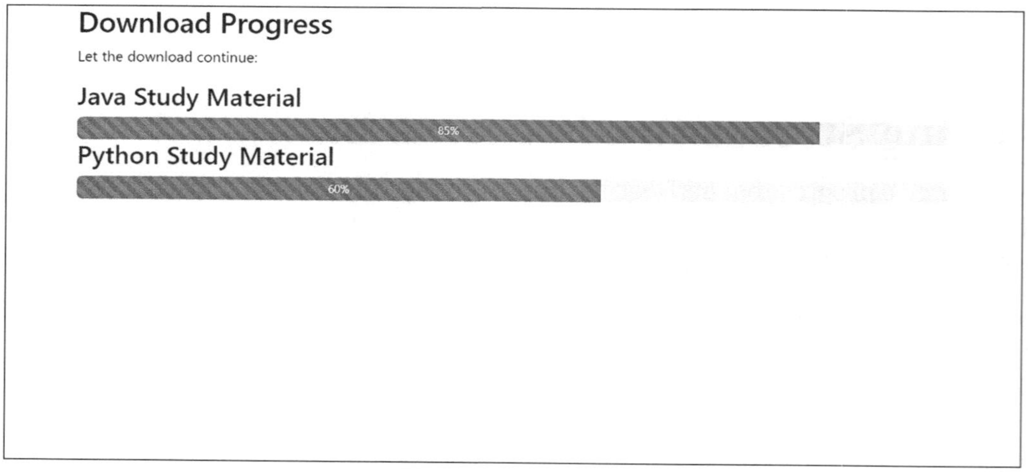

Figure 5.7*: Add stripes to a Progress Bar*

Animating Progress Bar

On a web page, you must have seen animated progress bars. To animate a progress bar, use the **`.progress-bar-animated`** class. Set it with a striped progress bar:

```
<div class="progress-bar progress-bar-striped progress-bar-animated"
style="width:40%;">40%</div>
```

Let us see an example to animate a progress bar on a web page:

```
<!DOCTYPE html>
<html lang="en">
<head>
  <title>Bootstrap Progress Bar</title>
  <meta charset="utf-8">
  <meta name="viewport" content="width=device-width, initial-scale=1">
  <link
href="https://cdn.jsdelivr.net/npm/bootstrap@5.3.3/dist/css/bootstrap.
min.css" rel="stylesheet">
  <script
src="https://cdn.jsdelivr.net/npm/bootstrap@5.3.3/dist/js/bootstrap.
bundle.min.js"></script>
</head>
<body>
<div class="container">
  <h2>Download Progress</h2>
  <p>Let the download continue:</p>
  <h3>CSS Study Material</h3>
  <div class="progress" style="height:25px">
    <div class="progress-bar progress-bar-striped progress-bar-animated"
style="width:40%;">40%</div>
  </div>
  <h3>SQL Study Material</h3>
  <div class="progress" style="height:25px">
    <div class="progress-bar progress-bar-striped progress-bar-animated"
style="width:55%;">55%</div>
  </div>
<div class="container">
</body>
</html>
```

After running the code, the web page will look as follows. The progress bar animates:

Screen Size: 1366 x 633

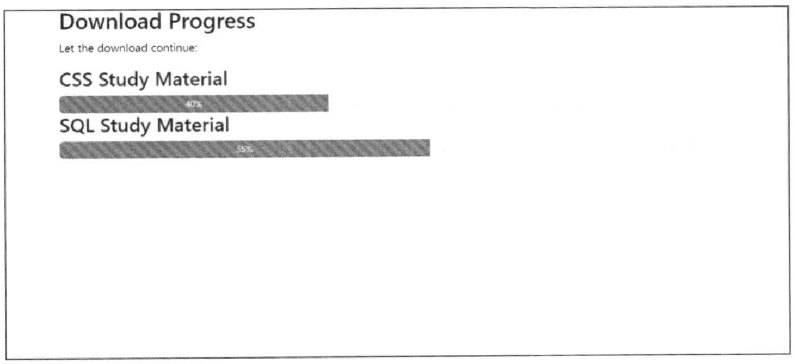

Figure 5.8: *Animate Progress Bar*

Cards

Learn what a card is in Bootstrap and how to create one. With that, get a thorough understanding of the following in this lesson:

- Creating a card
- Card Header and Footer
- Adding color to the card
- Adding an image to the card background
- Setting an image at the top of the card
- Setting an image at the bottom of the card

On a web page, consider a card as a box. It has borders and adds padding around the content to make it look amazing. Cards came to replace the Bootstrap 4 components, such as panels, wells, and thumbnails.

Create a Card

To create a card on a web page, use the **`.card`** class. The content of the card, that is, the body, can be set using the **`.card-body`** class.

Let us see how to create a card on a web page with Bootstrap:

```
<!DOCTYPE html>
<html lang="en">
<head>
  <title>Bootstrap Cards</title>
  <meta charset="utf-8">
  <meta name="viewport" content="width=device-width, initial-scale=1">
  <link
href="https://cdn.jsdelivr.net/npm/bootstrap@5.3.3/dist/css/bootstrap.
min.css" rel="stylesheet">
  <script
src="https://cdn.jsdelivr.net/npm/bootstrap@5.3.3/dist/js/bootstrap.
bundle.min.js"></script>
</head>
<body>
<div class="container">
  <h2>Bootstrap Card</h2>
  <div class="card">
    <div class="card-body">Amit Diwan is an Entrepreneur.</div>
  </div>
</div>
</body>
</html>
```

After running the code, the web page will look as follows:

Screen Size: 1366 x 633

***Figure 5.9**: Create a card*

We created a card and now, to make it more sensible, let us add a header and footer.

Card Header and Footer

Adding a header and footer to a card makes it more sensible and easier to understand. To create a card header, use the Bootstrap **`.card-header`** class. With that, the card footer is set using the **`.card-footer`** class. The footer can be used to place the social media links:

Let us see an example of adding a header and footer to a card:

```
<!DOCTYPE html>
<html lang="en">
<head>
  <title>Bootstrap Cards</title>
  <meta charset="utf-8">
  <meta name="viewport" content="width=device-width, initial-scale=1">
  <link
href="https://cdn.jsdelivr.net/npm/bootstrap@5.3.3/dist/css/bootstrap.
min.css" rel="stylesheet">
  <script
src="https://cdn.jsdelivr.net/npm/bootstrap@5.3.3/dist/js/bootstrap.
bundle.min.js"></script>
</head>
<body>
<div class="container">
  <h2>Bootstrap Card</h2>
```

```
  <div class="card">
    <div class="card-header">Amit Diwan</div>
    <div class="card-body">Amit is an Entrepreneur. He has launched over 40 courses on programming, web development and database technologies.</div>
    <div class="card-footer">Follow for more</div>
  </div>
</div>
</body>
</html>
```

After running the code, the web page will look as follows:

Screen Size: 1366 x 633

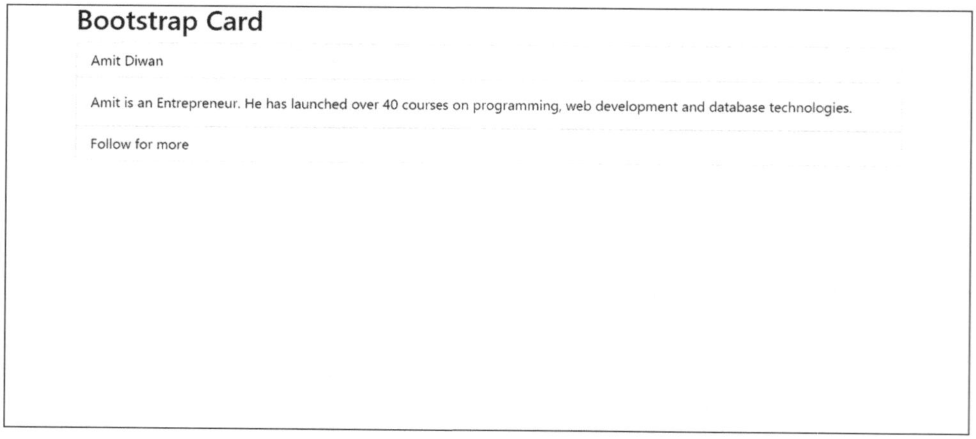

***Figure 5.10**: Add a header and footer to a card*

The card is now having a header and footer. The visible background color on the card is the default, which can be easily changed. Let's see how.

Adding a Color to a Card

Use the contextual classes to add a background color to the cards. The contextual classes are used here to add a color to a card. Each class represents a color to provide a meaning, that is, a representation.

Note: *We have discussed the contextual classes in the section* **Background Color** *of Chapter 9,* **Bootstrap Utilities**.

Let us see all the contextual classes:

- **`.bg-primary`:** Represents important text.
- **`.bg-secondary`:** Represents secondary text.
- **`.bg-success`:** Represents a successful action.

- **.bg-danger**: Represents danger.
- **.bg-warning**: Represents warning.
- **.bg-info**: Represents information.
- **.bg-light**: Light grey
- **.bg-dark**: Dark grey

For example, here we are using the **.bg-primary** class to set a blue color to the car. Also, the **text-white** is used to set the text color to white:

```
<div class="card bg-primary text-white">
```

Let us see an example of adding a color to a card on a web page:

```
<!DOCTYPE html>
<html lang="en">
<head>
  <title>Bootstrap Cards</title>
  <meta charset="utf-8">
  <meta name="viewport" content="width=device-width, initial-scale=1">
  <link
href="https://cdn.jsdelivr.net/npm/bootstrap@5.3.3/dist/css/bootstrap.
min.css" rel="stylesheet">
  <script
src="https://cdn.jsdelivr.net/npm/bootstrap@5.3.3/dist/js/bootstrap.
bundle.min.js"></script>
</head>
<body>
<div class="container">
  <h2>Bootstrap Card</h2>
  <div class="card bg-primary text-white">
    <div class="card-header">Amit Diwan</div>
    <div class="card-body">Amit is an Entrepreneur. He has launched over
40 courses on programming, web development and database technologies.</
div>
    <div class="card-footer">Follow for more</div>
  </div>
  <br>
   <div class="card bg-secondary text-white">
    <div class="card-header">David Ritter</div>
    <div class="card-body">David is an Author. He has written over 10
books on Marketing and Finance.</div>
    <div class="card-footer">Follow for more</div>
  </div>
</div>
</body>
</html>
```

After running the code, the web page will look as follows:

Screen Size: 1366 x 633

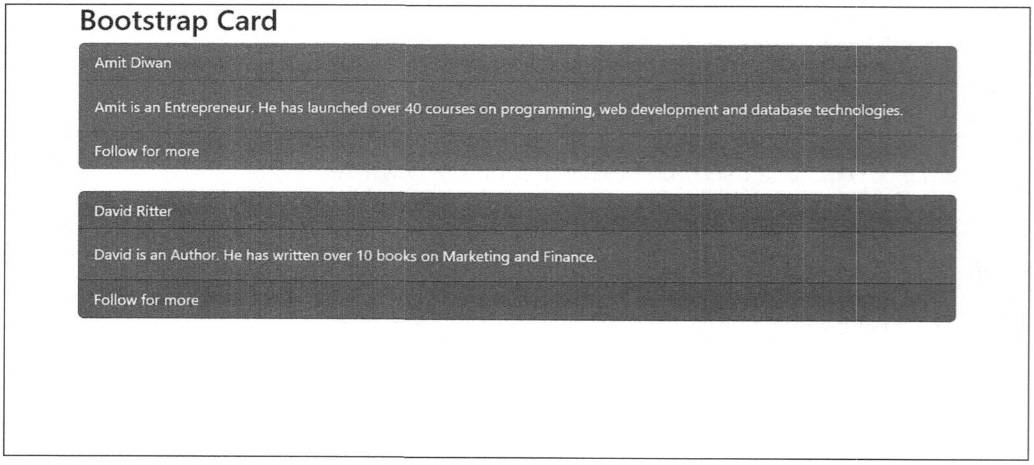

***Figure 5.11**: Add a color to a card*

We created a card above and added color to it. With Bootstrap, an image can also be set as a card background. Let us see.

Adding an Image to the Card Background

Set an image as a card background using the **`.card-img-overlay`** Bootstrap class:

```
<div class="card-img-overlay">
```

Let us see an example to add an image to the card background:

```
<!DOCTYPE html>
<html lang="en">
<head>
  <title>Bootstrap Cards</title>
  <meta charset="utf-8">
  <meta name="viewport" content="width=device-width, initial-scale=1">
  <link
href="https://cdn.jsdelivr.net/npm/bootstrap@5.3.3/dist/css/bootstrap.
min.css" rel="stylesheet">
  <script
src="https://cdn.jsdelivr.net/npm/bootstrap@5.3.3/dist/js/bootstrap.
bundle.min.js"></script>
</head>
<body>
<div class="container">
  <h2>Profile</h2>
```

```
  <p>Here is the profile of our team members:</p>
  <div class="card img-fluid" style="width:350px">
    <img class="card-img" src="http://studyopedia.com/wp-content/uploads
/2024/05/Amit-Diwan.png" alt="Amit Diwan" style="width:100%">
    <div class="card-img-overlay">
      <h4 class="card-title">Amit Diwan</h4>
      <p class="card-text">Amit is an Entrepreneur. He has launched over
40 courses on programming, web development and database technologies.</
p>
      <a href="#" class="btn btn-secondary">More Info</a>
    </div>
  </div>
</div>
</body>
</html>
```

After running the code, the web page will look as follows:

Screen Size: 1366 x 633

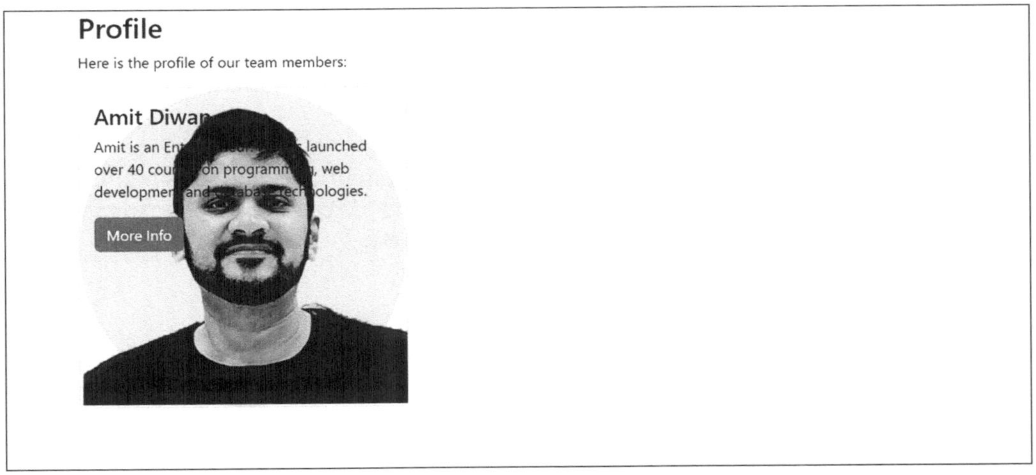

***Figure 5.12**: Add an image to the card background*

We added an image to the Bootstrap Card background. Similarly, the image can be set on the top of the card. Let us see how.

Setting an Image at the Top of the Card

Set an image at the top of the card using the **`.card-img-top`** Bootstrap class

```
<img class="card-img-top" src="http://studyopedia.com/wp-content/uploads
/2024/05/Amit-Diwan.png" alt="Amit Diwan" style="width:100%">
```

Let us see an example to set an image at the top of the card on a web page:

```
<!DOCTYPE html>
<html lang="en">
<head>
  <title>Bootstrap Cards</title>
  <meta charset="utf-8">
  <meta name="viewport" content="width=device-width, initial-scale=1">
  <link
href="https://cdn.jsdelivr.net/npm/bootstrap@5.3.3/dist/css/bootstrap.
min.css" rel="stylesheet">
  <script
src="https://cdn.jsdelivr.net/npm/bootstrap@5.3.3/dist/js/bootstrap.
bundle.min.js"></script>
</head>
<body>
<div class="container">
  <h2>Profile</h2>
  <p>Here is the profile of our team members:</p>
  <div class="card" style="width:350px">
    <img class="card-img-top" src="http://studyopedia.com/wp-content/up-
loads/2024/05/Amit-Diwan.png" alt="Amit Diwan" style="width:100%">
    <div class="card-body">
      <h4 class="card-title">Amit Diwan</h4>
      <p class="card-text">Amit is an Entrepreneur. He has launched over
40 courses on programming, web development and database technologies.</p>
      <a href="#" class="btn btn-secondary">More Info</a>
    </div>
  </div>
</div>
</body>
</html>
```

After running the code, the web page will look as follows:

Screen Size: 1366 x 633

***Figure 5.13**: Set an image at the top of the card*

Setting an Image at the Bottom of the Card

Set an image at the bottom of the card using the **`.card-img-bottom`** Bootstrap class:

```
<img class="card-img-bottom" src="http://studyopedia.com/wp-content/up-
loads/2024/05/Amit-Diwan.png" alt="Amit Diwan" style="width:100%">
```

Let us see an example to set an image at the bottom of the card on a web page:

```
<!DOCTYPE html>
<html lang="en">
<head>
  <title>Bootstrap Cards</title>
  <meta charset="utf-8">
  <meta name="viewport" content="width=device-width, initial-scale=1">
  <link
href="https://cdn.jsdelivr.net/npm/bootstrap@5.3.3/dist/css/bootstrap.
min.css" rel="stylesheet">
  <script
src="https://cdn.jsdelivr.net/npm/bootstrap@5.3.3/dist/js/bootstrap.
bundle.min.js"></script>
</head>
<body>
<div class="container">
  <h2>Profile</h2>
  <p>Here is the profile of our team members:</p>
  <div class="card" style="width:350px">
    <div class="card-body">
      <h4 class="card-title">Amit Diwan</h4>
      <p class="card-text">Amit is an Entrepreneur. He has launched over
40 courses on programming, web development and database technologies.</p>
      <a href="#" class="btn btn-secondary">More Info</a>
```

```
    </div>
     <img class="card-img-bottom" src="http://studyopedia.com/
wp-content/uploads/2024/05/Amit-Diwan.png" alt="Amit Diwan"
style="width:100%">
  </div>
</div>
</body>
</html>
```

After running the code, the web page will look as follows:

Screen Size: 1366 x 633

Figure 5.14: *Set an image at the bottom of the card*

We saw how to create a Card on a web page with Bootstrap. An image was also added to the card. Now let us see how to create a list group on a web page.

List Groups

To create lists on a web page, we use either the **<ul>** or the **<ol>**. This creates an unordered list or an ordered list, respectively. Using the **<ul>** and some Bootstrap classes, we can also create list groups.

Learn how to work with list groups in Bootstrap. You will understand:

- Creating list groups
- Highlight list group items
- Disabling list group item
- Coloring list items
- Create a Horizontal List Group

Creating List Groups

The **<ul>** element is used to create list groups with the Bootstrap **.list-group** class. Also, for the list of group items, use the **<li>** with the **.list-group-items** class.

Let us see an example of creating list groups on a web page:

```
<!DOCTYPE html>
<html lang="en">
<head>
  <title>Bootstrap List Groups</title>
  <meta charset="utf-8">
  <meta name="viewport" content="width=device-width, initial-scale=1">
  <link
href="https://cdn.jsdelivr.net/npm/bootstrap@5.3.3/dist/css/bootstrap.
min.css" rel="stylesheet">
  <script
src="https://cdn.jsdelivr.net/npm/bootstrap@5.3.3/dist/js/bootstrap.
bundle.min.js"></script>
</head>
<body>
<div class="container">
  <h2>Products</h2>
  <p>The following are our products:</p>
  <ul class="list-group">
    <li class="list-group-item">Furniture</li>
    <li class="list-group-item">Cameras</li>
    <li class="list-group-item">Laptops</li>
    <li class="list-group-item">Toys</li>
    <li class="list-group-item">Appliances</li>
  </ul>
</div>
</body>
</html>
```

After running the code, the web page will look as follows:

Screen Size: 1366 x 633

***Figure* 5.15**: *Create list groups*

Highlight the List Group Item

To set the active state of a list group item, use the **`.active`** class. This highlights the group list item:

```
<li class="list-group-item active">Furniture</li>
```

Let us see an example to highlight the list group item on a web page:

```
<!DOCTYPE html>
<html lang="en">
<head>
  <title>Bootstrap List Groups</title>
  <meta charset="utf-8">
  <meta name="viewport" content="width=device-width, initial-scale=1">
  <link
href="https://cdn.jsdelivr.net/npm/bootstrap@5.3.3/dist/css/bootstrap.
min.css" rel="stylesheet">
  <script
src="https://cdn.jsdelivr.net/npm/bootstrap@5.3.3/dist/js/bootstrap.
bundle.min.js"></script>
</head>
<body>
<div class="container">
  <h2>Products</h2>
  <p>The following are our products:</p>
  <ul class="list-group">
    <li class="list-group-item active">Furniture</li>
    <li class="list-group-item">Cameras</li>
    <li class="list-group-item">Laptops</li>
    <li class="list-group-item">Toys</li>
```

```
    <li class="list-group-item">Appliances</li>
  </ul>
</div>
</body>
</html>
```

After running the code, the web page will look as follows:

Screen Size: 1366 x 633

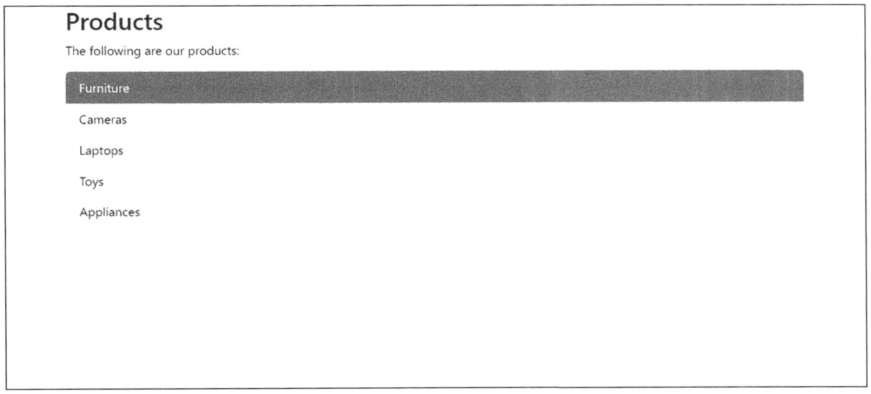

***Figure 5.16**: Highlight the list group items*

Disabling List Group Item

To set the disabled state of a list group item, use the **.disabled** class. This disables the list group item.

Let us see an example of disabling list group items on a web page:

```
<!DOCTYPE html>
<html lang="en">
<head>
  <title>Bootstrap List Groups</title>
  <meta charset="utf-8">
  <meta name="viewport" content="width=device-width, initial-scale=1">
  <link
href="https://cdn.jsdelivr.net/npm/bootstrap@5.3.3/dist/css/bootstrap.
min.css" rel="stylesheet">
  <script src="https://cdn.jsdelivr.net/npm/bootstrap@5.3.3/dist/js/
bootstrap.bundle.min.js"></script>
</head>
<body>
<div class="container">
  <h2>Products</h2>
  <p>The following are the available products:</p>
  <ul class="list-group">
```

```
    <li class="list-group-item active">Furniture</li>
    <li class="list-group-item disabled">Cameras</li>
    <li class="list-group-item active">Laptops</li>
    <li class="list-group-item disabled">Toys</li>
    <li class="list-group-item disabled">Appliances</li>
  </ul>
</div>
</body>
</html>
```

After running the code, the web page will look as follows:

Screen Size: 1366 x 633

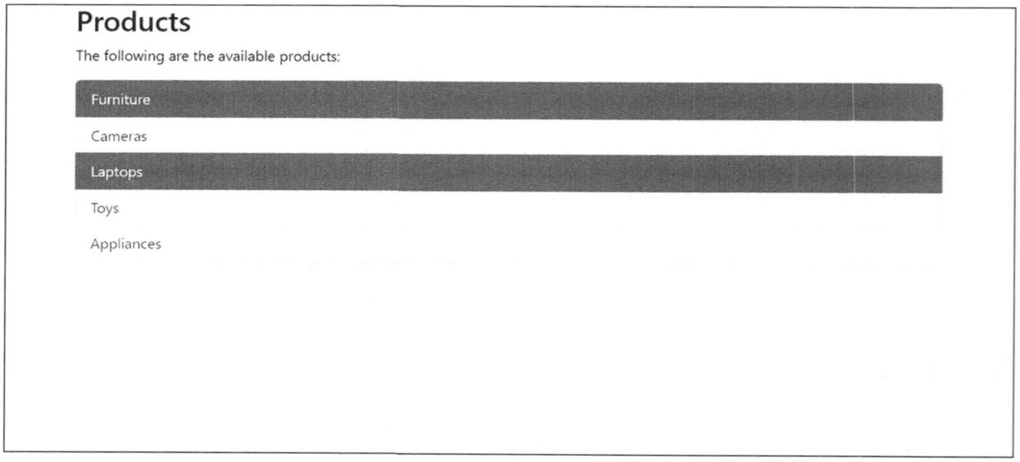

***Figure 5.17**: Disabling list group item*

Coloring List Items

Use the contextual classes to add color to the list items. Let us see all the contextual classes:

- **`.list-group-item-primary`:** Represents important text
- **`.list-group-item-secondary`:** Represents secondary text
- **`.list-group-item-success`:** Represents a successful action
- **`.list-group-item-warning`:** Represents warning
- **`.list-group-item-danger`:** Represents danger
- **`.list-group-item-info`:** Represents information
- **`.list-group-item-dark`:** Dark grey
- **`.list-group-item-light`:** Light grey

Let us see an example of coloring list items on a web page:

```
<!DOCTYPE html>
<html lang="en">
<head>
  <title>Bootstrap List Groups</title>
  <meta charset="utf-8">
  <meta name="viewport" content="width=device-width, initial-scale=1">
  <link
href="https://cdn.jsdelivr.net/npm/bootstrap@5.3.3/dist/css/bootstrap.
min.css" rel="stylesheet">
  <script
src="https://cdn.jsdelivr.net/npm/bootstrap@5.3.3/dist/js/bootstrap.
bundle.min.js"></script>
</head>
<body>
  <div class="container">
    <h2>Products</h2>
    <p>The following are the available products:</p>
    <ul class="list-group">
      <li class="list-group-item list-group-item-primary">Furniture</li>
      <li class="list-group-item list-group-item-secondary">Cameras</li>
      <li class="list-group-item list-group-item-dark">Laptops</li>
      <li class="list-group-item list-group-item-info">Toys</li>
      <li class="list-group-item list-group-item-warning">Appliances</li>
    </ul>
  </div>
</body>
</html>
```

After running the code, the web page will look as follows:

Screen Size: 1366 x 633

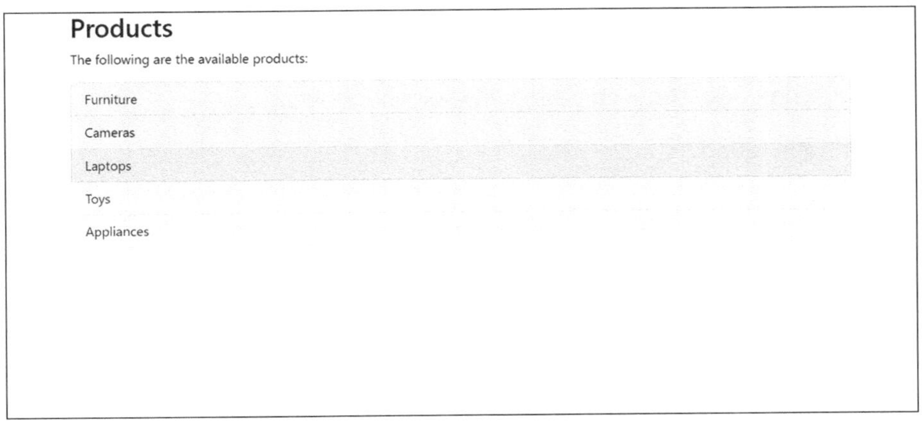

Figure 5.18: *Coloring list items on a web page*

Create a Horizontal List Group

The **.list-group-horizontal** class is used to create horizontal list groups:

```
<ul class="list-group list-group-horizontal">
```

Let us see an example of creating horizontal list groups:

```
<!DOCTYPE html>
<html lang="en">
<head>
  <title>Bootstrap List Groups</title>
  <meta charset="utf-8">
  <meta name="viewport" content="width=device-width, initial-scale=1">
  <link
href="https://cdn.jsdelivr.net/npm/bootstrap@5.3.3/dist/css/bootstrap.
min.css" rel="stylesheet">
  <script
src="https://cdn.jsdelivr.net/npm/bootstrap@5.3.3/dist/js/bootstrap.
bundle.min.js"></script>
</head>
<body>
<div class="container">
  <h2>Products</h2>
  <p>The following are the available products:</p>
  <ul class="list-group list-group-horizontal">
    <li class="list-group-item active">Furniture</li>
    <li class="list-group-item disabled">Cameras</li>
    <li class="list-group-item active">Laptops</li>
    <li class="list-group-item disabled">Toys</li>
    <li class="list-group-item disabled">Appliances</li>
  </ul>
</div>
</body>
</html>
```

After running the code, the web page will look as follows:

Screen Size: 1366 x 633

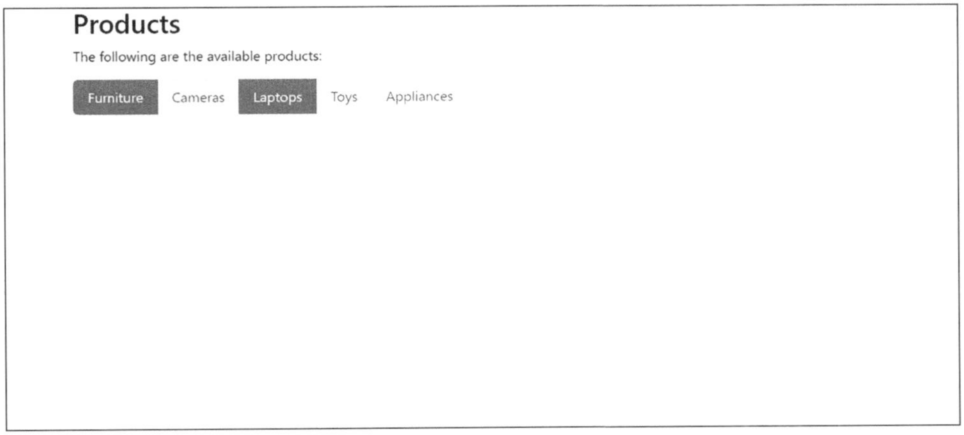

***Figure 5.19**: Create horizontal list groups*

Spinners

A spinner on a web page is used to display the loading stage of your project, let's say loading an image or downloadable content. It is also called a loader. Generally, a border spinner is visible on a web page.

Learn how to work with spinners in Bootstrap. You will understand:

- Creating a Spinner
- Customizing Spinner Color
- Setting Smaller Spinner
- Growing a Spinner
- Adding Spinner to a Button

Creating a Spinner

To create a spinner on a web page, use the **`.spinner-border`** Bootstrap class. This creates a border spinner, that is, a loader.

```
<div class="spinner-border"></div>
```

Let us see an example of creating a spinner on a web page:

```
<!DOCTYPE html>
<html>
<head>
  <title>Bootstrap Spinners</title>
  <meta name="viewport" content="width=device-width, initial-scale=1">
```

```
  <link
href="https://cdn.jsdelivr.net/npm/bootstrap@5.3.3/dist/css/bootstrap.
min.css" rel="stylesheet">
  <script
src="https://cdn.jsdelivr.net/npm/bootstrap@5.3.3/dist/js/bootstrap.
bundle.min.js"></script>
</head>
<body>
<div class="container">
  <h2>Java Course</h2>
  <p>The following course includes video lectures, quizzes, and
interview questions: </p>
  <div class="spinner-border"></div>
</div>
</body>
</html>
```

After running the code, the web page will look as follows:

Screen Size: 1366 x 633

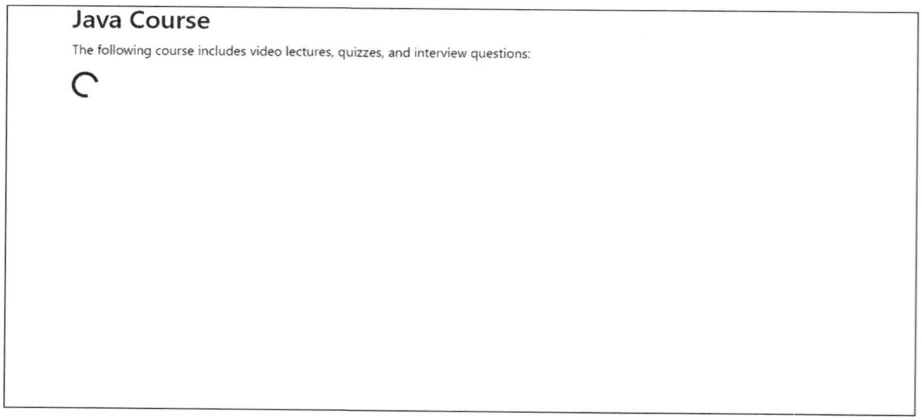

***Figure 5.20**: Create a Spinner*

Customizing Spinner Color

The default color of a spinner is black. Change it using the following text color utilities:

- **`.text-primary`:** Represents important text
- **`.text-secondary`:** Represents secondary text
- **`.text-success`:** Represents a successful action
- **`.text-danger`:** Represents danger
- **`.text-warning`:** Represents warning

- **`.text-info`**: Represents information
- **`.text-light`**: Light grey
- **`.text-bg-dark`**: Dark grey

Let us see an example of customizing spinner color:

```
<!DOCTYPE html>
<html>
<head>
  <title>Bootstrap Spinners</title>
  <meta name="viewport" content="width=device-width, initial-scale=1">
  <link
href="https://cdn.jsdelivr.net/npm/bootstrap@5.3.3/dist/css/bootstrap.
min.css" rel="stylesheet">
  <script
src="https://cdn.jsdelivr.net/npm/bootstrap@5.3.3/dist/js/bootstrap.
bundle.min.js"></script>
</head>
<body>
<div class="container">
  <h2>Java Course</h2>
  <p>The following course includes video lectures, quizzes, and
interview questions: </p>
  <div class="spinner-border text-primary"></div>
  <div class="spinner-border text-secondary"></div>
  <div class="spinner-border text-success"></div>
  <div class="spinner-border text-info"></div>
  <div class="spinner-border text-warning"></div>
  <div class="spinner-border text-danger"></div>
  <div class="spinner-border text-dark"></div>
  <div class="spinner-border text-light"></div>
</div>
</body>
</html>
```

After running the code, the web page will look as follows:

Screen Size: 1366 x 633

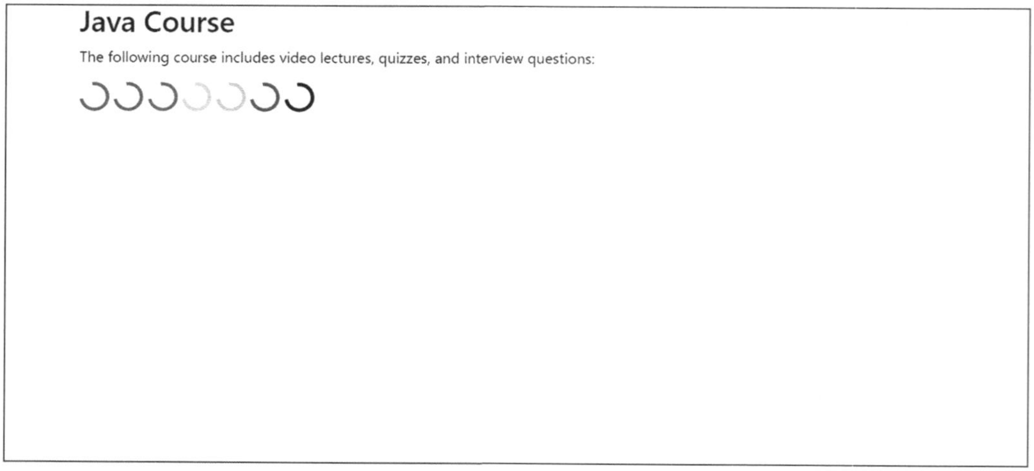

Figure 5.21: *Customizing Spinner color*

Setting Smaller Spinner

Bootstrap has provided the following class to set a spinner smaller than the default size:

.spinner-border-sm

Let us see an example to set a smaller size spinner on a web page:

```
<!DOCTYPE html>
<html>
<head>
  <title>Bootstrap Spinners</title>
  <meta name="viewport" content="width=device-width, initial-scale=1">
  <link
href="https://cdn.jsdelivr.net/npm/bootstrap@5.3.3/dist/css/bootstrap.
min.css" rel="stylesheet">
  <script
src="https://cdn.jsdelivr.net/npm/bootstrap@5.3.3/dist/js/bootstrap.
bundle.min.js"></script>
</head>
<body>
<div class="container">
  <h2>Java Course</h2>
  <p>The following course includes video lectures, quizzes, and inter-
view questions: </p>
  <div class="spinner-border spinner-border-sm"></div>
  <div class="spinner-grow spinner-grow-sm"></div>
</div>
</body>
</html>
```

After running the code, the web page will look as follows:

Screen Size: 1366 x 633

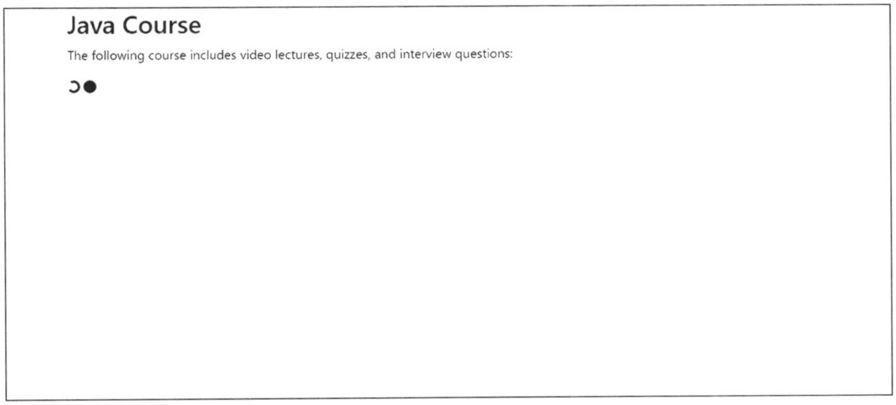

Figure 5.22: *Set a smaller spinner on a web page*

Growing a Spinner

To repeatedly grow a spinner, use the **`.spinner-grow`** Bootstrap class. This will not allow the spinner to spin. Also, set the spinner color using the text color utilities shown earlier.

Let us see an example of growing a spinner on a web page:

```
<!DOCTYPE html>
<html>
<head>
  <title>Bootstrap Spinners</title>
  <meta name="viewport" content="width=device-width, initial-scale=1">
  <link
href="https://cdn.jsdelivr.net/npm/bootstrap@5.3.3/dist/css/bootstrap.
min.css" rel="stylesheet">
  <script
src="https://cdn.jsdelivr.net/npm/bootstrap@5.3.3/dist/js/bootstrap.
bundle.min.js"></script>
</head>
<body>
<div class="container">
  <h2>Java Course</h2>
  <p>The following course includes video lectures, quizzes, and inter-
view questions: </p>
  <div class="spinner-grow text-primary"></div>
</div>
</body>
</html>
```

After running the code, the web page will look as follows:

Screen Size: 1366 x 633

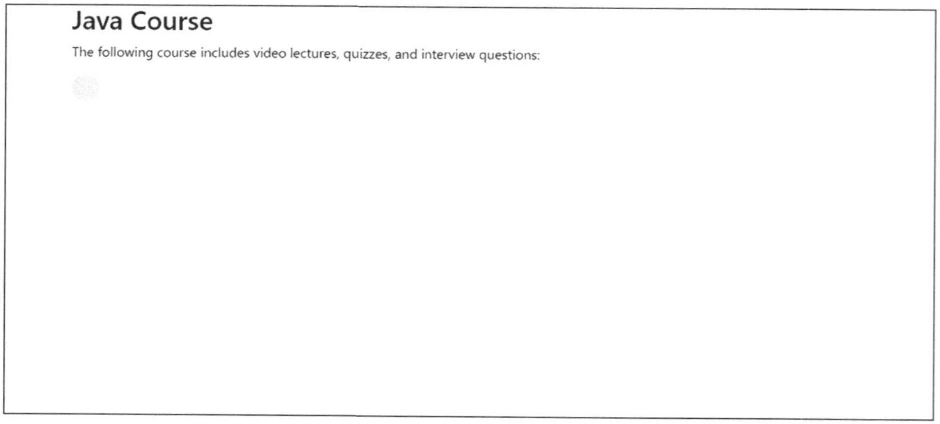

***Figure 5.23**: Grow a spinner on a web page*

Adding Spinner to a Button

To display an action currently taking place on a web page, add a spinner to a button. Add the text **`Loading...`** or leave it black to make only the spinner visible.

Let us see an example of adding a spinner to a button on a web page:

```
<!DOCTYPE html>
<html>
<head>
  <title>Bootstrap Spinners</title>
  <meta name="viewport" content="width=device-width, initial-scale=1">
  <link
href="https://cdn.jsdelivr.net/npm/bootstrap@5.3.3/dist/css/bootstrap.
min.css" rel="stylesheet">
  <script
src="https://cdn.jsdelivr.net/npm/bootstrap@5.3.3/dist/js/bootstrap.
bundle.min.js"></script>
</head>
<body>
<div class="container">
  <h2>Java Course</h2>
  <p>The following course includes video lectures, quizzes, and
interview questions: </p>
<button class="btn btn-secondary">
  <span class="spinner-border spinner-border-sm"></span>
</button>
```

```
<button class="btn btn-danger">
  <span class="spinner-border spinner-border-sm"></span>
  Loading..
</button>
</div>
</body>
</html>
```

After running the code, the web page will look as follows:

Screen Size: 1366 x 633

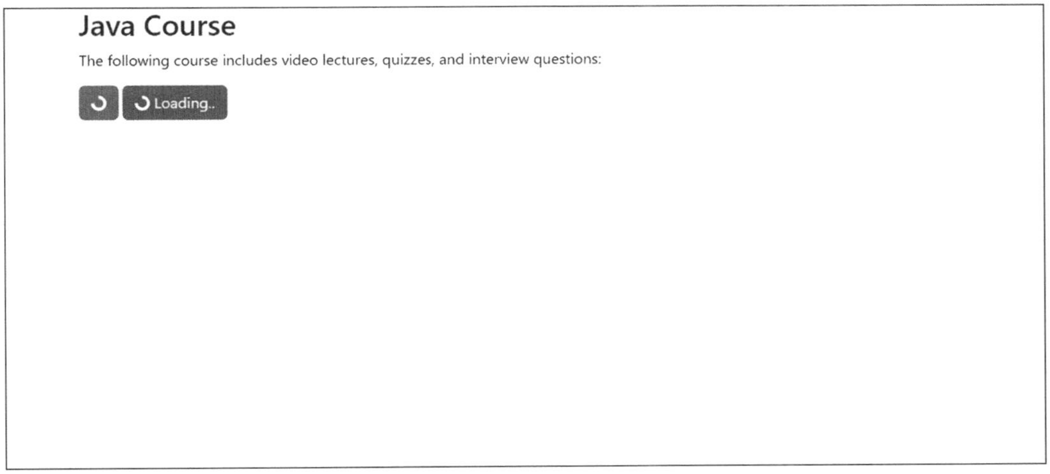

***Figure 5.24**: Add a spinner to a button*

Buttons

Buttons are a key part of a web page. Also, on forms, a submit button is a must. Such buttons can be easily created and styled using Bootstrap classes.

Learn how to add a new button with Bootstrap using the following classes:

- **`.btn`:** Create a button
- **`.btn-primary`:** Blue colored
- **`.btn-success`:** Success action on a button
- **`.btn-info`:** Set info messages on a button
- **`.btn-warning`:** Sets a warning action on a button
- **`.btn-danger`:** Sets danger action on a button
- **`.btn-dark`:** Sets a dark-colored button
- **`.btn-link`:** Sets a light-colored button

Creating a Button

We will create a button using the **`.btn`** Bootstrap class. Set it like the following:

```
<button type="button" class="btn">Next</button>
```

The **`.btn`** class would create a button but would not add any color to the button. To add a color, we will use a contextual class.

In the following example, the color will be set to the button using the **`.btn-primary`** contextual class:

```
<!DOCTYPE html>
<html lang="en">
<head>
  <title>Bootstrap Button</title>
  <meta charset="utf-8">
  <meta name="viewport" content="width=device-width, initial-scale=1">
  <link
href="https://cdn.jsdelivr.net/npm/bootstrap@5.3.3/dist/css/bootstrap.
min.css" rel="stylesheet">
  <script
src="https://cdn.jsdelivr.net/npm/bootstrap@5.3.3/dist/js/bootstrap.
bundle.min.js"></script>
</head>
<body>
<div class="container">
  <h1>Create a Button</h2>
  <p>Click the below button to proceed:</p>
  <button type="button" class="btn btn-primary">Next</button>
</div>
</body>
</html>
```

After running the code, the web page will look as follows:

Screen Size: 1366 x 633

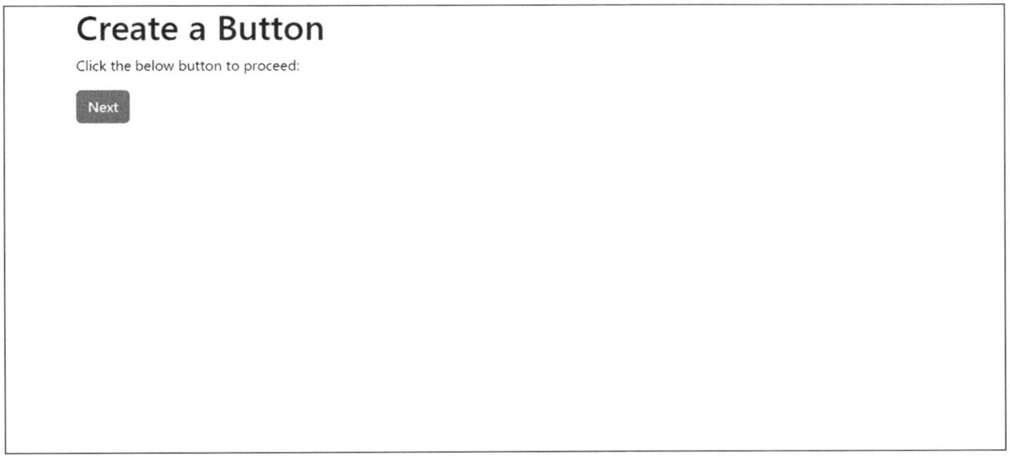

***Figure* 5.25**: *Create a Button on a web page*

Color a Button with Contextual Classes

To provide different colors to buttons, use the Bootstrap contextual classes. We used the contextual class earlier to add a color to a button. Let us see some more examples of adding different colors using contextual classes:

Set it like the following:

```
<button type="button" class="btn btn-success">Next</button>
```

```
<button type="button" class="btn btn-info">Next</button>
```

Let us see an example of coloring a button with contextual classes:

```
<!DOCTYPE html>
<html lang="en">
<head>
  <title>Bootstrap Button</title>
  <meta charset="utf-8">
  <meta name="viewport" content="width=device-width, initial-scale=1">
  <link
href="https://cdn.jsdelivr.net/npm/bootstrap@5.3.3/dist/css/bootstrap.
min.css" rel="stylesheet">
  <script
src="https://cdn.jsdelivr.net/npm/bootstrap@5.3.3/dist/js/bootstrap.
bundle.min.js"></script>
</head>
<body>
<div class="container">
  <h1>Create a Button</h2>
  <p>Click the below button to proceed with your favorite sports:</p>
```

```
  <button type="button" class="btn btn-primary">Cricket</button>
  <button type="button" class="btn btn-secondary">Football</button>
  <button type="button" class="btn btn-success">Archery</button>
  <button type="button" class="btn btn-info">Tennis</button>
  <button type="button" class="btn btn-warning">Golf</button>
  <button type="button" class="btn btn-danger">Table Tennis</button>
</div>
</body>
</html>
```

After running the code, the web page will look as follows:

Screen Size: 1366 x 633

***Figure 5.26**: Color a Button with Contextual Classes*

Converting a Button into a Link

Use the Bootstrap **`.btn-link`** to make a button look like a link on a web page:

```
<button type="button" class="btn btn-link">Link1</button>
```

You can use the **`<a>`** tag with the Bootstrap **`.btn`** class as well:

```
<a href="#" class="btn btn-primary">Link2</a>
```

Let us see the example of converting a button into a link:

```
<!DOCTYPE html>
<html lang="en">
<head>
  <title>Bootstrap Button Link</title>
  <meta charset="utf-8">
  <meta name="viewport" content="width=device-width, initial-scale=1">
```

```
  <link
href="https://cdn.jsdelivr.net/npm/bootstrap@5.3.3/dist/css/bootstrap.
min.css" rel="stylesheet">
  <script src="https://cdn.jsdelivr.net/npm/bootstrap@5.3.3/dist/js/
bootstrap.bundle.min.js"></script>
</head>
<body>
<div class="container">
  <h1>Create a Button like a link</h2>
  <p>Click any of the below links to proceed:</p>
  <button type="button" class="btn btn-link">Link1</button>
  <a href="#" class="btn btn-primary">Link2</a>
</div>
</body>
</html>
```

After running the code, the web page will look as follows:

Screen Size: 1366 x 633

***Figure** 5.27: Convert a Button into a Link*

Resizing Buttons

We can also easily specify the size of a button on a web page using the following Bootstrap classes:

- **`.btn-lg`:** Large Button
- **`.btn-md`:** Medium Button
- **`.btn-sm`:** Small Button

Let us see an example of resizing buttons on a web page:

```
<!DOCTYPE html>
<html lang="en">
<head>
  <title>Bootstrap Button</title>
  <meta charset="utf-8">
  <meta name="viewport" content="width=device-width, initial-scale=1">
  <link
href="https://cdn.jsdelivr.net/npm/bootstrap@5.3.3/dist/css/bootstrap.
min.css" rel="stylesheet">
  <script
src="https://cdn.jsdelivr.net/npm/bootstrap@5.3.3/dist/js/bootstrap.
bundle.min.js"></script>
</head>
<body>
<div class="container">
  <h1>Resize Buttons</h2>
  <p>Click the below button to proceed with your favorite sports:</p>
  <button type="button" class="btn btn-primary btn-lg">Cricket</button>
  <button type="button" class="btn btn-secondary btn-md">Football
</button>
  <button type="button" class="btn btn-success btn-sm">Archery</button>
</div>
</body>
</html>
```

After running the code, the web page will look as follows:

Screen Size: 1366 x 633

Figure 5.28: *Resizing buttons on a web page*

Set a Button to be Active

Learn how to set an active button using the `.active` Bootstrap class:

```
<button type="button" class="btn btn-secondary active">Cricket</button>
```

In the following example, we have two similar buttons, and one of them is set to active. You can easily check if the active button looks darker:

```
<!DOCTYPE html>
<html lang="en">
<head>
  <title>Bootstrap Button</title>
  <meta charset="utf-8">
  <meta name="viewport" content="width=device-width, initial-scale=1">
  <link
href="https://cdn.jsdelivr.net/npm/bootstrap@5.3.3/dist/css/bootstrap.
min.css" rel="stylesheet">
  <script
src="https://cdn.jsdelivr.net/npm/bootstrap@5.3.3/dist/js/bootstrap.
bundle.min.js"></script>
</head>
<body>
<div class="container">
  <h1>Active Button</h2>
  <p>Click the below button to proceed with your favorite sports:</p>
  <button type="button" class="btn btn-secondary active">Cricket</button>
  <button type="button" class="btn btn-secondary">Football</button>
</div>
</body>
</html>
```

After running the code, the web page will look as follows:

Screen Size: 1366 x 633

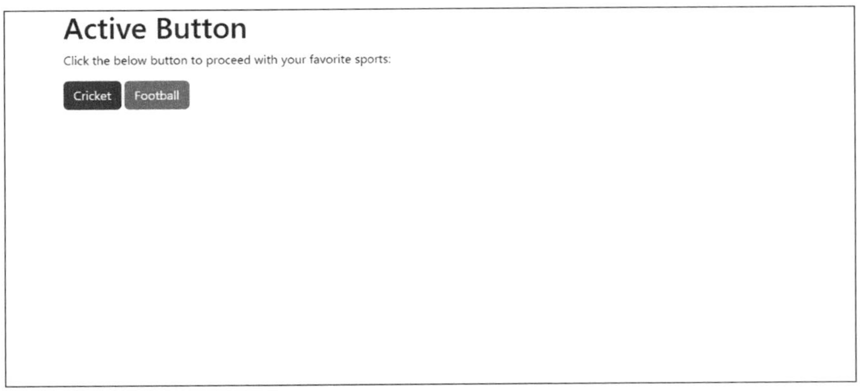

Figure 5.29: *Set an active button*

Disabling a Button

Learn how to disable a button in Bootstrap using the disabled attribute:

```
<button type="button" class="btn btn-secondary disabled">Cricket</button>
```

In the following example, we have two similar buttons, and one of them is set to disabled. You can easily check that the disabled button looks lightened and dull. This is done to make it look disabled:

```
<!DOCTYPE html>
<html lang="en">
<head>
  <title>Bootstrap Button</title>
  <meta charset="utf-8">
  <meta name="viewport" content="width=device-width, initial-scale=1">
  <link
href="https://cdn.jsdelivr.net/npm/bootstrap@5.3.3/dist/css/bootstrap.
min.css" rel="stylesheet">
  <script
src="https://cdn.jsdelivr.net/npm/bootstrap@5.3.3/dist/js/bootstrap.
bundle.min.js"></script>
</head>
<body>
<div class="container">
  <h1>Disabled Button</h2>
  <p>Click the below button to proceed with your favorite sports:</p>
  <button type="button" class="btn btn-secondary disabled">Cricket</button>
  <button type="button" class="btn btn-secondary">Football</button>
</div>
</body>
</html>
```

After running the code, the web page will look as follows:

Screen Size: 1366 x 633

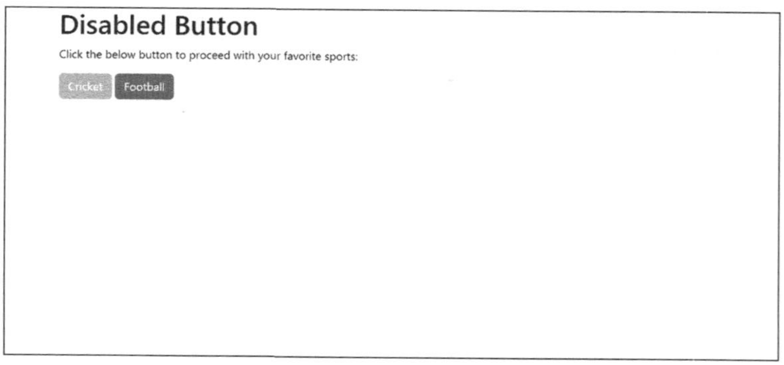

Figure 5.30: *Disable a button on a web page*

Setting Outlines to a Button

The buttons can also be outlined using the **.btn-online** class with the contextual classes, like:

```
class="btn btn-outline-secondary"
class="btn btn-outline-info"
class="btn btn-outline-success"
class="btn btn-outline-warning"
class="btn btn-outline-danger"
```

The outline classes also provide a hover effect to the buttons on mouseover. Let us see an example to set outlines to a button:

```
<!DOCTYPE html>
<html lang="en">
<head>
  <title>Bootstrap Button</title>
  <meta charset="utf-8">
  <meta name="viewport" content="width=device-width, initial-scale=1">
  <link
href="https://cdn.jsdelivr.net/npm/bootstrap@5.3.3/dist/css/bootstrap.
min.css" rel="stylesheet">
  <script
src="https://cdn.jsdelivr.net/npm/bootstrap@5.3.3/dist/js/bootstrap.
bundle.min.js"></script>
</head>
<body>
<div class="container">
  <h1>Create outlines for buttons</h2>
  <p>Click the below button to proceed with your favorite sports:</p>
  <button type="button" class="btn btn-outline-primary">Cricket</button>
  <button type="button" class="btn btn-outline-secondary">Football</button>
  <button type="button" class="btn btn-outline-success">Archery</button>
  <button type="button" class="btn btn-outline-info">Tennis</button>
  <button type="button" class="btn btn-outline-warning">Golf</button>
  <button type="button" class="btn btn-outline-danger">Table Tennis</
button>
</div>
</body>
</html>
```

After running the code, the web page will look as follows:

Screen Size: 1366 x 633

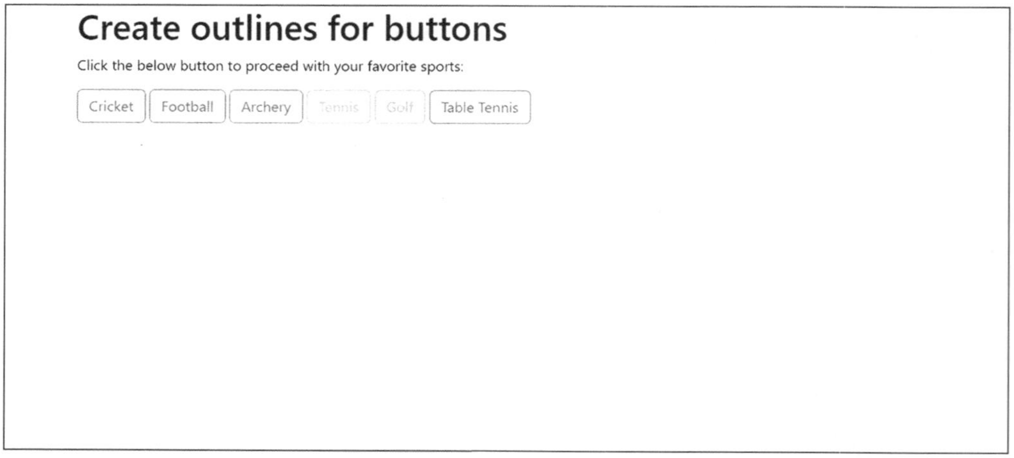

***Figure 5.31**: Set outlines to a button*

Let us hover over any of the buttons:

Screen Size: 1366 x 633

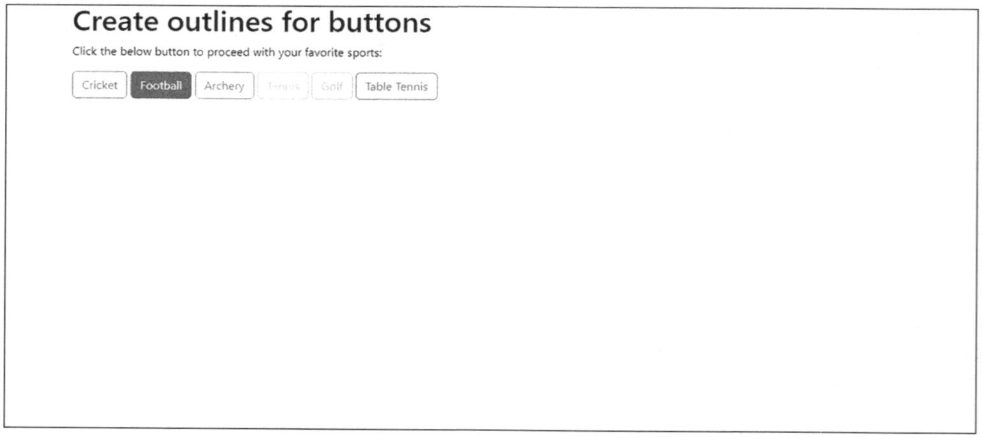

***Figure 5.32**: Hover the mouse cursor on any of the buttons*

Button Groups

Button groups are a series of buttons. Learn how to create button groups in Bootstrap and resize them. We will also learn how to vertically align buttons in a button group.

Create a Button Group

The **btn-group** Bootstrap class is used to add a new button group:

```
<div class="btn-group">
```

Let us see an example of creating a button group:

```
<!DOCTYPE html>
<html lang="en">
<head>
  <title>Bootstrap Button Group</title>
  <meta charset="utf-8">
  <meta name="viewport" content="width=device-width, initial-scale=1">
  <link
href="https://cdn.jsdelivr.net/npm/bootstrap@5.3.3/dist/css/bootstrap.
min.css" rel="stylesheet">
  <script
src="https://cdn.jsdelivr.net/npm/bootstrap@5.3.3/dist/js/bootstrap.
bundle.min.js"></script>
</head>
<body>
<div class="container">
  <h1>Cricket Leagues</h1>
  <p>Select your favorite team from the respective leagues:</p>
  <h2>Indian Premier League</h2>
  <div class="btn-group">
    <button type="button" class="btn btn-primary">Mumbai Indians</button>
    <button type="button" class="btn btn-primary">Chennai Super Kings</
button>
    <button type="button" class="btn btn-primary">Royal Challengers
Bangalore</button>
  </div>
  <h2>Big Bash League</h2>
  <div class="btn-group">
    <button type="button" class="btn btn-secondary">Brisbane Heat</button>
    <button type="button" class="btn btn-secondary">Perth Scorchers</
button>
    <button type="button" class="btn btn-secondary">Adelaide Strikers</
button>
  </div>
</div>
</body>
</html>
```

After running the code, the web page will look as follows:

Screen Size: 1366 x 633

***Figure* 5.33**: *Create a Button Group*

Creating a Vertical Button Group

We can easily convert a horizontal button group to a vertical one. The following is the class to add a vertical button group:

`.btn-group-vertical`

Let us see an example to create a vertical button group:

```
<!DOCTYPE html>
<html lang="en">
<head>
  <title>Bootstrap Button Group</title>
  <meta charset="utf-8">
  <meta name="viewport" content="width=device-width, initial-scale=1">
  <link
href="https://cdn.jsdelivr.net/npm/bootstrap@5.3.3/dist/css/bootstrap.
min.css" rel="stylesheet">
  <script
src="https://cdn.jsdelivr.net/npm/bootstrap@5.3.3/dist/js/bootstrap.
bundle.min.js"></script>
</head>
<body>
<div class="container">
  <h1>Cricket Leagues</h1>
  <p>Select your favorite team from the respective leagues:</p>
  <h2>Indian Premier League</h2>
  <div class="btn-group-vertical">
    <button type="button" class="btn btn-primary">Mumbai Indians</button>
    <button type="button" class="btn btn-primary">Chennai Super Kings</
button>
    <button type="button" class="btn btn-primary">Royal Challengers
Bangalore</button>
```

```
  </div>
  <h2>Big Bash League</h2>
  <div class="btn-group-vertical">
    <button type="button" class="btn btn-secondary">Brisbane Heat</button>
    <button type="button" class="btn btn-secondary">Perth Scorchers</
button>
    <button type="button" class="btn btn-secondary">Adelaide Strikers</
button>
  </div>
</div>
</body>
</html>
```

After running the code, the web page will look as follows:

Screen Size: 1366 x 633

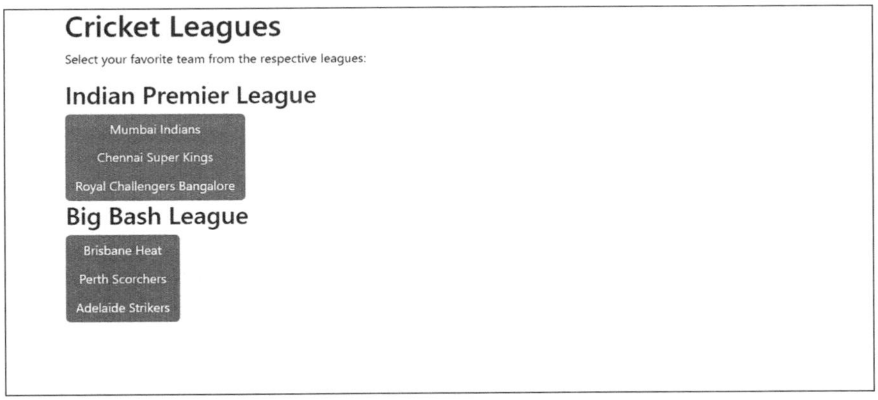

Figure 5.34: *Create a Vertical Button Group*

Resizing a Button Group

We can easily resize a button group and give it a smaller or larger size. The following are the classes to resize a button group:

- **`.btn-group-lg`**: Large Button Group
- **`.btn-group-sm`**: Small Button Group

Let us see an example of resizing a button group:

```
<!DOCTYPE html>
<html lang="en">
<head>
  <title>Bootstrap Button Group</title>
  <meta charset="utf-8">
  <meta name="viewport" content="width=device-width, initial-scale=1">
```

```
  <link
href="https://cdn.jsdelivr.net/npm/bootstrap@5.3.3/dist/css/bootstrap.
min.css" rel="stylesheet">
  <script
src="https://cdn.jsdelivr.net/npm/bootstrap@5.3.3/dist/js/bootstrap.
bundle.min.js"></script>
</head>
<body>
<div class="container">
  <h1>Cricket Leagues</h1>
  <p>Select your favorite team from the respective leagues:</p>
  <h2>Indian Premier League</h2>
  <div class="btn-group btn-group-lg">
    <button type="button" class="btn btn-primary">Mumbai Indians</button>
    <button type="button" class="btn btn-primary">Chennai Super Kings</
button>
    <button type="button" class="btn btn-primary">Royal Challengers
Bangalore</button>
  </div>
  <h2>Big Bash League</h2>
  <div class="btn-group btn-group-sm">
    <button type="button" class="btn btn-secondary">Brisbane Heat</button>
    <button type="button" class="btn btn-secondary">Perth Scorchers</
button>
    <button type="button" class="btn btn-secondary">Adelaide Strikers</
button>
  </div>
</div>
</body>
</html>
```

After running the code, the web page will look as follows:

Screen Size: 1366 x 633

***Figure 5.35**: Resize a Button Group*

Alerts

Learn how to work with the alerts in Bootstrap and set alert messages. Use different classes to create different types of alert boxes. Also, you need to set the alert color using the contextual classes.

Note: *The background contextual class is not used here because Bootstrap Alerts components have their background color utility with the prefix* ***`.alert`***.

Create an Alert Box

To create an alert box, use the **`.alert`** Bootstrap class. You need to also set a color for the alert. For that, use the following contextual classes for alerts with the prefix **`.alert`**:

- **`.alert-success`**: Success alert box
- **`.alert-info`**: Info alert box
- **`.alert-warning`**: Warning alert box
- **`.alert-danger`**: Danger alert box
- **`.alert-primary`**: Key information
- **`.alert-secondary`**: Less important info
- **`.alert-light`**: Light-colored alert
- **`.alert-dark`**: Dark-colored alert

Let's say you opted for an alert for a key informational message, that is, a blue-colored alert. For that, use the **`.alert`** class, followed by the contextual class:

```
<div class="alert alert-primary">
```

Let us see an example to create an alert box:

```
<!DOCTYPE html>
<html lang="en">
<head>
  <title>Bootstrap Alert</title>
  <meta charset="utf-8">
  <meta name="viewport" content="width=device-width, initial-scale=1">
  <link
href="https://cdn.jsdelivr.net/npm/bootstrap@5.3.3/dist/css/bootstrap.
min.css" rel="stylesheet">
  <script
src="https://cdn.jsdelivr.net/npm/bootstrap@5.3.3/dist/js/bootstrap.
bundle.min.js"></script>
</head>
<body>
<div class="container mt-3">
```

```
  <h1>Alerts</h1>
  <p>Here are some key points:</p>
  <div class="alert alert-primary">
    <strong>Timings!</strong> Reach the examination center before 9 AM.
  </div>
  <div class="alert alert-info">
    <strong>Exam format!</strong> The exam format is now MCQs.
  </div>
</div>

</body>
</html>
```

After running the code, the web page will look as follows:

Screen Size: 1366 x 633

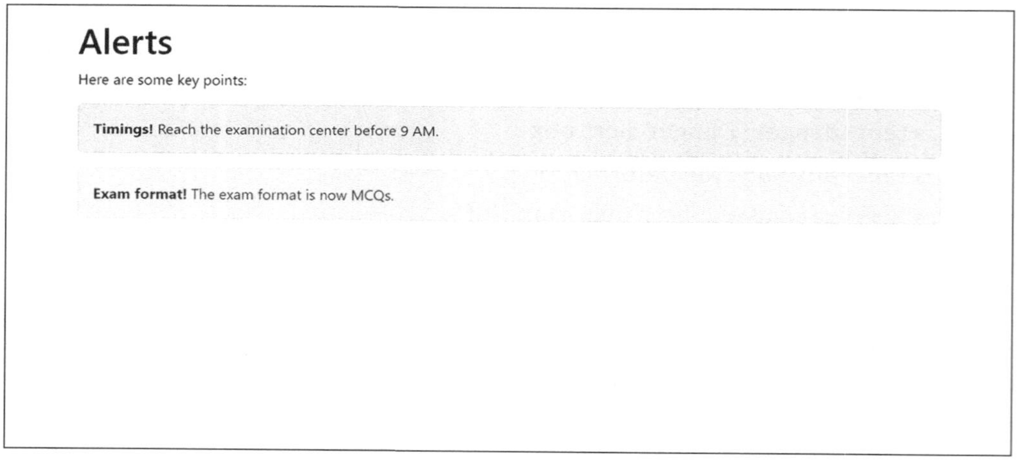

Figure 5.36: *Create an Alert Box*

Add a Close (x) Symbol in the Top-Right Corner of the Alert

The alerts can have a close symbol, which is a button or a link set with Bootstrap classes. The following class and attribute are added to make it look and work like a close symbol. The attribute is used as a JavaScript hook:

- **Class**: **`btn-close`**
- **Attribute**: **`data-bs-dismiss="alert"`**

For the alert symbol to work perfectly, you must also use the **`.alert-dismissible`** Bootstrap class with the **`.alert`** class.

Also, adding a fading effect is a good option to make the alert look like it is closing with a fading transition. To achieve this, use the **.fade** and **.show** classes.

```
<div class="alert alert-primary alert-dismissible fade show">
```

Let us see an example of creating an alert box and set a close button:

```
<!DOCTYPE html>
<html lang="en">
<head>
  <title>Bootstrap Alerts</title>
  <meta charset="utf-8">
  <meta name="viewport" content="width=device-width, initial-scale=1">
  <link
href="https://cdn.jsdelivr.net/npm/bootstrap@5.3.3/dist/css/bootstrap.
min.css" rel="stylesheet">
  <script
src="https://cdn.jsdelivr.net/npm/bootstrap@5.3.3/dist/js/bootstrap.
bundle.min.js"></script>
</head>
<body>
<div class="container mt-3">
  <h1>Alerts</h1>
  <p>Here are some key points:</p>
  <div class="alert alert-primary alert-dismissible fade show">
     <button type="button" class="btn-close" data-bs-dismiss="alert"></
button>
     <strong>Timings!</strong> Reach the examination center before 9 AM.
  </div>
  <div class="alert alert-info alert-dismissible fade show">
     <button type="button" class="btn-close" data-bs-dismiss="alert"></
button>
     <strong>Exam format!</strong> The exam format is now MCQs.
  </div>
</div>

</body>
</html>
```

After running the code, the web page will look as follows:

Screen Size: 1366 x 633

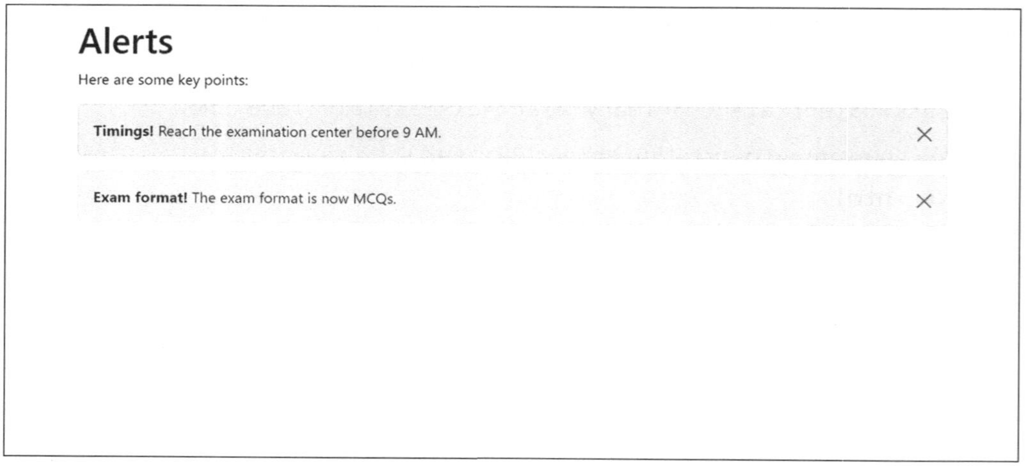

***Figure* 5.37**: *Close button for the Alert Box*

After clicking the close symbol on the second alert it disappears from the page:

Screen Size: 1366 x 633

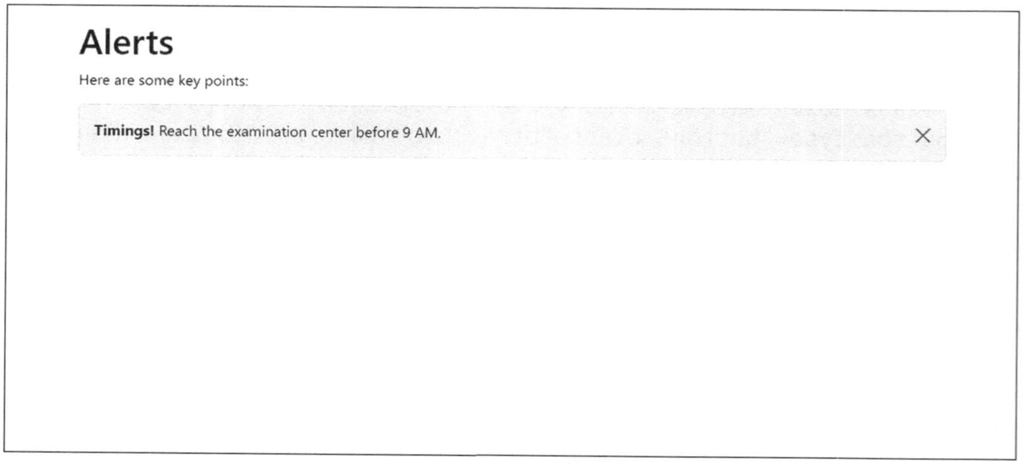

***Figure* 5.38**: *Closing one of the alert boxes*

Conclusion

We are now familiar with how to work with Bootstrap components on a web page. Beginning with the Badges and Progress Bars, we learned how to create a card on a web page. Along with setting list groups, spinners, and toast messages, we also learned the creation and styling of Buttons and Button Groups on a web page.

In the next chapter, we will learn how to work with Bootstrap popup components on a web page, such as models, offcanvas, tooltips, and more.

Points to Remember

- A badge is used to add any extra information to a piece of content. Use the **`.badge`** Bootstrap class to create a badge on a web page.
- To create a progress bar on a web page, use the **`.progress`** and **`.progress-bar`** classes.
- To set the tooltip, use the **`data-bs-toggle`** attribute.
- Consider a card on a web page as a box. The box has borders. To create a card on a web page, use the **`.card`** class.
- Create list groups with the **`.list-group`** class.
- To create a spinner on a web page, use the **`.spinner-border`** Bootstrap class.
- A spinner on a web page is used to display the loading stage of your project.
- Create a button using the **`.btn`** class.
- The **`.btn-group`** Bootstrap class is used to add a new button group.
- To create an alert box, use the **`.alert`** class.
- To set the alert color, use the contextual classes.

Multiple Choice Questions

1. How is the Badge made round on a web page with Bootstrap?
   a. `badge-pill`
   b. `round-pill`
   c. `badge-rounded`
   d. `rounded-pill`
2. Which class is used in Bootstrap to animate a progress bar?
   a. `progress-animated`
   b. `progress-bar-animated`
   c. `progress-bar-animation`
   d. `progress-animation`
3. Which class is used in Bootstrap to overlay the text on the top of the image?
   a. `card-background`
   b. `card-overlay`

   c. `card-img-background`

   d. `card-img-overlay`

4. Which class is used in Bootstrap to add a vertical button group?

   a. `group-vertical`

   b. `btngroup-vertical`

   c. `btn-group-vertical`

   d. `btn -vertical`

5. Which class in Bootstrap creates an alert box on a web page?

   a. `alert`

   b. `alert-box`

   c. `alert-msg`

   d. `alert-message`

Answers

1. d
2. b
3. d
4. c
5. a

Questions

1. How is a Badge created on a web page?
2. Set a label to the progress bar
3. How is an image set at the bottom of the card?
4. How is a spinner created on a web page?
5. What is a Button Group?
6. What is an alert on a web page?
7. How is a color added to an alert?
8. How is a close (x) symbol added in the top right corner of the alert?

Key Terms

- **Badge**: It allows a user to set predefined alert messages on a web page.
- **Card:** A card is a box that has borders. It adds padding around the content to make it look amazing.
- **Spinner:** A spinner on a web page is used to display the loading stage of your project.
- **Alert**: It allows a user to set predefined alert messages on a web page.

CHAPTER 6
Bootstrap Popup Components

Introduction

This chapter covers pop-up components in Bootstrap. Understand what collapsible content is and learn to set it. The concept of Offcanvas is also covered with examples. Also, create a modal dialog box on a web page and customize it.

We have implemented dropdown menus, tooltips, and toasts as well. Toast displays a message that mimics a Push Notification and displays a lightweight solution for it.

Structure

In this chapter, we will discuss the following topics:

- Collapse
- Modal
- Offcanvas
- Dropdown Menu
- Tooltips
- Toasts

Collapse

On a web page, visible content that becomes hidden when clicking a button or a section is called collapsible. Learn how to collapse content on a web page.

To collapse content on a web page, use the Bootstrap `.collapse` class. Also, the following two attributes are used:

- `data-bs-toggle`: This attribute is a JavaScript hook to call JavaScript when the button is clicked. This toggles between the content, that is, display or hide.

- **data-bs-target:** This attribute includes the CSS selector to link.

Use an explicit value **collapse** for the **data-bs-toggle** attribute to make it work:

```
data-bs-toggle="collapse"
```

Let us see an example:

```
<!DOCTYPE html>
<html lang="en">
<head>
  <title>Bootstrap Collapse</title>
  <meta charset="utf-8">
  <meta name="viewport" content="width=device-width, initial-scale=1">
  <link
href="https://cdn.jsdelivr.net/npm/bootstrap@5.3.3/dist/css/bootstrap.
min.css" rel="stylesheet">
  <script
src="https://cdn.jsdelivr.net/npm/bootstrap@5.3.3/dist/js/bootstrap.
bundle.min.js"></script>
</head>
<body>
<div class="container">
  <h1>Match Tickets</h1>
  The match tickets are limited. The tickets will be available next
week.<br>
  <button type="button" class="btn btn-danger" data-bs-toggle="collapse"
data-bs-target="#test">More Details</button>
  <div id="test" class="collapse">
    The tickets will be sold from 2PM TO 5PM. The last day to buy the
tickets is 15th June.
  </div>
</div>
</body>
</html>
```

After running the code, the web page will look as follows:

Screen Size: 1366 x 633

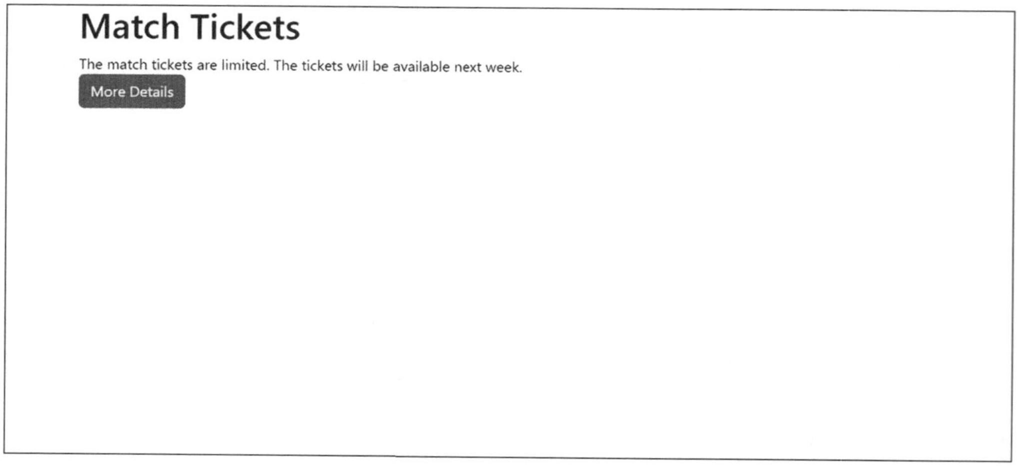

Figure 6.1: *Create collapsible content*

Click the **`More Details`** button to display the collapsed content:

Screen Size: 1366 x 633

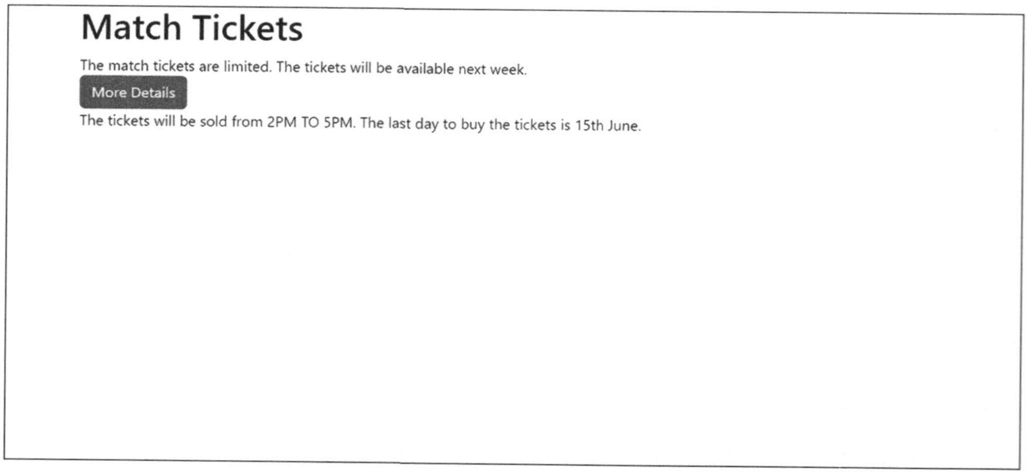

Figure 6.2: *Collapsible content appears*

Horizontal Collapsing

Transition the width while displaying the content with horizontal collapse. Bootstrap provides the **`.collapse-horizontal`** class to achieve this:

```
<div id="test" class="collapse collapse-horizontal">
```

To set the collapsed content width, we have set a Bootstrap class using the **.card** class. Remember, a width needs to be also set initially:

```
<div class="card card-body" style="width: 350px;">
```

Let us now see an example of horizontal collapsing:

```
<!DOCTYPE html>
<html lang="en">
<head>
  <title>Bootstrap Collapse</title>
  <meta charset="utf-8">
  <meta name="viewport" content="width=device-width, initial-scale=1">
  <link
href="https://cdn.jsdelivr.net/npm/bootstrap@5.3.3/dist/css/bootstrap.
min.css" rel="stylesheet">
  <script
src="https://cdn.jsdelivr.net/npm/bootstrap@5.3.3/dist/js/bootstrap.
bundle.min.js"></script>
</head>
<body>
<div class="container">
  <h1>Match Tickets</h1>
  The match tickets are limited. The tickets will be available next
week.<br>
  <p><button type="button" class="btn btn-danger" data-bs-toggle="
collapse" data-bs-target="#test">More Details</button></p>
  <div>
    <div id="test" class="collapse collapse-horizontal">
      <div class="card card-body" style="width: 350px;">
        The tickets will be sold from 2PM TO 5PM. The last day to buy
the tickets is 15th June.
      </div>
    </div>
  </div>
</div>
</body>
</html>
```

After running the code, the web page will look as follows:

Screen Size: 1366 x 633

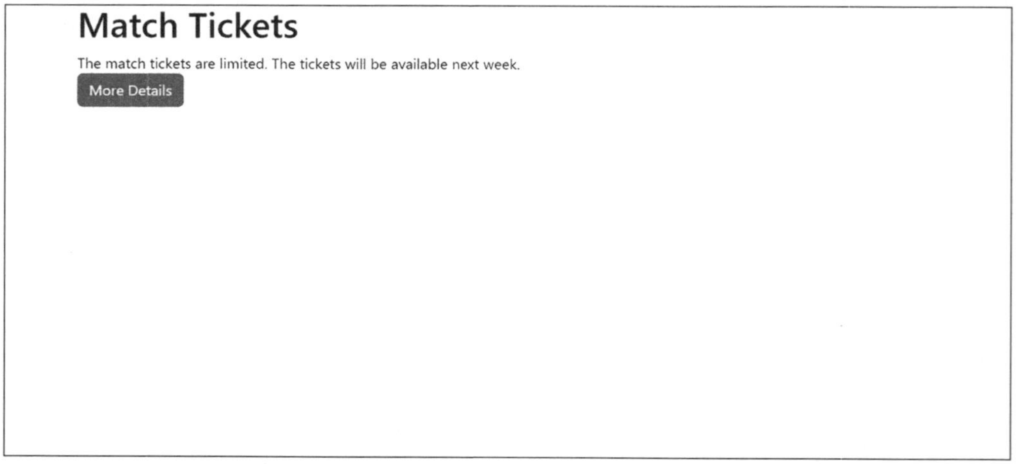

Figure 6.3: *Collapsible content*

Click the **`More Details`** button. The content would be displayed with a horizontal collapse:

Screen Size: 1366 x 633

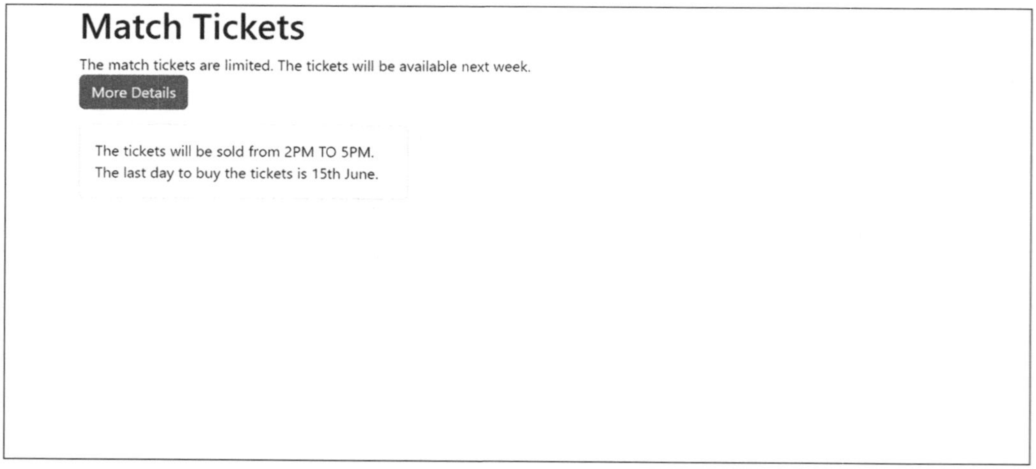

Figure 6.4: *Set the collapsible content width*

Multiple Toggles

We can also set multiple toggles using the same attributes for the collapsible content. Here, each button toggles its card component, referencing their **`data-bs-target`** attributes:

```
<button type="button" class="btn btn-primary" data-bs-toggle="collapse"
data-bs-target="#matchCollapse1">Match Details</button>
```

```
        <button class="btn btn-primary" type="button" data-bs-toggle
="collapse" data-bs-target="#matchCollapse2">Venue Details</button>
```

```
        <button class="btn btn-primary" type="button" data-bs-toggle
="collapse" data-bs-target="#matchCollapse3">Team Details</button>
```

Let us see an example of setting multiple toggles for collapsible content:

```
<!DOCTYPE html>
<html lang="en">
  <head>
    <title>Bootstrap Collapse</title>
    <meta charset="utf-8">
    <meta name="viewport" content="width=device-width, initial-scale=1">
    <link
href="https://cdn.jsdelivr.net/npm/bootstrap@5.3.3/dist/css/bootstrap.
min.css" rel="stylesheet">
    <script
src="https://cdn.jsdelivr.net/npm/bootstrap@5.3.3/dist/js/bootstrap.
bundle.min.js"></script>
  </head>
  <body>
    <div class="container">
      <h1>Match Tickets</h1>
      The match tickets are limited. The tickets will be available next
week.<br>
      <p>
        <button type="button" class="btn btn-primary" data-bs-toggle
="collapse" data-bs-target="#matchCollapse1">Match Details</button>
        <button class="btn btn-primary" type="button" data-bs-toggle
="collapse" data-bs-target="#matchCollapse2">Venue Details</button>
        <button class="btn btn-primary" type="button" data-bs-toggle
="collapse" data-bs-target="#matchCollapse3">Team Details</button>
        <button class="btn btn-info" type="warning" data-bs-toggle
="collapse" data-bs-target=".multi-collapse">All the info (Toggle)</button>
      </p>
      <div class="row">
        <div class="col">
          <div class="collapse multi-collapse" id="matchCollapse1">
            <div class="card card-body">
              Match between India and Australia on 9th June<br>
              Timings: 7PM - 11:30PM
            </div>
          </div>
        </div>
        <div class="col">
          <div class="collapse multi-collapse" id="matchCollapse2">
            <div class="card card-body">
```

```
              Venue: Eden Gardens, Kolkatta
            </div>
          </div>
        </div>
          <div class="col">
          <div class="collapse multi-collapse" id="matchCollapse3">
            <div class="card card-body">
              Captain (India): Rohit Sharma<br>Captain (Australia): Pat
              Cummins
            </div>
          </div>
        </div>
      </div>
    </div>
  </body>
</html>
```

After running the code, the web page will look as follows:

Screen Size: 1366 x 633

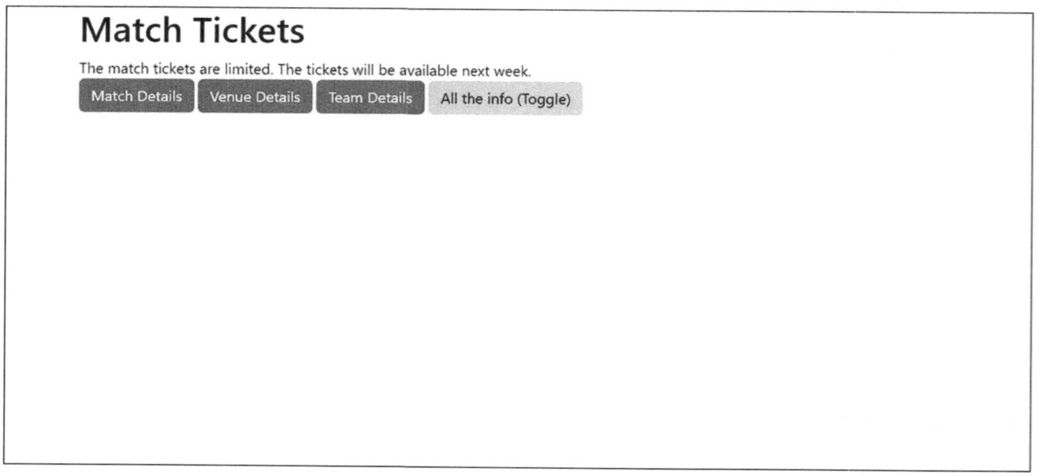

***Figure 6.5**: Multiple buttons set with individual collapsible content*

Click each button, and the content will be visible. When you click the last button, the entire collapsed content from all the buttons can be seen:

Screen Size: 1366 x 633

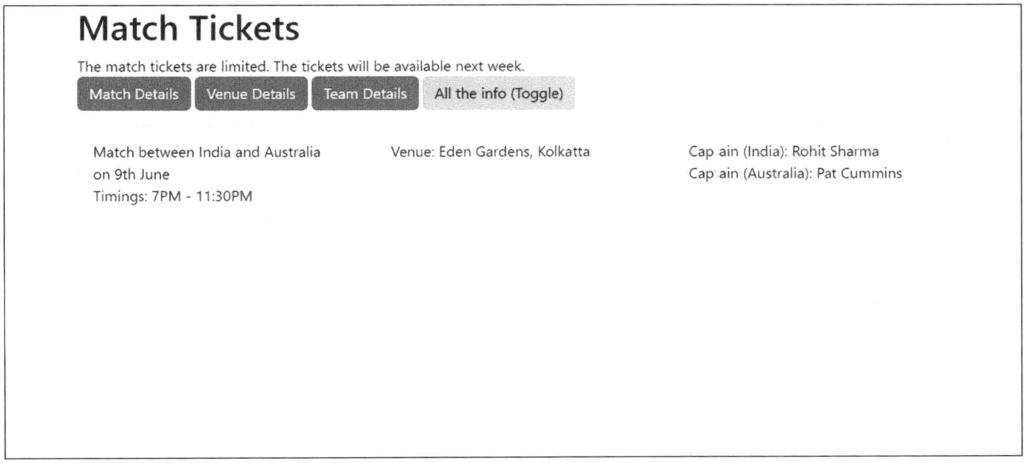

Figure 6.6: *Display collapsible content by clicking each button*

Modal

A modal is a dialog box on a web page. It appears at the top of a web page. Learn how to implement Modal in Bootstrap. With this lesson, you can learn how to:

- Create a Modal
- Create a Modal Dialog
- Modal Content

Create a Modal

To create a modal on a web page, use the Bootstrap **`.modal`** class. The Modal Dialog is created using the Bootstrap **`.modal-dialog`** class and it needs to be inside the **`.modal`** class. Use the Bootstrap **`.modal-dialog-centered`** with the **`.modal`** class to center the modal on the web page.

To set the content of the modal, that is, the header, title, body, footer, and so on, use the following classes:

- **`.modal-content`:** For modal header, body, and footer.
- **`.modal-header`:** The header of the modal.
- **`.modal-title`:** The title of the modal.
- **`.modal-body`:** The body of the modal.
- **`.modal-footer`:** The footer of the modal.

A fading effect is set for the modal using the Bootstrap **`.fade`** class. This will appear when you open or close the modal. Let us see an example and create a modal on a web page:

```
<!DOCTYPE html>
<html lang="en">
<head>
  <title>Bootstrap Modal</title>
  <meta charset="utf-8">
  <meta name="viewport" content="width=device-width, initial-scale=1">
  <link
href="https://cdn.jsdelivr.net/npm/bootstrap@5.3.3/dist/css/bootstrap.
min.css" rel="stylesheet">
  <script
src="https://cdn.jsdelivr.net/npm/bootstrap@5.3.3/dist/js/bootstrap.
bundle.min.js"></script>
</head>
<body>
<div class="container mt-2">
  <h1>Warning</h1>
  <p>Check the below warning:</p>
  <button type="button" class="btn btn-warning" data-bs-toggle="modal"
data-bs-target="#demoModal">
  Avoid system issues
  </button>
</div>
<div class="modal" id="demoModal">
  <div class="modal-dialog">
    <div class="modal-content">
      <div class="modal-header">
        <h4 class="modal-title">Warning</h4>
        <button type="button" class="btn-close" data-bs-dismiss="modal">
</button>
      </div>
      <div class= "modal-body">
        Restart the system to avoid any failed updates!
      </div>
      <div class= "modal-footer">
        <button type="button" class="btn btn-danger" data-bs-dismiss="-
modal">Close</button>
      </div>
    </div>
  </div>
</div>
</body>
</html>
```

After running the code, the web page will look as follows:

Screen Size: 1366 x 633

***Figure 6.7**: Button set to open the modal*

Click the **`Avoid system issues`** button:

Screen Size: 1366 x 633

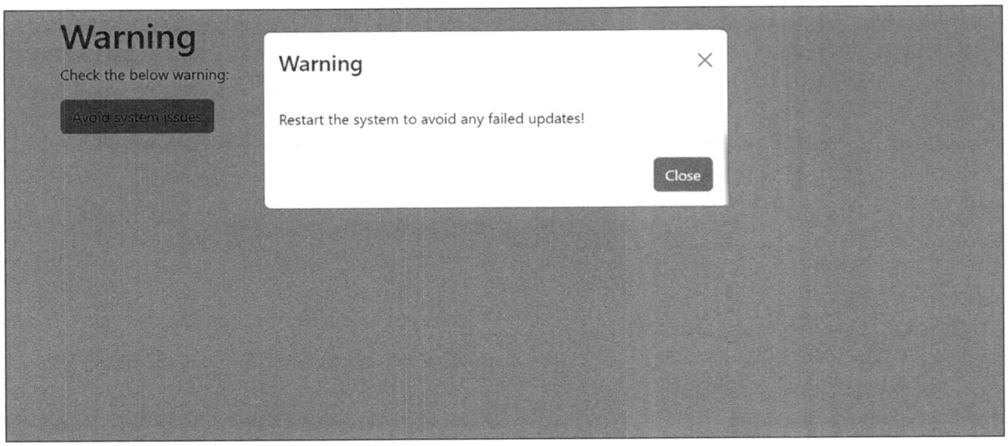

***Figure 6.8**: The button is clicked and the modal dialog box is visible*

Resize a Modal in Bootstrap

To resize a modal based on the screen size, put a max-width on a modal for specific breakpoints and up, such as, for small modals (max-width 300px), for large modals (max-width 800px), and so on.

Use the following Bootstrap classes to resize a modal. Add them with the **`.modal-dialog`** class:

- **Small modal:** The **`.modal-sm`** class, that is, max-width 300px will be visible when the screen size is >=576px.

- **Large Modal:** The **.modal-lg** class, that is, max-width 800px will be visible when the screen size is >=768px.
- **Extra Large Modal:** The **.modal-xl** class, that is, max-width 1140px will be visible when the screen size is >=992px.

Note: *We have discussed the screen sizes in the section* **Bootstrap Grids** *of Chapter 2,* **Bootstrap Layouts***.*

The default size of a modal is medium, that is, 500px max-width.

Let us see an example and a small modal. The small modal will be visible when the screen size is >= 576px.

```
<!DOCTYPE html>
<html lang="en">
<head>
  <title>Bootstrap Modal</title>
  <meta charset="utf-8">
  <meta name="viewport" content="width=device-width, initial-scale=1">
  <link
href="https://cdn.jsdelivr.net/npm/bootstrap@5.3.3/dist/css/bootstrap.
min.css" rel="stylesheet">
  <script
src="https://cdn.jsdelivr.net/npm/bootstrap@5.3.3/dist/js/bootstrap.
bundle.min.js"></script>
</head>
<body>
<div class="container mt-2">
  <h1>Warning</h1>
  <p>Check the below warning:</p>
  <button type="button" class="btn btn-info" data-bs-toggle="modal"
data-bs-target="#demoModal">
  Avoid system issues
  </button>
</div>
<div class="modal fade" id="demoModal">
  <div class="modal-dialog modal-sm">
    <div class="modal-content">
      <div class="modal-header">
        <h4 class="modal-title">Warning</h4>
        <button type="button" class="btn-close" data-bs-dismiss="modal">
</button>
      </div>
      <div class= "modal-body">
        Restart the system to avoid any failed updates!
      </div>
```

```
      <div class= "modal-footer">
        <button type="button" class="btn btn-danger" data-bs-dismiss
="modal">Close</button>
      </div>
    </div>
  </div>
</div>
</body>
</html>
```

After running the code, the web page will look as follows:

Screen Size: 1366 x 633

***Figure 6.9**: Click the button to open the modal dialog box*

Click the **`Avoid system issues`** button. A small modal will be visible:

Screen Size: 1366 x 633

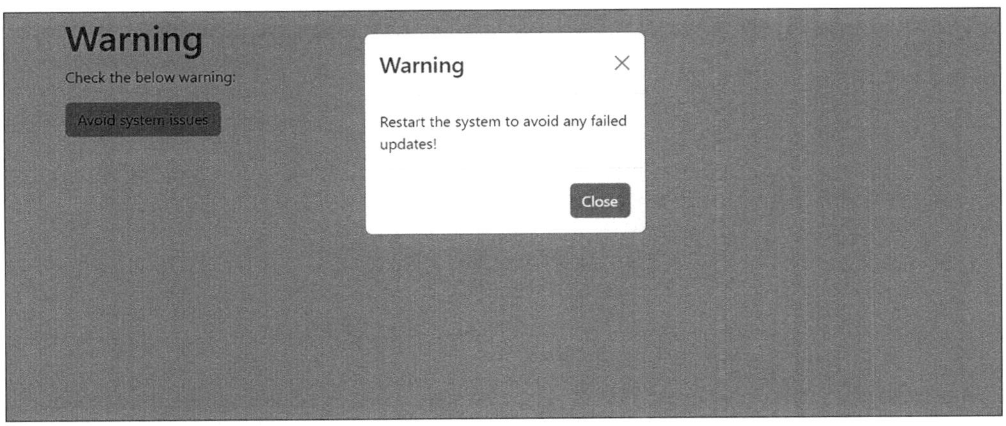

***Figure 6.10**: Click the button to open the modal dialog box smaller than the default*

Offcanvas

A toggleable sidebar component is called offcanvas on a web page. The sidebar can appear from a web page's left, right, top, or bottom. To call JavaScript, the data attributes are used:

```
data-bs-dismiss="offcanvas"
```

Set the following if you want to display the offcanvas by default:

```
div class="offcanvas offcanvas-start show"
```

Only a single offcanvas can be shown at a time on a web page. The offcanvas is a Bootstrap component.

By default, the state of the offcanvas can be hidden or shown:

- **`.offcanvas`**: This will hide the content. This is the default.
- **`.offcanvas.show`**: This will display the content.

Let us see an example of displaying an offcanvas with the click of a button:

```
<!DOCTYPE html>
<html lang="en">
  <head>
    <title>Bootstrap Offcanvas</title>
    <meta charset="utf-8">
    <meta name="viewport" content="width=device-width, initial-scale=1">
    <link
href="https://cdn.jsdelivr.net/npm/bootstrap@5.3.3/dist/css/bootstrap.
min.css" rel="stylesheet">
    <script
src="https://cdn.jsdelivr.net/npm/bootstrap@5.3.3/dist/js/bootstrap.
bundle.min.js"></script>
  </head>
  <body>
    <div class="container mt-3">
      <h4>Examination</h4>
      <div class="container">
        <button class="btn btn-primary" type="button" data-bs-toggle
="offcanvas" data-bs-target="#offcanvas">
        Exam Quick Info
        </button>
      </div>
      <div class="offcanvas offcanvas-end" id="offcanvas">
        <div class="offcanvas-header">
          <h5 class="offcanvas-title">
            Examination Information
```

```
          </h5>
          <button type="button" class="btn-close text-reset"
data-bs-dismiss="offcanvas" aria-label="Close"></button>
        </div>
        <div class="offcanvas-body">
          <p>The exam will begin at 9AM on 20th November. Bring your
admit card and a government official ID.</p>
        </div>
      </div>
    </div>
  </body>
</html>
```

After running the code, the web page will look as follows:

Screen Size: 1366 x 633

Figure 6.11: *Click the button to open the sidebar*

Click the **`Exam Quick Info`** button to open the sidebar component:

Screen Size: 1366 x 633

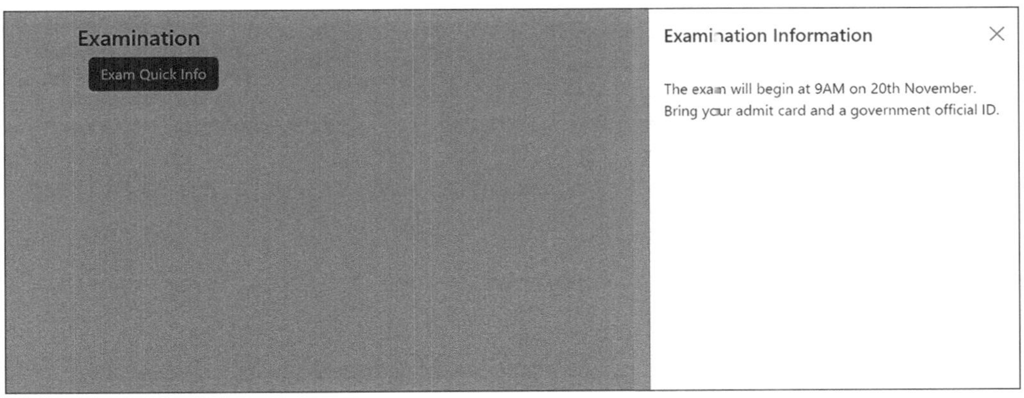

Figure 6.12: *The sidebar component is visible*

Dropdown Menu

You must have seen a menu on a web page. This menu provides navigation and helps you reach other pages of the website. Also, a sub-category is displayed as a drop-down menu. This menu has a predefined list. A user can access any one at a time after clicking this toggleable menu. Learn how to create a drop-down menu in Bootstrap. With that, learn the following in this lesson:

- Creating a drop-down menu
- Separating links in a drop-down menu
- Adding a header to the drop-down menu
- Setting Active for the drop-down menu item
- Disabling a drop-down menu item
- Creating a drop-up menu
- Creating a drop-left menu
- Aligning the drop-down menu to the right

Creating a Dropdown Menu

A dropdown menu can be a button or a link. To create a dropdown menu, various Bootstrap classes and attributes are considered. A button is turned into a trigger for a dropdown menu using the following:

- **.dropdown-toggle** class, and
- **.data-bs-toggle="dropdown"** attribute

Let us see an example to create a dropdown menu:

```
<!DOCTYPE html>
<html lang="en">
<head>
  <title>Bootstrap Dropdown Menu</title>
  <meta charset="utf-8">
  <meta name="viewport" content="width=device-width, initial-scale=1">
  <link
href="https://cdn.jsdelivr.net/npm/bootstrap@5.3.3/dist/css/bootstrap.
min.css" rel="stylesheet">
  <script
src="https://cdn.jsdelivr.net/npm/bootstrap@5.3.3/dist/js/bootstrap.
bundle.min.js"></script>
</head>
<body>
<div class="container">
  <div class="dropdown">
```

```
    <button type="button" class="btn btn-info dropdown-toggle"
data-bs-toggle="dropdown">
    Sports
    </button>
    <div class="dropdown-menu">
      <a class="dropdown-item" href="#">Football</a>
      <a class="dropdown-item" href="#">Cricket</a>
      <a class="dropdown-item" href="#">Archery</a>
      <a class="dropdown-item" href="#">Fencing</a>
    </div>
  </div>
</div>
</body>
</html>
```

After running the code, the web page will look as follows. Click the button to display the dropdown menu:

Screen Size: 1366 x 633

***Figure 6.13**: Create a dropdown menu*

Separating Links in a Dropdown Menu

If you have similar menus from different categories, then you can place them in a dropdown and separate them using the **`.dropdown-divider`** class.

Let us see an example of separating links in a dropdown menu on a web page:

```
<!DOCTYPE html>
<html lang="en">
<head>
  <title>Bootstrap Dropdown Menu</title>
```

```
  <meta charset="utf-8">
  <meta name="viewport" content="width=device-width, initial-scale=1">
  <link
href="https://cdn.jsdelivr.net/npm/bootstrap@5.3.3/dist/css/bootstrap.
min.css" rel="stylesheet">
  <script
src="https://cdn.jsdelivr.net/npm/bootstrap@5.3.3/dist/js/bootstrap.
bundle.min.js"></script>
</head>
<body>
<div class="container">
  <div class="dropdown">
    <button type="button" class="btn btn-info dropdown-toggle" data-bs
-toggle="dropdown">
    Sports
    </button>
    <div class="dropdown-menu">
      <a class="dropdown-item" href="#">Football</a>
      <a class="dropdown-item" href="#">Cricket</a>
      <hr class="dropdown-divider">
      <a class="dropdown-item" href="#">Archery</a>
      <a class="dropdown-item" href="#">Fencing</a>
    </div>
  </div>
</div>
</body>
</html>
```

After running the code, the web page will look as follows. Click the button to display the dropdown menu. The divider is also visible:

Screen Size: 1366 x 633

Figure 6.14: *The menu is visible*

Expand the dropdown menu. Now the separator is visible:

Screen Size: 1366 x 633

Figure 6.15: *Separate links in a dropdown menu*

Adding a Header to the Dropdown Menu

The dropdown menu may need headers to categorize and classify. Let's say you have menus for outdoor as well as indoor sports, then you can easily set different headers for each category with Bootstrap.

To add a header to the dropdown menu, use the **`.dropdown-header`** class. Let us see an example to add a header on a web page:

```
<!DOCTYPE html>
<html lang="en">
<head>
  <title>Bootstrap Dropdown Menu</title>
  <meta charset="utf-8">
  <meta name="viewport" content="width=device-width, initial-scale=1">
  <link
href="https://cdn.jsdelivr.net/npm/bootstrap@5.3.3/dist/css/bootstrap.
min.css" rel="stylesheet">
  <script
src="https://cdn.jsdelivr.net/npm/bootstrap@5.3.3/dist/js/bootstrap.
bundle.min.js"></script>
</head>
<body>
<div class="container">
  <div class="dropdown">
```

```
    <button type="button" class="btn btn-info dropdown-toggle" data-bs
-toggle="dropdown">
    Sports
    </button>
    <div class="dropdown-menu">
      <h5 class="dropdown-header">Outdoor</h5>
      <a class="dropdown-item" href="#">Football</a>
      <a class="dropdown-item" href="#">Cricket</a>
      <h5 class="dropdown-header">Indoor</h5>
      <a class="dropdown-item" href="#">Chess</a>
      <a class="dropdown-item" href="#">Table Tennis</a>
    </div>
  </div>
</div>
</body>
</html>
```

After running the code, the web page will look as follows. Click the button to display the dropdown menu. The header in the dropdown menu is also visible:

Screen Size: 1366 x 633

***Figure 6.16**: Add a header to the dropdown menu*

Creating a Drop-Right Menu

A default dropdown menu expands downwards, however, with Bootstrap, the dropdown can be expanded to the right. To create a dropright menu, use the **`.dropend`** class on a web page. Let us see an example of creating a drop-right menu:

```
<!DOCTYPE html>
<html lang="en">
<head>
```

```
  <title>Bootstrap Dropdown Menu</title>
  <meta charset="utf-8">
  <meta name="viewport" content="width=device-width, initial-scale=1">
  <link
href="https://cdn.jsdelivr.net/npm/bootstrap@5.3.3/dist/css/bootstrap.
min.css" rel="stylesheet">
  <script
src="https://cdn.jsdelivr.net/npm/bootstrap@5.3.3/dist/js/bootstrap.
bundle.min.js"></script>
</head>
<body>
<div class="container">
  <div class="dropdown dropend">
    <button type="button" class="btn btn-info dropdown-toggle" data-bs
-toggle="dropdown">
    Sports
    </button>
    <div class="dropdown-menu">
      <h5 class="dropdown-header">Outdoor</h5>
      <a class="dropdown-item" href="#">Football</a>
      <a class="dropdown-item" href="#">Cricket</a>
      <h5 class="dropdown-header">Indoor</h5>
      <a class="dropdown-item" href="#">Chess</a>
      <a class="dropdown-item" href="#">Table Tennis</a>
    </div>
  </div>
</div>
</body>
</html>
```

After running the code, the web page will look as follows. Click the button to display the dropdown menu. The menu is visible on the right:

Screen Size: 1366 x 633

***Figure 6.17**: Create a drop-right menu*

Creating a Drop-Left Menu

A default dropdown menu expands downwards, however, with Bootstrap, the dropdown can be expanded to the left. To create a drop-left menu, use the **`.dropstart`** class. Let us see an example of creating a drop-left menu on a web page:

```
<!DOCTYPE html>
<html lang="en">
<head>
  <title>Bootstrap Dropdown Menu</title>
  <meta charset="utf-8">
  <meta name="viewport" content="width=device-width, initial-scale=1">
  <link
href="https://cdn.jsdelivr.net/npm/bootstrap@5.3.3/dist/css/bootstrap.
min.css" rel="stylesheet">
  <script
src="https://cdn.jsdelivr.net/npm/bootstrap@5.3.3/dist/js/bootstrap.
bundle.min.js"></script>
</head>
<body>
<div class="container">
  <div class="dropdown dropstart text-end">
    <button type="button" class="btn btn-info dropdown-toggle" data-bs
-toggle="dropdown">
    Sports
    </button>
    <div class="dropdown-menu">
      <h5 class="dropdown-header">Outdoor</h5>
```

```
      <a class="dropdown-item" href="#">Football</a>
      <a class="dropdown-item" href="#">Cricket</a>
      <h5 class="dropdown-header">Indoor</h5>
      <a class="dropdown-item" href="#">Chess</a>
      <a class="dropdown-item" href="#">Table Tennis</a>
    </div>
  </div>
</div>
</body>
</html>
```

After running the code, the web page will look as follows. Click the button to display the dropdown menu. The menu is visible on the left:

Screen Size: 1366 x 633

Figure 6.18: *Create a drop-left menu*

Tooltips

Tooltip is a popover that appears when you hover the cursor. Learn how to create a tooltip in Bootstrap and how to position a tooltip, with the following:

- Creating Tooltip
- Positioning Tooltip Text

Creating Tooltip

To set the tooltip on an element, use the following attributes:

```
data-bs-toggle="tooltip"
```

Bootstrap components don't require JavaScript to run, but Tooltips require it. The following script will enable the tooltips on the web page:

```
<script>
var tooltipTrigger = [].slice.call(document.querySelectorAll
('[data-bs-toggle="mytooltip"]'))
var tooltipList = tooltipTrigger.map(function (tooltipTriggerEl) {
  return new bootstrap.Tooltip(tooltipTriggerEl)
})
</script>
```

Let us understand the preceding code. The following line selects all elements in the DOM (Document Object Model) that have the attribute **data-bs-toggle="mytooltip"**:

```
var tooltipTrigger = [].slice.call(document.querySelectorAll('[da-
ta-bs-toggle="mytooltip"]')):
```

The **`.slice.call`** turns the NodeList returned by **`querySelectorAll`** into an array.

The following line creates an array (tooltipList) by mapping over each **`tooltipTriggerEl`** (element from the tooltipTrigger array). For each element, a new Bootstrap Tooltip is instantiated and attached to that element.

```
var tooltipList = tooltipTrigger.map(function (tooltipTriggerEl)
{ return new bootstrap.Tooltip(tooltipTriggerEl) }):
```

The tooltip title is set using the title attribute:

```
title="New"
```

Let us see an example of creating a tooltip on a button. Keep the cursor on the button to view the tooltip text:

```
<!DOCTYPE html>
<html lang="en">
<head>
  <title>Bootstrap Tooltip</title>
  <meta charset="utf-8">
  <meta name="viewport" content="width=device-width, initial-scale=1">
  <link
href="https://cdn.jsdelivr.net/npm/bootstrap@5.3.3/dist/css/bootstrap.
min.css" rel="stylesheet">
  <script
src="https://cdn.jsdelivr.net/npm/bootstrap@5.3.3/dist/js/bootstrap.
bundle.min.js"></script>
</head>
<body>
<div class="container">
  <h2>Programming Cheat Sheets</h2>
  <p>Here are some cheat sheets:</p>
```

```
  <p>Keep the mouse cursor on the button to check the cheat sheet
status:</p>
<button type="button" class="btn btn-secondary" data-bs-toggle="mytooltip"
title="UPDATED">
   Python Cheat Sheet
  </button>
<button type="button" class="btn btn-dark" data-bs-toggle="mytooltip"
title="NEW">
    Java Cheat Sheet
  </button>
 <script>
var tooltipTrigger = [].slice.call(document.querySelectorAll
('[data-bs-toggle="mytooltip"]'))
var tooltipList = tooltipTrigger.map(function (tooltipTriggerEl) {
  return new bootstrap.Tooltip(tooltipTriggerEl)
})
</script>
</div>
</body>
</html>
```

After running the code, the web page will look as follows. On keeping the cursor on the button, the tooltip becomes visible:

Screen Size: 1366 x 633

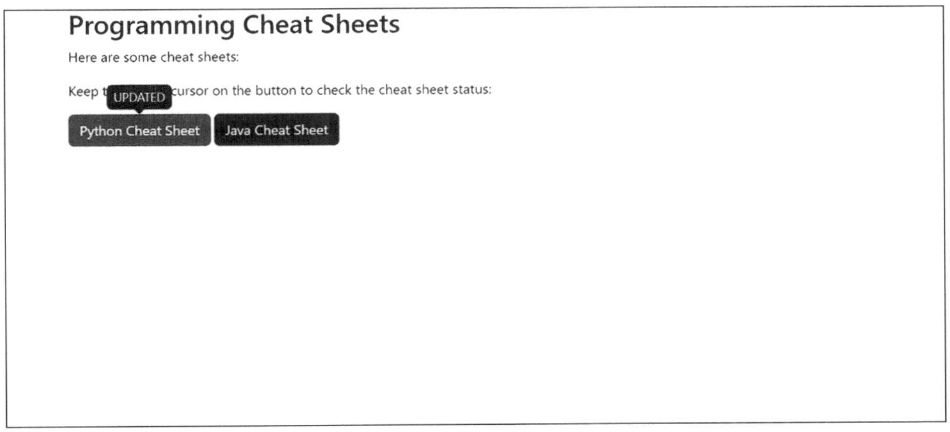

Figure 6.19: *Create a Tooltip*

Positioning Tooltip Text

The **`data-bs-placement`** attribute is used to set the position of the tooltip text. To set the position of the tooltip on the left of an element, use the left value:

```
data-bs-placement="left"
```

To set the position of the tooltip on the right of an element, use the **right** value:

```
data-bs-placement="right"
```

To set the position of the tooltip on the top of an element, use the **top** value:

```
data-bs-placement="top"
```

To set the position of the tooltip on the bottom of an element, use the **bottom** value:

```
data-bs-placement="bottom"
```

Let us see an example of how tooltips on a web page are positioned:

```
<!DOCTYPE html>
<html lang="en">
<head>
  <title>Bootstrap Tooltip</title>
  <meta charset="utf-8">
  <meta name="viewport" content="width=device-width, initial-scale=1">
  <link
href="https://cdn.jsdelivr.net/npm/bootstrap@5.3.3/dist/css/bootstrap.
min.css" rel="stylesheet">
  <script
src="https://cdn.jsdelivr.net/npm/bootstrap@5.3.3/dist/js/bootstrap.
bundle.min.js"></script>
</head>
<body>
<div class="container">
  <h2>Programming Cheat Sheets</h2>
  <p>Here are some cheat sheets:</p>
  <p>Keep the mouse cursor on the button to check the cheat sheet status:
</p>
  <button type="button" class="btn btn-secondary"  data-bs-placement
="top" data-bs-toggle="mytooltip" title="UPDATED">
   Python Cheat Sheet
  </button>
  <button type="button" class="btn btn-dark"  data-bs-placement="left"
data-bs-toggle="mytooltip" title="NEW">
    Java Cheat Sheet
  </button>
  <button type="button" class="btn btn-primary"  data-bs-placement
="bottom" data-bs-toggle="mytooltip" title="UPDATED">
   Data Science Cheat Sheet
  </button>
  <button type="button" class="btn btn-success"  data-bs-placement
="right" data-bs-toggle="mytooltip" title="NEW">
    AI Cheat Sheet
  </button>
 <script>
```

```
var tooltipTrigger = [].slice.call(document.querySelectorAll
('[data-bs-toggle="mytooltip"]'))
var tooltipList = tooltipTrigger.map(function (tooltipTriggerEl) {
  return new bootstrap.Tooltip(tooltipTriggerEl)
})
</script>
</div>
</body>
</html>
```

After running the code, the web page will look as follows. By keeping the cursor on each button, the individual tooltip text will be visible on the left, right, top, and bottom positions:

Screen Size: 1366 x 633

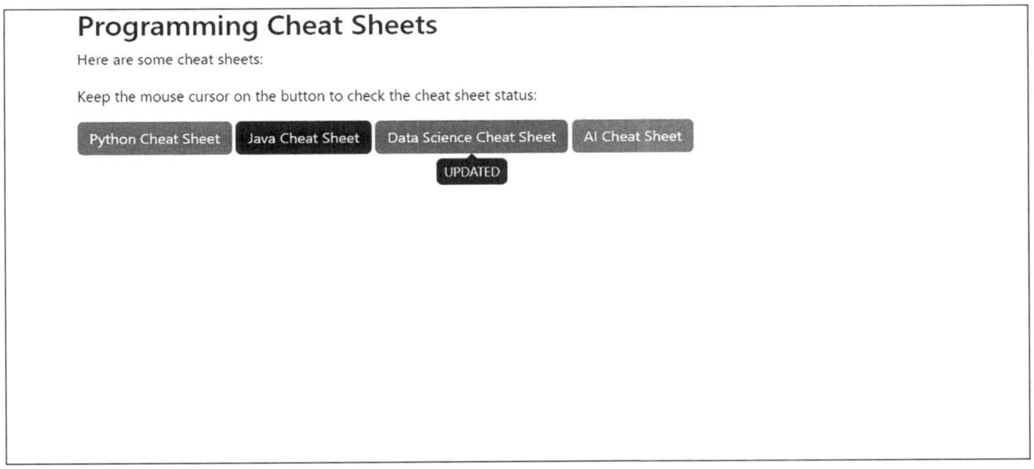

***Figure 6.20**: Positioning Tooltip Text*

We saw how to create a tooltip on a web page and position it. Now, let us see what a toast is, and how it is created on a web page.

Toasts

Toast displays a message that mimics a Push Notification message and displays a lightweight solution. Let's say you filled out a contact form, and after clicking submit, a message becomes visible: **`Submitted Successfully`**.

Learn how to work with Toasts in Bootstrap. You will understand:

- Creating a Toast
- Toast Color
- Stack Toasts

Creating a Toast

The **.toast** class is used to create a toast. You can also add a header to the toast using the **.toast-header** class. The toast message is set using **.toast-body** class.

Let us see an example of creating a toast on a web page. We have displayed the toast using the **.show** class:

```
<!DOCTYPE html>
<html lang="en">
<head>
  <title>Bootstrap Toasts</title>
  <meta charset="utf-8">
  <meta name="viewport" content="width=device-width, initial-scale=1">
  <link
href="https://cdn.jsdelivr.net/npm/bootstrap@5.3.3/dist/css/bootstrap.
min.css" rel="stylesheet">
  <script
src="https://cdn.jsdelivr.net/npm/bootstrap@5.3.3/dist/js/bootstrap.
bundle.min.js"></script>
</head>
<body>
<div class="container">
  <h2>Contact Us</h2>
  <div class="toast show">
    <div class="toast-header">
      <strong class="me-auto">Form Submitted</strong>
      <button type="button" class="btn-close" data-bs-dismiss="toast"></
button>
    </div>
    <div class="toast-body">
      <p>Thank you for submitting the form.</p>
    </div>
  </div>
</div>

</body>
</html>
```

After running the code, the web page will look as follows:

Screen Size: 1366 x 633

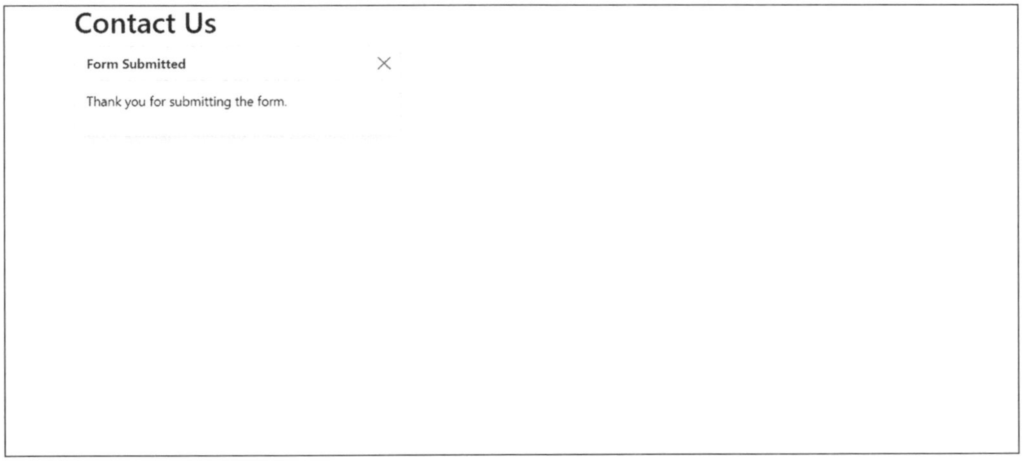

***Figure 6.21**: Create a Toast on a web page*

Toast Color

Use the contextual classes and set any background color for the Toast message:

- **`.text-bg-primary`:** Represents important text. Applies a blue color text background color to an element.
- **`.text-bg-secondary`:** Represents secondary text. Applies a green color text background color to an element.
- **`.text-bg-success`:** Represents a successful action. Applies a green color text background color to an element.
- **`.text-bg-danger`:** Represents danger. Applies a red color text background color to an element.
- **`.text-bg-warning`:** Represents warning. Applies a yellow color text background color to an element.
- **`.text-bg-info`:** Represents information. Applies a light blue color text background color to an element.
- **`.text-bg-light`:** Applies a light grey color
- **`.text-bg-dark`:** Applies a dark grey color

Let us see an example to set the background color for the toast message:

```
<!DOCTYPE html>
<html lang="en">
<head>
  <title>Bootstrap Toasts</title>
  <meta charset="utf-8">
```

```
  <meta name="viewport" content="width=device-width, initial-scale=1">
  <link
href="https://cdn.jsdelivr.net/npm/bootstrap@5.3.3/dist/css/bootstrap.
min.css" rel="stylesheet">
  <script
src="https://cdn.jsdelivr.net/npm/bootstrap@5.3.3/dist/js/bootstrap.
bundle.min.js"></script>
</head>
<body>
<div class="container">
  <h2>Contact Us</h2>
  <div class="toast show text-bg-dark">
    <div class="toast-header">
      <strong class="me-auto">Form Submitted</strong>
      <button type="button" class="btn-close" data-bs-dismiss="toast"></
button>
    </div>
    <div class="toast-body">
      <p>Thank you for submitting the form.</p>
    </div>
  </div>
</div>

</body>
</html>
```

After running the code, the web page will look as follows:

Screen Size: 1366 x 633

Figure 6.22: *Set the color of a Toast*

Stack Toasts

Create multiple toasts and stack them easily with Bootstrap. We will set both the toasts within a parent container. The **.toast-container** class sets the spacing between the containers:

```
<div class="toast-container position-static">
```

Let us see an example of stacking toasts on a web page:

```
<!DOCTYPE html>
<html lang="en">
  <head>
    <title>Bootstrap Toasts</title>
    <meta charset="utf-8">
    <meta name="viewport" content="width=device-width, initial-scale=1">
    <link
href="https://cdn.jsdelivr.net/npm/bootstrap@5.3.3/dist/css/bootstrap.
min.css" rel="stylesheet">
    <script
src="https://cdn.jsdelivr.net/npm/bootstrap@5.3.3/dist/js/bootstrap.
bundle.min.js"></script>
  </head>
  <body>
    <div class="container">
      <h2>Contact Us</h2>
      <div class="toast-container position-static">
        <div class="toast show">
          <div class="toast-header">
            <strong class="me-auto">Form Submitted</strong>
            <button type="button" class="btn-close" data-bs-dismiss
="toast"></button>
          </div>
          <div class="toast-body">
            <p>Thank you for submitting the form.</p>
          </div>
        </div>
        <div class="toast show">
          <div class="toast-header">
            <strong class="me-auto">Expect a Revert</strong>
            <button type="button" class="btn-close" data-bs-dismiss
="toast"></button>
          </div>
          <div class="toast-body">
            <p>We will call you shortly.</p>
          </div>
        </div>
```

```
      </div>
    </div>
  </body>
</html>
```

After running the code, the web page will look as follows:

Screen Size: 1366 x 633

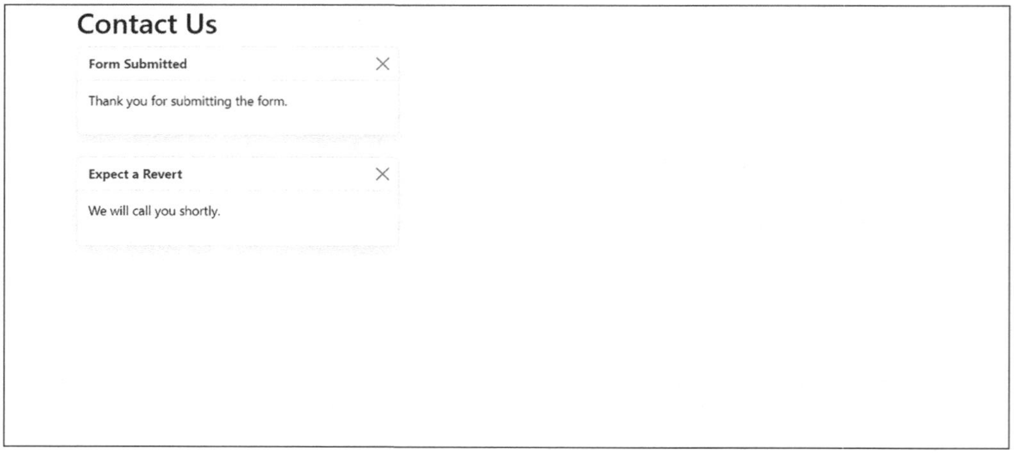

***Figure 6.23**: Stack Toasts on a web page*

Conclusion

Now we are familiar with working Bootstrap popup components on a web page. Beginning with collapsible content to show or hide content with the click of a button, we also learned to create tooltips and toasts. Offcanvas was generated at the click of a button. Modal was also created, and the content was set. We also created tooltips and dropdown menus.

In the next chapter, we will learn how to create forms on a web page. We will also create form controls, such as checkboxes, and radio buttons, and set validations.

Points to Remember

- To collapse content on a web page, use the **`.collapse`** class with the **`data-bs-toggle`** and the **`data-bs-target`** attributes. Use an explicit value **`collapse`** for the **`data-bs-toggle`** attribute.
- Multiple toggles can also be set on a web page with Bootstrap.
- To create a modal on a web page, use the **`.modal`** class.

- Create a small modal using the **`.modal-sm`** class. It will be visible when the screen size is >=576px.
- Create a large modal using the **`.modal-lg`** class. It will be visible when the screen size is >=768px.
- Create an extra-large modal using the **`.modal-xl`** class. It will be visible when the screen size is >=992px.
- The default size of a modal is medium, that is, 500px.
- A toggleable sidebar component is called offcanvas on a web page.
- To create a dropdown menu, use the **`.dropdown-toggle`** class and **`data-bs-toggle="dropdown"`** attribute.
- Toast mimics a push notification message and displays a lightweight solution.
- The **`.toast`** class is used to create a toast.

Multiple Choice Questions

1. Which attribute in Bootstrap is used to toggle collapsible content?
    a. `data-toggle`
    b. `data-collapse-toggle`
    c. `collapse-bs-toggle`
    d. `data-bs-toggle`
2. What is the default size of a modal set on a web page with Bootstrap?
    a. 300px max-width
    b. 500px max-width
    c. 800px max-width
    d. 1140px max-width
3. Which class in Bootstrap sets a small modal on a web page?
    a. `modal-small`
    b. `modal`
    c. `modal-sm`
    d. `modal-shrink`

4. Which class in Bootstrap centers a modal on the web page?
    a. `modal-dialog-centered`
    b. `modal-centered`
    c. `dialog-center`
    d. `modal-center`
5. Which class is used in Bootstrap to separate links in a Dropdown Menu?
    a. `dropdown-divider`
    b. `dropdown-separator`
    c. `dropdown-menu-divider`
    d. `dropdown-menu-separator`

Answers

1. d
2. b
3. c
4. a
5. a

Questions

- What is a collapsible on a web page?
- How to collapse content on a web page
- How is a modal on a web page created?
- What are the Bootstrap classes to resize a modal based on the screen size?
- What is an Offcanvas on a web page?
- How to position the tooltip text?
- Define toast on a web page.

Key Terms

- **Collapsible:** Visible content that becomes hidden when clicking a button or a section is called collapsible
- **Modal:** A modal is a dialog box on a web page. It appears on the top of a web page.
- **Offcanvas:** A toggleable sidebar component is called offcanvas on a web page.
- **Tooltip**: The tooltip is a popover that appears when you hover the cursor.
- **Toast:** Toast displays a message. It mimics a push notification message and displays a lightweight solution for it.

CHAPTER 7
Bootstrap Forms

Introduction

This chapter covers creating forms on a web page. A form can be stacked on a web page or it can be an inline form. With that, the working of form controls on a web page is also covered with validations.

The checkboxes and radio buttons are implemented with examples. We can also group input and validate a form easily.

Structure

In this chapter, we will discuss the following topics:

- Forms
- Custom Select Menu
- Checkboxes
- Radio Buttons
- Input Groups
- Floating Labels
- Form Validation

Forms

Learn how to create a form on a web page with Bootstrap. The `<form>` element is used to create a form. We can create any of the following forms:

- **Stacked Forms:** Form elements are horizontally stacked
- **Inline Forms:** Form elements appear side by side

Stacked Forms

The form elements can be stacked vertically. In the following example, we are creating a form with some input fields for email-id, password, and so on.

The following creates a label for the input field. The **for="email"** attribute links the label to the input field with the **id="email"**, ensuring users know which label corresponds to which input:

```
<label for="email">Email:</label>
```

Then, we created an input field where users can type their email address. The **type="email"** specifies that this input is for email addresses, enabling built-in validation for email formats. The **id="email"** gives this input field a unique identifier. The **placeholder="Enter the email"** provides placeholder text that appears inside the input field, guiding users on what to enter:

```
<input type="email" id="email" placeholder="Enter the email"
name="emailid">
```

The **name="emailid"** assigns a name to the input field, which is useful when submitting the form data.

Let us create a form on a web page:

```
<!DOCTYPE html>
<html lang="en">
<head>
  <title>Bootstrap Forms</title>
  <meta charset="utf-8">
  <meta name="viewport" content="width=device-width, initial-scale=1">
  <link
href="https://cdn.jsdelivr.net/npm/bootstrap@5.3.3/dist/css/bootstrap.
min.css" rel="stylesheet">
  <script
src="https://cdn.jsdelivr.net/npm/bootstrap@5.3.3/dist/js/bootstrap.
bundle.min.js"></script>
</head>
<body>
<div class="container">
  <h2>Login</h2>
  <form action="/next.php">
    <div>
      <label for="email">Email:</label>
      <input type="email" id="email" placeholder="Enter the email"
name="emailid">
    </div>
    <div>
      <label for="pwd">Password:</label>
      <input type="password" id="pwd" placeholder="Enter the password"
name="passwd">
    </div>
    <button type="submit" class="btn btn-secondary">Submit</button>
```

```
  </form>
</div>
</body>
</html>
```

After running the code, the web page will look as follows:

Screen Size: 1366 x 633

***Figure 7.1**: Creating a form on a web page*

In the preceding form, we have not aligned or styled the form input elements such as input, label, and so on. Now, let us style the elements.

Form Control

Use the following Bootstrap classes to align and style the form controls, such as:

- **`.form-control`**: Style the **`<input>`** as well as **`<textarea>`** elements.
- **`.form-label`**: Set the correct padding for the **`<label>`** elements.

The following example is somewhat different than the previous example. Here, we have added a textarea for the user to enter a text with multiple paragraphs:

```
<textarea class="form-control" rows="3" id="comment" placeholder
="Describe our website experience here..." name="text"></textarea>:
```

Above,

- **`textarea`**: The tag defines a multi-line input field.
- **`class="form-control"`**: Applies Bootstrap's styling for form elements, ensuring it looks neat and consistent with the rest of the Bootstrap-styled form.

- **`rows="3"`**: Specifies the number of visible text lines in the text area. It starts with three lines visible, but users can add more text.
- **`id="comment"`**: A unique identifier for this text area, useful for linking the label or JavaScript functionality.
- **`placeholder="Describe our website experience here..."`**: Provides a hint to the user about what to type inside the text area.
- **`name="text"`**: The name attribute is used to reference the form data after submission.

Let us now see an example of creating a stacked form with styled and aligned elements:

```
<!DOCTYPE html>
<html lang="en">
<head>
  <title>Bootstrap Forms</title>
  <meta charset="utf-8">
  <meta name="viewport" content="width=device-width, initial-scale=1">
  <link
href="https://cdn.jsdelivr.net/npm/bootstrap@5.3.3/dist/css/bootstrap.
min.css" rel="stylesheet">
  <script
src="https://cdn.jsdelivr.net/npm/bootstrap@5.3.3/dist/js/bootstrap.
bundle.min.js"></script>
</head>
<body>
<div class="container">
  <h2>Login</h2>
  <form action="/next.php">
    <div>
      <label class="form-label">Email:</label>
      <input type="email" class="form-control" id="email" placeholder
="Enter the email" name="emailid">
    </div>
    <div>
      <label for="pwd" class="form-label">Password:</label>
      <input type="password" class="form-control" id="pwd" placeholder
="Enter the password" name="passwd">
    </div>
     <div>
      <label for="comment">Describe:</label>
      <textarea class="form-control" rows="3" id="comment" placeholder
="Describe our website experience here..." name="text"></textarea>
    </div>
    <button type="submit" class="btn btn-secondary">Submit</button>
  </form>
```

```
</div>
</body>
</html>
```

After running the code, the web page will look as follows:

Screen Size: 1366 x 633

***Figure 7.2**: Creating a form and styling it*

Inline Forms

With Inline Forms, you can easily let the form elements appear side by side. For this, use the **.row** and **.col** Bootstrap classes. Let us see the example to create an inline form:

```
<!DOCTYPE html>
<html lang="en">
<head>
  <title>Bootstrap Forms</title>
  <meta charset="utf-8">
  <meta name="viewport" content="width=device-width, initial-scale=1">
  <link
href="https://cdn.jsdelivr.net/npm/bootstrap@5.3.3/dist/css/bootstrap.
min.css" rel="stylesheet">
  <script
src="https://cdn.jsdelivr.net/npm/bootstrap@5.3.3/dist/js/bootstrap.
bundle.min.js"></script>
</head>
<body>
<div class="container">
  <h2>Login</h2>
  <form>
```

```
    <div class="row">
      <div class="col">
        <label class="form-label">Email:</label>
        <input type="email" class="form-control" id="email" placeholder
="Enter the email" name="emailid">
      </div>
    <div class="col">
      <label for="pwd" class="form-label">Passworc:</label>
      <input type="password" class="form-control" id="pwd" placeholder
="Enter the password" name="passwd">
    </div>
   </div>
  </form>
</div>
</body>
</html>
```

After running the code, the web page will look as follows:

Screen Size: 1366 x 633

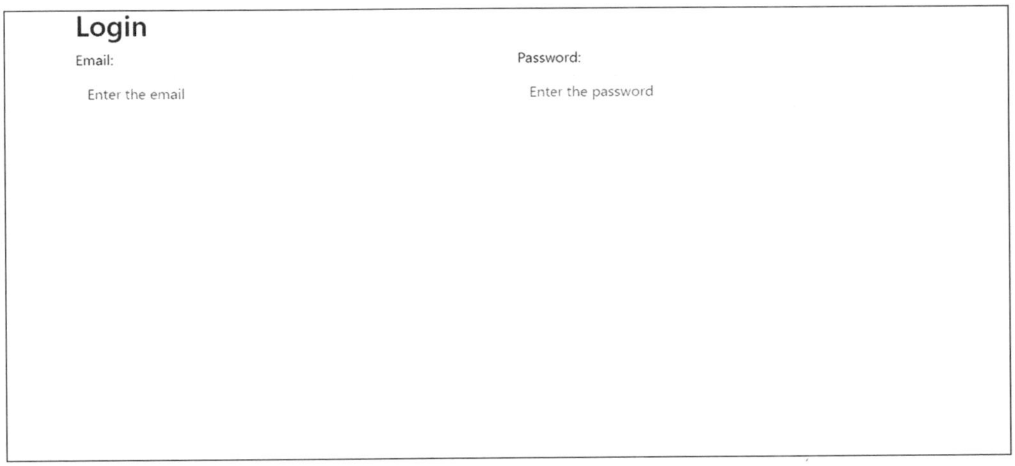

Figure 7.3: *Creating inline forms*

Resize Form Control

Resize the form controls easily on a web page using the following Bootstrap classes:

- **`.form-control-sm`:** A form input control smaller than the default size.
- **`.form-control-lg`:** A form input control bigger than the default size

Let us see an example to resize the form controls. We have created an inline form here:

```
<!DOCTYPE html>
<html lang="en">
<head>
  <title>Bootstrap Forms</title>
  <meta charset="utf-8">
  <meta name="viewport" content="width=device-width, initial-scale=1">
  <link
href="https://cdn.jsdelivr.net/npm/bootstrap@5.3.3/dist/css/bootstrap.
min.css" rel="stylesheet">
  <script
src="https://cdn.jsdelivr.net/npm/bootstrap@5.3.3/dist/js/bootstrap.
bundle.min.js"></script>
</head>
<body>
<div class="container">
  <h2>Login</h2>
  <form>
    <div class="row">
      <div class="col">
        <label class="form-label">Email:</label>
        <input type="email" class="form-control form-control-lg"
id="email" placeholder="Enter the email" name="emailid">
      </div>
    <div class="col">
      <label for="pwd" class="form-label">Password:</label>
      <input type="password" class="form-control form-control-sm"
id="pwd" placeholder="Enter the password" name="passwd">
    </div>
   </div>
  </form>
</div>
</body>
</html>
```

After running the code, the web page will look as follows:

Screen Size: 1366 x 633

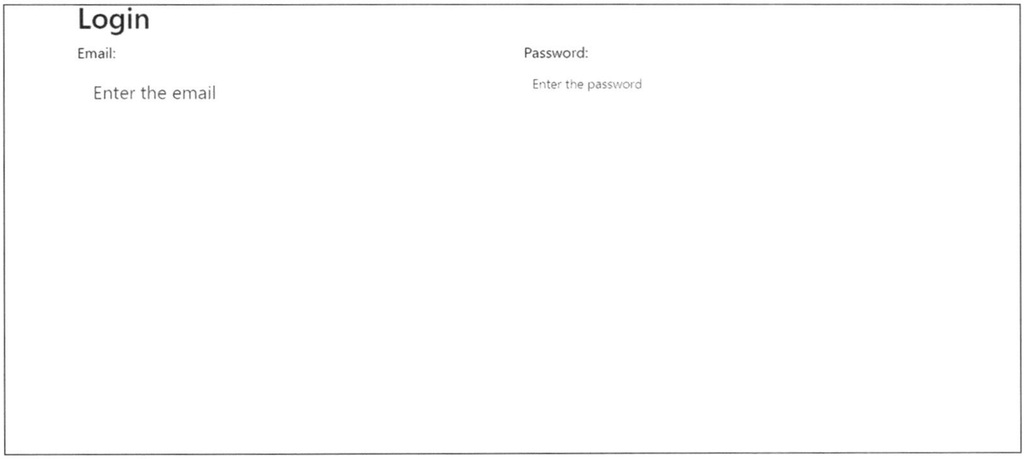

***Figure 7.4**: Form controls of different sizes*

Setting Range Input

To create an input element with range, use the following input type:

```
<input type ="range">
```

The range is styled using the **`.form-range`** class. Let us see an example:

```
<!DOCTYPE html>
<html lang="en">
<head>
  <title>Bootstrap Range Input</title>
  <meta charset="utf-8">
  <meta name="viewport" content="width=device-width, initial-scale=1">
  <link
href="https://cdn.jsdelivr.net/npm/bootstrap@5.3.3/dist/css/bootstrap.
min.css" rel="stylesheet">
  <script
src="https://cdn.jsdelivr.net/npm/bootstrap@5.3.3/dist/js/bootstrap.
bundle.min.js"></script>
</head>
<body>
<div class="container mt-3">
  <h2>Feedback</h2>
  <p>Did you liked the website experience?</p>
  <form action="/next.php">
    <label for="newRange" class="form-label">Submit your feedback</label>
    <input type="range" class="form-range" id="newRange" name="points">
    <button type="submit" class="btn btn-secondary mt-3">Submit</button>
  </form>
```

```
</div>
</body>
</html>
```

After running the code, the web page will look as follows:

Screen Size: 1366 x 633

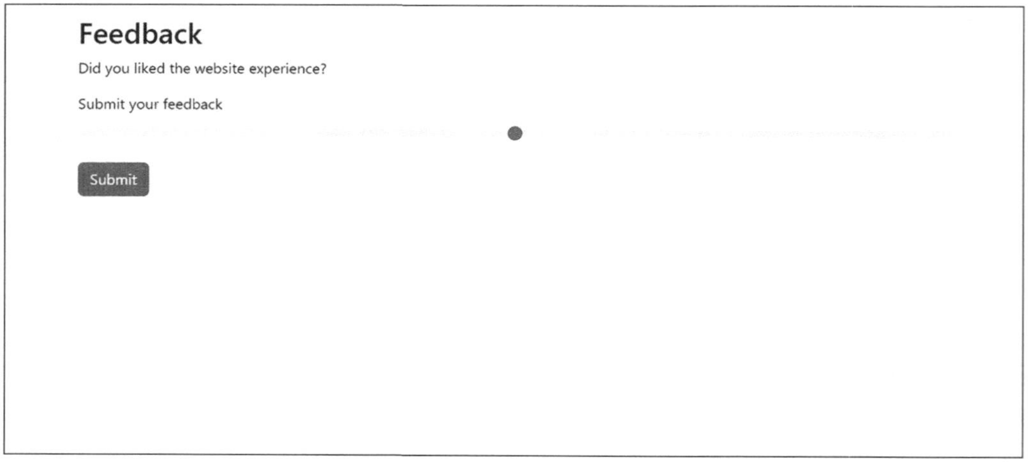

***Figure 7.5**: Input element with range*

Custom Select Menu

With Bootstrap, create a select menu like a dropdown easily and style it using the **.form-select** class.

Users can either be given an option to select a single menu or multiple menus. Let us see both the examples.

Creating a Single Select Menu

The user can select only one option from the select menu. At a time, only a single option can be selected.

Let us see an example to create a single select menu on a web page:

```
<!DOCTYPE html>
<html lang="en">
<head>
  <title>Bootstrap Select Menu</title>
  <meta charset="utf-8">
  <meta name="viewport" content="width=device-width, initial-scale=1">
```

```
  <link
href="https://cdn.jsdelivr.net/npm/bootstrap@5.3.3/dist/css/bootstrap.
min.css" rel="stylesheet">
  <script
src="https://cdn.jsdelivr.net/npm/bootstrap@5.3.3/dist/js/bootstrap.
bundle.min.js"></script>
</head>
<body>

<div class="container mt-3">
  <h2>Favourite Sports</h2>
  <p>Select any of the following sports you love to play and watch:</p>
  <form action="next.php">
    <label for="sel" class="form-label">Sports</label>
    <select class="form-select" id="sel" name="selmenu">
      <option>Football</option>
      <option>Cricket</option>
      <option>Tennis</option>
      <option>Badminton</option>
      <option>Table Tennis</option>
    </select>
    <button type="submit" class="btn btn-secondary mt-3">Submit</button>
  </form>
</div>

</body>
</html>
```

After running the code, the web page will look as follows:

Screen Size: 1366 x 633

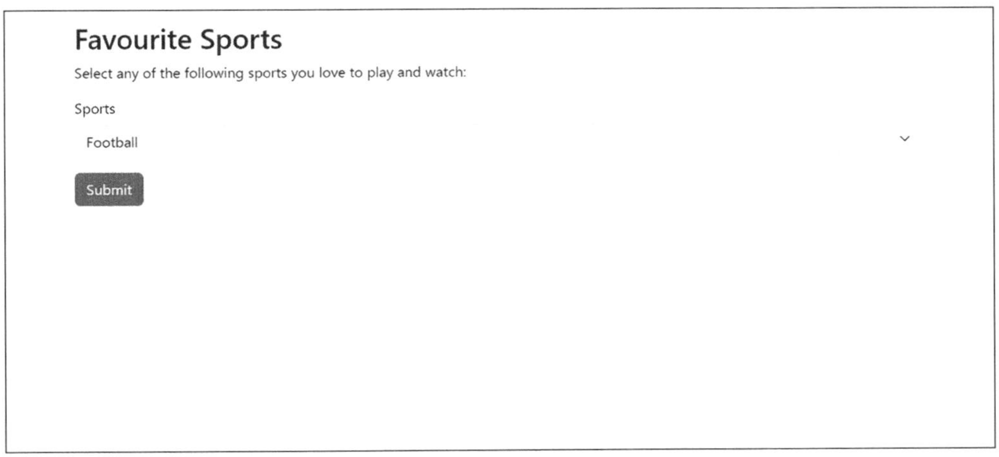

***Figure 7.6**: Creating a select menu on a web page*

Select any of the sports from the options:

Screen Size: 1366 x 633

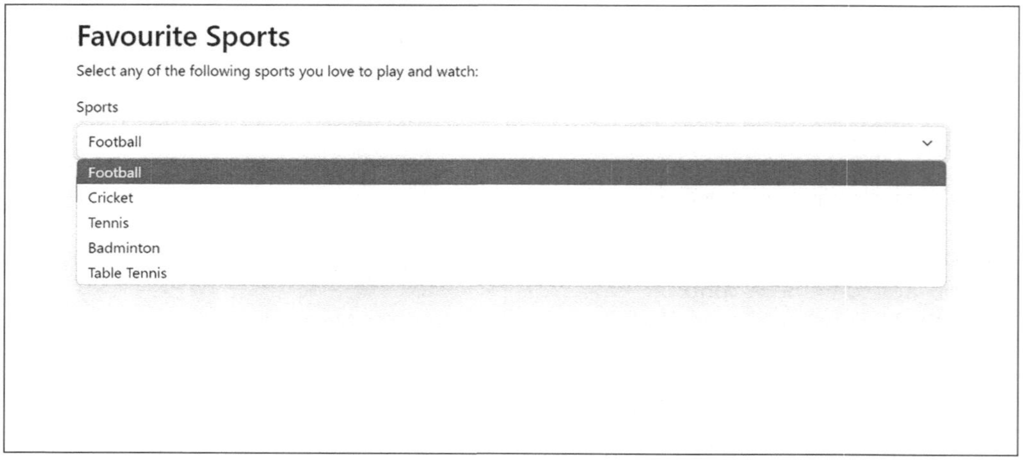

***Figure 7.7**: Selecting from the select menu*

Creating a Multiple-Select Menu

The user can select one or multiple options from the select menu by pressing the *CTRL* or *SHIFT* keys.

Let us see an example of creating a multiple select menu on a web page:

```
<!DOCTYPE html>
<html lang="en">
<head>
  <title>Bootstrap Select Menu</title>
  <meta charset="utf-8">
  <meta name="viewport" content="width=device-width, initial-scale=1">
  <link
href="https://cdn.jsdelivr.net/npm/bootstrap@5.3.3/dist/css/bootstrap.
min.css" rel="stylesheet">
  <script
src="https://cdn.jsdelivr.net/npm/bootstrap@5.3.3/dist/js/bootstrap.
bundle.min.js"></script>
</head>
<body>
<div class="container mt-3">
  <h2>Favourite Sports</h2>
  <p>Select the sports you love to play and watch:</p>
  <form action="next.php">
```

```
    <label for="sel" class="form-label">Sports: Press the CTRL or SHIFT
key to select more than one option:</label>
    <select multiple class="form-select" id="sel" name="selmenu">
      <option>Football</option>
      <option>Cricket</option>
      <option>Tennis</option>
      <option>Badminton</option>
      <option>Table Tennis</option>
    </select>
    <button type="submit" class="btn btn-secondary mt-3">Submit</button>
  </form>
</div>
</body>
</html>
```

After running the code, the web page will look as follows:

Screen Size: 1366 x 633

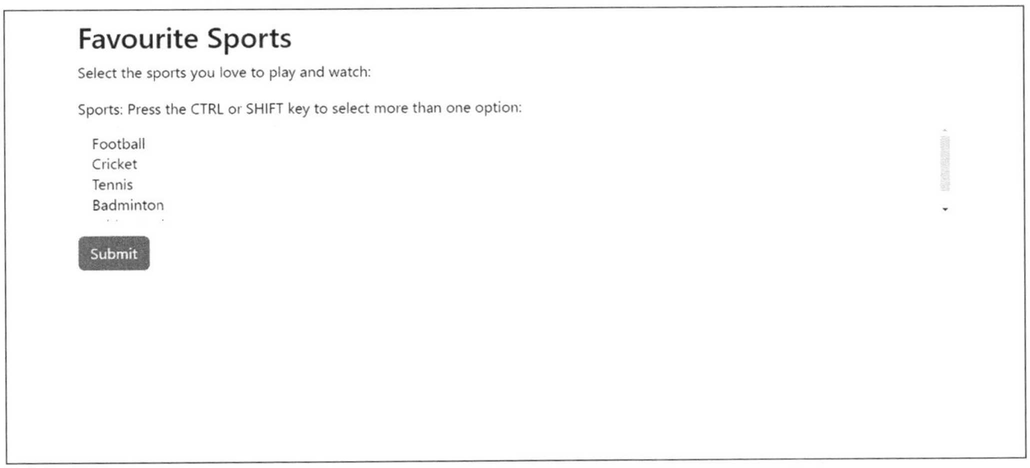

Figure 7.8: *Creating a Select Menu*

Select multiple options now using the CTRL or SHIFT keys:

Screen Size: 1366 x 633

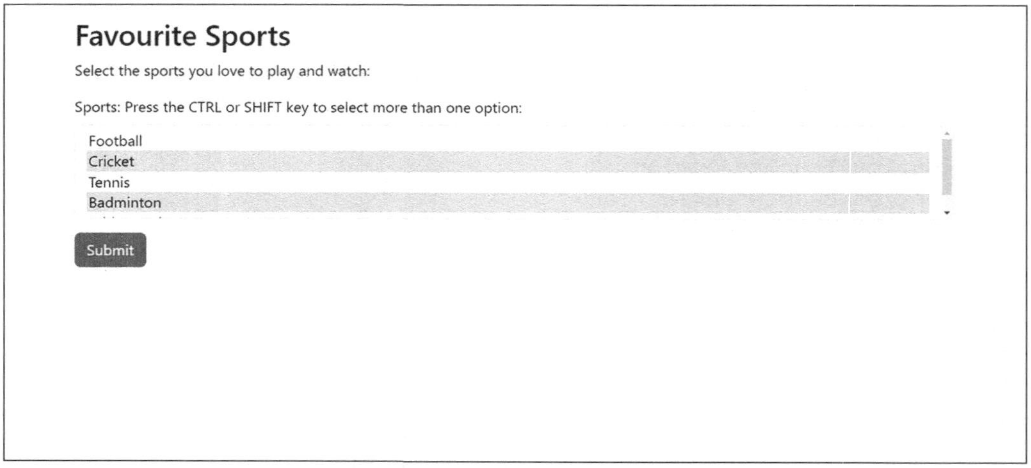

***Figure 7.9**: Selecting multiple options from a select menu*

Resizing the Select Menu

Resize the select menu easily using the following Bootstrap classes:

- **`.form-select-sm`:** A select menu smaller than the default size.
- **`.form-select-lg`:** A select menu bigger than the default size

Let us see an example to resize the form controls on a web page. We have created a form:

```
<!DOCTYPE html>
<html lang="en">
<head>
  <title>Bootstrap Select Menu</title>
  <meta charset="utf-8">
  <meta name="viewport" content="width=device-width, initial-scale=1">
  <link
href="https://cdn.jsdelivr.net/npm/bootstrap@5.3.3/dist/css/bootstrap.
min.css" rel="stylesheet">
  <script
src="https://cdn.jsdelivr.net/npm/bootstrap@5.3.3/dist/js/bootstrap.
bundle.min.js"></script>
</head>
<body>
<div class="container mt-3">
  <h2>Favourites</h2>
  <p>Select what you like:</p>
  <form action="next.php">
```

```
    <label for="sel" class="form-label">Subject (any one)</label>
    <select class="form-select form-select-sm" id="sel" name="selmenu">
      <option>Maths</option>
      <option>Science</option>
      <option>IT</option>
      <option>English</option>
    </select>
    <label for="sel2" class="form-label">Sports: (one or more) Press the
CTRL or SHIFT key to select more than one option:</label>
    <select multiple class="form-select form-select-lg" id="sel2"
name="selmenu2">
      <option>Football</option>
      <option>Cricket</option>
      <option>Tennis</option>
      <option>Badmintion</option>
      <option>Table Tennis</option>
    </select>
    <button type="submit" class="btn btn-secondary mt-3">Submit</button>
  </form>
</div>
</body>
</html>
```

After running the code, the web page will look as follows:

Screen Size: 1366 x 633

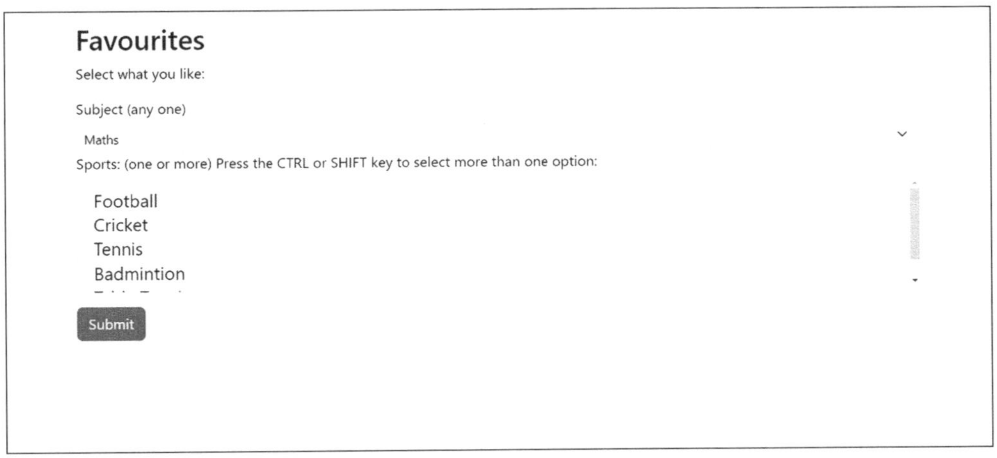

***Figure 7.10**: Select Menu is resized*

Here we saw that the select menu has been resized.

Now, select any one of the subjects:

Screen Size: 1366 x 633

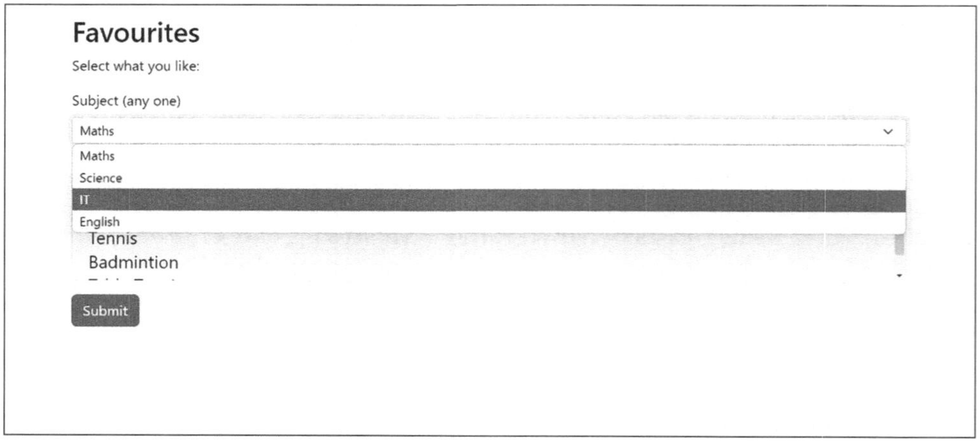

Figure 7.11: *Selecting from the resized select menu*

Select multiple sports:

Screen Size: 1366 x 633

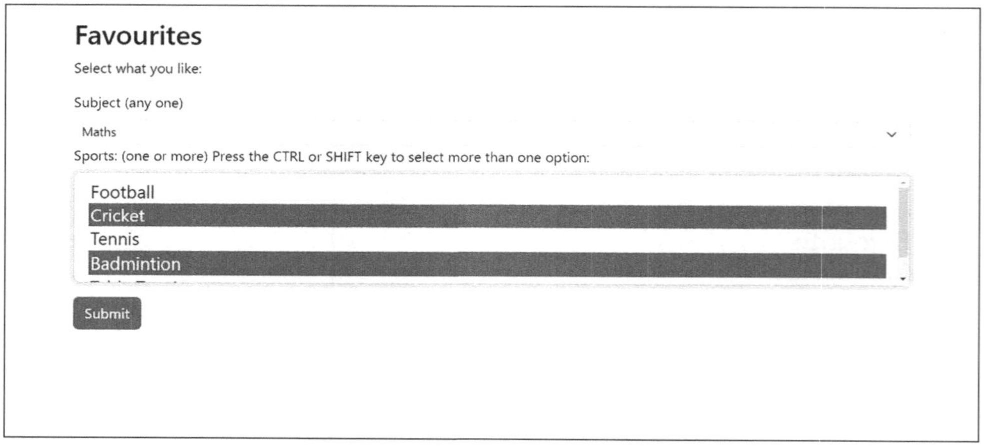

Figure 7.12: *Select multiple options*

Above, we selected multiple sports with CTRL or SHIFT keys.

Checkboxes

A checkbox is an interactive element in graphical user interfaces that allows users to make binary choices–typically, a selection or deselection.

The role of checkboxes is often seen on a web page with a form. Select multiple options with the checkbox; however, you can only select a single option with a radio button.

Creating a Checkbox

Create a container with a **.form-check** class. This helps to set margins and padding. For the labels, use the **.form-check-label**:

```
label class="form-check-label"
```

For the checkbox on a web page, we use the **input type="checkbox"** with the **.form check-input** class:

```
<input class="form-check-input" type="checkbox">
```

To display it checked by default, set the input type with the **checked** attribute:

```
<input class="form-check-input" type="checkbox" checked>
```

Let us see how we can style different types of checkboxes with Bootstrap:

```
<!DOCTYPE html>
<html lang="en">
<head>
  <title>Bootstrap Checkboxes</title>
  <meta charset="utf-8">
  <meta name="viewport" content="width=device-width, initial-scale=1">
  <link
href="https://cdn.jsdelivr.net/npm/bootstrap@5.3.3/dist/css/bootstrap.
min.css" rel="stylesheet">
  <script
src="https://cdn.jsdelivr.net/npm/bootstrap@5.3.3/dist/js/bootstrap.
bundle.min.js"></script>
</head>
<body>
<div class="container mt-3">
  <h2>Pizza Toppings</h2>
  <form action="/next.php">
   <div class="form-check">
     <input class="form-check-input" type="checkbox" value="" id="check1">
     <label class="form-check-label" for="CheckDefault">
     Black Olive
     </label>
   </div>
   <div class="form-check">
     <input class="form-check-input" type="checkbox" value="" id="check2">
     <label class="form-check-label" for="CheckDefault">
    Jalapeno
     </label>
   </div>
   <div class="form-check">
```

```
     <input class="form-check-input" type="checkbox" value="" id=
"checkedID" checked>
     <label class="form-check-label" for="newChecked">
      Red Pepper
   </label>
</div>
    <button type="submit" class="btn btn-secondary mt-3">Submit</button>
  </form>
</div>
</body>
</html>
```

After running the code, the web page will look as follows:

Screen Size: 1366 x 633

***Figure 7.13**: Create a checkbox on a web page*

Select any other checkbox:

Screen Size: 1366 x 633

***Figure 7.14**: Select multiple options in a checkbox*

Creating an Inline Checkbox

With Inline Checkboxes, you can easily let the checkboxes appear side by side on the same horizontal row. For this, use the **`.form-check-inline`** Bootstrap class for the container with the **`.form-check`** class:

```
<div class="form-check form-check-inline">
```

Let us see the example of creating inline checkboxes on a web page:

```
<!DOCTYPE html>
<html lang="en">
<head>
  <title>Bootstrap Checkboxes</title>
  <meta charset="utf-8">
  <meta name="viewport" content="width=device-width, initial-scale=1">
  <link
href="https://cdn.jsdelivr.net/npm/bootstrap@5.3.3/dist/css/bootstrap.
min.css" rel="stylesheet">
  <script
src="https://cdn.jsdelivr.net/npm/bootstrap@5.3.3/dist/js/bootstrap.
bundle.min.js"></script>
</head>
<body>
<div class="container mt-3">
  <h2>Pizza Toppings</h2>
  <form action="/next.php">
   <div class="form-check form-check-inline">
     <input class="form-check-input" type="checkbox" value="" id="check1">
     <label class="form-check-label" for="CheckDefault">
     Black Olive
     </label>
   </div>
   <div class="form-check form-check-inline">
     <input class="form-check-input" type="checkbox' value="" id="check2">
     <label class="form-check-label" for="CheckDefault">
    Jalapeno
     </label>
   </div>
   <div class="form-check form-check-inline">
     <input class="form-check-input" type="checkbox" value="" id="-
checkedID" checked>
     <label class="form-check-label" for="newChecked">
      Red Pepper
   </label>
</div>
    <button type="submit" class="btn btn-secondary mt-3">Submit</button>
```

```
  </form>
</div>
</body>
</html>
```

After running the code, the web page will look as follows:

Screen Size: 1366 x 633

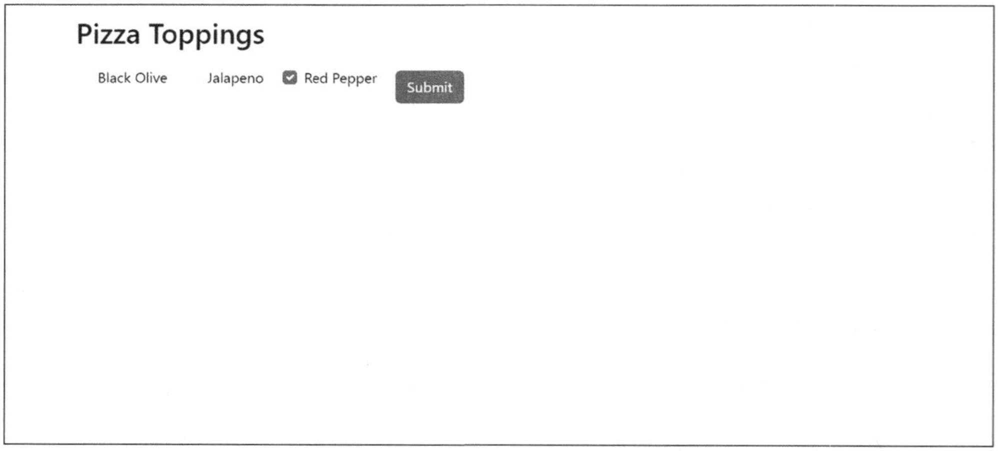

Figure 7.15: *Creating an inline checkbox*

Select any other checkbox:

Screen Size: 1366 x 633

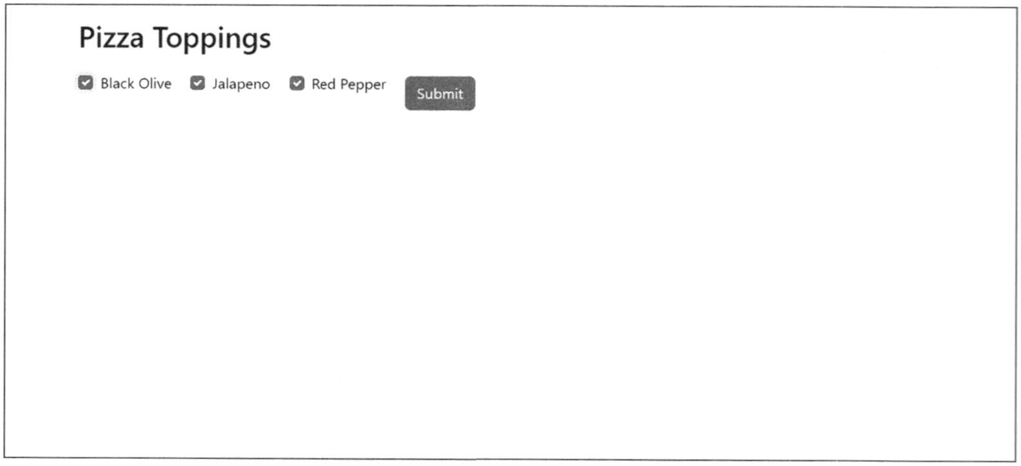

Figure 7.16: *Select multiple options in an inline checkbox*

Creating Reverse Checkboxes

With Bootstrap, create checkboxes easily on the opposite side using the **`.form-check-reverse`** class:

```
<div class="form-check form-check-reverse">
```

Let us see an example of creating reverse checkboxes on a web page:

```
<!DOCTYPE html>
<html lang="en">
<head>
  <title>Bootstrap Checkboxes</title>
  <meta charset="utf-8">
  <meta name="viewport" content="width=device-width, initial-scale=1">
  <link
href="https://cdn.jsdelivr.net/npm/bootstrap@5.3.3/dist/css/bootstrap.
min.css" rel="stylesheet">
  <script
src="https://cdn.jsdelivr.net/npm/bootstrap@5.3.3/dist/js/bootstrap.
bundle.min.js"></script>
</head>
<body>
<div class="container mt-3">
  <h2>Pizza Toppings</h2>
  <form action="/next.php">
   <div class="form-check form-check-reverse">
     <input class="form-check-input" type="checkbox' value="" id="check1">
     <label class="form-check-label" for="CheckDefault">
     Black Olive
     </label>
   </div>
   <div class="form-check form-check-reverse">
     <input class="form-check-input" type="checkbox' value="" id="check2">
     <label class="form-check-label" for="CheckDefault">
    Jalapeno
     </label>
   </div>
   <div class="form-check form-check-reverse">
     <input class="form-check-input" type="checkbox" value="" id="-
checkedID" checked>
     <label class="form-check-label" for="newChecked">
      Red Pepper
   </label>
</div>
    <button type="submit" class="btn btn-secondary mt-3">Submit</button>
  </form>
```

```
</div>
</body>
</html>
```

After running the code, the web page will look as follows:

Screen Size: 1366 x 633

***Figure 7.17**: Creating Reverse Checkboxes*

Select any other checkbox:

Screen Size: 1366 x 633

***Figure 7.18**: Select multiple options from a reverse checkbox*

Radio Buttons

A radio button is an interactive element in graphical user interfaces that allows users to select one option from a predefined set of choices.

The role of radio buttons is often seen on a web page with a form. Select a single option with a radio button, such as Gender: Male or Female.

Creating Radio Buttons

The concept works like a checkbox to create a radio button on a web page. Create a container with a **.form-check** class. This helps to set margins and padding. For the labels, use the **.form-check-label** class:

```
label class="form-check-label"
```

For the radio button on a web page, we use the **input type="radio"** with the **.form-check-input** class:

```
input class="form-check-input" type="radio"
```

To display it selected by default, set the input type with the **checked** attribute:

```
<input class="form-check-input" type="radio" checked>
```

Let us see how we can style different types of radio buttons on a web page with Bootstrap:

```
<!DOCTYPE html>
<html lang="en">
<head>
  <title>Bootstrap Radio Buttons</title>
  <meta charset="utf-8">
  <meta name="viewport" content="width=device-width, initial-scale=1">
  <link
href="https://cdn.jsdelivr.net/npm/bootstrap@5.3.3/dist/css/bootstrap.
min.css" rel="stylesheet">
  <script
src="https://cdn.jsdelivr.net/npm/bootstrap@5.3.3/dist/js/bootstrap.
bundle.min.js"></script>
</head>
<body>
<div class="container mt-3">
  <h2>Educational Qualification</h2>
  <form action="/next.php">
   <div class="form-check">
  <input class="form-check-input" type="radio" name="RadioDefault"
id="DefaultRadio1">
  <label class="form-check-label" for="DefaultRadio1">
    Undergraduate
  </label>
</div>
<div class="form-check">
```

```
  <input class="form-check-input" type="radio" name="RadioDefault"
id="DefaultRadio2" checked>
  <label class="form-check-label" for="DefaultRadio2">
    Graduate
  </label>
</div>
    <button type="submit" class="btn btn-secondary mt-3">Submit</button>
  </form>
</div>
</body>
</html>
```

After running the code, the web page will look as follows:

Screen Size: 1366 x 633

***Figure 7.19**: Creating radio buttons on a web page*

Select any other radio button:

Screen Size: 1366 x 633

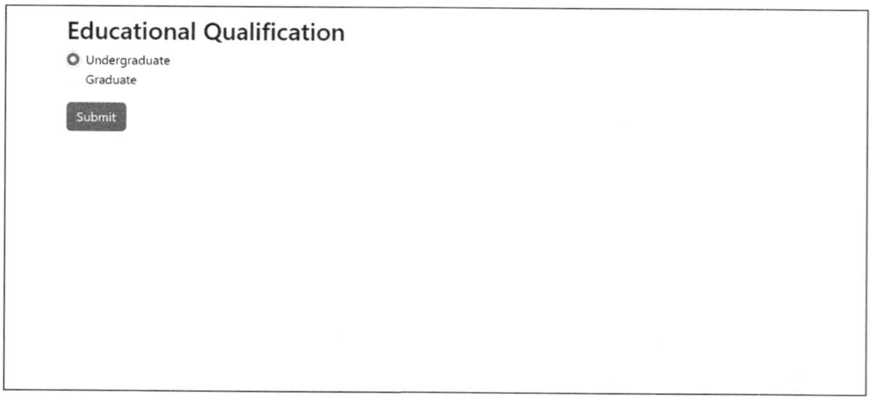

***Figure 7.20**: Selecting another option of a radio button*

Creating Inline Radio Buttons

With Inline Radio Buttons, you can easily let the radio button appear side by side on the same horizontal row. For this, use the **.form-check-inline** Bootstrap class for the container:

```
<div class="form-check form-check-inline">
```

Let us see the example of creating inline radio buttons on a web page:

```
<!DOCTYPE html>
<html lang="en">
<head>
  <title>Bootstrap Radio Buttons</title>
  <meta charset="utf-8">
  <meta name="viewport" content="width=device-width, initial-scale=1">
  <link
href="https://cdn.jsdelivr.net/npm/bootstrap@5.3.3/dist/css/bootstrap.
min.css" rel="stylesheet">
  <script
src="https://cdn.jsdelivr.net/npm/bootstrap@5.3.3/dist/js/bootstrap.
bundle.min.js"></script>
</head>
<body>
<div class="container mt-3">
  <h2>Educational Qualification</h2>
  <form action="/next.php">
   <div class="form-check form-check-inline">
  <input class="form-check-input" type="radio" name="RadioDefault"
id="DefaultRadio1">
  <label class="form-check-label" for="DefaultRadio1">
    Undergraduate
  </label>
</div>
<div class="form-check form-check-inline">
  <input class="form-check-input" type="radio" name="RadioDefault"
id="DefaultRadio2" checked>
  <label class="form-check-label" for="DefaultRadio2">
    Graduate
  </label>
</div>
    <button type="submit" class="btn btn-secondary mt-3">Submit</button>
  </form>
</div>
</body>
</html>
```

After running the code, the web page will look as follows:

Screen Size: 1366 x 633

***Figure 7.21**: Creating inline checkboxes*

Creating Reverse Radio Buttons

With Bootstrap, create radio buttons on the opposite side using the **`.form-check-reverse`** class:

```
<div class="form-check form-check-reverse">
```

Let us see an example of creating reverse radio buttons on a web page:

```
<!DOCTYPE html>
<html lang="en">
<head>
  <title>Bootstrap Radio Buttons</title>
  <meta charset="utf-8">
  <meta name="viewport" content="width=device-width, initial-scale=1">
  <link
href="https://cdn.jsdelivr.net/npm/bootstrap@5.3.3/dist/css/bootstrap.
min.css" rel="stylesheet">
  <script
src="https://cdn.jsdelivr.net/npm/bootstrap@5.3.3/dist/js/bootstrap.
bundle.min.js"></script>
</head>
<body>
<div class="container mt-3">
  <h2>Educational Qualification</h2>
  <form action="/next.php">
   <div class="form-check form-check-reverse">
```

```
  <input class="form-check-input" type="radio" name="RadioDefault"
id="DefaultRadio1">
  <label class="form-check-label" for="DefaultRadio1">
    Undergraduate
  </label>
</div>
<div class="form-check form-check-reverse">
  <input class="form-check-input" type="radio" name="RadioDefault"
id="DefaultRadio2" checked>
  <label class="form-check-label" for="DefaultRadio2">
    Graduate
  </label>
</div>
    <button type="submit" class="btn btn-secondary mt-3">Submit</button>
  </form>
</div>
</body>
</html>
```

After running the code, the web page will look as follows:

Screen Size: 1366 x 633

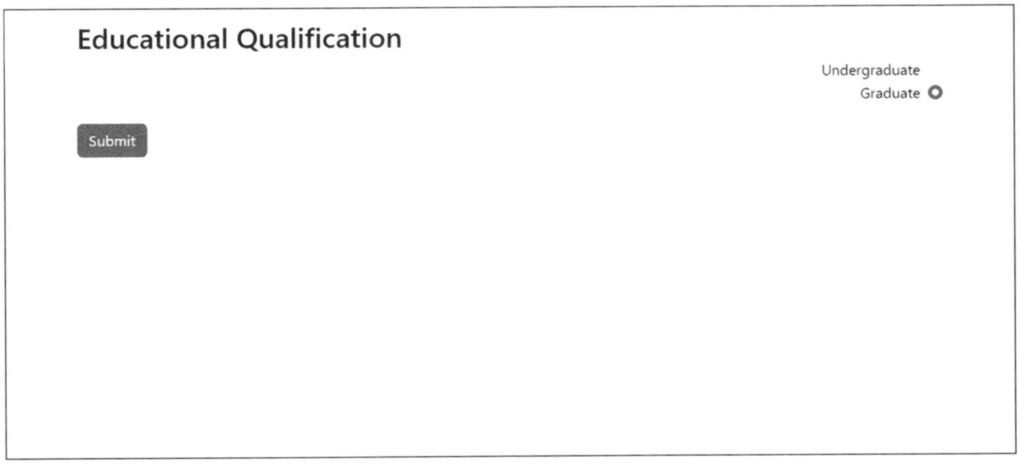

***Figure 7.22**: Creating reverse radio button*

Select any other radio button:

Screen Size: 1366 x 633

***Figure* 7.23**: *Selecting any other option from the reverse radio button*

Input Groups

With Bootstrap, design the input fields by placing an icon, button, and so on, before or after the input fields. This is achieved using the **`.input-group`** class that acts like a container.

Creating Input Group

To create an input group, create a container with the class **`.input-group`**:

```
<div class="input-group">
```

You can also use the **`.input-group-text`** class to set the text before or after the input field:

```
<span class="input-group-text">.com</span>
```

Let us see an example to create an input group on a web page:

```
<!DOCTYPE html>
<html lang="en">
<head>
  <title>Bootstrap Input Group</title>
  <meta charset="utf-8">
  <meta name="viewport" content="width=device-width, initial-scale=1">
  <link
href="https://cdn.jsdelivr.net/npm/bootstrap@5.3.3/dist/css/bootstrap.
min.css" rel="stylesheet">
  <script
src="https://cdn.jsdelivr.net/npm/bootstrap@5.3.3/dist/js/bootstrap.
bundle.min.js"></script>
```

```
</head>
<body>
<div class="container mt-3">
  <h2>Details</h2>
  <form action="/next.php">
    <div class="input-group mb-3">
      <span class="input-group-text">@</span>
      <input type="text" class="form-control" placeholder="Employee
Username" name="empname">
    </div>

    <div class="input-group mb-3">
      <input type="text" class="form-control" placeholder="Employee
Email" name="empemail">
      <span class="input-group-text">@studyopedia.com</span>
    </div>

     <div class="input-group mb-3">
      <input type="text" class="form-control" placeholder="Employee's
Personal Blog" name="empblog">
      <span class="input-group-text">.com</span>
    </div>

    <button type="submit" class="btn btn-secondary">Submit</button>
  </form>
</div>
</body>
</html>
```

After running the code, the web page will look as follows:

Screen Size: 1366 x 633

***Figure 7.24**: Creating input groups*

Resizing Input Groups

Resize the input groups using the following Bootstrap classes:

- **`.input-group-sm`**: An input group smaller than the default size.
- **`.input-group-lg`**: An input group bigger than the default size

Let us see an example of resizing a web page's input groups. Here, we have three input groups with different sizes:

```
<!DOCTYPE html>
<html lang="en">
<head>
  <title>Bootstrap Input Group</title>
  <meta charset="utf-8">
  <meta name="viewport" content="width=device-width, initial-scale=1">
  <link
href="https://cdn.jsdelivr.net/npm/bootstrap@5.3.3/dist/css/bootstrap.
min.css" rel="stylesheet">
  <script
src="https://cdn.jsdelivr.net/npm/bootstrap@5.3.3/dist/js/bootstrap.
bundle.min.js"></script>
</head>
<body>
<div class="container mt-3">
  <h2>Details</h2>
  <form action="/next.php">
    <div class="input-group mb-3">
      <span class="input-group-text">@</span>
      <input type="text" class="form-control" placeholder="Employee
Username" name="empname">
    </div>
    <div class="input-group mb-3  input-group-sm">
      <input type="text" class="form-control" placeholder="Employee
Email" name="empemail">
      <span class="input-group-text">@studyopedia.com</span>
    </div>
     <div class="input-group mb-3  input-group-lg">
      <input type="text" class="form-control" placeholder="Employee's
Personal Blog" name="empblog">
      <span class="input-group-text">.com</span>
    </div>
    <button type="submit" class="btn btn-secondary">Submit</button>
  </form>
</div>
</body>
</html>
```

After running the code, the web page will look as follows:

Screen Size: 1366 x 633

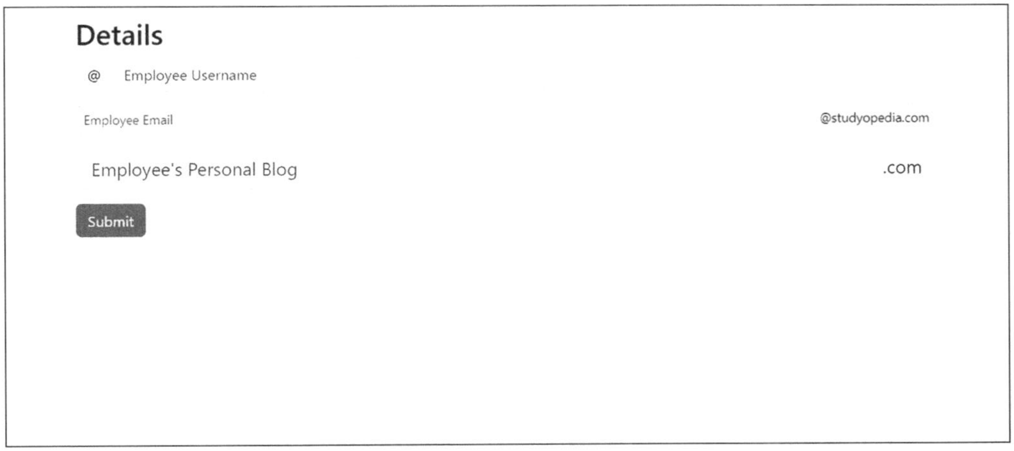

***Figure 7.25**: Input Groups of different sizes*

Floating Labels

The labels we saw appeared on the input element's top or left side. With Bootstrap, we can also animate the input fields by clicking them. This is achieved using the Floating Labels concept, that is, the **`.form-floating`** class in Bootstrap.

Floating Labels for Input Field

To set the floating labels for input type text, password, and so on, place the input fields in a container with the class **`.form-floating`**:

```
<div class="form-floating">
```

Also, the label is placed after the input field. Let us see an example to set the floating labels on a web page:

```
<!DOCTYPE html>
<html lang="en">
<head>
  <title>Bootstrap Forms</title>
  <meta charset="utf-8">
  <meta name="viewport" content="width=device-width, initial-scale=1">
  <link
href="https://cdn.jsdelivr.net/npm/bootstrap@5.3.3/dist/css/bootstrap.
min.css" rel="stylesheet">
```

```
  <script
src="https://cdn.jsdelivr.net/npm/bootstrap@5.3.3/dist/js/bootstrap.
bundle.min.js"></script>
</head>
<body>
<div class="container">
  <h2>Login</h2>
  <form action="/next.php">
    <div class="form-floating">
     <input type="email" class="form-control" id="email" placeholder
="Enter the email" name="emailid">
 <label class="form-label">Email:</label>
    </div>
    <div>
     <div class="form-floating">
          <input type="password" class="form-control" id="pwd"
placeholder="Enter the password" name="passwd">
 <label for="pwd" class="form-label">Password:</label>
     </div>
    </div>
    <button type="submit" class="btn btn-secondary">Submit</button>
  </form>
</div>
</body>
</html>
```

After running the code, the web page will look as follows:

Screen Size: 1366 x 633

Figure 7.26: *From input fields*

On clicking the text box, the input is focused. The label is transitioned to the top of the input.

Screen Size: 1366 x 633

***Figure 7.27**: The label transitioned to the top of the input.*

Floating Label for textarea

To set the floating labels for the textarea, place the input fields in a container with the class **`.form-floating`**:

```
<div class="form-floating">
```

Also, the label is placed after the input field. Let us see an example of setting the floating labels for the textarea on a web page:

```
<!DOCTYPE html>
<html lang="en">
<head>
  <title>Bootstrap Forms</title>
  <meta charset="utf-8">
  <meta name="viewport" content="width=device-width, initial-scale=1">
  <link
href="https://cdn.jsdelivr.net/npm/bootstrap@5.3.3/dist/css/bootstrap.
min.css" rel="stylesheet">
  <script
src="https://cdn.jsdelivr.net/npm/bootstrap@5.3.3/dist/js/bootstrap.
bundle.min.js"></script>
</head>
<body>
<div class="container">
  <h2>Login</h2>
  <form action="/next.php">
```

```
     <div class="form-floating mb-3 mt-3">
      <input type="email" class="form-control" id="email" placeholder
="Enter the email" name="emailid">
      <label class="form-label">Email:</label>
    </div>
    <div class="form-floating mb-3 mt-3">
      <input type="password" class="form-control" id="pwd" placeholder
="Enter the password" name="passwd">
      <label for="pwd" class="form-label">Password:</label>
    </div>
     <div class="form-floating mb-3 mt-3">
      <textarea class="form-control" rows="4" id="comment" placeholder
="Describe our website experience here..." name="text"></textarea>
      <label for="comment">Describe:</label>
    </div>
    <button type="submit" class="btn btn-secondary">Submit</button>
  </form>
</div>
</body>
</html>
```

After running the code, the web page will look as follows:

Screen Size: 1366 x 633

***Figure 7.28**: Input field including text area*

On clicking the text box, the input is focused. The label is transitioned to the top of the input.

Screen Size: 1366 x 633

***Figure 7.29**: The label transitioned to the top of the input.*

Form Validation

This helps provide validations easily for your users on a web page with a form. With Bootstrap, the validations on a form can be easily achieved.

Use the **was-validated** class in the **<form>** if you want to provide the validation feedback before submitting the form. It should be added if you want to display the validation styles after a form is tried to be submitted.

```
<form action="/next.php" class="was-validated">
```

Use the **needs-validation** in the **<form>** if you want to provide the validation feedback after submitting the form. It prevents form submission if there's invalid fields:

```
<form action="/next.php" class="needs-validation">
```

The div with a class **.valid-feedback** is used to set the validation success message:

```
<div class="valid-feedback">
Successfully added.
</div>
```

The div with a class **.invalid-feedback** is used to set the validation error message:

```
<div class="valid-feedback">
Please provide a valid name.
</div>
```

In the following example, the validation feedback is visible before submitting the form because we have used the **was-validated** class:

```
<!DOCTYPE html>
<html lang="en">
<head>
```

```
  <title>Bootstrap Form Validation</title>
  <meta charset="utf-8">
  <meta name="viewport" content="width=device-width, initial-scale=1">
  <link
href="https://cdn.jsdelivr.net/npm/bootstrap@5.3.3/dist/css/bootstrap.
min.css" rel="stylesheet">
  <script
src="https://cdn.jsdelivr.net/npm/bootstrap@5.3.3/dist/js/bootstrap.
bundle.min.js"></script>
</head>
<body>
<div class="container mt-3">
  <h3>Login</h3>
  <form action="next.php" class="was-validated">
    <div class="mb-3 mt-3">
      <label for="name" class="form-label">Username:</label>
      <input type="text" class="form-control" id="name" placeholder
="Enter the username" name="uname" required>
      <div class="valid-feedback">Successfully added.</div>
      <div class="invalid-feedback">Please enter the username.</div>
    </div>
    <div class="mb-3">
      <label for="pwd" class="form-label">Password:</label>
      <input type="password" class="form-control" id="pwd" placeholder
="Enter the password" name="passwd" required>
      <div class="valid-feedback">Successfully added.</div>
      <div class="invalid-feedback">Please enter the correct password.
</div>
    </div>
  <button type="submit" class="btn btn-secondary">Submit</button>
  </form>
</div>
</body>
</html>
```

After running the code, the web page will look as follows:

Screen Size: 1366 x 633

***Figure 7.30**: Validating a form*

Only add the username and leave the password box empty. The validation feedback can be seen accordingly:

Screen Size: 1366 x 633

***Figure 7.31**: The messages appear when a field is left empty*

After adding both fields, the valid feedback becomes visible:

Screen Size: 1366 x 633

Figure 7.32: *The validation feedback is visible when both the fields are filled*

Conclusion

We are now familiar with creating a form on a web page. Beginning with adding form input controls, such as input type text and password, we also saw how to create radio boxes, checkboxes, and so on. We also saw how to add validations, select, range, input groups, and floating labels to a form.

In the next chapter, we will learn about helper classes with Bootstrap.

Points to Remember

- The **`<form>`** element is used to create a form.
- Form elements appear side by side in inline forms.
- Style a select menu using the **`.form-select`** class.
- To set and style checkboxes or/and radio boxes on a web page, create a container with a **`.form-check`** class and set it within.
- Create checkboxes and radio boxes on the opposite side using the **`.form-check-reverse`** class.
- Input groups place an icon, button, or text before or after the input fields.
- Use the **`.was-validated`** class in the **`<form>`** to provide the validation feedback before submitting the form.
- Use the **`.needs-validation`** class in the **`<form>`** to provide the validation feedback after submitting the form.

Multiple Choice Questions

1. The ______ attribute is used to reference the form data after submission.

    a. `placeholder`

    b. `name`

    c. `id`

    d. `class`

2. Which class is used in Bootstrap to easily position the label inside an input field and then animate/ transition the label when the input field is focused?

    a. `form-animate`

    b. `form-animation`

    c. `form-float`

    d. `form-floating`

3. Which class is used in Bootstrap to create inline checkboxes and radioboxes?

    a. `check-inline`

    b. `form-inline`

    c. `form-check-inline`

    d. `form-inline-check`

4. Use the _______ class in the **`<form>`** to provide the validation feedback before submitting the form.

    a. `need-validation`

    b. `was-validated`

Answer

1. b.
2. d.
3. c.
4. b.

Questions

- How the correct padding for the `<label>` elements in a form set?
- What are the steps to let the form elements appear side by side?
- What is an inline checkbox?
- How to create a reverse checkbox?
- What is an input group?
- How are floating labels for textarea created?
- How are validations in a form added?

Key Terms

- **Inline Forms:** The form elements appear side by side with inline forms
- **Input Groups:** Design the input fields by placing an icon, button, or text before or after the input fields
- **Floating Labels:** Easily position the label inside an input field and then animate/ transition the label when the input field is focused
- **Reverse Checkbox:** Creates a checkbox on the opposite side
- **Reverse Radiobox:** Creates radio buttons on the opposite side

CHAPTER 8
Bootstrap Helpers

Introduction

This chapter covers Helper classes in Bootstrap, whether it is clearfix, aspect ratio, vertical rule, focus ring, and so on. These classes ease the work of web page layout and styling for web developers. Bootstrap includes dozens of helper classes. The visually hidden class assists screen readers and is a crucial class to understand and implement on a web page.

The position of an element can be set at the top or bottom. With that, like <hr>, you can also set a vertical divider on a web page.

Structure

In this chapter, we will discuss the following topics:

- Clearfix
- Colored links
- Aspect Ratio
- Visually hidden
- Text Truncation
- Set the Position
- Vertical Rule
- Stretched link
- Focus Ring

Clearfix

Floats are a layout mechanism that is used to position elements to the left or right of their container, allowing text and inline elements to wrap around them.

However, floats can cause some layout issues, such as collapsing parent containers or overflowing content. This is where clearfix comes in to "clear" the floats, ensuring that the parent element properly contains the floated elements. Just set the **.clearfix** class to the parent element:

```
<div class="clearfix">
```

In the following example, we will float a button to the left using the **.float-start** and to the right using the **.float-end** classes respectively.

Let us see an example to implement clearfix. We have added color to the div and button to make the things easier:

```
<!DOCTYPE html>
<html lang="en">
<head>
  <title>Bootstrap Clearfix</title>
  <meta charset="utf-8">
  <meta name="viewport" content="width=device-width, initial-scale=1">
  <link
href="https://cdn.jsdelivr.net/npm/bootstrap@5.3.3/dist/css/bootstrap.
min.css" rel="stylesheet">
  <script
src="https://cdn.jsdelivr.net/npm/bootstrap@5.3.3/dist/js/bootstrap.
bundle.min.js"></script>
</head>
<body>
<div class="container mt-3">
  <h2>Demo Heading</h2>
  <div class="bg-danger  clearfix">
   <button type="button" class="btn btn-primary float-start">Left
Button</button>
   <button type="button" class="btn btn-primary float-end">Right Button</
button>
  </div>
</div>
</body>
</html>
```

After running the code, the web page will look as follows:

Screen Size: 1366 x 633

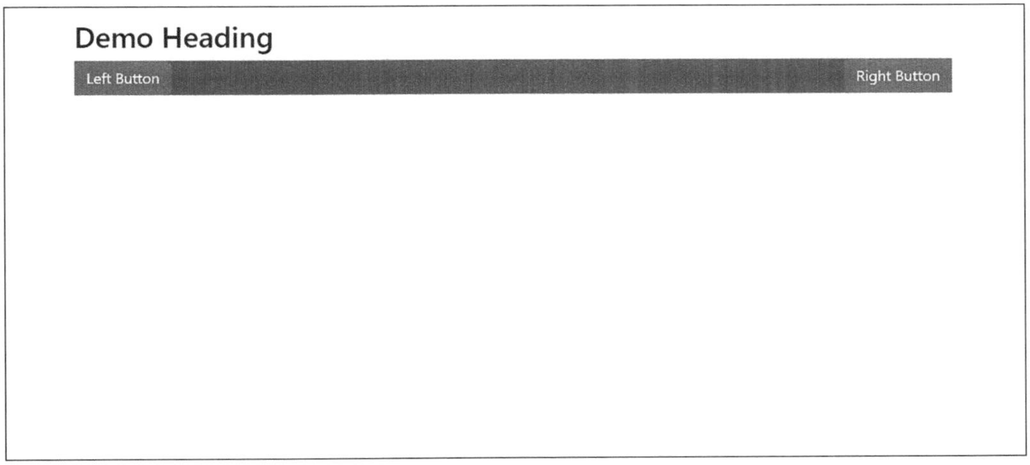

Figure 8.1: *Clearing the floats*

Colored Links

The **`.link-*`** classes are used in Bootstrap to color links. For example, **`.link-primary`**, **`.link-secondary`**, and so on. Here are some:

```
<a href="#" class="link-primary">Primary link</a>
<a href="#" class="link-secondary">Secondary link</a>
<a href="#" class="link-success">Success link</a>
```

Let us see an example of color links on a web page:

```
<!DOCTYPE html>
<html lang="en">
<head>
  <title>Bootstrap Link Color</title>
  <meta charset="utf-8">
  <meta name="viewport" content="width=device-width, initial-scale=1">
  <link
href="https://cdn.jsdelivr.net/npm/bootstrap@5.3.3/dist/css/bootstrap.
min.css" rel="stylesheet">
  <script
src="https://cdn.jsdelivr.net/npm/bootstrap@5.3.3/dist/js/bootstrap.
bundle.min.js"></script>
</head>
<body>
<div class="container mt-3">
  <h2>Link Color</h2>
  <p>Here, the different color for links is demonstrated:<p>
  <div>
   <a href="#" class="link-primary">The primary link</a>
```

```
    <a href="#" class="link-secondary">The secondary link</a>
    <a href="#" class="link-dark">The dark link</a>
    <a href="#" class="link-success">The success link</a>
    <a href="#" class="link-danger">The danger link</a>
    <a href="#" class="link-warning">The warning link</a>
    <a href="#" class="link-info">The info link</a>
    <a href="#" class="link-light">The light link</a>
  </div>
</div>
</body>
</html>
```

After running the code, the web page will look as follows:

Screen Size: 1366 x 633

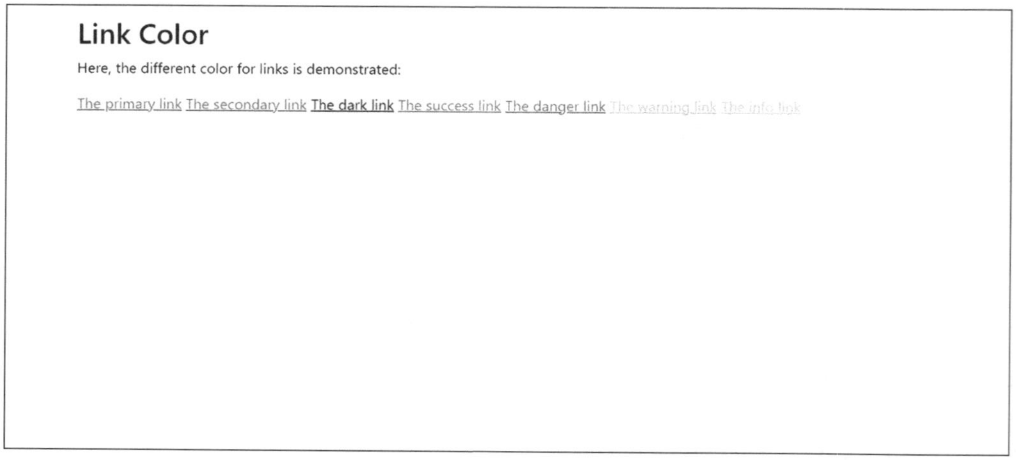

Figure 8.2: *Different colors for links*

Aspect Ratio

Manage the aspect ratio of external content, such as iframe, video, and so on, easily with Bootstrap. Use the **`.ratio`** class with the below ratio classes for aspect ratio. These are aspect ratio classes:

- **`ratio-1x1`**
- **`ratio-4x3`**
- **`ratio-16x9`**
- **`ratio-21x9`**

We will use the **`.ratio`** class and an aspect ratio class to wrap an iframe or a video. The following is set with an aspect ratio of **`4:3`** to wrap an iframe:

```
<div class="ratio ratio-4x3">
    <iframe src="https://www.youtube.com/embed/sgpDAiF-18o" title
="MySQL"></iframe>
  </div>
```

Let us see an example of managing different aspect ratios on a web page:

```
<!DOCTYPE html>
<html lang="en">
<head>
  <title>Bootstrap Aspect Ratio</title>
  <meta charset="utf-8">
  <meta name="viewport" content="width=device-width, initial-scale=1">
  <link
href="https://cdn.jsdelivr.net/npm/bootstrap@5.3.3/dist/css/bootstrap.
min.css" rel="stylesheet">
  <script
src="https://cdn.jsdelivr.net/npm/bootstrap@5.3.3/dist/js/bootstrap.
bundle.min.js"></script>
</head>
<body>
<div class="container mt-3">
  <h2>MySQL Course</h2>
  <p>The video in different aspect ratios scaling to the parent element.</
p>

  <h2>1:1</h2>
  <div class="ratio ratio-1x1">
    <iframe src="https://www.youtube.com/embed/sgpDAiF-18o" title
="MySQL"></iframe>
  </div>
  <br>

  <h2>4:3</h2>
  <div class="ratio ratio-4x3">
    <iframe src="https://www.youtube.com/embed/sgpDAiF-18o" title
="MySQL"></iframe>
  </div>
  <br>

  <h2>16:9</h2>
  <div class="ratio ratio-16x9">
    <iframe src="https://www.youtube.com/embed/sgpDAiF-18o" title
="MySQL"></iframe>
  </div>
```

```
  <br>

  <h2>21:9</h2>
  <div class="ratio ratio-21x9">
    <iframe src="https://www.youtube.com/embed/sgpDAiF-18o" title
="MySQL"></iframe>
  </div>
</div>
</body>
</html>
```

After running the code, the web page will look as follows:

Screen Size: 1366 x 633

Figure 8.3: *Managing the aspect ratio of iframes*

Visually Hidden

For screen readers, Bootstrap came up with the **.visually-hidden** class. Use this class to visually hide an element on all screen sizes, except assistive technologies such as screen readers. It is also visible for web crawlers and useful for search engine optimization.

Let us see an example. Here, we are showing how to display text only for the screen readers on a web page:

```
<!DOCTYPE html>
<html lang="en">
<head>
  <title>Bootstrap Visually Hidden</title>
  <meta charset="utf-8">
  <meta name="viewport" content="width=device-width, initial-scale=1">
  <link
href="https://cdn.jsdelivr.net/npm/bootstrap@5.3.3/dist/css/bootstrap.
min.css" rel="stylesheet">
  <script
src="https://cdn.jsdelivr.net/npm/bootstrap@5.3.3/dist/js/bootstrap.
bundle.min.js"></script>
</head>
<body>
<div class="container mt-3">
  <h2>Demo Text</h2>
  <span class="visually-hidden">This text will be hidden on all screens
except screen readers.</span>
</div>
</body>
</html>
```

After running the code, the web page will look as follows:

Screen Size: 1366 x 633

Figure 8.4: *Displaying text for screen readers*

Text Truncation

Ellipses can be set for long strings of text with Bootstrap. Use the **`.text-truncate`** class to truncate long strings of text with ellipses. Let us see how to truncate text:

- Block-Level
- Inline-Level

Let us see an example of truncating long strings of text with block-level text truncation on a web page:

```
<!DOCTYPE html>
<html lang="en">
<head>
  <title>Bootstrap Text Truncate</title>
  <meta charset="utf-8">
  <meta name="viewport" content="width=device-width, initial-scale=1">
  <link
href="https://cdn.jsdelivr.net/npm/bootstrap@5.3.3/dist/css/bootstrap.
min.css" rel="stylesheet">
  <script
src="https://cdn.jsdelivr.net/npm/bootstrap@5.3.3/dist/js/bootstrap.
bundle.min.js"></script>
</head>
<body>
<div class="container mt-3">
 <div class="row">
   <div class="col-2 text-truncate">
     Neque porro quisquam est qui dolorem
   </div>
```

```
 </div>
</div>
</body>
</html>
```

After running the code, the web page will look as follows:

Screen Size: 1366 x 633

Figure 8.5: *Block-level text truncation*

Let us see an example of inline-level text truncation. Here, we have used the **d-inline-block** class to make an element display inline-block because the truncate helper class only works for inline-block and block elements, and not inline elements:

```
<!DOCTYPE html>
<html lang="en">
<head>
  <title>Bootstrap Text Truncate</title>
  <meta charset="utf-8">
  <meta name="viewport" content="width=device-width, initial-scale=1">
  <link
href="https://cdn.jsdelivr.net/npm/bootstrap@5.3.3/dist/css/bootstrap.
min.css" rel="stylesheet">
  <script
src="https://cdn.jsdelivr.net/npm/bootstrap@5.3.3/dist/js/bootstrap.
bundle.min.js"></script>
</head>
<body>
<div class="container mt-3">
  <span class="d-inline-block text-truncate" style="max-width: 150px;">
  Neque porro quisquam est qui dolorem
  </span>
```

```
</div>
</body>
</html>
```

After running the code, the web page will look as follows:

Screen Size: 1366 x 633

Figure 8.6: *Inline-level text truncation*

Set the Position

To set the position of an element on a web page, Bootstrap came up with the following classes:

- **`.fixed-top`:** Sets the position at the top
- **`.fixed-bottom`:** Sets the position at the bottom
- **`.sticky-top`:** Sets the element to remain at the top, that is, a sticky element
- **`.sticky-bottom`:** Sets the element to remain at the bottom, that is, a sticky element

Top Position

To set the element's position to the top, use the **`.fixed-top`** Bootstrap class. Even when the page is scrolled, the element set with **`.fixed-top`** remains at the top.

Let us see an example to set an element's position to the top:

```
<!DOCTYPE html>
<html lang="en">
<head>
  <title>Bootstrap Position</title>
```

```
  <meta charset="utf-8">
  <meta name="viewport" content="width=device-width, initial-scale=1">
  <link
href="https://cdn.jsdelivr.net/npm/bootstrap@5.3.3/dist/css/bootstrap.
min.css" rel="stylesheet">
  <script
src="https://cdn.jsdelivr.net/npm/bootstrap@5.3.3/dist/js/bootstrap.
bundle.min.js"></script>
</head>
<body style="height:1400px">
  <nav class="navbar navbar-expand-lg text-bg-warring navbar-dark
fixed-top">
    <div class="container-fluid">
      <a class="navbar-brand" href="#">Get 50% Off: Coupon Code LEARN
50</a>
    </div>
  </nav>
  <div class="container-fluid" style="margin-top:100px">
    <h4>Demo Text</h4>
    <p>The top bar remains fixed.</p>
  </div>
</body>
</html>
```

After running the code, the web page will look as follows:

Screen Size: 1366 x 633

Figure 8.7: *Element is positioned at the top*

Scroll the web page and you can see the element's position on the top:

Screen Size: 1366 x 633

Figure 8.8: *Element is still positioned at the top even when the web page is scrolled*

Bottom Position

To set the element's position to the bottom, use the **`.fixed-bottom`** Bootstrap class. Even when the page is scrolled, the element set with **`.fixed-bottom`** remains at the bottom.

Let us see an example to set an element's position to the bottom:

```
<!DOCTYPE html>
<html lang="en">
<head>
  <title>Bootstrap Position</title>
  <meta charset="utf-8">
  <meta name="viewport" content="width=device-width, initial-scale=1">
  <link
href="https://cdn.jsdelivr.net/npm/bootstrap@5.3.3/dist/css/bootstrap.
min.css" rel="stylesheet">
  <script
src="https://cdn.jsdelivr.net/npm/bootstrap@5.3.3/dist/js/bootstrap.
bundle.min.js"></script>
</head>
<body style="height:1400px">
  <nav class="navbar navbar-expand-lg text-bg-warning navbar-dark
fixed-bottom">
    <div class="container-fluid">
      <a class="navbar-brand" href="#">All Rights Reserved &#169;
Studyopedia</a>
    </div>
  </nav>
  <div class="container-fluid" style="margin-top:100px">
    <h4>Demo Text</h4>
```

```
    <p>The bottom bar remains fixed.</p>
  </div>
</body>
</html>
```

After running the code, the web page will look as follows:

Screen Size: 1366 x 633

Figure 8.9: *Element is positioned at the bottom*

Scroll the web page and you can see the element's position at the bottom:

Screen Size: 1366 x 633

Figure 8.10: *Element is still positioned at the bottom even when the web page is scrolled*

Top Position for a Sticky Element

To position a sticky element at the top of the screen, use the **.sticky-top** Bootstrap class. When the page is scrolled, the element set with **.sticky-top** moves to the top.

Let us see an example to set a sticky element's position to the top:

```
<!DOCTYPE html>
<html lang="en">
<head>
  <title>Bootstrap Position</title>
  <meta charset="utf-8">
  <meta name="viewport" content="width=device-width, initial-scale=1">
  <link
href="https://cdn.jsdelivr.net/npm/bootstrap@5.3.3/dist/css/bootstrap.
min.css" rel="stylesheet">
  <script
src="https://cdn.jsdelivr.net/npm/bootstrap@5.3.3/dist/js/bootstrap.
bundle.min.js"></script>
</head>
<body style="height:1500px">
  <div class="container-fluid mt-3">
    <h3>Demo Heading</h3>
    <p>Scroll to the bottom of the page</p>
  </div>
  <nav class="navbar navbar-expand-lg bg-dark navbar-dark sticky-top">
    <div class="container-fluid">
      <a class="navbar-brand" href="#">Sticky Nav</a>
    </div>
  </nav>
  <div class="container-fluid">
    <p>Demo text</p>
  </div>
</body>
</html>
```

After running the code, the web page will look as follows:

Screen Size: 1366 x 633

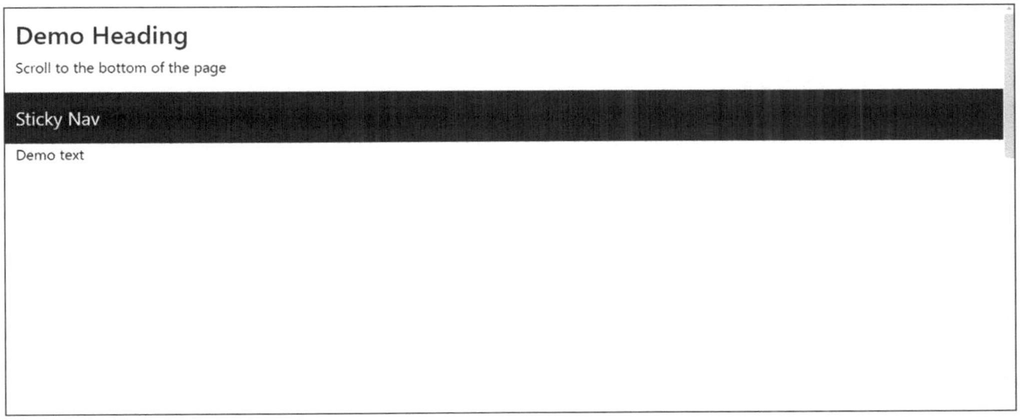

Figure 8.11: *The element is positioned at the top*

Scroll the web page and you can see the element's position sticks to the top:

Screen Size: 1366 x 633

Figure 8.12: *The element's position sticks to the top*

Bottom Position for a Sticky Element

To position a sticky element at the bottom of the screen, use the **`.sticky-bottom`** Bootstrap class. When the page is scrolled, the element set with **`.sticky-bottom`** moves to the bottom.

Let us see an example to set a sticky element's position to the bottom:

```
<!DOCTYPE html>
<html lang="en">
<head>
  <title>Bootstrap Position</title>
  <meta charset="utf-8">
```

```
  <meta name="viewport" content="width=device-width, initial-scale=1">
  <link
href="https://cdn.jsdelivr.net/npm/bootstrap@5.3.3/dist/css/bootstrap.
min.css" rel="stylesheet">
  <script
src="https://cdn.jsdelivr.net/npm/bootstrap@5.3.3/dist/js/bootstrap.
bundle.min.js"></script>
</head>
<body style="height:1400px" class="d-flex flex-column">
  <nav class="navbar navbar-expand-lg bg-dark navbar-dark">
    <div class="container-fluid">
      <a class="navbar-brand" href="#">Nav</a>
    </div>
  </nav>
  <div class="container-fluid flex-grow-1">
    <h3>Demo Text</h3>
    <p>Scroll the page</p>
  </div>
  <footer class="footer text-bg-warning py-3 sticky-bottom">
    <div class="container">
      <span class="display-8 text-dark">Sticky bottom</span>
    </div>
  </footer>
</body>
</html>
```

After running the code, the web page will look as follows:

Screen Size: 1366 x 633

Figure 8.13: *The element is positioned*

Scroll the web page and you can see the element's position sticks to the bottom:

Screen Size: 1366 x 633

Figure 8.14: *The element's position sticks to the bottom*

Vertical Rule

To set vertical dividers on a web page like the **<hr>**, use the vertical rule in Bootstrap. The Bootstrap class **.vr** is used for this purpose. They are **1px** wide with **min-height** of **1em**.

Let us see an example of setting a vertical rule and creating a vertical divider:

```
<!DOCTYPE html>
<html lang="en">
<head>
  <title>Bootstrap Vertical Rule</title>
  <meta charset="utf-8">
  <meta name="viewport" content="width=device-width, initial-scale=1">
  <link
href="https://cdn.jsdelivr.net/npm/bootstrap@5.3.3/dist/css/bootstrap.
min.css" rel="stylesheet">
  <script
src="https://cdn.jsdelivr.net/npm/bootstrap@5.3.3/dist/js/bootstrap.
bundle.min.js"></script>
</head>
<body>
<h4>Entrance</h4>
<div class="container">
  <div class="row">
    <div class="col-md-3 text-bg-primary">
      <p>Left (Before the Vertical rule)</p>
    </div>
```

```
    <div class="col-md-1">
      <hr class="vr">
    </div>
    <div class="col-md-3 text-bg-primary">
      <p>Right (After the vertical rule)</p>
    </div>
  </div>
</div>
</body>
</html>
```

After running the code, the web page will look as follows:

Screen Size: 1366 x 633

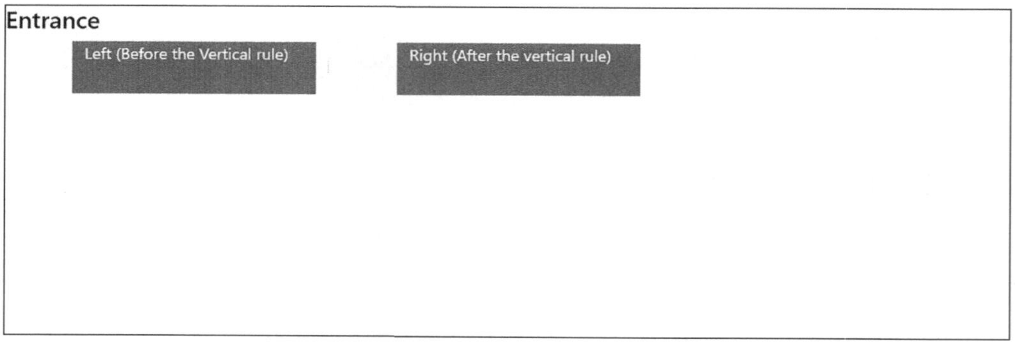

Figure 8.15: *Vertical dividers on a web page*

Resize the web browser and decrease the size:

Screen size: 760x633

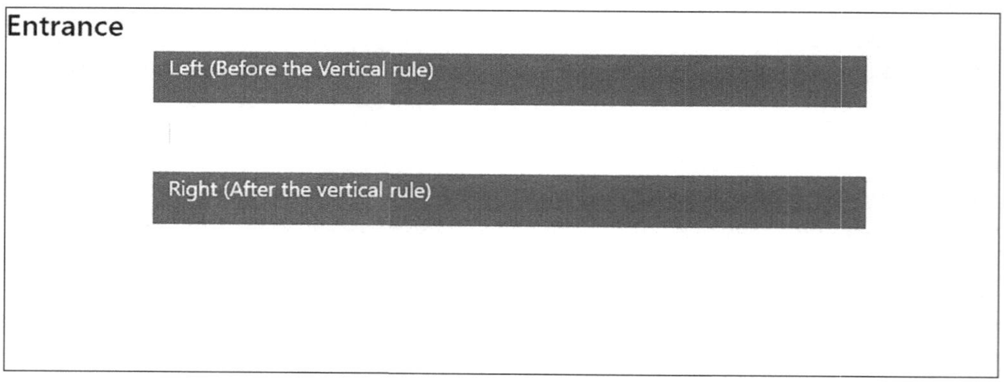

Figure 8.16: *The web browser is resized*

Vertical Rule in Stacks

Let us see another example and use the vertical rule in stacks. Here we have used the **.hstack** class:

```
<!DOCTYPE html>
<html lang="en">
<head>
  <title>Bootstrap Vertical Rule</title>
  <meta charset="utf-8">
  <meta name="viewport" content="width=device-width, initial-scale=1">
  <link
href="https://cdn.jsdelivr.net/npm/bootstrap@5.3.3/dist/css/bootstrap.
min.css" rel="stylesheet">
  <script
src="https://cdn.jsdelivr.net/npm/bootstrap@5.3.3/dist/js/bootstrap.
bundle.min.js"></script>
</head>
<body>
<h2>Products</h2>
<div class="hstack gap-2">
  <div class="p-2 text-bg-primary">Furniture</div>
  <div class="vr"></div>
  <div class="p-2 text-bg-secondary">Accessories</div>
  <div class="vr"></div>
  <div class="p-2 text-bg-info">Electronics</div>
  <div class="vr"></div>
  <div class="p-2 text-bg-danger">Equipments</div>
  <div class="vr"></div>
  <div class="p-2 text-bg-warning">Books</div>
</div>
</body>
</html>
```

After running the code, the web page will look as follows:

Screen Size: 1366 x 633

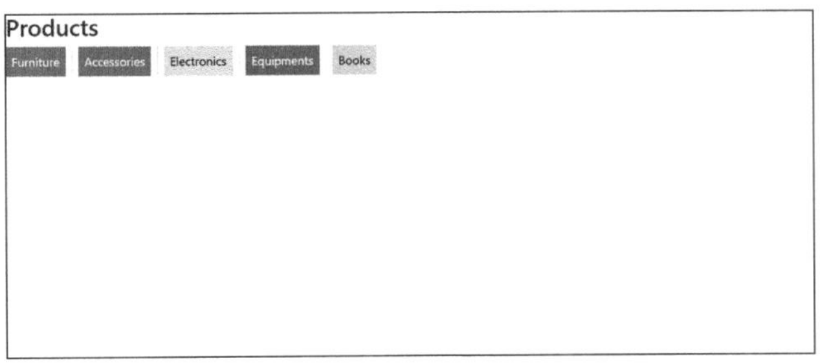

Figure 8.17: *The vertical rule in stacks*

Stretched Link

The **.stretched-link** class in Bootstrap makes any HTML element or Bootstrap component clickable. This is done by "stretching" a nested link. Let us see some examples.

Make the Entire Card Stretchable

The Bootstrap card component can be made clickable completely using the **.stretched-link** class. Set the class under the **<a>** tag in the card body:

```
<a href="#" class="btn btn-secondary stretched-link"">More Info</a>
```

Let us see an example to make the entire card stretchable:

```
<!DOCTYPE html>
<html lang="en">
<head>
  <title>Bootstrap Stretchable Link</title>
  <meta charset="utf-8">
  <meta name="viewport" content="width=device-width, initial-scale=1">
  <link
href="https://cdn.jsdelivr.net/npm/bootstrap@5.3.3/dist/css/bootstrap.
min.css" rel="stylesheet">
  <script
src="https://cdn.jsdelivr.net/npm/bootstrap@5.3.3/dist/js/bootstrap.
bundle.min.js"></script>
</head>
<body>
<div class="container">
  <h2>Profile</h2>
  <p>Here is the profile of our team members:</p>
  <div class="card" style="width:350px">
      <img class="card-img-top" src="http://studyopedia.com/wp-content/
uploads/2024/05/Amit-Diwan.png" alt="Amit Diwan" style="width:100%">
      <div class="card-body">
      <h4 class="card-title">Amit Diwan</h4>
      <p class="card-text">Amit is an Entrepreneur. He has launched
over 40 courses on programming, web development and database technolo-
gies.</p>
      <a href="#" class="btn btn-secondary stretched-link">More Info</a>
      </div>
  </div>
</div>
</body>
</html>
```

After running the code, the web page will look as follows:

Screen Size: 1366 x 633

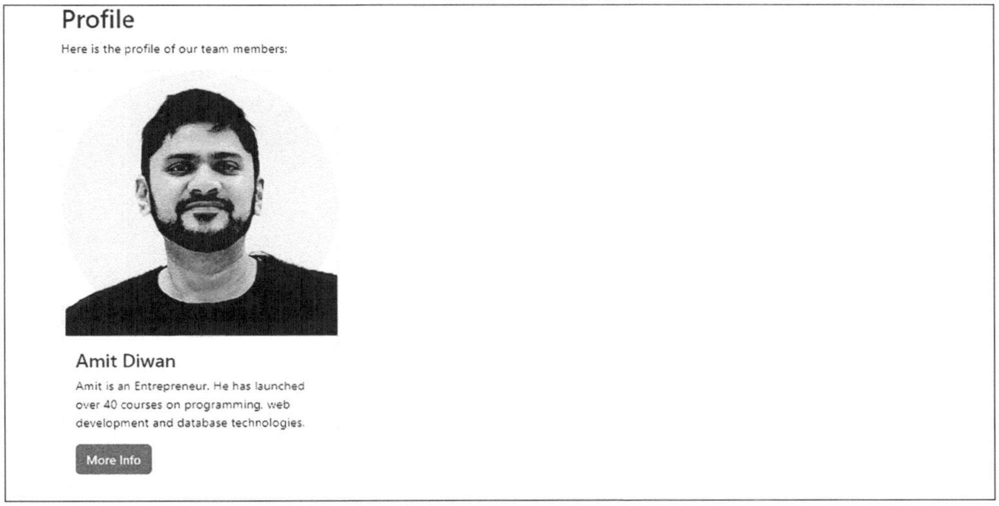

***Figure 8.18:** A bootstrap card is made clickable*

Set the Columns with Stretched Link

Here, we will set the columns with stretched links. We will use the **`.position-relative`** class and then set the **`.stretched-link`** class with position-relative to make the element clickable.

Let us see an example of setting the columns with stretched links in Bootstrap:

```
<!DOCTYPE html>
<html lang="en">
<head>
  <title>Bootstrap Stretched Link</title>
  <meta charset="utf-8">
  <meta name="viewport" content="width=device-width, initial-scale=1">
  <link
href="https://cdn.jsdelivr.net/npm/bootstrap@5.3.3/dist/css/bootstrap.
min.css" rel="stylesheet">
  <script
src="https://cdn.jsdelivr.net/npm/bootstrap@5.3.3/dist/js/bootstrap.
bundle.min.js"></script>
</head>
<body>
<h2>Profile</h2>
<div class="row g-0 bg-body-secondary position-relative">
      <div class="col-md-4 mb-md-0 p-md-4">
```

```
      <img src="http://studyopedia.com/wp-content/uploads/2024/05/
Amit-Diwan.png" class="w-100" alt="Amit Diwan">
      </div>
      <div class="col-md-4 p-4 ps-md-0">
      <h4 class="mt-0">Amit Diwan</h4>
      <p>Amit is an Entrepreneur. He has launched over 40 courses on
programming, web development and database technologies.</p>
      <a href="#" class="stretched-link">More Info</a>
      </div>
      </div>
  </body>
</html>
```

After running the code, the web page will look as follows:

Screen Size: 1366 x 633

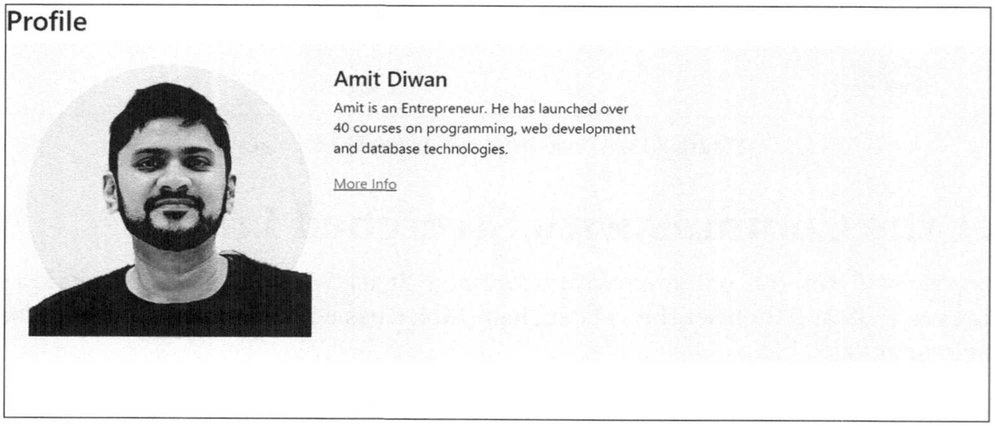

Figure 8.19: *The columns with stretched link*

Focus Ring

The Focus Ring is an indicator visible when an element receives focus and shows that the element is active. An outline is visible around the element therefore the name focus ring.

The helper class **`.focus-ring`** removes the default outline on **`:focus`**. To modify the default settings, Bootstrap also came up with some utilities **`.focus-ring-*`**.

Focus Ring on a Button

In this example, we have set the focus ring on a button. Click the button and the focus ring will be visible:

```
<!DOCTYPE html>
<html lang="en">
<head>
  <title>Bootstrap Focus Ring</title>
  <meta charset="utf-8">
  <meta name="viewport" content="width=device-width, initial-scale=1">
  <link
href="https://cdn.jsdelivr.net/npm/bootstrap@5.3.3/dist/css/bootstrap.
min.css" rel="stylesheet">
  <script
src="https://cdn.jsdelivr.net/npm/bootstrap@5.3.3/dist/js/bootstrap.
bundle.min.js"></script>
</head>
<body>
  <div class="container-fluid">
       <h4>Final Call</h4>
       <p>Click the below button for verification:</p>
       <button class="button focus-ring py-1 px-2 text-bg-light border
rounded-2">Submit</button>
       </div>
       </body>
</html>
```

After running the code, the web page will look as follows:

Screen Size: 1366 x 633

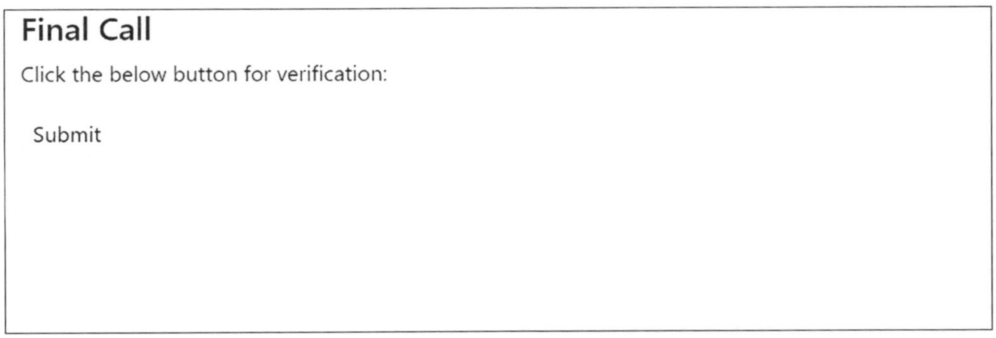

***Figure 8.20:** Click on the button to see the focus rings*

Click the **`Submit`** button and now you can see the focus ring:

Screen Size: 1366 x 633

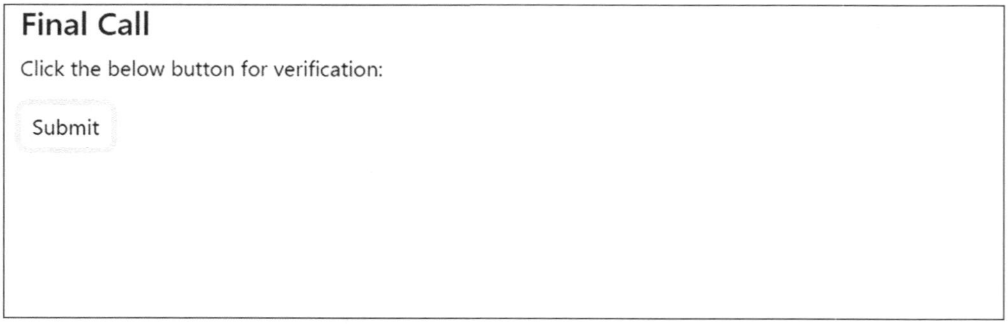

***Figure 8.21:** The focus ring is visible*

Focus Ring on a Link

We can also set a focus ring on a link in Bootstrap. In the following example, we have set the focus ring on a link. Click the link and the focus ring will be visible:

```
<!DOCTYPE html>
<html lang="en">
<head>
  <title>Bootstrap Focus Ring</title>
  <meta charset="utf-8">
  <meta name="viewport" content="width=device-width, initial-scale=1">
  <link
href="https://cdn.jsdelivr.net/npm/bootstrap@5.3.3/dist/css/bootstrap.
min.css" rel="stylesheet">
  <script
src="https://cdn.jsdelivr.net/npm/bootstrap@5.3.3/dist/js/bootstrap.
bundle.min.js"></script>
</head>
<body>
 <div class="container-fluid">
       <h4>Final Call</h4>
       <p>Click the below link for verification:</p>
       <a href="#" class="d-inline-flex focus-ring py-1 px-2 text-decora-
tion-none border rounded-2">
       Submit</a>
</div>
</body>
</html>
```

After running the code, the web page will look as follows:

Screen Size: 1366 x 633

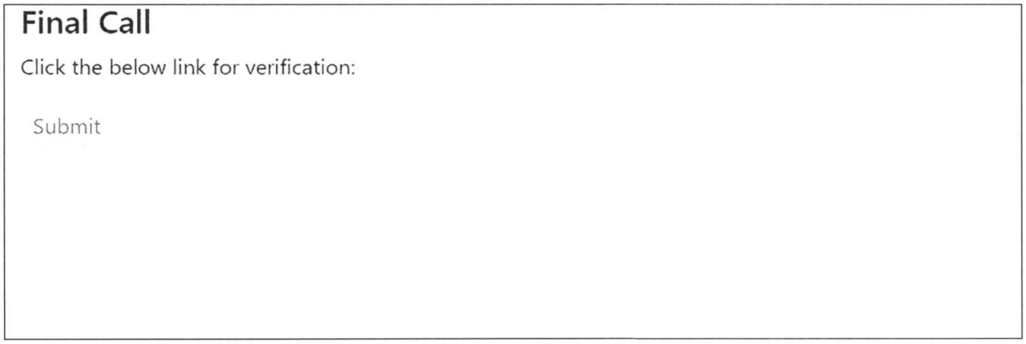

Figure 8.22: *Click on the link to see the focus rings*

Click the link with the text **`Submit`** and now you can see the focus ring:

Screen Size: 1366 x 633

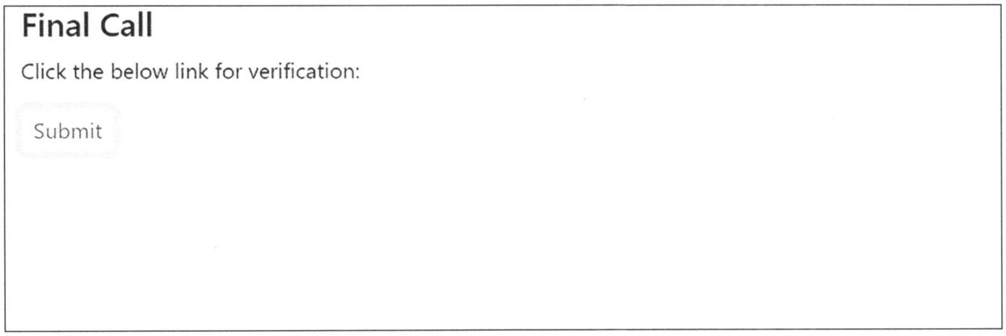

Figure 8.23: *The focus ring on the link is visible*

Customize the Focus Ring using the CSS Variable

To change the default look of the focus ring, use the **`-bs-focus-ring-*`** CSS variable. Let us see an example to customize the focus ring:

```
<!DOCTYPE html>
<html lang="en">
<head>
  <title>Bootstrap Focus Ring</title>
  <meta charset="utf-8">
  <meta name="viewport" content="width=device-width, initial-scale=1">
  <link
href="https://cdn.jsdelivr.net/npm/bootstrap@5.3.3/dist/css/bootstrap.
min.css" rel="stylesheet">
```

```
  <script
src="https://cdn.jsdelivr.net/npm/bootstrap@5.3.3/dist/js/bootstrap.
bundle.min.js"></script>
</head>
<body>
  <div class="container-fluid">
       <h4>Final Call</h4>
       <p>Click the below link for verification:</p>
<a href="#" class="d-inline-flex focus-ring py-1 px-2 text-decora-
tion-none border rounded-2" style="--bs-focus-ring-color: rgba(var(--bs-
warning-rgb), .25)">
       Submit</a>
</div>
       </body>
</html>
```

After running the code, the web page will look as follows:

Screen Size: 1366 x 633

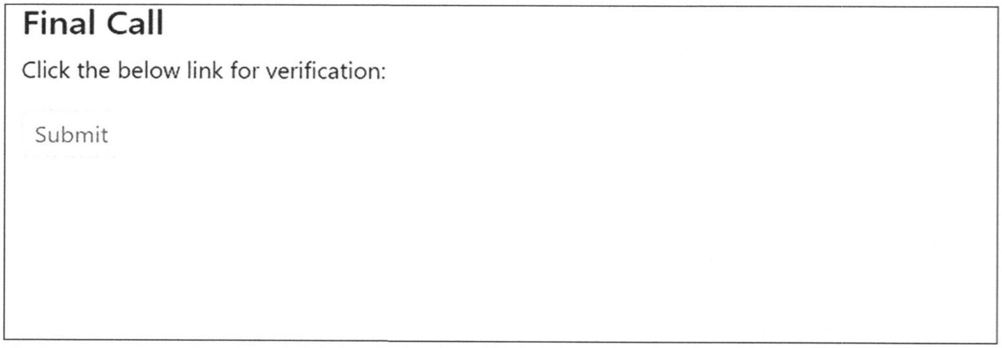

Figure 8.24: *Click on the link to see the customized focus ring*

Click the link with the text **`Submit`** and now you can see the customized focus ring:

Screen Size: 1366 x 633

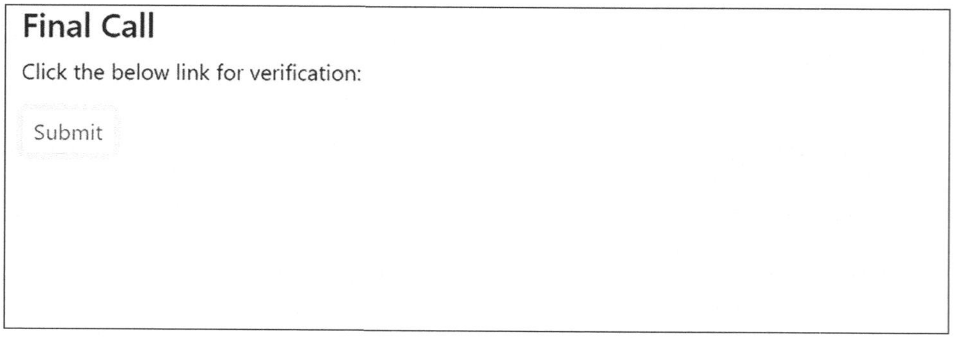

Figure 8.25: *The customized focus ring is visible*

Change the Color with Utility Classes

Use the following **.focus-ring-*** utility classes to change the focus ring color:

- **.focus-ring-primary**
- **.focus-ring-secondary**
- **.focus-ring-info**
- **.focus-ring-success**
- **.focus-ring-warning**
- **.focus-ring-danger**

Let us now see an example and change the color of the focus ring with utility classes:

```
<!DOCTYPE html>
<html lang="en">
<head>
  <title>Bootstrap Focus Ring</title>
  <meta charset="utf-8">
  <meta name="viewport" content="width=device-width, initial-scale=1">
  <link
href="https://cdn.jsdelivr.net/npm/bootstrap@5.3.3/dist/css/bootstrap.
min.css" rel="stylesheet">
  <script
src="https://cdn.jsdelivr.net/npm/bootstrap@5.3.3/dist/js/bootstrap.
bundle.min.js"></script>
</head>
<body>
  <div class="container-fluid">
      <h4>Final Call</h4>
      <p>Click the below links for verification:</p>
      <p><a href="#" class="d-inline-flex focus-ring focus-ring-primary
py-1 px-2">Submit</a></p>
      <p><a href="#" class="d-inline-flex focus-ring focus-ring-second-
ary py-1 px-2">Submit</a></p>
      <p><a href="#" class="d-inline-flex focus-ring focus-ring-info
py-1 px-2">Submit</a></p>
      <p><a href="#" class="d-inline-flex focus-ring focus-ring-warning
py-1 px-2">Submit</a></p>
      <p><a href="#" class="d-inline-flex focus-ring focus-ring-danger
py-1 px-2">Submit</a></p>
      <p><a href="#" class="d-inline-flex focus-ring focus-ring-success
py-1 px-2">Submit</a></p>
  </div>
</body>
</html>
```

After running the code, the web page will look as follows:

Screen Size: 1366 x 633

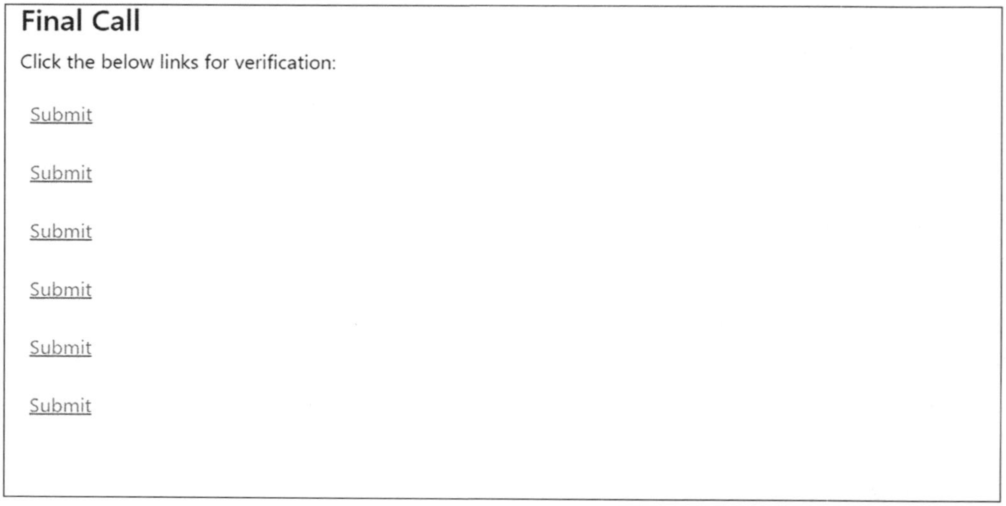

Figure 8.26: *Click on the links to change the color of the focus ring*

Click any of the links with the text **`Submit`** and now you can see the customized focus ring:

Screen Size: 1366 x 633

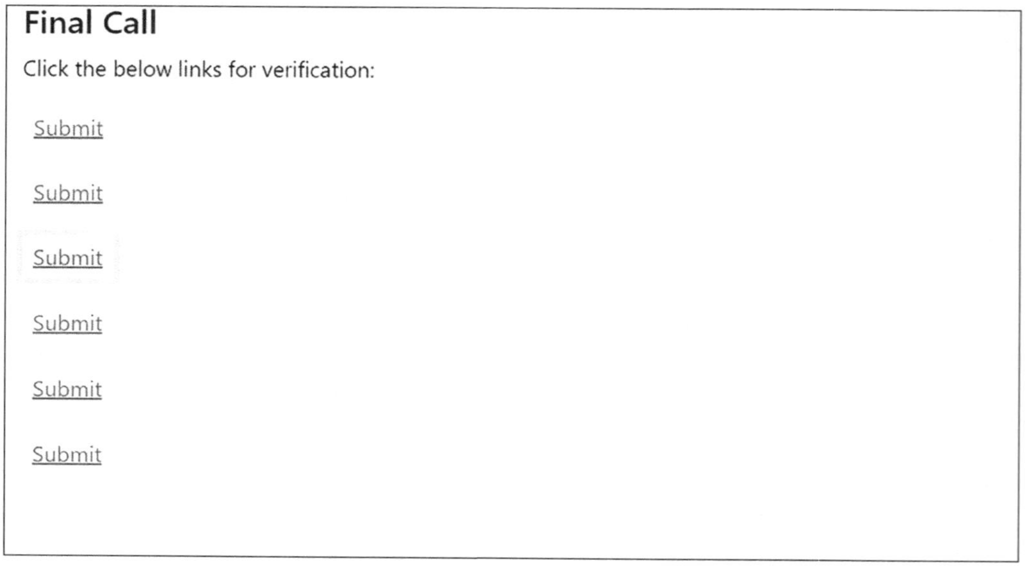

Figure 8.27: *The customized focus ring is visible on clicking*

Now click any of the other links with the text **`Submit`** to see a different colored focus ring:

Screen Size: 1366 x 633

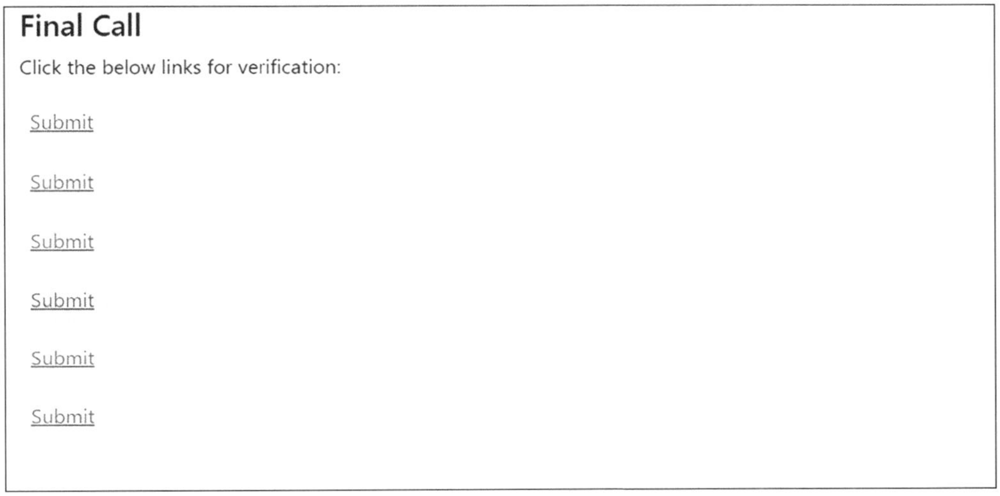

Figure 8.28: *Click on any other link to see the customized focus ring*

Conclusion

We are now familiar with how to work with the Helper classes in Bootstrap. Beginning with clearing floats, we saw how to color links, set aspect ratios, alignment, and so on. To set accessibility for screen readers, we worked on the **`.visually-hidden`** class. The long strings of text were set with ellipses.

We also saw how to position an element at the top and bottom. Also, some concepts, such as stretched link and focus ring were also discussed with examples.

In the next chapter, we will learn about utility classes with Bootstrap.

Points to Remember

- Helper classes ease the work of web developers.
- Clear the floats using the Bootstrap **`.clearfix`** class
- The **`.link-*`** classes are used in Bootstrap to color links.
- Manage the aspect ratio of external content, such as iframe, video, and so on, easily with Bootstrap **`.ratio`** classes.
- Bootstrap came up with the **`visually-hidden`** class for the screen readers.

- Use the Bootstrap **`.text-truncate`** class to truncate long strings of text with ellipsis.
- To set the position of an element at the top, use the **`.fixed-top`** class.
- To set the position of an element at the top, use the **`.fixed-bottom`** class.

Multiple Choice Questions

1. Which of the following Bootstrap classes clear the floats on a web page?
   a. `.clear`
   b. `.clearfix`
   c. `.floats-clear`
   d. `.floats-clearfix`
2. Which of the following Bootstrap class sets a frame's aspect ratio to 4:3?
   a. `ratio43`
   b. `ratio4x3`
   c. `ratio-43`
   d. `ratio-4x3`
3. Which Bootstrap class visually hides an element on all devices, except assistive technologies such as screen readers?
   a. `.visually-hidden`
   b. `.hidden`
   c. `.hide`
   d. `.assistive`
4. Which Bootstrap class should be used to truncate text?
   a. `.truncate`
   b. `.text-truncate`
   c. `.truncation`
   d. `.text-truncation`

5. Which Bootstrap class makes any HTML element or Bootstrap component clickable?
    a. `.stretch-link`
    b. `.stretched-clickable`
    c. `.stretched-click`
    d. `.stretched-link`
6. Can a focus ring be set on a link in a web page?
    a. `Yes`
    b. `No`

Answers

1. b
2. d
3. a
4. b
5. d
6. a

Questions

- What is the purpose of Helper classes?
- How are floats cleared on a web page?
- How is the aspect ratio of iframes on a web page set?
- How is text-only available for screen readers set?
- How are long strings of text truncated?
- What is a stretched link?
- What is a Focus Ring?

Key Terms

- **Helper classes**: Eases the work of web developers for the web page layout and styling.

- **Clearfix**: Clears floats on a web page.
- **Aspect Ratio:** The proportional relationship between the width and height of an element.
- **Visually hidden:** To hide an element on all devices, except assistive technologies such as screen readers. It is also visible for web crawlers and helpful for search engine optimization.
- **Focus Ring**: It is an indicator visible when an element receives focus like it shows that the element is active.

CHAPTER 9
Bootstrap Utilities

Introduction

This chapter covers utility classes in Bootstrap. These are used on a web page for the content to display, hide, or align. The overflowing content is also controlled with these utility classes.

The Utility classes provide predefined CSS classes to manage everything from spacing, alignment, display properties, and more without writing custom CSS.

Structure

In this chapter, we will discuss the following topics:

- Borders
- Background Color
- Text Color
- Flex
- Float
- Interactions
- Spacing
- Width Sizing
- Height Sizing
- Overflow
- Display
- Vertical Align

Borders

Borders are visual boundaries around elements. They are used to frame content, create separation, or enhance visual aesthetics.

We will see different Bootstrap classes to add or remove borders on a web page.

Adding Borders

To add borders on a web page with Bootstrap, use the border classes. To set borders in different directions, use the following classes:

- **`border`:** All the four borders
- **`border-top`:** The top border
- **`border-end`:** The right border
- **`border-bottom`:** The bottom border
- **`border-start`:** The left border

Let us see an example of adding borders to elements with Bootstrap:

```
<!DOCTYPE html>
<html lang="en">
<head>
  <title>Bootstrap Borders</title>
  <meta charset="utf-8">
  <meta name="viewport" content="width=device-width, initial-scale=1">
  <link
href="https://cdn.jsdelivr.net/npm/bootstrap@5.3.3/dist/css/bootstrap.
min.css" rel="stylesheet">
  <script
src="https://cdn.jsdelivr.net/npm/bootstrap@5.3.3/dist/js/bootstrap.
bundle.min.js"></script>
  <style>
  span {
    display: inline-block;
    width: 100px;
    height: 100px;
    margin: 10px;
    background-color: #fcf5f5;
  }
  </style>
</head>
<body>

<div class="container mt-3">
  <h2>Add Borders</h2>
  <span class="border">1</span>
  <span class="border-top">2</span>
  <span class="border-end">3</span>
  <span class="border-bottom">4</span>
  <span class="border-start">5</span>
</div>
```

```
</body>
</html>
```

After running the code, the web page will look as follows:

Screen Size: 1366 x 633

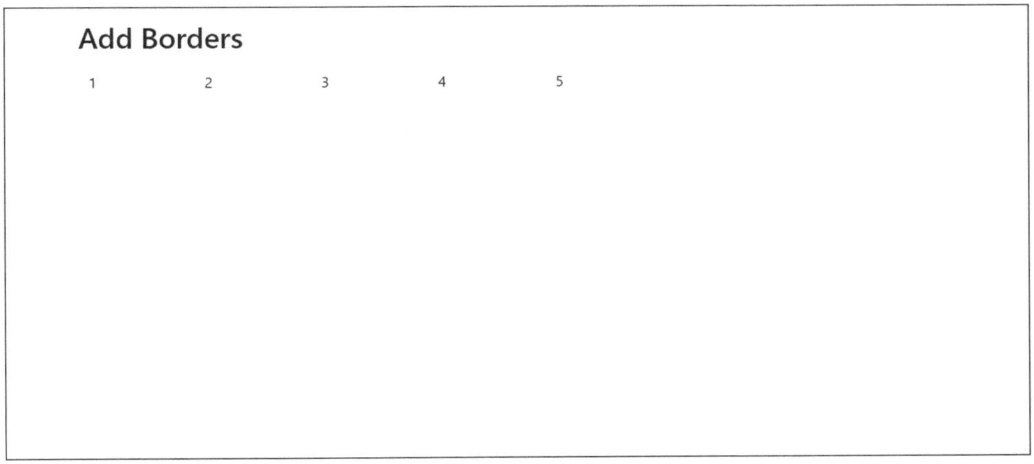

Figure 9.1: *Add borders to an element on a web page*

Removing Borders

To remove borders from an element with Bootstrap, use the border classes. To remove borders from different directions, use the following classes with the border class:

- **`border-0`:** Remove all the four borders
- **`border-top-0`:** Remove the top border
- **`border-end-0`:** Remove the right border
- **`border-bottom-0`:** Remove the bottom border
- **`border-start-0`:** Remove the left border

Let us see an example of removing borders:

```
<!DOCTYPE html>
<html lang="en">
<head>
  <title>Bootstrap Borders</title>
  <meta charset="utf-8">
  <meta name="viewport" content="width=device-width, initial-scale=1">
  <link
href="https://cdn.jsdelivr.net/npm/bootstrap@5.3.3/dist/css/bootstrap.
min.css" rel="stylesheet">
```

```
  <script
src="https://cdn.jsdelivr.net/npm/bootstrap@5.3.3/dist/js/bootstrap.
bundle.min.js"></script>
  <style>
  span {
    display: inline-block;
    width: 100px;
    height: 100px;
    margin: 10px;
    background-color: #fcf5f5;
  }
  </style>
</head>
<body>

<div class="container mt-3">
  <h2>Remove Borders</h2>
  <span class="border border-0">1</span>
  <span class="border border-top-0">2</span>
  <span class="border border-end-0">3</span>
  <span class="border border-bottom-0">4</span>
  <span class="border border-start-0">5</span>
</div>

</body>
</html>
```

After running the code, the web page will look as follows:

Screen Size: 1366 x 633

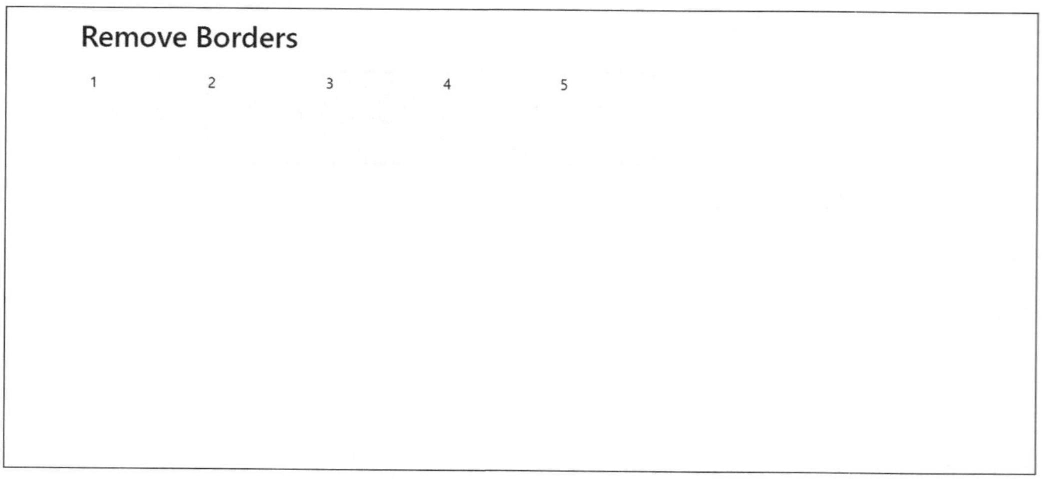

Figure 9.2: *Remove borders from elements*

Setting Border Width

To set the border width, use the border class with the width. The increase in number increases the width as well:

- **border-1**
- **border-2**
- **border-3**
- **border-4**
- **border-5**

Let us see an example of setting the border width:

```
<!DOCTYPE html>
<html lang="en">
<head>
  <title>Bootstrap Borders</title>
  <meta charset="utf-8">
  <meta name="viewport" content="width=device-width, initial-scale=1">
  <link
href="https://cdn.jsdelivr.net/npm/bootstrap@5.3.3/dist/css/bootstrap.
min.css" rel="stylesheet">
  <script
src="https://cdn.jsdelivr.net/npm/bootstrap@5.3.3/dist/js/bootstrap.
bundle.min.js"></script>
  <style>
  span {
    display: inline-block;
    width: 100px;
    height: 100px;
    margin: 10px;
    background-color: #fcf5f5;
  }
  </style>
</head>
<body>

<div class="container mt-3">
  <h2>Border Width</h2>
  <span class="border border-1">1</span>
  <span class="border border-2">2</span>
  <span class="border border-3">3</span>
  <span class="border border-4">4</span>
  <span class="border border-5">5</span>
</div>
```

```
</body>
</html>
```

After running the code, the web page will look as follows:

Screen Size: 1366 x 633

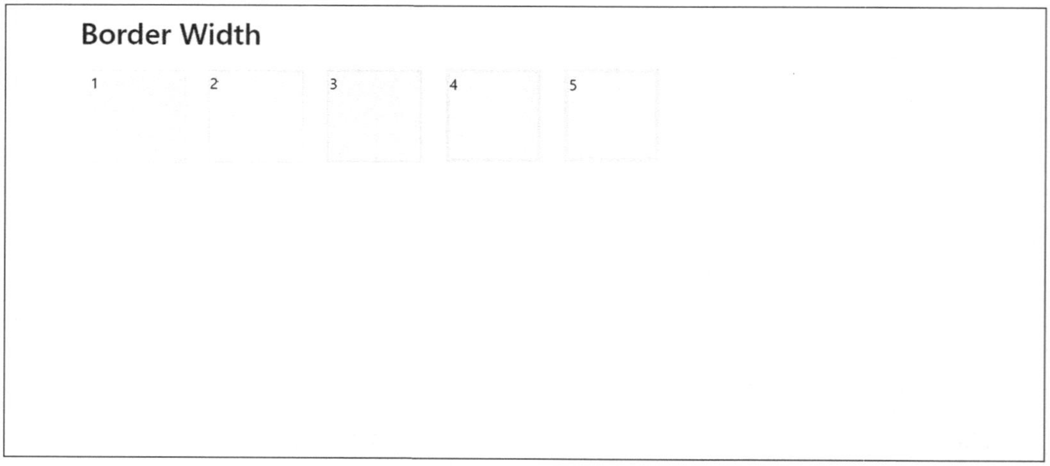

Figure 9.3: *Set the border width*

Setting Border Color

To set the border color, use the contextual border classes. Use it with the border class:

- **`border-primary`**
- **`border-secondary`**
- **`border-success`**
- **`border-danger`**
- **`border-warning`**
- **`border-info`**
- **`border-light`**
- **`border-dark`**
- **`border-white`**

Let us now see an example of setting the border color:

```
<!DOCTYPE html>
<html lang="en">
<head>
  <title>Bootstrap Borders</title>
  <meta charset="utf-8">
```

```
  <meta name="viewport" content="width=device-width, initial-scale=1">
  <link
href="https://cdn.jsdelivr.net/npm/bootstrap@5.3.3/dist/css/bootstrap.
min.css" rel="stylesheet">
  <script
src="https://cdn.jsdelivr.net/npm/bootstrap@5.3.3/dist/js/bootstrap.
bundle.min.js"></script>
  <style>
  span {
    display: inline-block;
    width: 100px;
    height: 100px;
    margin: 10px;
    background-color: #fcf5f5;
  }
  </style>
</head>
<body>

<div class="container mt-3">
  <h2>Border Color</h2>
  <span class="border border-primary">1</span>
  <span class="border border-secondary">2</span>
  <span class="border border-success">3</span>
  <span class="border border-danger">4</span>
  <span class="border border-warning">5</span>
  <span class="border border-info">6</span>
  <span class="border border-light">7</span>
  <span class="border border-dark">8</span>
  <span class="border border-white">9</span>
</div>

</body>
</html>
```

After running the code, the web page will look as follows:

Screen Size: 1366 x 633

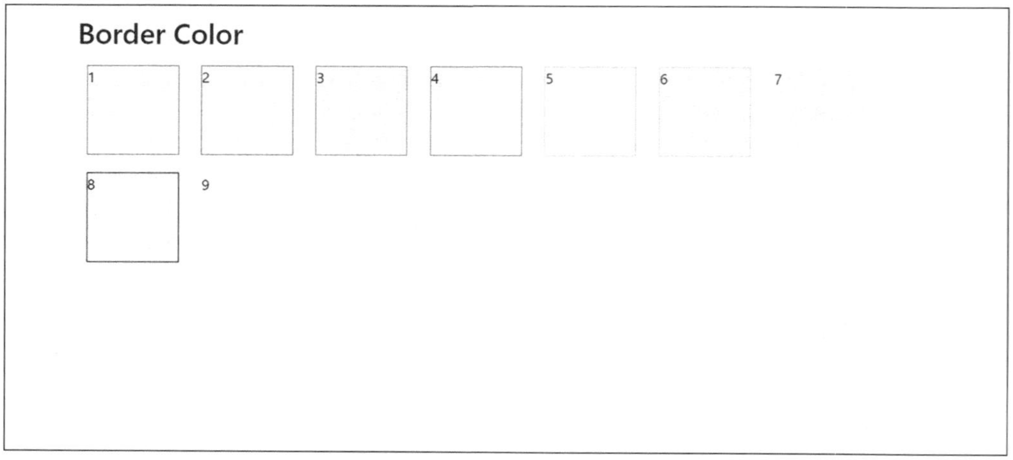

Figure 9.4: *Set the color of the border*

Setting the Border's Radius

To set the border's radius means to make the corners rounded. Use the rounded classes to set the border's radius. The corners are rounded based on the direction:

- **`rounded`**
- **`rounded-top`**
- **`rounded-end`**
- **`rounded-bottom`**
- **`rounded-start`**
- **`rounded-circle`**

Let us see an example of setting the border's radius:

```
<!DOCTYPE html>
<html lang="en">
<head>
  <title>Bootstrap Borders</title>
  <meta charset="utf-8">
  <meta name="viewport" content="width=device-width, initial-scale=1">
  <link
href="https://cdn.jsdelivr.net/npm/bootstrap@5.3.3/dist/css/bootstrap.
min.css" rel="stylesheet">
  <script
src="https://cdn.jsdelivr.net/npm/bootstrap@5.3.3/dist/js/bootstrap.
bundle.min.js"></script>
  <style>
  span {
```

```
    display: inline-block;
    width: 100px;
    height: 100px;
    margin: 10px;
    background-color: orange;
  }
  </style>
</head>
<body>

<div class="container mt-3">
  <h2>Border with rounded corners</h2>
  <span class="rounded"></span>
  <span class="rounded-top"></span>
  <span class="rounded-end"></span>
  <span class="rounded-bottom"></span>
  <span class="rounded-start"></span>
  <span class="rounded-circle"></span>
</div>

</body>
</html>
```

After running the code, the web page will look as follows:

Screen Size: 1366 x 633

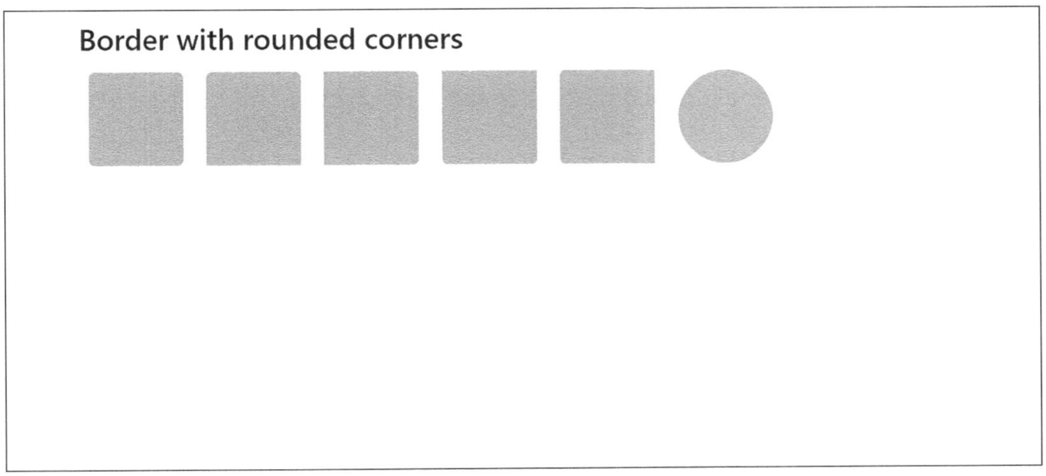

Figure 9.5: *Set the border's radius*

Setting Background Color

Learn how to set the background color for text using the contextual classes **.bg-*** in Bootstrap.

The following are the contextual classes for background color:

- **.bg-primary**: Key information. Blue color.
- **.bg-success**: Success action. Green color.
- **.bg-info**: Set information. Teal color.
- **.bg-warning**: Set warning message. Yellow color.
- **.bg-danger**: Set danger message. Red color.
- **.bg-secondary**: Less important info. Gray color.
- **.bg-dark**: Dark background color. Dark gray.
- **.bg-light**: Light background color. Light gray.

Setting the Text Background Color

Let us see an example of setting the background color for text:

```
<!DOCTYPE html>
<html lang="en">
<head>
  <title>Bootstrap Text Background Color</title>
  <meta charset="utf-8">
  <meta name="viewport" content="width=device-width, initial-scale=1">
  <link
href="https://cdn.jsdelivr.net/npm/bootstrap@5.3.3/dist/css/bootstrap.
min.css" rel="stylesheet">
  <script
src="https://cdn.jsdelivr.net/npm/bootstrap@5.3.3/dist/js/bootstrap.
bundle.min.js"></script>
</head>
<body>
<div class="container mt-3">
  <h2>Text Background Color</h2>
  <div class="p-2 mb-2 bg-primary text-white">.bg-primary</div>
  <div class="p-2 mb-2 bg-secondary text-white">.bg-secondary</div>
  <div class="p-2 mb-2 bg-success text-white">.bg-success</div>
  <div class="p-2 mb-2 bg-danger text-white">.bg-danger</div>
  <div class="p-2 mb-2 bg-warning text-dark">.bg-warning</div>
  <div class="p-2 mb-2 bg-info text-dark">.bg-info</div>
  <div class="p-2 mb-2 bg-light text-dark">.bg-light</div>
  <div class="p-2 mb-2 bg-dark text-white">.bg-dark</div>
```

```
</div>
</body>
</html>
```

After running the code, the web page will look as follows:

Screen Size: 1366 x 633

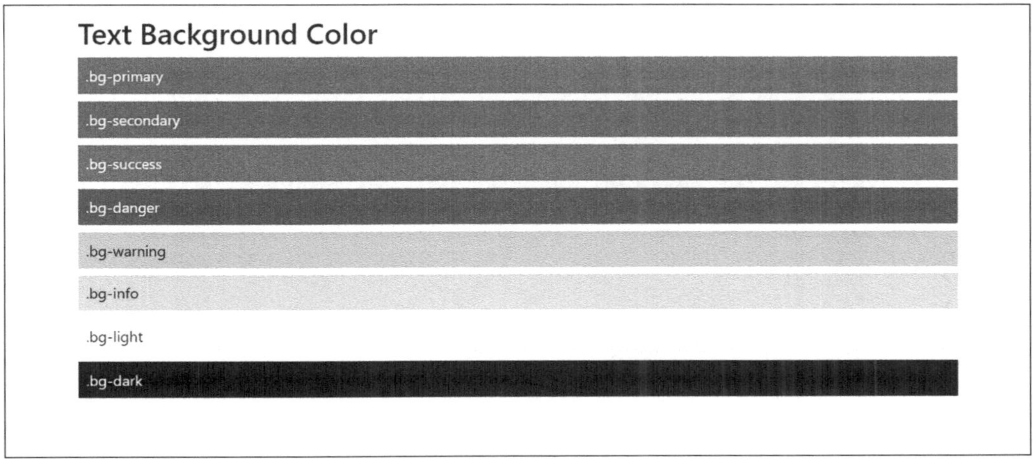

Figure 9.6: *Set the background color*

Setting the Gradient Background Color

To set the gradient background color, use the **`.bg-gradient`** class. The following is the gradient set with the **`bg-primary`** contextual class:

```
<div class="p-2 mb-2 bg-primary bg-gradient text-white">.bg-primary</div>
```

Let us see an example of setting the gradient background color:

```
<!DOCTYPE html>
<html lang="en">
<head>
  <title>Bootstrap Text Background Color</title>
  <meta charset="utf-8">
  <meta name="viewport" content="width=device-width, initial-scale=1">
  <link
href="https://cdn.jsdelivr.net/npm/bootstrap@5.3.3/dist/css/bootstrap.
min.css" rel="stylesheet">
  <script
src="https://cdn.jsdelivr.net/npm/bootstrap@5.3.3/cist/js/bootstrap.
bundle.min.js"></script>
</head>
<body>
<div class="container mt-3">
```

```
  <h2>Text Background Color</h2>
  <div class="p-2 mb-2 bg-primary bg-gradient text-white">.bg-primary</
div>
  <div class="p-2 mb-2 bg-secondary bg-gradient text-white">.bg-second-
ary</div>
  <div class="p-2 mb-2 bg-success bg-gradient text-white">.bg-success</
div>
  <div class="p-2 mb-2 bg-danger bg-gradient text-white">.bg-danger</
div>
  <div class="p-2 mb-2 bg-warning bg-gradient text-dark">.bg-warning</
div>
  <div class="p-2 mb-2 bg-info bg-gradient text-dark">.bg-info</div>
  <div class="p-2 mb-2 bg-light bg-gradient text-dark">.bg-light</div>
  <div class="p-2 mb-2 bg-dark bg-gradient text-white">.bg-dark</div>
</div>
</body>
</html>
```

After running, the web page will look as follows:

Screen Size: 1366 x 633

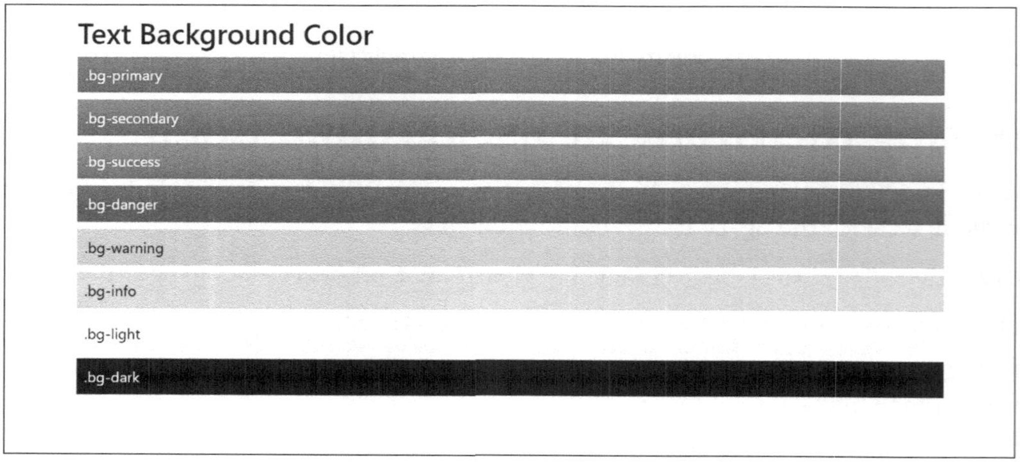

Figure 9.7: *Set the gradient background color*

Text Color

Learn how to set the text color using the contextual classes **`.text-*`** in Bootstrap. The following are the contextual classes for text color:

- **`.text-muted`:** Gray Color
- **`.text-primary`:** Blue Color - Key Content
- **`.text-success`:** Success Action - Green Color

- **.text-info**: Set Information - Teal Color
- **.text-warning**: Set Warning Message - Orange Color
- **.text-danger**: Set Danger Message - Red Color
- **.text-secondary:** Less Key Content - Gray Color
- **.text-white:** White Color Text
- **.text-body:** Normal Body
- **.text-light**: Light Color - Light Gray Color
- **.text-dark:** Dark Text - Dark Gray Color

Let us see an example of setting the text color:

```
<!DOCTYPE html>
<html lang="en">
<head>
  <title>Bootstrap Text Color</title>
  <meta charset="utf-8">
  <meta name="viewport" content="width=device-width, initial-scale=1">
  <link
href="https://cdn.jsdelivr.net/npm/bootstrap@5.3.3/dist/css/bootstrap.
min.css" rel="stylesheet">
  <script
src="https://cdn.jsdelivr.net/npm/bootstrap@5.3.3/dist/js/bootstrap.
bundle.min.js"></script>
</head>
<body>
<div class="container mt-3">
  <h2>Text Color</h2>
  <p class="text-primary">Important Text</p>
  <p class="text-success">Indicates success.</p>
  <p class="text-info">Represents information.</p>
  <p class="text-warning">Represents a warning.</p>
  <p class="text-danger">Represents danger.</p>
  <p class="text-secondary">Secondary text.</p>
  <p class="text-dark">Dark grey text.</p>
  <p class="text-light">Light grey text.</p>
</div>
</body>
</html>
```

After running the code, the web page will look as follows:

Screen Size: 1366 x 633

Figure 9.8: *Set the text color*

Flex

The flexbox layout model allows designing a flexible responsive layout structure. Let us create a flex container and set flex items. Transform direct children's elements into flex items using **d-flex**:

```
<!DOCTYPE html>
<html lang="en">
<head>
  <title>Bootstrap Flexbox</title>
  <meta charset="utf-8">
  <meta name="viewport" content="width=device-width, initial-scale=1">
  <link
href="https://cdn.jsdelivr.net/npm/bootstrap@5.3.3/dist/css/bootstrap.
min.css" rel="stylesheet">
  <script
src="https://cdn.jsdelivr.net/npm/bootstrap@5.3.3/dist/js/bootstrap.
bundle.min.js"></script>
</head>
<body>

<div class="container mt-3">
  <h2>Flex</h2>
  <div class="d-flex p-3 bg-primary text-white">
    <div class="p-3 bg-secondary">Flex Item 1</div>
    <div class="p-3 bg-danger">Flex Item 2</div>
    <div class="p-3 bg-info">Flex Item 3</div>
    <div class="p-3 bg-warning">Flex Item 4</div>
  </div>
</div>
```

```
</body>
</html>
```

After running the code, the web page will look as follows:

Screen Size: 1366 x 633

***Figure 9.9**: Displaying the flex items*

Direction of Flex Item

We can easily display the flex items horizontally or vertically using the Bootstrap classes:

- **flex-row:** Horizontal direction. Default.
- **flex-column:** Vertical direction

Displaying Horizontal Flex Items

Let us see an example of displaying the flex item horizontally using the **.flex-row** class. This is the default, that is, even if you won't add the **.flex-row** class, it will work.

Also, the flex items will be right-aligned using the **.flex-row-reverse**:

```
<!DOCTYPE html>
<html lang="en">
<head>
  <title>Bootstrap Flex Direction</title>
  <meta charset="utf-8">
  <meta name="viewport" content="width=device-width, initial-scale=1">
  <link
href="https://cdn.jsdelivr.net/npm/bootstrap@5.3.3/dist/css/bootstrap.
min.css" rel="stylesheet">
```

```
  <script
src="https://cdn.jsdelivr.net/npm/bootstrap@5.3.3/dist/js/bootstrap.
bundle.min.js"></script>
</head>
<body>
<div class="container mt-3">
  <h2>Horizontal Direction</h2>
  <p>The flex items are displayed horizontally using the .flex-row
class:</p>
  <div class="d-flex flex-row bg-primary text-white">
    <div class="p-2 bg-secondary">Flex Item 1</div>
    <div class="p-2 bg-danger">Flex Item 2</div>
    <div class="p-2 bg-info">Flex Item 3</div>
    <div class="p-2 bg-warning">Flex Item 4</div>
  </div>
  <p>The flex items are displayed horizontally and right-aligned using
the .flex-row-reverse class:</p>
  <div class="d-flex flex-row-reverse bg-primary text-white">
    <div class="p-2 bg-secondary">Flex Item 1</div>
    <div class="p-2 bg-danger">Flex Item 2</div>
    <div class="p-2 bg-info">Flex Item 3</div>
    <div class="p-2 bg-warning">Flex Item 4</div>
  </div>
</div>
</body>
</html>
```

After running the code, the web page will look as follows:

Screen Size: 1366 x 633

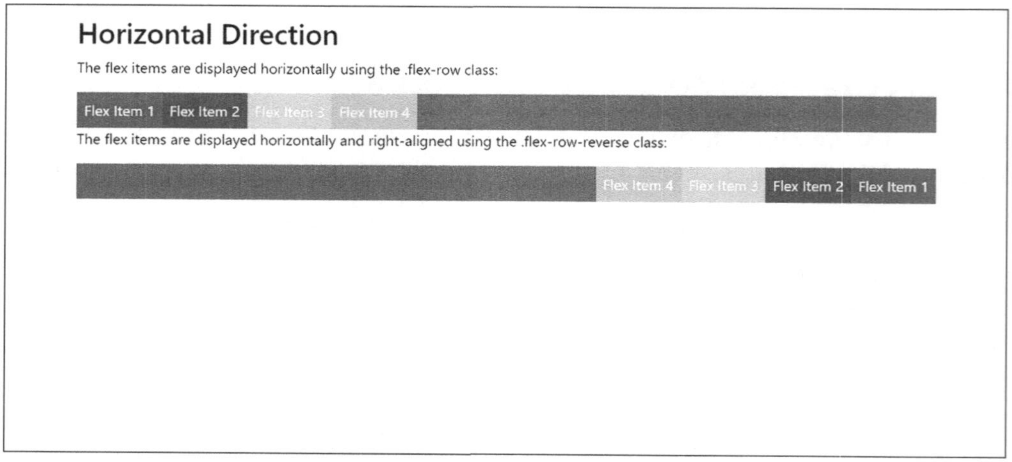

Figure 9.10: *Displaying horizontal flex items*

Displaying Vertical Flex Items

Let us see an example of displaying the flex item vertically using the **flex-column** class. Also, it can be reversed using the **flex-column-reverse** class:

```
<!DOCTYPE html>
<html lang="en">
<head>
  <title>Bootstrap Flex Direction</title>
  <meta charset="utf-8">
  <meta name="viewport" content="width=device-width, initial-scale=1">
  <link
href="https://cdn.jsdelivr.net/npm/bootstrap@5.3.3/dist/css/bootstrap.
min.css" rel="stylesheet">
  <script
src="https://cdn.jsdelivr.net/npm/bootstrap@5.3.3/dist/js/bootstrap.
bundle.min.js"></script>
</head>
<body>

<div class="container mt-3">
  <h2>Vertical Direction</h2>
  <p>The flex items are displayed vertically using the .flex-column
class:</p>
  <div class="d-flex flex-column bg-primary text-white">
    <div class="p-2 bg-secondary">Flex Item 1</div>
    <div class="p-2 bg-danger">Flex Item 2</div>
    <div class="p-2 bg-info">Flex Item 3</div>
    <div class="p-2 bg-warning">Flex Item 4</div>
  </div>
  <p>The flex items are displayed vertically and reversed direction using
the .flex-column-reverse class:</p>
  <div class="d-flex flex-column-reverse bg-primary text-white">
    <div class="p-2 bg-secondary">Flex Item 1</div>
    <div class="p-2 bg-danger">Flex Item 2</div>
    <div class="p-2 bg-info">Flex Item 3</div>
    <div class="p-2 bg-warning">Flex Item 4</div>
  </div>
</div>

</body>
</html>
```

After running the code, the web page will look as follows:

Screen Size: 1366 x 633

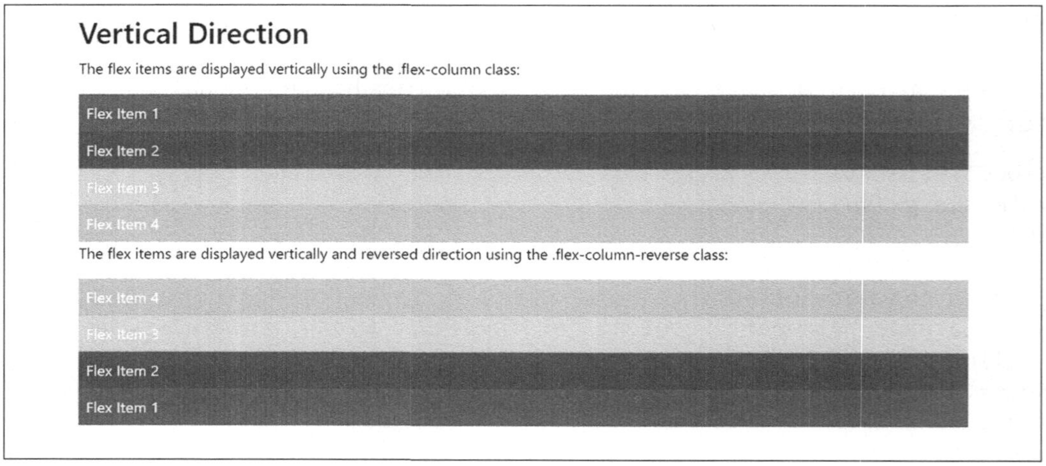

Figure 9.11: *Displaying vertical flex items*

Using Justify content

The alignment of the flex items can be easily changed using the **`.justify-content-*`** classes. In Bootstrap, the **`justify-content`** class is used to control the alignment of flex items along the main axis (horizontal by default). The flex items can be aligned in any direction using the following Bootstrap classes:

- **`justify-content-start`:** Align flex items to the beginning. This is the default.
- **`justify-content-end`:** Align flex items to the end.
- **`justify-content-center`:** Align flex items to the center.
- **`justify-content-between`:** Distributes items evenly with the first item at the start and the last item at the end.
- **`justify-content-around`:** Distributes items evenly with equal space around them.
- **`justify-content-evenly`:** Distributes items so that the spacing between any two items is equal.

Let us also understand cross and main axis:

- **Main Axis:** This is the primary axis along which flex items are placed. By default, it runs horizontally from left to right. When you use flex-direction: row, the main axis is the horizontal axis. If you switch to flex-direction: column, the main axis becomes vertical.
- **Cross Axis:** This is perpendicular to the main axis. So, if your main axis is horizontal (row), the cross axis is vertical. If your main axis is vertical (column), the cross axis is horizontal.

Let us see an example and align the flex items on a web page with Bootstrap:

```
<!DOCTYPE html>
<html lang="en">
<head>
  <title>Bootstrap Justify Content</title>
  <meta charset="utf-8">
  <meta name="viewport" content="width=device-width, initial-scale=1">
  <link
href="https://cdn.jsdelivr.net/npm/bootstrap@5.3.3/dist/css/bootstrap.
min.css" rel="stylesheet">
  <script
src="https://cdn.jsdelivr.net/npm/bootstrap@5.3.3/dist/js/bootstrap.
bundle.min.js"></script>
</head>
<body>
<div class="container mt-3">
  <h2>Align Flex Items</h2>
  <div class="d-flex justify-content-start bg-primary mb-3">
    <div class="p-2 bg-secondary">Flex Item 1</div>
    <div class="p-2 bg-danger">Flex Item 2</div>
    <div class="p-2 bg-info">Flex Item 3</div>
    <div class="p-2 bg-warning">Flex Item 4</div>
  </div>
  <div class="d-flex justify-content-end bg-primary mb-3">
    <div class="p-2 bg-secondary">Flex Item 1</div>
    <div class="p-2 bg-danger">Flex Item 2</div>
    <div class="p-2 bg-info">Flex Item 3</div>
    <div class="p-2 bg-warning">Flex Item 4</div>
  </div>
  <div class="d-flex justify-content-center bg-primary mb-3">
    <div class="p-2 bg-secondary">Flex Item 1</div>
    <div class="p-2 bg-danger">Flex Item 2</div>
    <div class="p-2 bg-info">Flex Item 3</div>
    <div class="p-2 bg-warning">Flex Item 4</div>
  </div>
  <div class="d-flex justify-content-between bg-primary mb-3">
    <div class="p-2 bg-secondary">Flex Item 1</div>
    <div class="p-2 bg-danger">Flex Item 2</div>
    <div class="p-2 bg-info">Flex Item 3</div>
    <div class="p-2 bg-warning">Flex Item 4</div>
  </div>
  <div class="d-flex justify-content-around bg-primary mb-3">
    <div class="p-2 bg-secondary">Flex Item 1</div>
    <div class="p-2 bg-danger">Flex Item 2</div>
    <div class="p-2 bg-info">Flex Item 3</div>
    <div class="p-2 bg-warning">Flex Item 4</div>
```

```
  </div>
</div>
</body>
</html>
```

After running the code, the web page will look as follows:

Screen Size: 1366 x 633

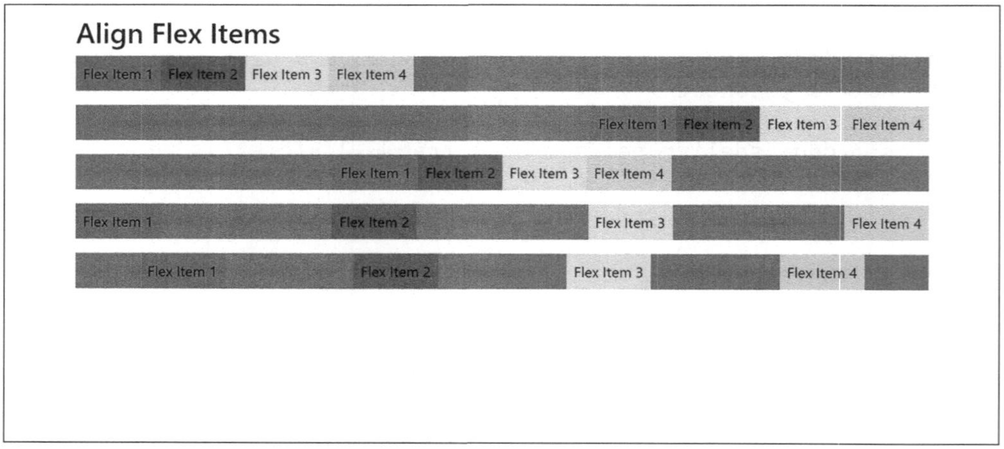

Figure 9.12: *Align the flex items in any direction*

Using Align Items

The vertical alignment of the flex items can be easily changed using the **`.align-items-*`** classes. In flexbox, the **`align-items`** are used to align flex items along the cross axis. It determines how flex items are positioned inside the flex container. Bootstrap provides several utility classes to apply different values of the align-items property.

The flex items can be aligned in any direction using the following Bootstrap classes:

- **`align-items-start`:** align flex items to the start of the cross axis
- **`align-items-end`:** align flex items to the end of the cross axis
- **`align- items-center`:** align flex items to the center of the cross axis
- **`align-items-baseline`:** align flex items along the baseline of their container
- **`align items-stretch`:** This is the default. Stretch the flex items to fill the height of the flex container.

Let us see an example of vertically aligning the flex items on a web page with Bootstrap:

```
<!DOCTYPE html>
<html lang="en">
<head>
```

```
  <title>Bootstrap Align Items</title>
  <meta charset="utf-8">
  <meta name="viewport" content="width=device-width, initial-scale=1">
  <link
href="https://cdn.jsdelivr.net/npm/bootstrap@5.3.3/dist/css/bootstrap.
min.css" rel="stylesheet">
  <script
src="https://cdn.jsdelivr.net/npm/bootstrap@5.3.3/dist/js/bootstrap.
bundle.min.js"></script>
</head>
<body>
<div class="container mt-3">
  <h2>Align Flex Items</h2>
  <p>Align Items Start</p>
  <div class="d-flex align-items-start bg-dark" style="height:150px;">
    <div class="p-2 bg-secondary">Flex Item 1</div>
    <div class="p-2 bg-danger">Flex Item 2</div>
    <div class="p-2 bg-info">Flex Item 3</div>
    <div class="p-2 bg-warning">Flex Item 4</div>
  </div>
  <p>Align Items End</p>
  <div class="d-flex align-items-end bg-dark" style="height:150px;">
    <div class="p-2 bg-secondary">Flex Item 1</div>
    <div class="p-2 bg-danger">Flex Item 2</div>
    <div class="p-2 bg-info">Flex Item 3</div>
    <div class="p-2 bg-warning">Flex Item 4</div>
  </div>
  <p>Align Items Center</p>
  <div class="d-flex align-items-center bg-dark" style="height:150px;">
    <div class="p-2 bg-secondary">Flex Item 1</div>
    <div class="p-2 bg-danger">Flex Item 2</div>
    <div class="p-2 bg-info">Flex Item 3</div>
    <div class="p-2 bg-warning">Flex Item 4</div>
  </div>
  <p>Align Items Baseline</p>
  <div class="d-flex align-items-baseline bg-dark" style="height:150px;">
    <div class="p-2 bg-secondary">Flex Item 1</div>
    <div class="p-2 bg-danger">Flex Item 2</div>
    <div class="p-2 bg-info">Flex Item 3</div>
    <div class="p-2 bg-warning">Flex Item 4</div>
  </div>
  <p>Align Items Stretch</p>
  <div class="d-flex align-items-stretch bg-dark" style="height:150px;">
    <div class="p-2 bg-secondary">Flex Item 1</div>
    <div class="p-2 bg-danger">Flex Item 2</div>
    <div class="p-2 bg-info">Flex Item 3</div>
    <div class="p-2 bg-warning">Flex Item 4</div>
```

```
  </div>
</div>
</body>
</html>
```

After running the code, the web page will look as follows:

Screen Size: 1366 x 633

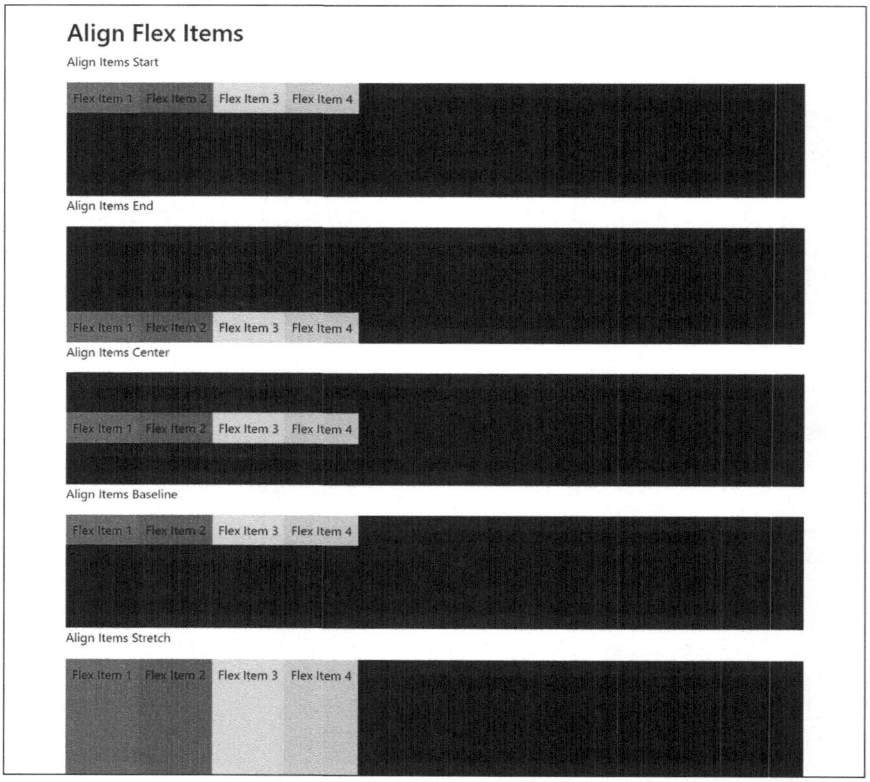

Figure 9.13: *Vertically align flex items*

Using Align Self

The vertical alignment of a particular flex item can be easily changed using the **`.align-self-*`** classes. The **`align-self`** in flexbox allows individual flex items to override the align-items property applied to the flex container. This gives you finer control over the alignment of specific items within the same flex container.

The following are the Bootstrap classes:

- **`.align-self-start`:** Aligns the item to the start of the cross-axis.
- **`.align-self-end`:** Aligns the item to the end of the cross-axis.

- **.align-self-center**: Centers the item along the cross-axis.
- **.align-self-baseline**: Aligns the item along the container's baseline.
- **.align-self-stretch**: This is the default. Stretches the item to fill the container.

Let us see an example of vertically aligning a particular flex item on a web page with Bootstrap:

```
<!DOCTYPE html>
<html lang="en">
<head>
  <title>Bootstrap Align Self</title>
  <meta charset="utf-8">
  <meta name="viewport" content="width=device-width, initial-scale=1">
  <link
href="https://cdn.jsdelivr.net/npm/bootstrap@5.3.3/dist/css/bootstrap.
min.css" rel="stylesheet">
  <script
src="https://cdn.jsdelivr.net/npm/bootstrap@5.3.3/dist/js/bootstrap.
bundle.min.js"></script>
</head>
<body>
<div class="container mt-3">
  <h2>Align Self</h2>
  <p>Align Self Start</p>
  <div class="d-flex bg-dark" style="height:150px;">
    <div class="p-2 bg-secondary">Flex Item 1</div>
    <div class="p-2 bg-danger">Flex Item 2</div>
    <div class="p-2 align-self-start bg-info">Flex Item 3</div>
    <div class="p-2 bg-warning">Flex Item 4</div>
  </div>
  <p>Align Self End</p>
  <div class="d-flex bg-dark" style="height:150px;">
    <div class="p-2 bg-secondary">Flex Item 1</div>
    <div class="p-2 bg-danger">Flex Item 2</div>
    <div class="p-2 align-self-end bg-info">Flex Item 3</div>
    <div class="p-2 bg-warning">Flex Item 4</div>
  </div>
  <p>Align Self Center</p>
  <div class="d-flex bg-dark" style="height:150px;">
    <div class="p-2 bg-secondary">Flex Item 1</div>
    <div class="p-2 bg-danger">Flex Item 2</div>
    <div class="p-2 align-self-center bg-info">Flex Item 3</div>
    <div class="p-2 bg-warning">Flex Item 4</div>
  </div>
  <p>Align Self Baseline</p>
```

```
  <div class="d-flex bg-dark" style="height:150px;">
    <div class="p-2 bg-secondary">Flex Item 1</div>
    <div class="p-2 bg-danger">Flex Item 2</div>
    <div class="p-2 bg-info align-self-baseline">Flex Item 3</div>
    <div class="p-2 bg-warning">Flex Item 4</div>
  </div>
  <p>Align Self Stretch</p>
  <div class="d-flex bg-dark" style="height:150px;">
    <div class="p-2 bg-secondary">Flex Item 1</div>
    <div class="p-2 bg-danger">Flex Item 2</div>
    <div class="p-2 bg-info align-self-stretch">Flex Item 3</div>
    <div class="p-2 bg-warning">Flex Item 4</div>
  </div>
</div>
</body>
</html>
```

After running the code, the web page will look as follows:

Screen Size: 1366 x 633

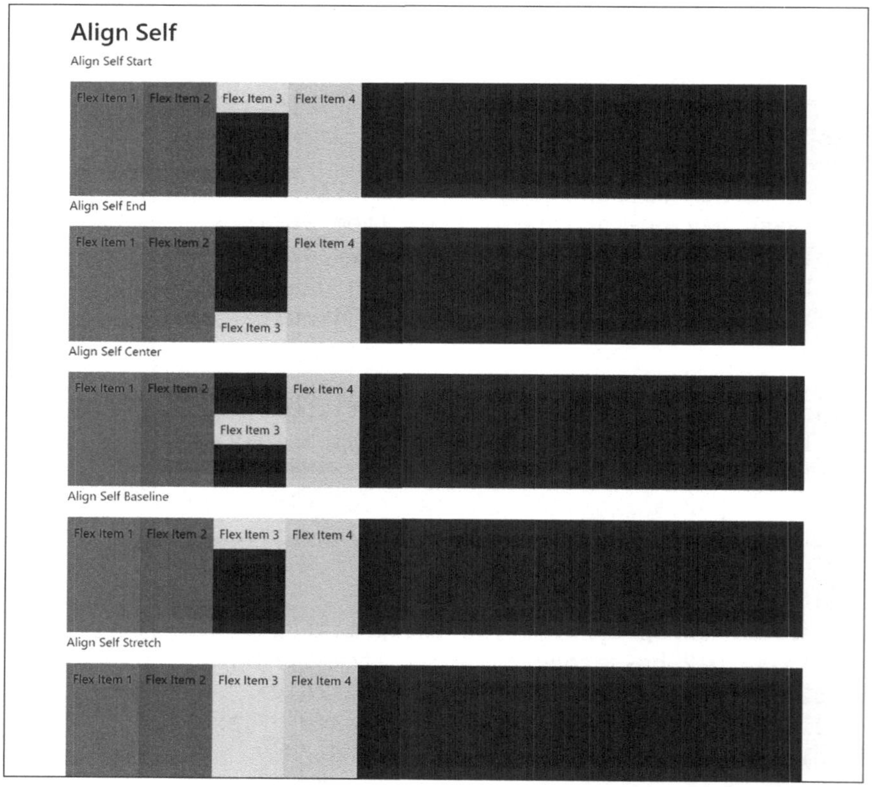

Figure 9.14: *Vertically align a particular flex item*

Using Flex Fill

To force the series of sibling elements that is the flex-items into equal widths, use the **.flex-fill** class.

Let us see an example without using flex fill. The flex items did not stretch to equal widths:

```
<!DOCTYPE html>
<html lang="en">
<head>
  <title>Bootstrap Flex Fill</title>
  <meta charset="utf-8">
  <meta name="viewport" content="width=device-width, initial-scale=1">
  <link
href="https://cdn.jsdelivr.net/npm/bootstrap@5.3.3/dist/css/bootstrap.
min.css" rel="stylesheet">
  <script
src="https://cdn.jsdelivr.net/npm/bootstrap@5.3.3/dist/js/bootstrap.
bundle.min.js"></script>
</head>
<body>
<div class="container mt-3">
  <h2>Without using flex-fill</h2>
  <div class="d-flex mb-3 bg-primary">
    <div class="p-2 bg-secondary">Flex Item 1</div>
    <div class="p-2 bg-danger">Flex Item 2</div>
    <div class="p-2 bg-info">Flex Item 3</div>
    <div class="p-2 bg-warning">Flex Item 4</div>
  </div>
</div>

</body>
</html>
```

After running the code, the web page will look as follows:

Screen Size: 1366 x 633

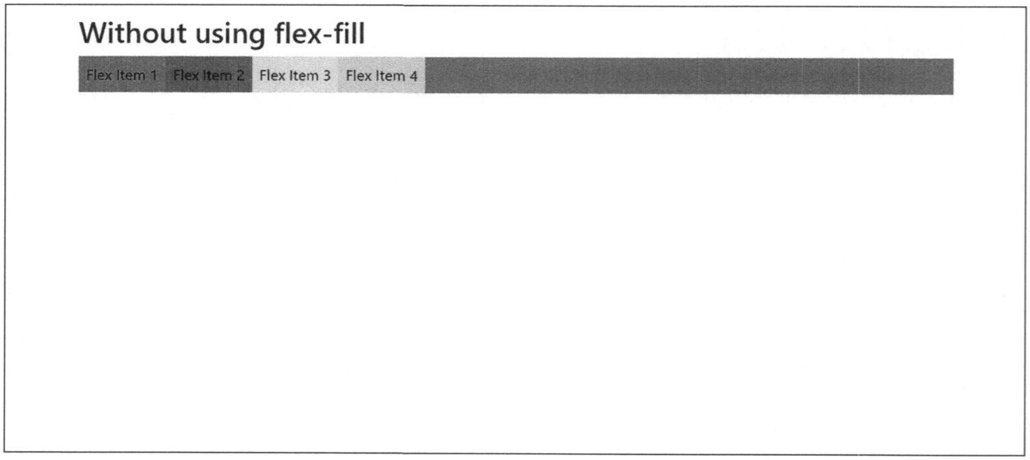

Figure 9.15: *The flex items did not stretch to equal widths*

Now, let us see an example using flex fill. You can easily spot the width differences:

```
<!DOCTYPE html>
<html lang="en">
<head>
  <title>Bootstrap Flex Fill</title>
  <meta charset="utf-8">
  <meta name="viewport" content="width=device-width, initial-scale=1">
  <link
href="https://cdn.jsdelivr.net/npm/bootstrap@5.3.3/dist/css/bootstrap.
min.css" rel="stylesheet">
  <script
src="https://cdn.jsdelivr.net/npm/bootstrap@5.3.3/dist/js/bootstrap.
bundle.min.js"></script>
</head>
<body>
<div class="container mt-3">
  <h2>Using flex-fill (Equal Width)</h2>
  <div class="d-flex mb-3 bg-primary">
    <div class="p-2 flex-fill bg-secondary">Flex Item 1</div>
    <div class="p-2 flex-fill bg-danger">Flex Item 2</div>
    <div class="p-2 flex-fill bg-info">Flex Item 3</div>
    <div class="p-2 flex-fill bg-warning">Flex Item 4</div>
  </div>
</div>

</body>
</html>
```

After running the code, the web page will look as follows:

Screen Size: 1366 x 633

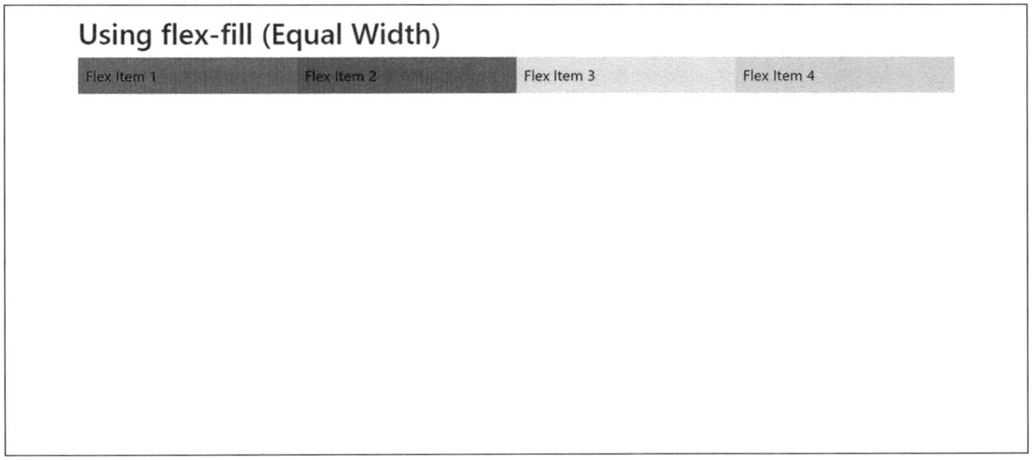

***Figure 9.16**: The flex fill is used to stretch to equal widths*

Growing a Flex item

To let a flex item take up the rest of the space, use the **.flex-grow-1** Bootstrap class.

Let us see an example in which a specific flex item takes up the remaining space. We have shown all the flex items one by one:

```
<!DOCTYPE html>
<html lang="en">
<head>
  <title>Bootstrap Flex Grow</title>
  <meta charset="utf-8">
  <meta name="viewport" content="width=device-width, initial-scale=1">
  <link
href="https://cdn.jsdelivr.net/npm/bootstrap@5.3.3/dist/css/bootstrap.
min.css" rel="stylesheet">
  <script
src="https://cdn.jsdelivr.net/npm/bootstrap@5.3.3/dist/js/bootstrap.
bundle.min.js"></script>
</head>
<body>
<div class="container mt-3">
  <h2>Flex Grow</h2>
  <p>The last flex item takes up the remaining space:</p>
  <div class="d-flex mb-3 bg-primary">
    <div class="p-2 bg-secondary">Flex Item 1</div>
    <div class="p-2 bg-danger">Flex Item 2</div>
    <div class="p-2 bg-info">Flex Item 3</div>
    <div class="p-2 flex-grow-1 bg-warning">Flex Item 4</div>
  </div>
```

```
  <p>The 2nd last flex item takes up the remaining space:</p>
  <div class="d-flex mb-3 bg-primary">
    <div class="p-2 bg-secondary">Flex Item 1</div>
    <div class="p-2 bg-danger">Flex Item 2</div>
    <div class="p-2 flex-grow-1  bg-info">Flex Item 3</div>
    <div class="p-2 bg-warning">Flex Item 4</div>
  </div>
  <p>The 2nd flex item takes up the remaining space:</p>
  <div class="d-flex mb-3 bg-primary">
    <div class="p-2 bg-secondary">Flex Item 1</div>
    <div class="p-2 flex-grow-1 bg-danger">Flex Item 2</div>
    <div class="p-2 bg-info">Flex Item 3</div>
    <div class="p-2 bg-warning">Flex Item 4</div>
  </div>
  <p>The 1st flex item takes up the remaining space:</p>
  <div class="d-flex mb-3 bg-primary">
    <div class="p-2 flex-grow-1 bg-secondary">Flex Item 1</div>
    <div class="p-2 bg-danger">Flex Item 2</div>
    <div class="p-2 bg-info">Flex Item 3</div>
    <div class="p-2 bg-warning">Flex Item 4</div>
  </div>
</div>

</body>
</html>
```

After running the code, the web page will look as follows:

Screen Size: 1366 x 633

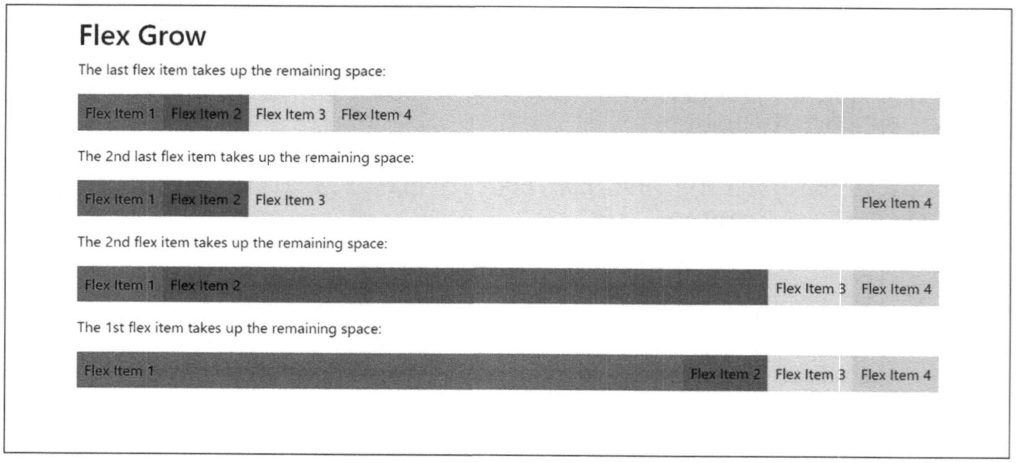

Figure 9.17: *The flex item takes up the rest of the space*

Shrinking a Flex item

To let a flex item shrink and wrap its content to a new line to allow more space for the other flex item, use the **.flex-shrink-1** Bootstrap class. Let us see an example.

In the following example, the second flex item with **flex-shrink** shrinks and allows more space for the previous flex item with **.w-100**. The second flex item wraps its content to a new line:

```
<!DOCTYPE html>
<html lang="en">
<head>
  <title>Bootstrap Flex Shrink</title>
  <meta charset="utf-8">
  <meta name="viewport" content="width=device-width, initial-scale=1">
  <link
href="https://cdn.jsdelivr.net/npm/bootstrap@5.3.3/dist/css/bootstrap.
min.css" rel="stylesheet">
  <script
src="https://cdn.jsdelivr.net/npm/bootstrap@5.3.3/dist/js/bootstrap.
bundle.min.js"></script>
</head>
<body>
<div class="container mt-3">
  <h2>Flex Shrink</h2>
  <p>The last flex item takes up the remaining space:</p>
  <div class="d-flex mt-4 bg-primary">
    <div class="p-2 w-100 bg-secondary">Flex Item 1</div>
    <div class="p-2 flex-shrink-1 bg-danger">Flex Item 2</div>
  </div>
</div>

</body>
</html>
```

After running the code, the web page will look as follows:

Screen Size: 1366 x 633

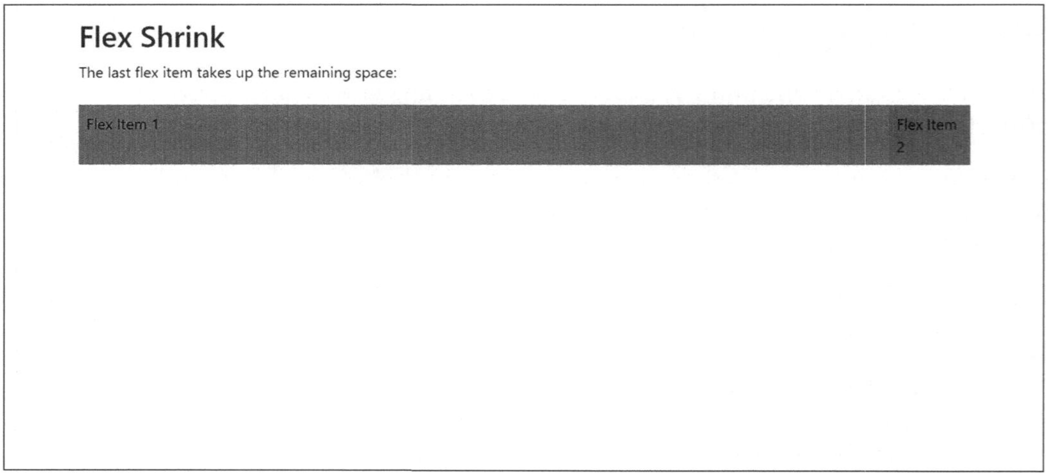

Figure 9.18: *Shrink a flex item*

Using Align Content

The flex items can be aligned together using the **`.align-content-*`** classes. The **`align-content`** in the flexbox is used to control the alignment of the entire flex container's lines when there's extra space on the cross-axis. It's particularly useful for multi-line flex containers, affecting the space between lines.

They can be aligned using the following Bootstrap classes:

- **`.align-content-start`:** Aligns the flex lines to the start of the container
- **`.align-content-end`:** Aligns the flex lines to the end of the container
- **`.align-content-center`:** Centers the flex lines in the container
- **`.align-content-between`:** Distributes the flex lines evenly, with the first line at the start and the last line at the end
- **`.align-content-around`:** Distributes the flex lines evenly, with equal space around each line
- **`.align-content-stretch`:** Stretches the flex lines to fill the container (default behavior)

Let us see an example of vertically aligning a specific flex item on a web page with Bootstrap:

```
<!DOCTYPE html>
<html lang="en">
<head>
  <title>Bootstrap Align Content</title>
  <meta charset="utf-8">
```

```
  <meta name="viewport" content="width=device-width, initial-scale=1">
  <link
href="https://cdn.jsdelivr.net/npm/bootstrap@5.3.3/dist/css/bootstrap.
min.css" rel="stylesheet">
  <script
src="https://cdn.jsdelivr.net/npm/bootstrap@5.3.3/dist/js/bootstrap.
bundle.min.js"></script>
</head>
<body>
<div class="container mt-3">
  <h2>Align Content</h2>
  <p>Align Content Start</p>
  <div class="d-flex flex-wrap align-content-start bg-dark"
style="height:200px;">
    <div class="p-2 bg-secondary">Flex Item 1</div>
    <div class="p-2 bg-danger">Flex Item 2</div>
    <div class="p-2 bg-info">Flex Item 3</div>
    <div class="p-2 bg-warning">Flex Item 4</div>
    <div class="p-2 bg-secondary">Flex Item 5</div>
    <div class="p-2 bg-danger">Flex Item 6</div>
    <div class="p-2 bg-info">Flex Item 7</div>
    <div class="p-2 bg-warning">Flex Item 8</div>
  </div>
  <p>Align Content End</p>
  <div class="d-flex flex-wrap align-content-end bg-dark"
style="height:200px;">
    <div class="p-2 bg-secondary">Flex Item 1</div>
    <div class="p-2 bg-danger">Flex Item 2</div>
    <div class="p-2 bg-info">Flex Item 3</div>
    <div class="p-2 bg-warning">Flex Item 4</div>
    <div class="p-2 bg-secondary">Flex Item 5</div>
    <div class="p-2 bg-danger">Flex Item 6</div>
    <div class="p-2 bg-info">Flex Item 7</div>
    <div class="p-2 bg-warning">Flex Item 8</div>
  </div>
  <p>Align Content Center</p>
  <div class="d-flex flex-wrap align-content-center bg-dark"
style="height:200px;">
    <div class="p-2 bg-secondary">Flex Item 1</div>
    <div class="p-2 bg-danger">Flex Item 2</div>
    <div class="p-2 bg-info">Flex Item 3</div>
    <div class="p-2 bg-warning">Flex Item 4</div>
    <div class="p-2 bg-secondary">Flex Item 5</div>
    <div class="p-2 bg-danger">Flex Item 6</div>
    <div class="p-2 bg-info">Flex Item 7</div>
    <div class="p-2 bg-warning">Flex Item 8</div>
  </div>
```

```
  <p>Align Content Between</p>
  <div class="d-flex flex-wrap align-content-between bg-dark"
style="height:200px;">
    <div class="p-2 bg-secondary">Flex Item 1</div>
    <div class="p-2 bg-danger">Flex Item 2</div>
    <div class="p-2 bg-info">Flex Item 3</div>
    <div class="p-2 bg-warning">Flex Item 4</div>
    <div class="p-2 bg-secondary">Flex Item 5</div>
    <div class="p-2 bg-danger">Flex Item 6</div>
    <div class="p-2 bg-info">Flex Item 7</div>
    <div class="p-2 bg-warning">Flex Item 8</div>
  </div>
  <p>Align Content Around</p>
  <div class="d-flex flex-wrap align-content-around bg-dark"
style="height:200px;">
    <div class="p-2 bg-secondary">Flex Item 1</div>
    <div class="p-2 bg-danger">Flex Item 2</div>
    <div class="p-2 bg-info">Flex Item 3</div>
    <div class="p-2 bg-warning">Flex Item 4</div>
    <div class="p-2 bg-secondary">Flex Item 5</div>
    <div class="p-2 bg-danger">Flex Item 6</div>
    <div class="p-2 bg-info">Flex Item 7</div>
    <div class="p-2 bg-warning">Flex Item 8</div>
  </div>
  <p>Align Content Stretch</p>
  <div class="d-flex flex-wrap align-content-stretch bg-dark"
style="height:200px;">
    <div class="p-2 bg-secondary">Flex Item 1</div>
    <div class="p-2 bg-danger">Flex Item 2</div>
    <div class="p-2 bg-info">Flex Item 3</div>
    <div class="p-2 bg-warning">Flex Item 4</div>
    <div class="p-2 bg-secondary">Flex Item 5</div>
    <div class="p-2 bg-danger">Flex Item 6</div>
    <div class="p-2 bg-info">Flex Item 7</div>
    <div class="p-2 bg-warning">Flex Item 8</div>
  </div>
</div>
</body>
</html>
```

After running the code, the web page will look as follows:

Screen Size: 1366 x 633

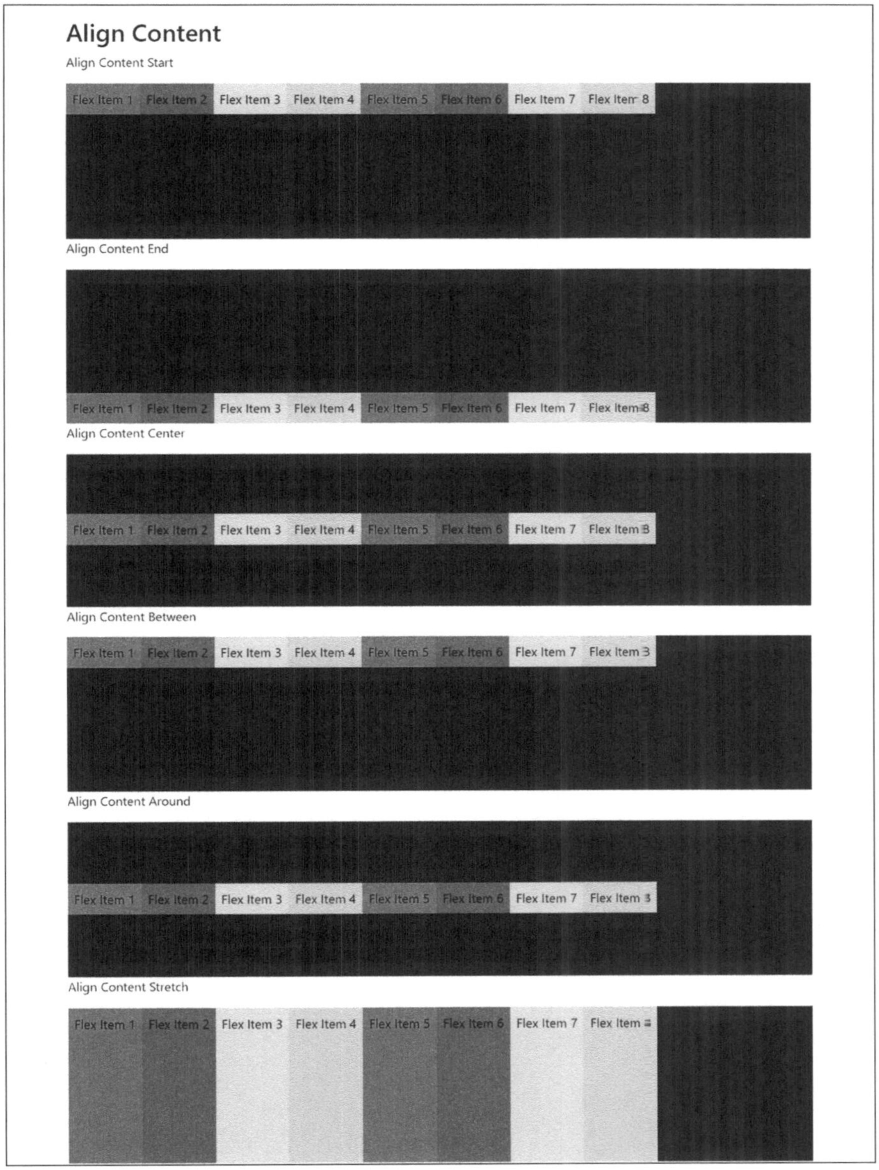

Figure 9.19: *Align the flex items together*

Float

Use the following utility classes to float an element to the left or right. You can also disable floating:

- **`float-start`:** Float to the left

- **float-end:** Float to the right
- **float-none:** Disable floating

Let us see an example of floating an element:

```
<!DOCTYPE html>
<html lang="en">
<head>
  <title>Bootstrap Float</title>
  <meta charset="utf-8">
  <meta name="viewport" content="width=device-width, initial-scale=1">
  <link
href="https://cdn.jsdelivr.net/npm/bootstrap@5.3.3/dist/css/bootstrap.
min.css" rel="stylesheet">
  <script
src="https://cdn.jsdelivr.net/npm/bootstrap@5.3.3/dist/js/bootstrap.
bundle.min.js"></script>
</head>
<body>

<div class="container mt-3">
  <h2>Float</h2>
  <div class="float-start">Float start </div><br>
  <div class="float-end">Float ends</div><br>
  <div class="float-none">Disable float</div>
</div>

</body>
</html>
```

After running the code, the web page will look as follows:

Screen Size: 1366 x 633

Figure 9.20: *Float elements on a web page*

Responsive Floats

The responsive floats also exist, that is, float elements to the right or left based on the screen size. The Bootstrap class is the following:

```
.float-*-start|end
```

Here, the * can be any of the following based on the screen width:

- **sm:** For screen size >=576px
- **md:** For screen size >=768px
- **lg:** For screen size >=992px
- **xl:** For screen size >=1200px
- **xxl:** For screen size >=1400px

Let us see an example and understand how responsive float works on a web page:

```
<!DOCTYPE html>
<html lang="en">
<head>
  <title>Bootstrap Responsive Floats</title>
  <meta charset="utf-8">
  <meta name="viewport" content="width=device-width, initial-scale=1">
  <link
href="https://cdn.jsdelivr.net/npm/bootstrap@5.3.3/dist/css/bootstrap.
min.css" rel="stylesheet">
  <script
src="https://cdn.jsdelivr.net/npm/bootstrap@5.3.3/dist/js/bootstrap.
bundle.min.js"></script>
</head>
<body>

<div class="container mt-3">
  <h2>Responsive Floats</h2>
  <p>Resize the browser window to see the effect.</p>
  <div>
    <div class="float-sm-end">Floats right on screen width >=576px</
div><br>
    <div class="float-md-end">Floats right on screen width >=768px</
div><br>
    <div class="float-lg-end">Floats right on screen width >=992px</
div><br>
    <div class="float-xl-end">Floats right on screen width >=1200px</
div><br>
    <div class="float-xxl-end">Floats right on screen width >=1400px</
div><br>
  </div>
```

```
</div>

</body>
</html>
```

After running the code, the web page will look as follows:

Screen Size: 1366 x 633

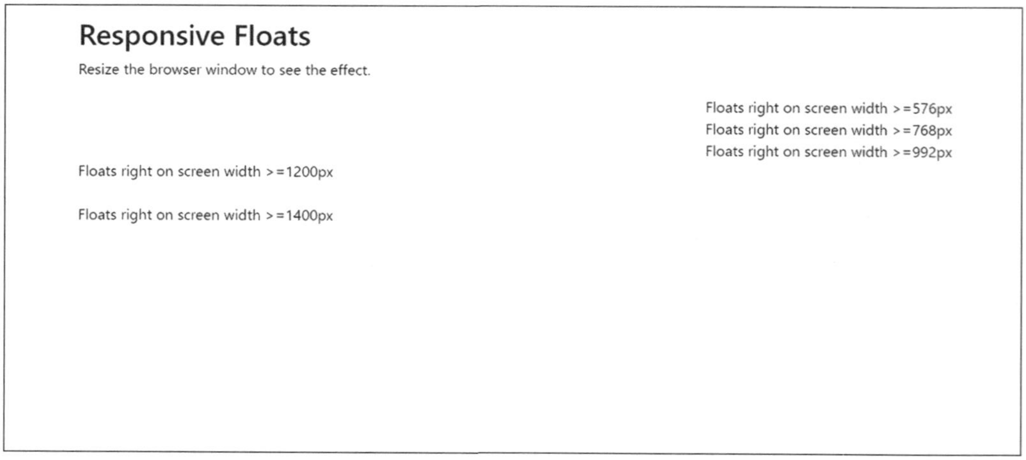

Figure 9.21: *Responsive Floats*

Interactions

Bootstrap also provides some classes for selecting text and element interactions. Let us see them with examples.

Text Selection

The content on a web page can be easily selected using a mouse, like double-clicking to copy the complete line or paragraph. However, with Bootstrap we can easily change the behavior using the following classes:

- **`user-select-all`:** Select the entire paragraph by clicking only
- **`user-select-auto`:** The default select behavior
- **`user-select-none`:** Disable selection

Let us see an example to change how text is selected on a web page with Bootstrap:

```
<!DOCTYPE html>
<html lang="en">
<head>
  <title>Bootstrap Text Selection</title>
```

```
  <meta charset="utf-8">
  <meta name="viewport" content="width=device-width, initial-scale=1">
  <link
href="https://cdn.jsdelivr.net/npm/bootstrap@5.3.3/dist/css/bootstrap.
min.css" rel="stylesheet">
  <script
src="https://cdn.jsdelivr.net/npm/bootstrap@5.3.3/dist/js/bootstrap.
bundle.min.js"></script>
</head>
<body>

<div class="container mt-3">
  <h2>Text Selection</h2>
  <p class="user-select-all">Select the entire paragraph on clicking.</p>
  <p class="user-select-auto">The default select behaviour. </p>
  <p class="user-select-none">Disable selection</p>
</div>

</body>
</html>
```

After running the code, the web page will look as follows: The last line won't get selected using a single or double-click because we have set **`user-select-none`**:

Screen Size: 1366 x 633

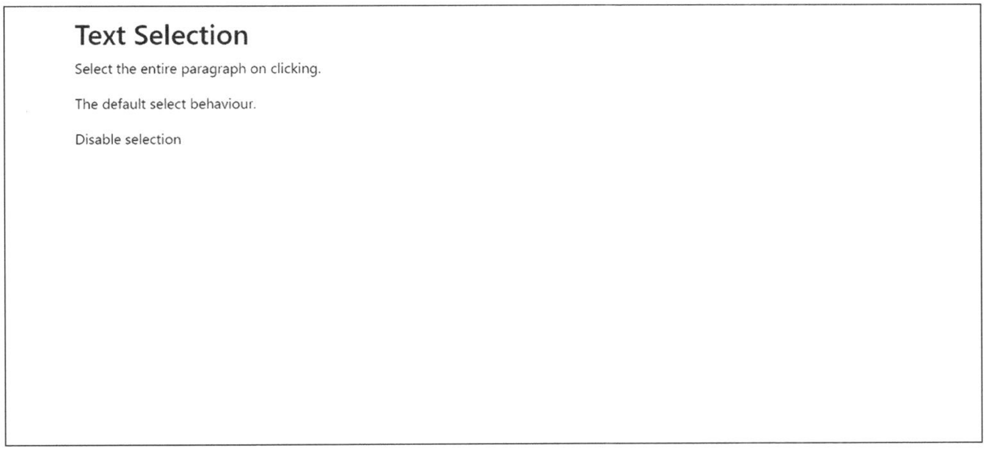

Figure 9.22: *The last line cannot be selected*

On clicking the first line, all the text gets selected completely as shown in the following figure because we have used the **`user-select-all`** class:

Screen Size: 1366 x 633

Figure 9.23: *Select the entire paragraph by clicking*

On clicking a word in the second line, only that specific word gets selected as shown in the following figure because we have set the default behavior using the **`user-select-auto`** class:

Screen Size: 1366 x 633

Figure 9.24: *Click any word to select it*

Pointer Events

The pointer events in Bootstrap include the **`.pe-none`** and **`.pe-auto`** Bootstrap classes. It allows a user to prevent or add element interactions on a web page.

Let us see an example where we will create a clickable and unclickable link on a web page. In the following example, we have set the pointer event to none and also set the class **pe-auto.** The link will remain clickable:

```
<a href="#" class="pe-auto" style="pointer-events: none;">This link</a>
is clickable.
```

Here is an example:

```
<!DOCTYPE html>
<html lang="en">
<head>
  <title>Bootstrap Pointer Events</title>
  <meta charset="utf-8">
  <meta name="viewport" content="width=device-width, initial-scale=1">
  <link
href="https://cdn.jsdelivr.net/npm/bootstrap@5.3.3/dist/css/bootstrap.
min.css" rel="stylesheet">
  <script
src="https://cdn.jsdelivr.net/npm/bootstrap@5.3.3/dist/js/bootstrap.
bundle.min.js"></script>
</head>
<body>

<div class="container mt-3">
  <h2>Text Selection</h2>
  <p><a href="#" class="pe-none">This link</a> is unclickable. </p>
  <p><a href="#" class="pe-auto" style="pointer-events: none;">This
link</a> is clickable. </p>
</div>

</body>
</html>
```

After running the code, the web page will look as follows:

Screen Size: 1366 x 633

Figure 9.25: *One of the links is unclickable*

Spacing

For responsive margin and padding, Bootstrap provides some utility classes for all screen sizes:

- **`xs`:** For screen size <576px
- **`sm`:** For screen size >=576px
- **`md`:** For screen size >=768px
- **`lg`:** For screen size >=992px
- **`xl`:** For screen size >=1200px
- **`xxl`:** For screen size >=1400px

The following is the format of the utility classes. For the **`xs`** breakpoint:

`{property}{sides}-{size}`

For the **`sm`, `md`, `lg`, `xl`** , and **`xxl`** breakpoints:

`{property}{sides}-{breakpoint}-{size}`

The **property** shown here can be any of the following:

- `m` : To set the margin
- `p` : To set the **padding**

The **sides** shown can be any of the following:

- **`t`** : Sets margin-top or padding-top
- **`b`** : Sets margin-bottom or padding-bottom
- **`s`** : Sets margin-left or padding-left

- **e** : Sets margin-right or padding-right
- **x** : Sets both padding-left and padding-right or margin-left and margin-right
- **y** ; Sets both padding-top and padding-bottom or margin-top and margin-bottom
- **blank** : Sets a margin or padding on all four sides of the element

Similarly, the size shown can be any of the following:

- **0** : sets margin or padding to 0
- **1** : sets margin or padding to .25rem
- **2** : sets margin or padding to .5rem
- **3** : sets margin or padding to 1rem
- **4** : sets margin or padding to 1.5rem
- **5** : sets margin or padding to 3rem
- **auto** : sets margin to auto

Let's see some quick examples. Follow what we mentioned earlier about property, sides, breakpoints, and size:

- **m-5:** Sets the margin on all sides to 3rem
- **p-5:** Sets the padding on all the sides to 3rem
- **pt-5:** Sets the top padding to 3rem
- **pb-4:** Sets the bottom padding to 1.5rem
- **mt-5:** Sets the top margin to 3rem

Let us implement this in our example and set the spacing on a web page:

```
<!DOCTYPE html>
<html lang="en">
<head>
  <title>Bootstrap Spacing</title>
  <meta charset="utf-8">
  <meta name="viewport" content="width=device-width, initial-scale=1">
  <link
href="https://cdn.jsdelivr.net/npm/bootstrap@5.3.3/dist/css/bootstrap.
min.css" rel="stylesheet">
  <script
src="https://cdn.jsdelivr.net/npm/bootstrap@5.3.3/dist/js/bootstrap.
bundle.min.js"></script>
</head>
<body>

<div class="container mt-3">
  <h1>Spacing</h1>
```

```
  <div class="m-5 bg-primary">Sets the margin on all sides to 3rem</div>
  <div class="p-5 bg-secondary">Sets the padding on all the sides to 
3rem</div>
  <div class="pt-5 bg-warning">Sets the top padding to 3rem</div>
  <div class="pb-4 bg-info">Sets the bottom padding to 1.5rem</div>
  <div class="mt-5 bg-danger">Sets the top margin to 3rem</div>
</div>

</body>
</html>
```

After running the code, the web page will look as follows:

Screen Size: 1366 x 633

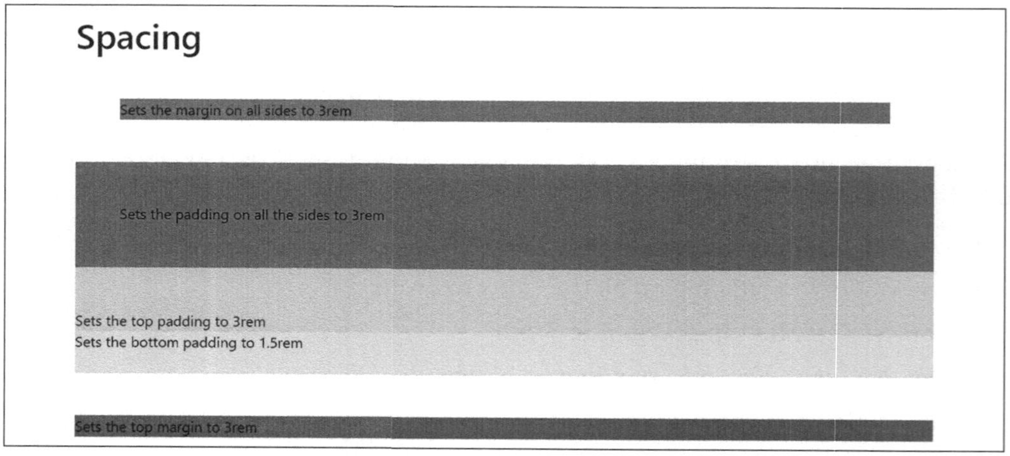

Figure 9.26: *Set the spacing*

Width Sizing

To set the size of an element's width, use the **`w-*`** classes. The width classes are utility classes. The classes include:

- **`.w-25`:** Width 25%
- **`.w-50`:** Width 50%
- **`.w-75`:** Width 75%
- **`.w-100`:** Width 100%
- **`.w-auto`:** Width Auto
- **`.mw-100`:** Max Width 100%

Let us see an example of setting the width size of an element on a web page:

```
<!DOCTYPE html>
<html lang="en">
<head>
  <title>Bootstrap Width Sizing</title>
  <meta charset="utf-8">
  <meta name="viewport" content="width=device-width, initial-scale=1">
  <link
href="https://cdn.jsdelivr.net/npm/bootstrap@5.3.3/dist/css/bootstrap.
min.css" rel="stylesheet">
  <script
src="https://cdn.jsdelivr.net/npm/bootstrap@5.3.3/dist/js/bootstrap.
bundle.min.js"></script>
</head>
<body>
<div class="container mt-2">
  <h1>Sizing (Width)</h1>
  <div class="w-25 bg-primary">25% Width</div>
  <div class="w-50 bg-secondary">50% Width</div>
  <div class="w-75 bg-info">75% Width</div>
  <div class="w-100 bg-warning">100% Width</div>
  <div class="w-auto bg-danger">Auto Width </div>
  <div class="mw-100 bg-primary">Max Width</div>
</div>
</body>
</html>
```

After running the code, the web page will look as follows:

Screen Size: 1366 x 633

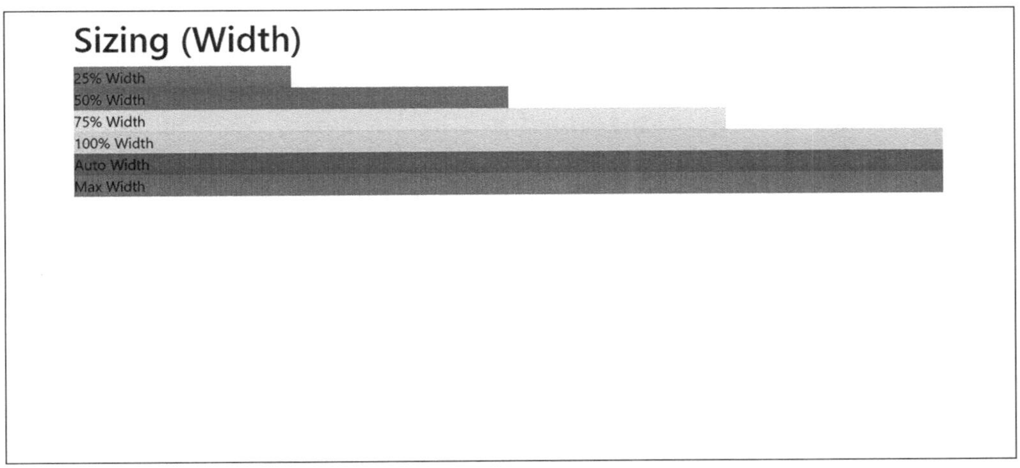

Figure 9.27: *Set the size of the element's width*

Height Sizing

To set the size of an element's height, use the **h-*** classes. The height classes are utility classes. The classes include:

- **.h-25**: Height 25%
- **.h-50**: Height 50%
- **.h-75**: Height 75%
- **.h-100**: Height 100%
- **.h-auto**: Height Auto
- **.mh-100**: Max Height 100%

Let us see an example of setting the height size of an element on a web page:

```
<!DOCTYPE html>
<html lang="en">
<head>
  <title>Bootstrap Height Sizing</title>
  <meta charset="utf-8">
  <meta name="viewport" content="width=device-width, initial-scale=1">
  <link
href="https://cdn.jsdelivr.net/npm/bootstrap@5.3.3/dist/css/bootstrap.
min.css" rel="stylesheet">
  <script
src="https://cdn.jsdelivr.net/npm/bootstrap@5.3.3/dist/js/bootstrap.
bundle.min.js"></script>
</head>
<body>
<div class="container mt-3">
  <h1>Sizing (Height)</h1>
  <div style="height:300px;background-color:orange">
    <div class="h-25 d-inline-block p-3 bg-primary">25% Height</div>
    <div class="h-50 d-inline-block p-3 bg-secondary">50% Height</div>
    <div class="h-75 d-inline-block p-3 bg-info">75% Height</div>
    <div class="h-100 d-inline-block p-3 bg-primary">100% Height</div>
    <div class="h-auto d-inline-block p-3 bg-warning">Auto Height</div>
    <div class="mh-100 d-inline-block p-3 bg-warning">100% Max Height</
div>
  </div>
</div>
</body>
</html>
```

After running the code, the web page will look as follows:

Screen Size: 1366 x 633

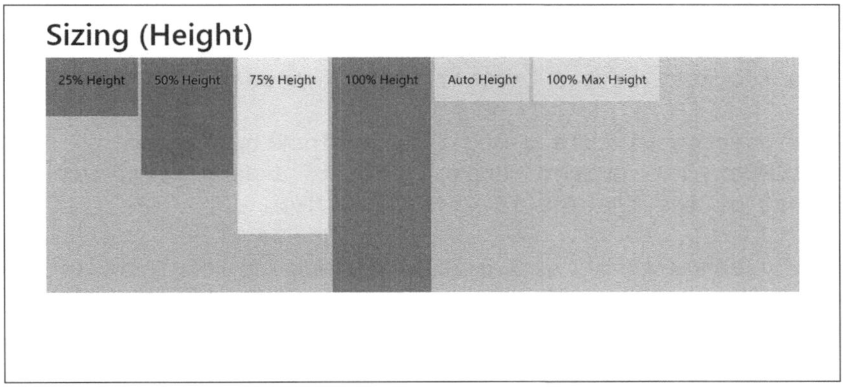

Figure 9.28: *Set the size of the element's height*

Overflow

With Bootstrap, easily set what happens when content overflows. Here are the classes:

- **overflow-auto:** Overflow is clipped but the scrollbar gets added if it is required
- **overflow-hidden:** Overflow is clipped and the rest of the content will be hidden
- **overflow-visible:** Overflow is not clipped
- **overflow-scroll:** Overflow is clipped, and scrollbar gets added.

Let us see an example of handling content overflow on a web page:

```
<!DOCTYPE html>
<html lang="en">
<head>
  <title>Bootstrap Handling Content Overflow</title>
  <meta charset="utf-8">
  <meta name="viewport" content="width=device-width, initial-scale=1">
  <link
href="https://cdn.jsdelivr.net/npm/bootstrap@5.3.3/dist/css/bootstrap.
min.css" rel="stylesheet">
  <script
src="https://cdn.jsdelivr.net/npm/bootstrap@5.3.3/dist/js/bootstrap.
bundle.min.js"></script>
</head>
<body>
<h1>Handling Content Overflow</h1>
<div class="overflow-auto p-2 d-inline-block bg-light" style="max-width:
200px; max-height: 80px;">This is a demo text. Overflow is clipped but
the scrollbar gets added if it is required.</div>
```

```
<div class="overflow-hidden p-2 d-inline-block bg-primary" style="-
max-width: 200px; max-height: 80px;">This is a demo text. Overflow is
clipped and the rest of the content will be hidden.</div>

<div class="overflow-visible p-2 d-inline-block bg-secondary" style="-
max-width: 200px; max-height: 80px;">This is a demo text. Overflow is not
clipped. Rest of the content is visible.</div>

<div class="overflow-scroll p-3 d-inline-block bg-info" style="max-width:
200px; max-height: 80px;">This is a demo text. Overflow is clipped and
scrollbar gets added.</div>

</body>
</html>
```

After running the code, the web page will look as follows:

Screen Size: 1366 x 633

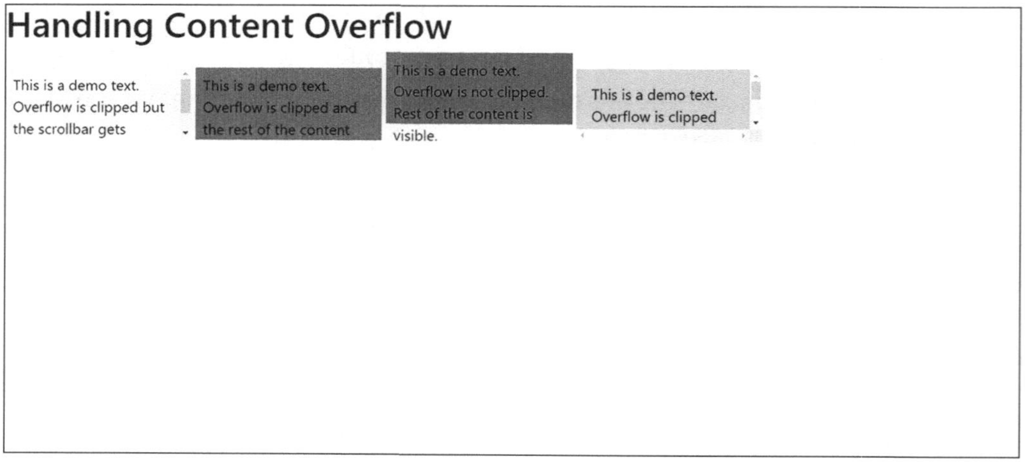

Figure 9.29: *Handling content overflow on a web page*

Display

The display value of components in Bootstrap can be toggled using the display utilities. With this, you can easily control the display when printing.

Consider changing the display property value using the display utility classes in Bootstrap. Name the classes using the following format:

```
.d-{value}
```

The value here can be:

- none
- inline
- inline-block
- block
- grid
- inline-grid
- table
- table-cell
- table-row
- flex
- inline-flex

Note: *You must have used some of the preceding values in CSS as well.*

Let us see an example of using the **`.d-inline-block`**:

```
<!DOCTYPE html>
<html lang="en">
<head>
  <title>Bootstrap Display</title>
  <meta charset="utf-8">
  <meta name="viewport" content="width=device-width, initial-scale=1">
  <link
href="https://cdn.jsdelivr.net/npm/bootstrap@5.3.3/dist/css/bootstrap.
min.css" rel="stylesheet">
  <script
src="https://cdn.jsdelivr.net/npm/bootstrap@5.3.3/dist/js/bootstrap.
bundle.min.js"></script>
</head>
<body>
<div class="container mt-3">
  <span class="d-inline-block text-truncate" style="max-width: 130px;">
  Neque porro quisquam est qui dolorem
  </span>
</div>
</body>
</html>
```

After running the code, the web page will look as follows:

Screen Size: 1366 x 633

Figure 9.30: *The display value*

Hide elements

Use responsive display classes for hiding elements on devices. To hide elements, use the **`.d-none`** class or one of the **`.d-{sm,md,lg,xl,xxl}-none`** classes for any responsive device.

The following are the classes based on the screen size:

Screen/ Device size	**Class**
Hidden on all devices	`.d-none`
Hidden only on `xs` device	`.d-none .d-sm-block`
Hidden only on `sm` device	`.d-sm-none .d-md-block`
Hidden only on `md` device	`.d-md-none .d-lg-block`
Hidden only on `lg` device	`.d-lg-none .d-xl-block`
Hidden only on `xl` device	`.d-xl-none .d-xxl-block`
Hidden only on `xxl` device	`.d-xxl-none`

Table 9.1: *Classes based on screen size*

Let us see an example of hiding elements on a web page with Bootstrap:

```
<!DOCTYPE html>
<html lang="en">
<head>
  <title>Bootstrap Display</title>
  <meta charset="utf-8">
  <meta name="viewport" content="width=device-width, initial-scale=1">
  <link
href="https://cdn.jsdelivr.net/npm/bootstrap@5.3.3/dist/css/bootstrap.
min.css" rel="stylesheet">
```

```
  <script
src="https://cdn.jsdelivr.net/npm/bootstrap@5.3.3/dist/js/bootstrap.
bundle.min.js"></script>
</head>
<body>
<div class="container mt-3">
  <div>This line is visible.</div>
  <div class="d-none">This line is hidden on all devices.</div>
  <div class="d-lg-none">This line is hidden on only large devices
(992px and above).</div>
</div>
</body>
</html>
```

After running the code, the web page will look as follows:

Screen Size: 1366 x 633

Figure 9.31: *One of the lines is invisible and cannot be seen on the web page*

Vertical Align

The alignment of the inline, inline-block, inline-table, or table-cell elements can be easily changed using the vertical alignment utilities.

The following are the classes:

- **`align-baseline`**: Aligns the element with the baseline of its parent.
- **`align-top`**: Aligns the element with the top of the tallest element on the line.
- **`align-middle`**: Vertically aligns the element with the middle of the line.
- **`align-bottom`**: Aligns the element with the bottom of the line.
- **`align-text-bottom`**: Aligns the element with the bottom of the text within it.
- **`align-text-top`**: Aligns the element with the top of the text within it.

Vertically Align span

We can easily vertically align the span with Bootstrap. Let us see an example and vertically align inline container elements on a web page:

```
<!DOCTYPE html>
<html lang="en">
<head>
  <title>Bootstrap Vertical Alignment</title>
  <meta charset="utf-8">
  <meta name="viewport" content="width=device-width, initial-scale=1">
  <link
href="https://cdn.jsdelivr.net/npm/bootstrap@5.3.3/dist/css/bootstrap.
min.css" rel="stylesheet">
  <script
src="https://cdn.jsdelivr.net/npm/bootstrap@5.3.3/dist/js/bootstrap.
bundle.min.js"></script>
</head>
<body>
<div class="container mt-3">
  <h1>Demo Heading</h1>
  <p>The following elements are vertically aligned: </p>
  <span class="align-baseline">baseline</span>
  <span class="align-top">top</span>
  <span class="align-middle">middle</span>
  <span class="align-bottom">bottom</span>
  <span class="align-text-top">text-top</span>
  <span class="align-text-bottom">text-bottom</span>
</div>
</body>
</html>
```

After running the code, the web page will look as follows:

Screen Size: 1366 x 633

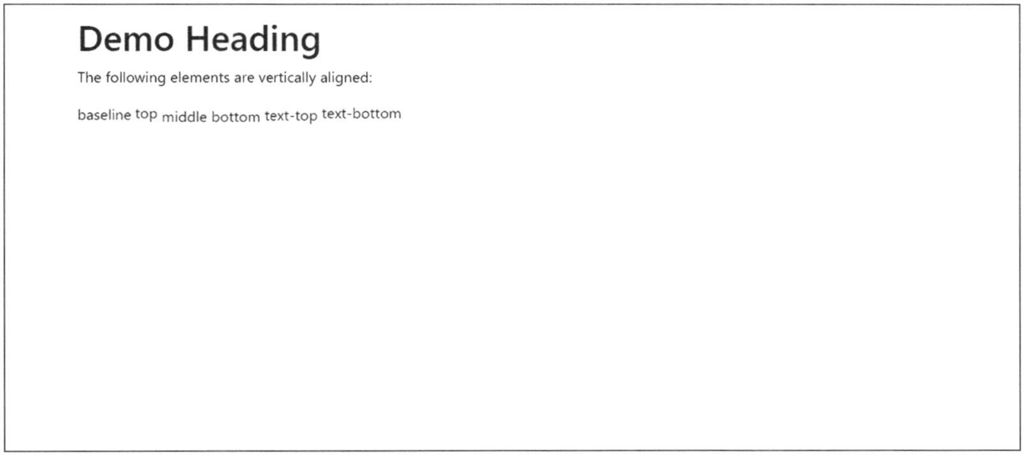

Figure 9.32: *Vertically align the span*

Vertically Align the Table Cells

The table cells can also be vertically aligned using the vertical-alignment utilities. Let us see an example of vertically aligning the table cells on a web page:

```
<!DOCTYPE html>
<html lang="en">
<head>
  <title>Bootstrap Vertical Alignment</title>
  <meta charset="utf-8">
  <meta name="viewport" content="width=device-width, initial-scale=1">
  <link
href="https://cdn.jsdelivr.net/npm/bootstrap@5.3.3/dist/css/bootstrap.
min.css" rel="stylesheet">
  <script
src="https://cdn.jsdelivr.net/npm/bootstrap@5.3.3/dist/js/bootstrap.
bundle.min.js"></script>
</head>
<body>
<div class="container mt-3">
  <h1>Demo Heading</h1>
  <table style="height: 200px;">
    <tbody>
      <tr>
        <td class="align-baseline">baseline</td>
        <td class="align-top">top</td>
        <td class="align-middle">middle</td>
        <td class="align-bottom">bottom</td>
        <td class="align-text-top">text-top</td>
```

```
        <td class="align-text-bottom">text-bottom</td>
      </tr>
    </tbody>
  </table>
</div>
</body>
</html>
```

After running the code, the web page will look as follows:

Screen Size: 1366 x 633

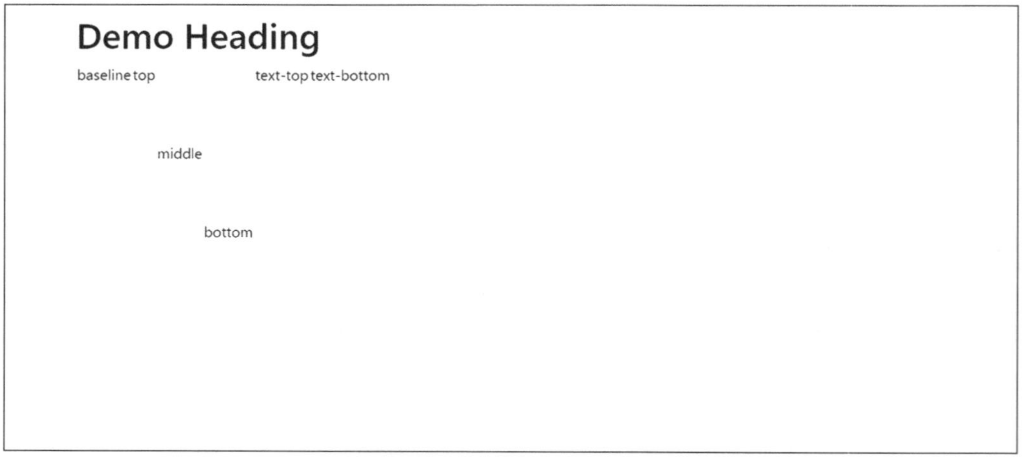

Figure 9.33: *Vertically align the table cells*

Conclusion

We are now familiar with how to work with borders and colors on a web page in Bootstrap. We also understood how to implement the Flexbox layout with Bootstrap to align content. With setting spacing and size elements, we also handled overflow content on a web page and toggled the display value of components.

In the next chapter, we will learn about optimizing websites with Bootstrap.

Points to Remember

- To add borders on a web page with Bootstrap, use the borders classes.
- Set the background color for text using the contextual classes **`.bg-*`** in Bootstrap.
- To set the gradient background color, use the **`.bg-gradient`** class.
- Set the text color using the contextual classes **`.text-*`** in Bootstrap.

- To transform direct children's elements into flex items using the class **`.d-flex`**.
- Display the flex items vertically using the **`.flex-column`** Bootstrap class.
- The **`justify-content`** class is used to control the alignment of flex items along the main axis.
- The **`align-items`** are used to align flex items along the cross-axis. It determines how flex items are positioned inside the flex container.
- The **`align-self`** in flexbox allows individual flex items to override the align-items property applied to the flex container.
- To force the flex-items into equal widths, use the **`.flex-fill`** class.
- To let a flex item take up the rest of the space, use the **`.flex-grow-1`** Bootstrap class.
- To let a flex item shrink and wrap its content to a new line to allow more space for the other flex item, use the **`.flex-shrink-1`** Bootstrap class.
- The **`.pe-none`** and **`.pe-auto`** Bootstrap classes allow a user to prevent or add element interactions on a web page.
- The display value of components in Bootstrap can be toggled using the display utilities.
- To hide elements, use the **`.d-none`** class in Bootstrap.
- The alignment of the elements can be easily changed using the vertical alignment utilities.

Multiple Choice Questions

1. Which Bootstrap class is used to remove all the borders from an element?
   a. `border-0`
   b. `border0`
   c. `border-none`
   d. `border-no`
2. Which Bootstrap class is used to set the text gradient background color?
   a. `bg-grad-color`
   b. `bg-grad`
   c. `gradient`
   d. `bg-gradient`

3. Which of the following classes is used to transform direct children's elements into flex items??
   a. `flex`
   b. `d-flex`
   c. `dflex-items`
   d. `flex-items`
4. Which of the following classes is used to display the flex item vertically?
   a. `flex-row`
   b. `flex-vertical`
   c. `flex-column`
   d. `flex-col`
5. How to disable a float on a web page with Bootstrap?
   a. `none`
   b. `float-none`
   c. `disable`
   d. `float-disable`
6. Which Bootstrap class is used to select the entire paragraph on clicking?
   a. `user-select-all`
   b. `user-select-auto`
   c. `user-select-none`
   d. `user-select`
7. Which Bootstrap class is used to make a link unclickable?
   a. `pe-unlink`
   b. `pe-link`
   c. `pe-all`
   d. `pe-none`
8. Can the vertical alignment be set for a table cell on a web page with Bootstrap?
   a. `Yes`
   b. `No`

Answers

1. a
2. d
3. b
4. c
5. b
6. a
7. d
8. a

Questions

- How are borders added to a web page?
- How are borders removed from a web page?
- How are the corners of the element rounded?
- Can a gradient color be set for the background on a web page?
- How are flex items displayed horizontally or vertically?
- How are flex items aligned in any direction?
- How are flex items set into equal widths?
- How do a flex item take up the rest of the space?
- How is selecting text on a web page disabled?
- How is a link made unclickable?
- How is content overflow on a web page handled?
- How are the elements on a web page hidden?
- How are the alignment of the elements changed?

Key Terms

- **Utility Classes:** Utility classes in Bootstrap are used on a web page for the content to display, hide, align, and much more.
- **Flexbox:** The flexbox layout model allows the designing of a flexible responsive layout structure.

- **Flex Fill:** To force the series of sibling elements, that is, the flex-items into equal widths, use the `.flex-fill` class.
- **Justify Content:** The alignment of the flex items can be easily changed using the `.justify-content-*` classes.
- **Align Items:** The `.align-items-*` classes are used to align flex items along the cross-axis.
- **Pointer Events:** The pointer events in Bootstrap that include the `.pe-none` and `.pe-auto` Bootstrap classes allow a user to prevent or add element interactions on a web page.

CHAPTER 10
Optimization Techniques for Bootstrap Websites

Introduction

This chapter covers some approaches and guiding principles, strategies, and techniques to build and maintain a responsive website with Bootstrap.

Structure

In this chapter, we will discuss the following topics:

- Techniques
- Optimizations
- Icons

Techniques

While working on Bootstrap, you should know the principles and techniques that built and maintained Bootstrap:

- Responsive
- Classes
- z-index scales

Responsive

Bootstrap responsive approach is referred to as mobile-first. Responsiveness is about reducing CSS overrides by pushing you to add styles as the viewport becomes larger.

Media queries, like min-width and max-width, are used to set the responsiveness for multiple devices, such as mobiles, tablets, desktops, large desktops, and more. They both allow for different layouts based on the viewport.

Let us see the usage of media queries, that is, the responsive breakpoints:

The `min-width`

The **`min-width`** media query triggers styles for screens when the device width is greater than a certain pixel. The media query for extra small devices, that is, **`xs`** is not provided. For the rest of the devices, such as mobile, laptops, and desktops, the breakpoints are as follows:

```
// Small devices (landscape phones, 576px and up)
@media (min-width: 576px) { ... }

// Medium devices (tablets, 768px and up)
@media (min-width: 768px) { ... }

// Large devices (desktops, 992px and up)
@media (min-width: 992px) { ... }

// Xlarge devices (large desktops, 1200px and up)
@media (min-width: 1200px) { ... }

// XXlarge devices (large desktops, 1400px and up)
@media (min-width: 1400px) { ... }
```

Let us see an example and use min-width. When the screen size is 992px and above, the background color will change to orange:

```
<!DOCTYPE html>
<html lang="en">
<head>
  <title>Bootstrap Responsiveness</title>
  <meta charset="utf-8">
  <meta name="viewport" content="width=device-width, initial-scale=1">
  <link
href="https://cdn.jsdelivr.net/npm/bootstrap@5.3.3/dist/css/bootstrap.
min.css" rel="stylesheet">
  <script
src="https://cdn.jsdelivr.net/npm/bootstrap@5.3.3/dist/js/bootstrap.
bundle.min.js"></script>
   <style>
            @media (min-width: 992px) {
                .container {
                    background: orange;
```

```
                }
            }
        </style>
</head>
<body>

<div class="container mt-3">
  <h2>Favourite Sports</h2>
  <p>Select any of the following sports you love to play and watch:</p>
  <form action="next.php">
    <label for="sel" class="form-label">Sports</label>
    <select class="form-select" id="sel" name="selmenu">
      <option>Football</option>
      <option>Cricket</option>
      <option>Tennis</option>
    </select>
    <button type="submit" class="btn btn-secondary mt-3">Submit</button>
  </form>
</div>

</body>
</html>
```

After running, the web page will look as follows: Here the screen size is less than 992px:

Screen Size: 980 x 633

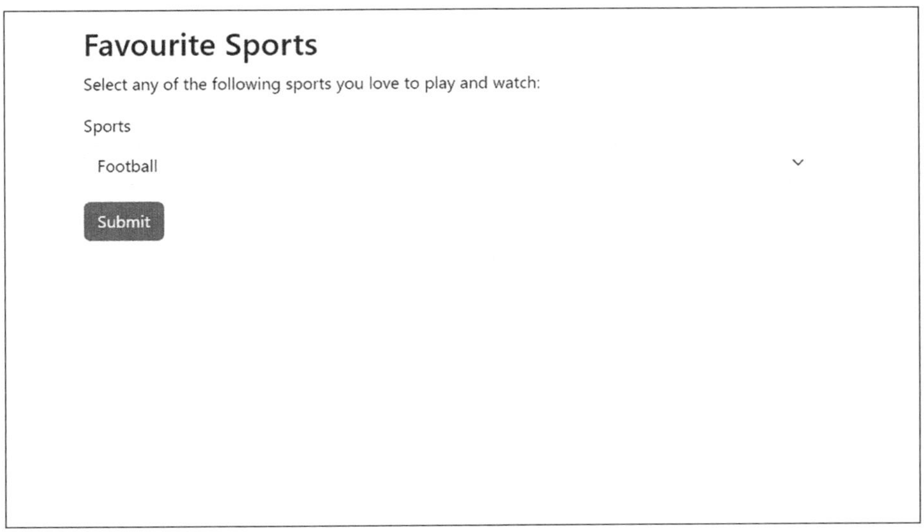

Figure 10.1: *The screen size is below 992px*

When the screen size is changed to 992px and above, the query will trigger and the background color will change to orange:

Screen Size: 1100x 633

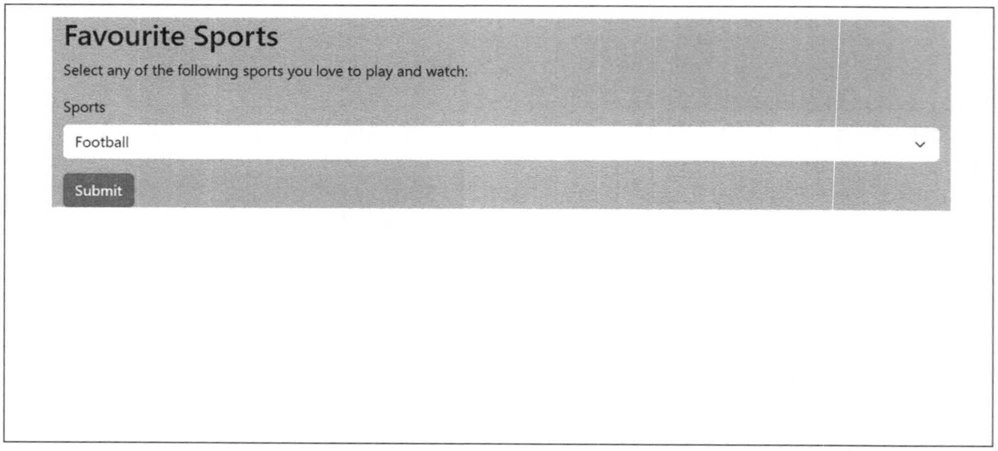

***Figure 10.2**: When the screen size is above 992px, the background color is changed*

The `max-width`

The media query for the opposite direction is occasionally used. For this, the **`max-width`** is used. The media query for extra-large devices is not provided. This query triggers styles for screens when the device width is less than a certain pixel:

```
// Extra small devices (portrait phones, less than 576px)
@media (max-width: 575.98px) { ... }

// Small devices (landscape phones, less than 768px)
@media (max-width: 767.98px) { ... }

// Medium devices (tablets, less than 992px)
@media (max-width: 991.98px) { ... }

// Large devices (desktops, less than 1200px)
@media (max-width: 1199.98px) { ... }
```

Let us see an example of using max-width. When the screen size is less than 992px, the background color will change to green:

```
<!DOCTYPE html>
<html lang="en">
<head>
  <title>Bootstrap Responsiveness</title>
```

```
  <meta charset="utf-8">
  <meta name="viewport" content="width=device-width, initial-scale=1">
  <link
href="https://cdn.jsdelivr.net/npm/bootstrap@5.3.3/dist/css/bootstrap.
min.css" rel="stylesheet">
  <script
src="https://cdn.jsdelivr.net/npm/bootstrap@5.3.3/dist/js/bootstrap.
bundle.min.js"></script>
   <style>
           @media (max-width: 992px) {
               .container {
                   background: green;
               }
           }
        </style>
</head>
<body>

<div class="container mt-3">
  <h2>Favourite Sports</h2>
  <p>Select any of the following sports you love to play and watch:</p>
  <form action="next.php">
    <label for="sel" class="form-label">Sports</label>
    <select class="form-select" id="sel" name="selmenu">
      <option>Football</option>
      <option>Cricket</option>
      <option>Tennis</option>
    </select>
    <button type="submit" class="btn btn-secondary mt-3">Submit</button>
  </form>
</div>

</body>
</html>
```

After running the code, the web page will look as follows: Here, the screen size is above 992px:

Screen Size: 1100 x 633

***Figure 10.3**: The screen size is above 992px*

When the screen size is less than 992px, the query will trigger and the background color will change to green:

Screen Size: 980 x 633

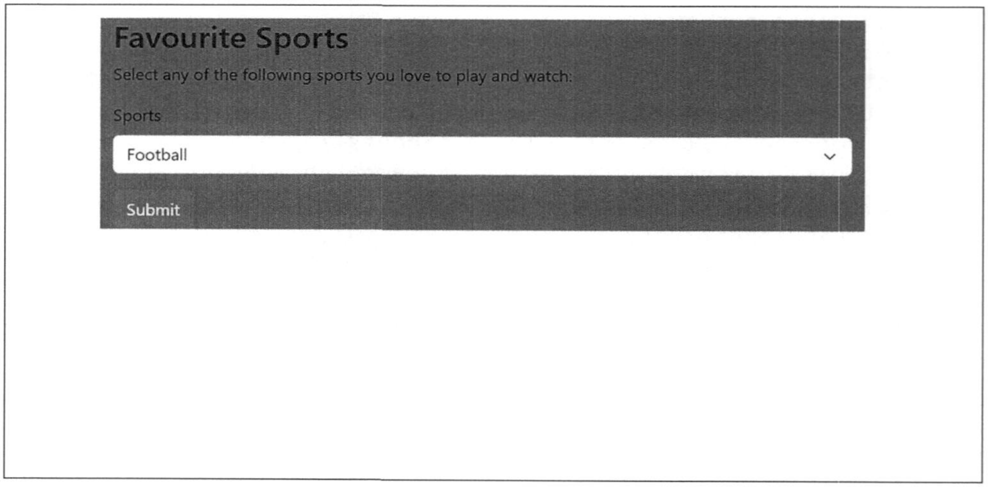

***Figure 10.4**: When the screen size is below 992px, the background color is changed*

Combine `min-width` and `max-width`

The **`min-width`** and **`max-width`** can be used together. You can easily target a single segment of screen size with the minimum and maximum breakpoint widths, that is, target a specific range of screen resolutions or viewport sizes:

```
// Extra small devices (portrait phones, less than 576px)
@media (max-width: 575.98px) { ... }

// Small devices (landscape phones, 576px and up)
@media (min-width: 576px) and (max-width: 767.98px) { ... }
```

```
// Medium devices (tablets, 768px and up)
@media (min-width: 768px) and (max-width: 991.98px) { ... }

// Large devices (desktops, 992px and up)
@media (min-width: 992px) and (max-width: 1199.98px) { ... }

// Extra large devices (large desktops, 1200px and up)
@media (min-width: 1200px) { ... }
```

Let us see an example and use both max-width and min-width:

```
<!DOCTYPE html>
<html lang="en">
<head>
  <title>Bootstrap Responsiveness</title>
  <meta charset="utf-8">
  <meta name="viewport" content="width=device-width, initial-scale=1">
  <link
href="https://cdn.jsdelivr.net/npm/bootstrap@5.3.3/dist/css/bootstrap.
min.css" rel="stylesheet">
  <script
src="https://cdn.jsdelivr.net/npm/bootstrap@5.3.3/dist/js/bootstrap.
bundle.min.js"></script>
   <style>
         @media (min-width: 768px) and (max-width: 991.98px) {
               .container {
                   background: green;
               }
           }
        </style>
</head>
<body>

<div class="container mt-3">
  <h2>Favourite Sports</h2>
  <p>Select any of the following sports you love to play and watch:</p>
  <form action="next.php">
    <label for="sel" class="form-label">Sports</label>
    <select class="form-select" id="sel" name="selmenu">
      <option>Football</option>
      <option>Cricket</option>
      <option>Tennis</option>
    </select>
    <button type="submit" class="btn btn-secondary mt-3">Submit</button>
  </form>
</div>
```

```
</body>
</html>
```

After running the code, the web page will look as follows: Here, the screen size is above 991.98px:

Screen Size: 1100 x 633

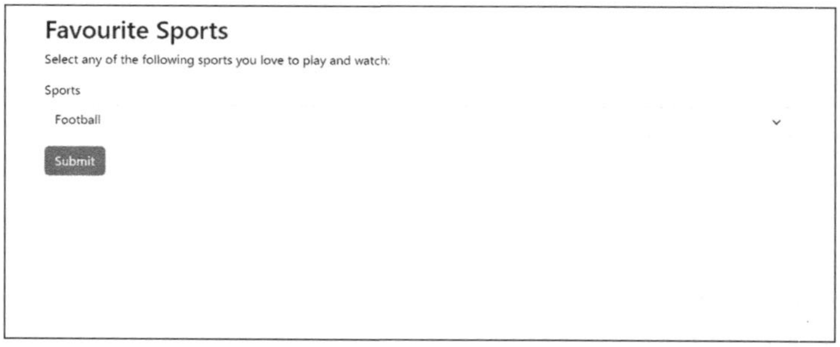

***Figure 10.5**: The screen size is above 991.98px*

Change the screen size. The query will trigger only for screen sizes between 768px and 991.98px and the background color will change:

Screen Size: 980 x 633

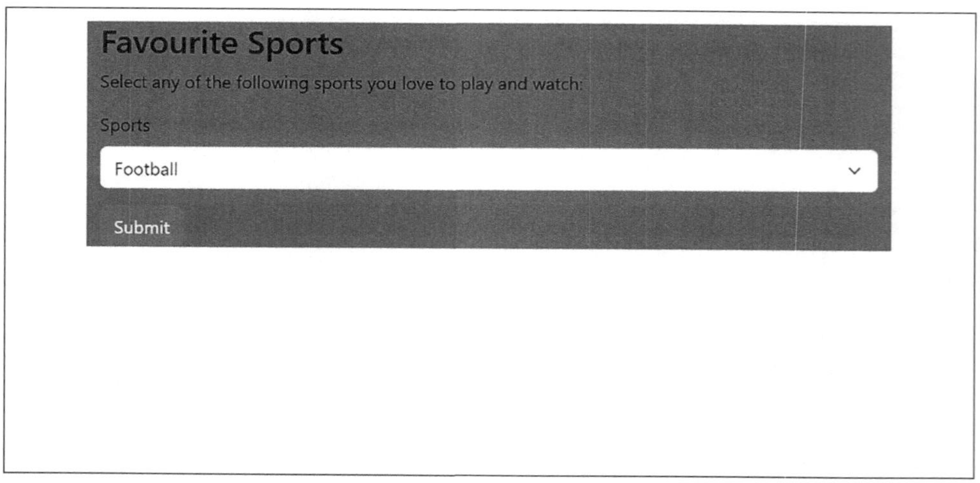

***Figure 10.6**: When the screen size is between 768 and 991.98, the background color is changed*

Classes

In Bootstrap 5, the components can be easily styled. The modifier classes are designed to provide an easy way to modify various properties of components, such as padding, margins, background color, and so on.

Let us see an example to set the button color on a web page with Bootstrap. For buttons, you can't use the background contextual classes, such as bg-primary, bg-secondary, and so on. Instead, use the **.btn-primary, btn-secondary,** class as a modifier class:

```
<!DOCTYPE html>
<html lang="en">
<head>
  <title>Bootstrap Classes</title>
  <meta charset="utf-8">
  <meta name="viewport" content="width=device-width, initial-scale=1">
  <link
href="https://cdn.jsdelivr.net/npm/bootstrap@5.3.3/dist/css/bootstrap.
min.css" rel="stylesheet">
  <script
src="https://cdn.jsdelivr.net/npm/bootstrap@5.3.3/dist/js/bootstrap.
bundle.min.js"></script>
</head>
<body>
<div class="container mt-3">
  <h1>Create a Button</h2>
  <p>Click the below button to proceed with your favorite sports:</p>
  <button type="button" class="btn btn-primary">Cricket</button>
  <button type="button" class="btn btn-secondary">Football</button>
  <button type="button" class="btn btn-success">Archery</button>
  <button type="button" class="btn btn-info">Tennis</button>
</div>
</body>
</html>
```

After running the code, the web page will look as follows:

Screen Size: 1366 x 633

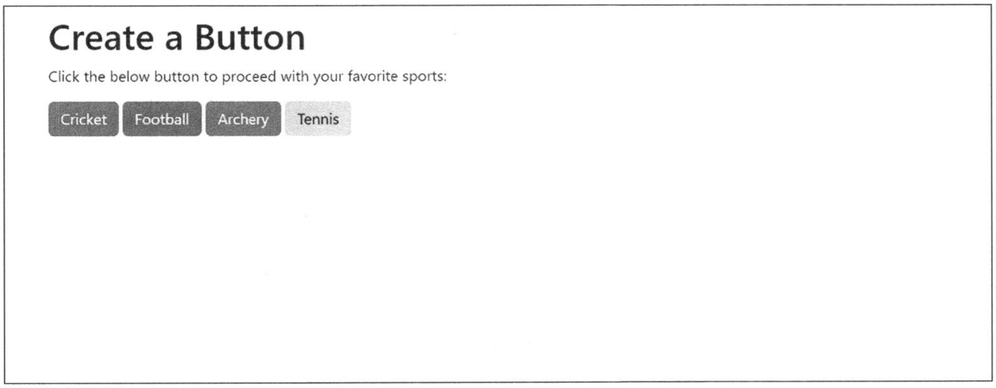

***Figure 10.7**: Changing the button color*

z-index scales

The z-index scales are to arrange elements on a web page. A lot of Bootstrap components use the CSS z-index property to control layout by providing a third axis for arranging the content. A higher z-index value means the component is on top of the component with a lower z-index value.

The z-index controls the stack order of elements. Higher z-index values are displayed in front of lower values.

Let us see the Bootstrap classes for z-index:

Bootstrap Class	Represents
z-n2	z-index is -2
z-n1	z-index is -1
z-0	z-index is 0
z-1	z-index is 1
z-2	z-index is 2

Table 10.1: *Bootstrap classes for z-index*

Here is an example displaying the usage of z-index. The divs are arranged accordingly based on the preceding table:

```
<!DOCTYPE html>
<html lang="en">
<head>
  <title>Bootstrap z-index</title>
  <meta charset="utf-8">
  <meta name="viewport" content="width=device-width, initial-scale=1">
  <link
href="https://cdn.jsdelivr.net/npm/bootstrap@5.3.3/dist/css/bootstrap.
min.css" rel="stylesheet">
   <link href=
"https://getbootstrap.com/docs/5.3/assets/css/docs.css"
          rel="stylesheet" />
  <script
src="https://cdn.jsdelivr.net/npm/bootstrap@5.3.3/dist/js/bootstrap.
bundle.min.js"></script>
</head>
<body>
```

```
  <div class="container mt-3">
    <h2>Demo Heading</h2>
  </div>
  <div class="p-3 m-0 border-0 bd-example bd-example-zindex-levels
position-relative">
    <div class="z-0 position-absolute bg-primary p-5">
    </div>
    <div class="z-n2 position-absolute bg-warning p-5">
    </div>
    <div class="z-n1 position-absolute bg-secondary p-5">
    </div>
    <div class="z-1 position-absolute bg-danger p-5">
    </div>
  </div>
</body>
</html>
```

After running the code, the web page will look as follows:

Screen Size: 1366 x 633

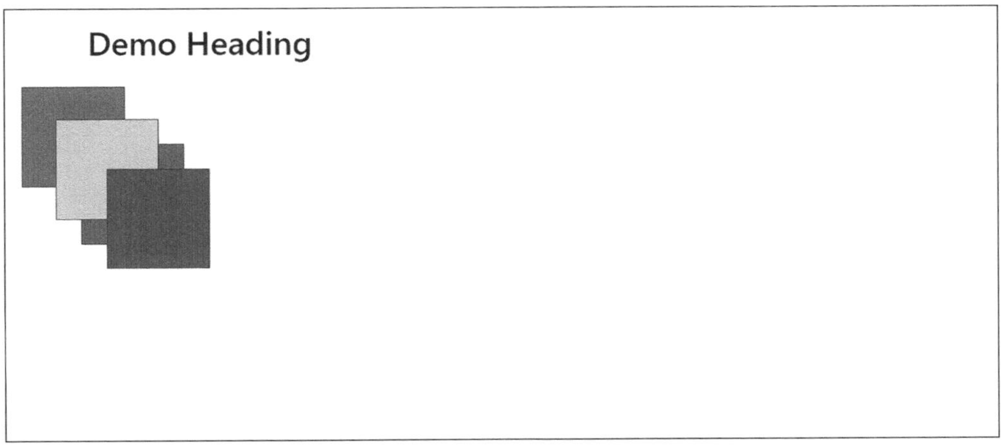

Figure 10.8: *Using z-index on a web page*

Types of z-index scales

Let us see the two types of z-index scales in Bootstrap:

- Elements within a component
- Overlay component

Elements within a component

The Bootstrap components button groups, input groups, and pagination are built with overlapping elements to prevent double borders without modifying the border property. Let us see their z-index scale:

- These components share a standard z-index scale of 0 through 3.
- The scale values:

  0 is **`default`**

  1 is **`:hover`**

  2 is **`:active/.active`**

  3 is **`:focus`**

Overlay components

Bootstrap components, such as dropdowns, fixed and sticky navbars, modals, tooltips, and popovers have their z-index scale beginning at 1000.

The overlay component increases its z-index value in such a way that common UI principles allow user-focused or hovered elements to always be visible.

Optimizations

While working on Bootstrap, always optimize your code to let the web pages load faster. Let us see some optimizations you can apply to your web project. Such optimization techniques reduce the loading time of a web page.

Sass Imports

Optimize Bootstrap while using Sass, by only @importing the components you require. Here are some:

// Configuration

```
@import "functions";
@import "variables";
@import "mixins";
@import "utilities";

// Layout & components
@import "root";
@import "reboot";
@import "type";
@import "images";
@import "containers";
@import "grid";
@import "tables";
```

Note: *If you are not using a component, comment it out or delete it entirely. This will surely save some file size in your compiled CSS.*

Minify

On a web page, minify the HTML, CSS, and JS for optimization. Minification means compressing the code served to the website visitors. If you are using Bootstrap dist files, try to use only the minified versions.

Note: *The minified versions are* `.min.css` and `.min.js` extension files.

Icons

Bootstrap came up with its icon library called Bootstrap Icons.

SVG implementations are suggested to use for their enhanced accessibility and vector support.

The official website to access Bootstrap icons is:

https://icons.getbootstrap.com/

The Bootstrap icons library is a free and open-source icon library with 2000+ icons. The SVG code to directly add the icons on your website is also provided. Let's say you want the SVG code for the Apple icon, then go to the website mentioned earlier and click the Apple icon:

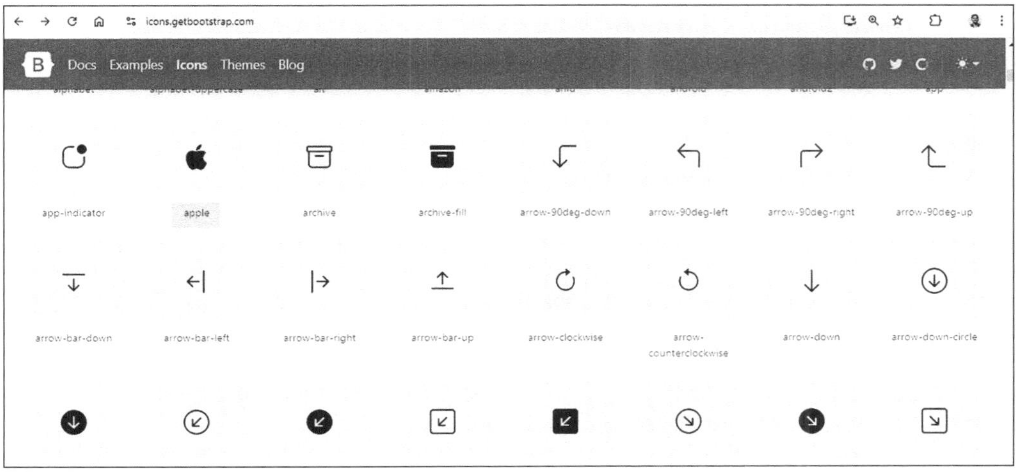

***Figure 10.9**: Icon Library*

After clicking the icon, you will reach the section where the SVG Download can be seen. Click it and download the SVG code:

***Figure 10.10**: SVG code for the icon*

Add an Icon

To add a Bootstrap icon, you need to add the CDN link under the **<head>** tag. The current version is v1.11.3:

```
<link rel="stylesheet" href="https://cdn.jsdelivr.net/npm/boot-
strap-icons@1.11.3/font/bootstrap-icons.css"/>
```

Let us see how to add a Bootstrap icon on a web page. We will add some icons like Bluetooth, Book, Laptop, and more.

```
<!DOCTYPE html>
<html lang="en">
<head>
  <title>Bootstrap Handling Content Overflow</title>
  <meta charset="utf-8">
  <meta name="viewport" content="width=device-width, initial-scale=1">
  <link
href="https://cdn.jsdelivr.net/npm/bootstrap@5.3.3/dist/css/bootstrap.
min.css" rel="stylesheet">
  <link
rel="stylesheet" href="https://cdn.jsdelivr.net/npm/boot-
strap-icons@1.11.3/font/bootstrap-icons.css" />
  <script src="https://cdn.jsdelivr.net/npm/bootstrap@5.3.3/dist/js/
bootstrap.bundle.min.js"></script>

</head>
<body>
<div class="container mt-3">
```

```
  <h1>Bootstrap Icons</h1>
  <h2 class="m-2">Bluetooth Icon:
    <i class="bi-globe"></i>
  </h2>
  <h2 class="m-2">Book Icon:
    <i class="bi-book"></i>
  </h2>
  <h2 class="m-2">Laptop Icon:
    <i class="bi-laptop"></i>
  </h2>
</div>
</body>
</html>
```

After running the code, the web page will look as follows:

Screen Size: 1366 x 633

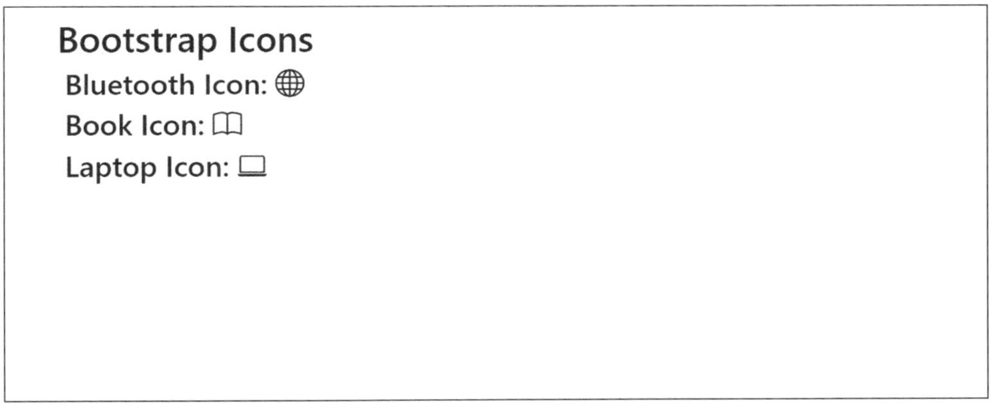

***Figure 10.11**: Adding icons on a web page*

Conclusion

We are now familiar with some techniques to be followed while designing a responsive website with Bootstrap. We also saw some optimization techniques to reduce the size of a web page leading to its faster loading. The concept of Bootstrap icons was also covered with examples.

Points to Remember

- Media queries, like min-width and max-width, are used to set the responsiveness for multiple devices.
- The z-index classes are to arrange elements on a web page.

- Optimize Bootstrap while using Sass, by only @importing the components you require.
- Minification means compressing the code served to the website visitors

Multiple Choice Questions

1. The media query for extra small devices, that is ___ is not provided.
    a. `xs`
    b. `sm`
    c. `md`
    d. `lg`
2. Can min-width and max-width be used together?
    a. Yes
    b. No
3. CSS z-index property controls the layout by providing ____ axis for arranging the content.
    a. First
    b. Second
    c. Third
    d. None of the above
4. What is the minified version of CSS?
    a. `minimum.css`
    b. `min.css`
    c. `minified.css`
    d. `style.css`

Answers

1. a
2. a
3. c
4. b

Questions

- What is a media query?
- How are media queries on a web page set?
- What is the difference between min-width and max-width?
- How are min-width and max-width combined?
- What is a z-index scale?
- What is the difference between higher z-index and lower z-index values?
- How is a Bootstrap icon added on a web page?

Key Terms

- **min-width:** The min-width media query triggers styles for screens when the device width is greater than a certain pixel.
- **max-width:** The max-width media query triggers styles for smaller screens when the device width is less than a certain pixel.
- **z-index:** The z-index scales are to arrange elements on a web page. A lot of Bootstrap components use the CSS z-index property to control layout by providing a third axis for arranging the content.
- **Minification:** Minification means compressing the code served to the website visitors.

Index

Symbols

A

B

P

R

S

T

V

W

Z